The Syntax of Italian Dialects

Recent Titles in
OXFORD STUDIES IN COMPARATIVE SYNTAX
Richard Kayne, General Editor

The Syntax of
Italian Dialects

Edited by

Christina Tortora

OXFORD
UNIVERSITY PRESS
2003

OXFORD
UNIVERSITY PRESS

Oxford   New York
Auckland   Bangkok   Buenos Aires   Cape Town   Chennai
Dar es Salaam   Delhi   Hong Kong   Istanbul   Karachi   Kolkata
Kuala Lumpur   Madrid   Melbourne   Mexico City   Mumbai   Nairobi
São Paulo   Shanghai   Taipei   Tokyo   Toronto

Copyright © 2003 by Oxford University Press, Inc.

Published by Oxford University Press, Inc.
198 Madison Avenue, New York, New York 10016

www.oup.com

Chapter 5, "Person Morphemes and Reflexives in Italian, French,
and Related Languages," by Richard Kayne, also appears as Chapter 8
in his *Parameters and Universals* (Oxford University Press, 2002).

Library of Congress Cataloging-in-Publication Data
The syntax of Italian dialects / edited by Christina Tortora.
p. cm.
Includes index.
ISBN 0-19-513645-4; 0-19-513646-2 (pbk.)
1. Italian Language—Dialects—Syntax. 2. Italian language—
Dialects—Morphology. I. Tortora, Christina.
PC1746 .S964 2002
457—dc21   2002025764

1 3 5 7 9 8 6 4 2

Printed in the United States of America
on acid-free paper

Photo by Giulio Lepschy, 1979

A Paola

un'insegnante, un'ispirazione, un'amica

Preface

This volume has been compiled in honor of Paola Benincà, Professor of Linguistics at the University of Padua, Italy.

As a collection of works that focuses on the syntax of Italian dialects, this book can serve only as a very small gesture of recognition of Paola's contribution to the field of linguistics; to recognize the contribution of Benincà the etymologist, or Benincà the morphologist, or Benincà the philologist, or Benincà the phonologist would take at least five more volumes. With this book the authors and I have decided to make a humble attempt to honor and thank Paola for the understated influence she has had specifically on the field of Italian dialect syntax.

The contributors to this volume accepted the invitation to contribute with an affection and a respect that has no doubt been inspired by the years of Paola's intellectual nurturing and camaraderie. As a consequence of this common inspiration, the chapters in this book share a significant property: they all deal with some aspect of syntax (and/or with some Italian dialect) that Paola herself has worked on—verbal morphology, modals, subject/object clitics, the syntax of CP, or pragmatics (and Paduan, Rhaetoromance, Piedmontese, or Italian, to name just a few). A further consequence of this commonality is that each chapter coheres with the other, both in terms of goals as well as in terms of content.

For example, chapters 6, 7, and 8 (authored by Nicola Munaro, Mair Parry, and Cecilia Poletto and Raffaella Zanuttini, respectively) each deal with the syntax of the Complementizer Phrase (CP). Munaro and Parry both examine different types of wh-phrases. While Parry's study on the development of a double-CP (i.e., wh+*that*) in Piedmontese varieties is from the point of view of pragmatic theory, Munaro takes a syntactic approach to providing evidence for a split-CP by looking at the syntactic difference in behavior between exclamatives and interrogatives in Bellunese. As a follow-up, Poletto and Zanuttini examine the syntax of imperatives in Badiotto (Central Rhaetoromance), providing yet another perspective on (and yet another body of evidence for) multiple CPs. Specifically, they convincingly argue that different (phonologically overt) C heads are reflexes of different types of pragmatic information. All three of these chapters successfully develop areas and ideas investigated by Paola in previous work (e.g., Benincà 1983a, 1995f, 1996a, & 1997f).

Three more chapters also deal with the syntax of functional heads, but further down the structure: Andrea Calabrese (chapter 1), Anna Cardinaletti and Giuliana Giusti (chapter 2), and Guglielmo Cinque (chapter 3) all examine the syntax of verbal heads, a topic which complements the topic of the CP domain discussed in chapters 6–8. Again, here we revisit issues previously investigated by Paola. Calabrese's contribution, which draws on Benincà (1996b), investigates the system behind the verbal morphology of Livinallongo. Calabrese's original morphological analysis of inflectional heads is followed by Cardinaletti and Giusti's syntactic analysis of verbal heads. Their proposal that certain motion verbs lose their lexical content in favor of expressing functional content in the dialect of Marsala (spoken in Sicily) is reminiscent of Paola's work on the verb *bisogna* and other modals in Italian (see Benincà & Poletto 1994c; 1997c). Cinque's chapter on restructuring verbs also makes use of the concept of verbal-functional structure to explain a previously unaccounted for set of facts concerning passives and causatives. To account for the data, Cinque makes use of the functional head Voice°, which is part of the same functional zone where we find the Modal° head of Benincà & Poletto's (1994c; 1997c) *bisogna*.

Moving on to a different lexical category, Diana Cresti (chapter 4), Richard Kayne (chapter 5), Giampaolo Salvi (chapter 9), and John Trumper (chapter 10) all investigate the syntax of nominal heads. Cresti discusses the behavior of *ghe/ne* in Paola's native language, Paduan, and provides a novel syntactic (and formal semantic) analysis which relates these clitics to locative elements in the Germanic languages. While Kayne also investigates the syntax of pronouns, in contrast with Cresti he focuses on their internal structure. In particular, he argues that contrary to appearances, the Italian and French nonclitic (singular) first, second, and reflexive pronouns are bimorphemic. His analysis is supported by facts exhibited in various Italian dialects (e.g., Milanese, Paduan, Piedmontese, and Sardinian). Trumper also examines the behavior of object clitics—this time in Southern Italian dialects (i.e., Sicilian and Calabrian). Specifically, he looks at how the semantic interpretation of clitics as [+human] in these dialects correlates with their co-occurrence with a preposition. Salvi's examination of pronominal heads focuses on the distribution and behavior of enclitic and proclitic subject pronouns in various Northern Italian dialects. Again, in these chapters we look at languages and topics that Paola herself has researched (e.g., Benincà 1983a; Benincà, Vanelli, and Renzi 1985b; and Benincà and Cinque 1993b).

From this brief preface, we see that all of the works in this volume cover languages and areas investigated by Paola in her own research. In addition to their coherent coverage, in the spirit of Paola's work, the contributions in this book also have the individual and collective goal of further informing the question of the universal nature of linguistic properties. While they all have similar concerns, some have a very different type of theoretical approach than others. In particular, while Parry's, Salvi's, and Trumper's chapters clearly reflect training in the European tradition, the other chapters emerge from the American generative tradition. This difference in traditions, yet similarity in terms of content and goals, is a non-accidental reflex of these scholars' connection to Paola Benincà.

Paola has a unique intellectual history that incorporates both traditions (I invite the reader to peruse the list of her publications in the appendix, a few of which are referred to in this preface). From her first lessons with Carlo Tagliavini as a student of glottology, to her development as a linguist under the mentoring of Giovan Battista Pellegrini and Manlio Cortelazzo, to her Professorship in Linguistics at the University of Padua, Paola has long been a part of the European Romance linguistics scholarly tradition. At the same time, since the mid 1970s she has also participated in core developments in American generative theory. Her interest in generative linguistics began with phonology (a natural affinity for which arose as a result of being trained by the likes of Pellegrini and Cortelazzo), but she became involved in generative syntax when, after reading Richard Kayne's doctoral thesis, she was inspired to examine the similarities and differences between Paduan *el* and French *il*. Her subsequent work on the syntax of subject clitics in Paduan (first published as Benincà 1983a) circulated in 1979, when she was a visitor in Linguistics at MIT. This 1979 visit to MIT was also instrumental in her development as a generative syntactician: it was the year that Noam Chomsky had just returned from giving his lectures in Pisa (notes of which Jean-Yves Pollock collected and passed on to Paola and a young Andrea Calabrese, working on his thesis at Padua). Thus, Paola began participating in the field during a crucial moment in its development at MIT (when the Pisa lectures where just going to press, Luigi Burzio was working on his doctoral thesis on the syntax of unaccusatives in Italian and Piedmontese, and Luigi Rizzi was working on small *pro*). Many of Paola's earlier works appear in her 1994 collection, *La Variazione Sintattica: Studi di Dialettologia Romanza* (a book which unfortunately has not yet been translated into English; however, interested non-Italian speakers may get an excellent idea of its contributions to the field from Richard Kayne's review, appearing in the Spring 2001 issue of *Romance Philology*, pp. 492–499).

While Paola has since worked closely with these and other Italian syntacticians, such as Guglielmo Cinque, her work has developed a character all its own. It is not just her scholarly background (both European and American generative), and her ongoing ties to both European and American linguists, which give her work its depth and its unique character; it is also her personal interpretation of her background—her synthesis of each tradition's approach to the systematicity and universal nature of linguistic properties. It is her personal understanding of the syntax of non-standard Romance varieties, such as Paduan (her native language), and her recognition of the distinctive role they play in the development of our theory of universal grammar. It is her (perhaps unconscious) understanding of her own role in the field, and what types of contributions will have a lasting impact (as such, she does not limit herself to theoretical work, as, for example, her instrumental role in the years-long development of the *Atlante Sintattico Italia Settentrionale*, which describes syntactic data from hundreds of Italian varieties, shows). In short, it is her unique scholarship that has made such an impact on the field. Her work, both theoretical and descriptive, has perhaps had more of an impact on the field than we realize (consider, for example, recent theoretical developments in the syntax of the left periphery of the clause; Paola's contribution to this area of knowledge long precedes its latest popularity; see, e.g., Benincà 1986a; 1988b).

Fortunately for all of us, her instrumental role in the development of the field of Italian dialect syntax, Romance syntax, and syntax in general continues, grows, and attracts scholars to her and her Paduan base from all over the world. Again, this volume serves as only a very small window onto the number and type of scholars that have assimilated her unique gift.

Acknowledgments

I owe a tremendous amount of gratitude to many friends and colleagues for their help and support in the conception and fruition of this project. I am particularly grateful to Anna Cardinaletti, a conversation with whom (years back) gave birth to the idea for this book, and who was also instrumental in ensuring the survival of the idea. In this regard, the book and I also owe a great deal to Giuliana Giusti, Cecilia Poletto, and Lori Repetti, who participated in countless hours of decision-making discussions. In fact, Anna, Giuliana, Cecilia, and Lori invested more in the development of this project than a few simple thanks here could ever be capable of acknowledging.

In addition, I thank Richard Kayne for his enthusiastic and affectionate proposal that this volume be published in OUP's Comparative Syntax series; I also thank him for his subsequent commitment to hours of consultation and opinion-sharing regarding the conceptual direction (and title) of the book. Guglielmo Cinque and Raffaella Zanuttini are also responsible for indispensable advice along the way. I also thank all of the contributors to this volume for their patience in its development, their conviction that the endeavor was a worthwhile one, and their faith that it would eventually be completed. I am indebted to Annemarie Toebosch, as well, for her help with the preparation of the camera-ready manuscript. I would also like to thank (with all my heart) Maddalena Cinque, Alice Ferraboschi, and Martina Ferraboschi (and little Agata, who came into the world with this book), for their moral support and advice. They are more responsible than they realize for the completion of this book. Finally, I thank Paola, for years of mentoring, inspiration, and friendship.

Christina Tortora
Staten Island, NY
June 2002

Contents

Contributors

ANDREA CALABRESE
University of Connecticut
Department of Linguistics
U-145
337 Mansfield Rd
Storrs, CT 06269
USA
calabres@uconnvm.uconn.edu

ANNA CARDINALETTI
Università di Venezia
Dipartimento di Scienze del linguaggio
G.B. Giustinian
Dorsoduro 1453
30123 Venezia
ITALY
cardin@unive.it

GUGLIELMO CINQUE
Università di Venezia
Dipartimento di Scienze del linguaggio
G.B. Giustinian
Dorsoduro 1453
30123 Venezia
ITALY
cinque@unive.it

DIANA CRESTI
Massachusetts Institute of Technology
Department of Linguistics and Philosophy
77 Massachusetts Avenue Bldg.E39-245
Cambridge, MA 02139
USA
cresti@alum.mit.edu

GIULIANA GIUSTI
Università di Venezia
Dipartimento di Scienze del linguaggio
G.B. Giustinian
Dorsoduro 1453
30123 Venezia
ITALY
giusti@unive.it

RICHARD S. KAYNE
New York University
Department of Linguistics
719 Broadway, 4th Floor
New York, NY 10003
USA
richard.kayne@nyu.edu

NICOLA MUNARO
Università di Venezia
Dipartimento di Scienze del linguaggio
G.B. Giustinian
Dorsoduro 1453
30123 Venezia
ITALY
munaro@unive.it

JOHN B. TRUMPER
Università della Calabria
Dipartimento di Linguistica
Laboratorio di Fonetica
Facoltà di Lettere e Filosofia
87036 Arcavacata di Rende (CS)
ITALY
trumper@unical.it

MAIR PARRY
University of Bristol
Department of Italian
19, Woodland Road
Bristol BS8 1TE
UNITED KINGDOM
m.m.parry@bristol.ac.uk

RAFFAELLA ZANUTTINI
Georgetown University
Department of Linguistics
Box 571051
Washington, D.C. 20057 USA
zanuttir@georgetown.edu

CECILIA POLETTO
Università di Padova
Istituto di Scienze e Tecnologie della
Cognizione , Dipartimento di Linguistica
Via B. Pellegrino, 1
35137 Padova
ITALY
cecilia.poletto@unipd.it

GIAMPAOLO SALVI
Eötvös Loránd University
Department of Romance Languages and
Literatures
Múzeum krt. 4/C
H-1088 Budapest
HUNGARY
gps@ludens.elte.hu

The Syntax of Italian Dialects

1

On Fission and Impoverishment in the Verbal Morphology of the Dialect of Livinallongo

Andrea Calabrese

1. Introduction

In her 1996 paper "Agglutination and Inflection in Northern Italian Dialects," Paola Benincà, with her usual insight, points to the importance of the verbal paradigm in (1) for a theory of the syntax-morphology interface:[1]

(1) *Livinallongo (Fodóm)*

    a.   *este* 'to be'

pres. ind.	pres. subj.	impf. subj.	impf. ind.
son	sombe	sonse	sonve
es	siebe	ese	eve
e	siebe	esa	eva
son	sombe	sonse	sonve
sei	siebe	seise	seive
e	siebe	esa	eva

    b.   *avej* 'to have'

pres. ind.	pres. subj.	impf. subj.	impf. ind.
e	ebe	ese	eve
as	abe	ase	ave
a	abe	asa	ava
on	onbe	onse	onve
ei	eibe	eise	eive
a	abe	asa	ava

3

c. *sauté* 'to jump'

pres. ind.	pres. subj.	impf. subj.	impf. ind.
saute	saute	sautase	sautave
saute	saute	sautase	sautave
sauta	saute	sautasa	sautava
sauton	sautombe	sautonse	sautonve
sautei	sauteibe	sauteise	sauteive
sauta	saute	sautasa	sautava

In this chapter I will develop some of Benincà's observations on (1) and propose a detailed account of the verbal morphology in (1) in the framework of Distributed Morphology (cf. Halle 1996, 1997, Halle and Marantz 1993, Harris 1994). In so doing, I will reformulate Impoverishment and Fission, two of the basic morphological operations of Distributed Morphology.

We can begin with a rough segmentation of the morphological material in (1) by focusing on the regular verb *sauté* to determine the various elements that play a role in the paradigm in (1). The present indicative and subjunctive are not identified by any markers except in the I and II plural of the latter, where a suffixal /-b-e/ appears. The imperfect subjunctive is identified by the suffix /-s/, the imperfect indicative by the suffix /-v-/, and both are followed by an ending which is /-a/ in the third person, otherwise /-e/. These endings are those that also appear in the present indicative of the regular verb *sauté*. The imperfect suffixes are added to the stem (=root + thematic vowel /-a-/), except for I and II plural. The endings of the I and II plural are /-on/ and /-ei/, respectively, and always appear adjacent to the stem.

The situation we find in the singular and in the third person plural of the regular verb imperfects is that characteristic of most other Romance varieties, where the imperfect suffixes appear between the stem and subject agreement, mirroring the order of functional heads in the syntactic structure, as shown in (2) (/-v-/ and /-ss-/ are the Italian imperfect suffixes; /-B-/ and /-s-/ are the Spanish ones; the post-root /-a-/ is the thematic vowel):

(2) Imperfect subjunctive: *cantare* 'sing'

    a.   Italian: sg. 1. cant-a-ss-i   2. cant-a-ss-i   3. cant-a-ss-e
                          pl. 1. cant-a-ss-imo 2. cant-a-s-te   3. cant-a-ss-ero

    b.   Spanish: sg. 1. cant-a-s-e   2. cant-a-s-es   3. cant-a-s-e
                          pl. 1. cant-a-s-emos 2. cant-a-s-eis 3. cant-a-s-en

(3) Imperfect indicative:

    a.   Italian: sg. 1. cant-a-v-o   2. cant-a-v-i   3. can-t-a-va
                          pl. 1. cant-a-v-amo 2. cant-a-v-ate 3. cant-a-v-ano

    b.   Spanish: sg. 1. cant-a-b-a   2. cant-a-b-as 3. cant-a-b-a
                          pl. 1. cant-a-b-amos 2. cant-a-b-ais 3. cant-a-b-an

The striking feature of the regular verbs in the Livinallongo dialect is that in the forms that appear in the first and second person plural of the present subjunctive, and imperfect indicative and subjunctive, the suffixal sequences, /-b-e/, /-v-e/, and /-s-e/ respectively, are added to what appears to be the corresponding inflected form of the present indicative.

We can now discuss the auxiliary verbs. Consider first the imperfect subjunctive of BE, and compare it with the present indicative. As in the regular verbs, the forms appearing in the first person singular and plural, and in the second person plural seem to be formed by adding a suffix string /-s-e/ to the corresponding inflected form of the present indicative.

The same happens with the imperfect indicative: in the first person singular and plural, and in the second person plural, it appears to be formed by attaching a suffix /-v-e/ to the corresponding inflected forms of the present indicative.

In the other persons, the imperfect suffixes /-s-/ and /-v-/ seem to be added to the stem /e-/. This is obviously clear in the case of the II singular forms. It is more difficult to determine, however, in the case of the III singular and plural forms *esa* and *eva*, since the present indicative is identical to the stem in this case. However, the fact that the suffixal /-a/ in this case is the agreement marker of the third person seen in the regular verbs leads us to opt for the null hypothesis, that expected by the morphological structure of the same persons in regular verbs, where, as we know, the imperfect suffixes /-v-/ and /-s-/ appear between the stem and subject agreement. I thus assume that suffixal /-s-a/-v-a/ are simply added to the stem in the case of the III singular and plural imperfect of BE.

The verb *have* behaves in the same way: as can be seen in (1b), the imperfect markers /-v/ and /-s/ are added to the inflected forms of the indicative present in the I singular and plural and in the II plural, but to the stem in the other persons.

In the case of the present subjunctive, seen in (1a, b), however, there is a striking difference between 'be' and 'have': the latter adds a suffixal string /-b-e/ to the inflected form of the present indicative, while the former in the II singular and III singular and plural adds the same sequence to a form that does not correspond to the present indicative but, rather, is a special stem allomorph.

As observed by Benincà (1996) (see also Benincà 1999), if we approach these phenomena within the framework of checking theory proposed by Chomsky (1995), we would probably say that a correspondence between the order of the features to check and the order of recognizable elements bearing those features is not strictly required. There is no reason to expect differences like the ones pointed out among the different persons in the Livinallongo verbal conjugations. Therefore, checking theory cannot provide an account for the different peculiar order of suffixes in the verbal morphology.

If we adopt a strictly syntactic theory of inflectional morphology, and we conceive of the order of inflectional formatives (following Baker's 1985 Mirror Principle) as mirroring the order of functional projections, we would be forced to conclude that, in the dialect of Livinallongo, there is a different order of functional projections— precisely that Tense is above Subject agreement, in the case of some persons, but not others, which is a rather idiosyncratic situation.

In order to account for the different ordering of the morphological elements in

(1), Benincà proposes to break down the process of word formation: some lexical forms are built in the syntax, whereas others come directly from a lexicon of morphologically related forms. In particular, she proposes that in the same conjugation, some forms can come directly from the lexicon with their endowment of features, whereas others can be incomplete for some purposes and require further movements in the structure and other morphemes, which are then morphologically incorporated. Thus, in the case of the imperfect subjunctive form *sautonve*, she hypothesizes that the imperfect form provided by the lexicon is morphologically incomplete—and, in fact, the inflected base in this case is that of the present indicative, the unmarked tense. To be completed, this form moves past the subject agreement position to a functional head Aspect marked [+imperfect]. In this dialect, when a functional projection of this type is activated, a suffix /-ve/ is inserted. Supposing that it is a head: the verb has to adjoin to its left, and then they move upward together. This is shown in (4):

(4)

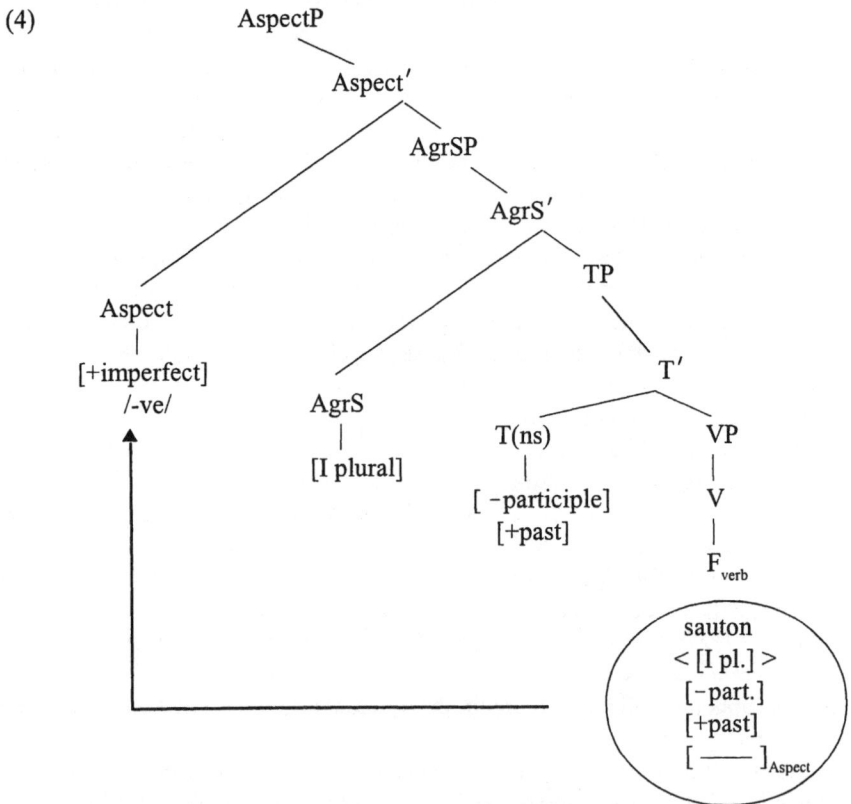

Despite its merits, I disagree with Benincà's solution for the following reasons. First, it does not account for the fact that the morphological structure of the form *sautonve* actually involves four morphological elements: (a) the stem /saut-/, (b) the I plural ending /-on/, (c) the imperfect marker /-v-/, and, crucially,

(d) the ending /-e/. Observe that the ending /-e/ also appears in the forms of the indicative present which according to Benincà should be stored in the lexicon. Thus we have a situation in which the identical morphological ending is inserted once in the lexicon and then later in the syntax. This problem is epitomized in the case of the form [e-v-e] 'have-Imperf. Ind. Isg.' where the ending /-e/ would be inserted twice, once in the lexicon after the stem /a/ "have"—which is deleted on the surface (cf. p.18) and then again in the syntax after the imperfect suffix /-v-/. The assumption that inflectional material can be inserted in two different derivational stages is thus problematic insofar as it is unable to express obvious generalizations on word structure.

Furthermore, it is unclear how to extend Benincà's analysis to other forms in the paradigm in (1). For example in the II and III singular and plural present subjunctive of BE, the suffix /-b-e/ is added to the form /si-e/. From the analysis given above, and from the I and II plural of the subjunctive present of regular verbs, we must conclude that the presence of this /-be/ must involve movement to the mood node so that the form is completed. This implies that the form /si-e/ is incomplete. It is unclear, however, in what sense it is incomplete insofar as it displays obvious subjunctive morphology in the stem allomorph.

Another possible problem for Benincà's theory involves the treatment of forms such as the imperfect indicative *sautava*, where the order of the suffixes is that expected by the Mirror Principle. Benincà seems to assume that we have to resort to word formation in the syntax only when we have a violation of the Mirror Principle such as that seen in *sautonve*. But this is counterintuitive because by having word formation in the syntax we can directly account for the order of the suffix we see in *sautava*. By relegating *sautava* to the lexicon, we are thus missing an important morphological generalization.

In order to account for the different ordering of the suffixes in (1), we have to look for a different theory of the syntax/morphology interface we observe in verbal morphology. This theory need not only account for order of the different suffixes however, but also for how these suffixes realize different morphosyntactic properties. It is well known that the Tense and Agreement morphemes of verbs have the status of independent syntactic elements that require separate nodes in the terminal string. And one of the goals of morphology is precisely that of accounting for the different ways in which different languages package these universal morphological entities into words. As an example, consider the finite verb forms of Italian in (5).

(5) a.   Maria parló con foga   'M. spoke with passion.'
    b.   Maria parlava con foga   'M. was speaking with passion.'
    c.   Maria parla con foga   'M. speaks with passion.'

The verb forms are composed of a stem and one or more suffixes. If we compare (5a) and (5b), we observe that in (5a) there is only the suffix /-ó/ which represents not only the fact that the subject of the sentence is III person and singular, but also that the tense is past. In contrast, in (5b), in addition to the thematic vowel /-a-/, we have two suffixes: the suffix /-v-/ which represents the imperfect and the suffix /-a/ which represents the fact that the subject of the sentence is III person and singular. Thus tense and agreement in (5a) are represented by only one morpheme, in (5b) by two different morphemes. In the case of (5c), we find the same ending /-a/ characterizing the III singular, which appears in the imperfect. We can assume that this is a subject agreement suffix. We can thus hypothesize the same structure as in the imperfect, but in which the present tense must be represented by a null morpheme Ø. A more explicit representation of the verbs in (5) is given in (6), where the angled brackets enclose the grammatical—that is, non-phonetic—information conveyed by the stem and the suffixes (from Halle's 1997 analysis of English verbal forms):[2]

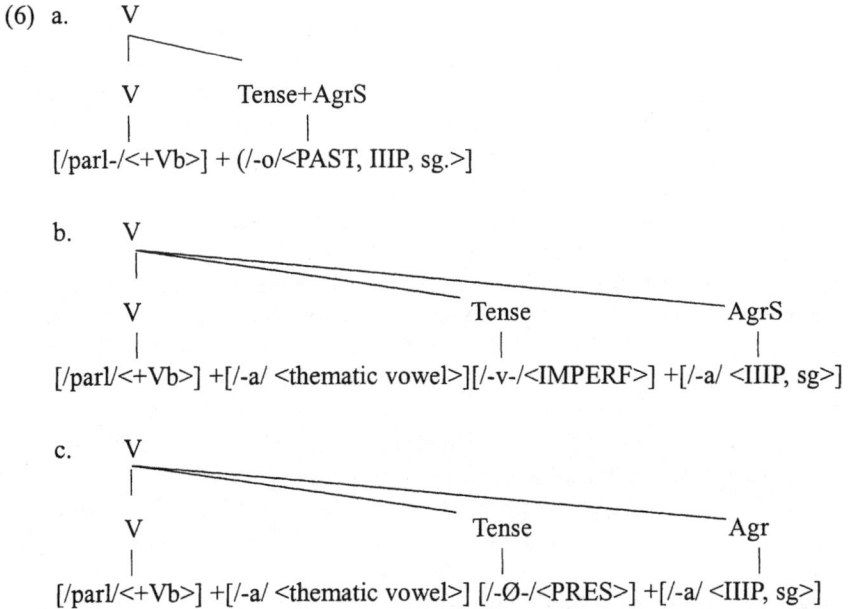

(6) a.   V
           ┌────────────────
           V   Tense+AgrS
           | |
     [/parl-/<+Vb>] + (/-o/<PAST, IIIP, sg.>]

    b.   V
           ┌──────────────────────────────────
           V   Tense   AgrS
           | | |
     [/parl/<+Vb>] +[/-a/ <thematic vowel>][/-v-/<IMPERF>] +[/-a/ <IIIP, sg>]

    c.   V
           ┌──────────────────────────────────
           V   Tense   Agr
           | | |
     [/parl/<+Vb>] +[/-a/ <thematic vowel>] [/-Ø-/<PRES>] +[/-a/ <IIIP, sg>]

Any theory of the syntax-morphology interface needs to account for the different morphosyntactic packaging that differentiate forms such as *parló* and *parlava* and for how these packagings relate to the terminal nodes of the syntax. I will now introduce a morphological theory that directly address these issues. This theory is Distributed Morphology (Halle 1997, Halle and Marantz 1994, Harris 1994).[3] As we will see by adopting this theory, a straightforward account of the different suffix ordering we observe in (1) can be proposed.

Distributed Morphology assumes that there is an autonomous morphological component where the hierarchical structures provided by the syntax can be manipulated in a variety of ways before lexical insertion, as shown diagrammatically in (7):

(7)

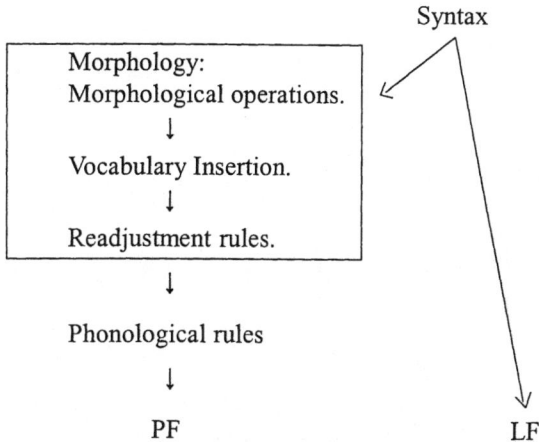

One of the morphological operations of the morphological component which plays an important role in the analysis proposed here is merger. Merger joins syntactic terminal nodes under a category node of a head (a "zero-level category node") but maintains two independent terminal nodes under this category node (see Halle and Marantz 1993). Thus, vocabulary insertion places two separate vocabulary items under the derived head, one for each of the merged terminal nodes. Merger forms a new morphological constituent from the heads of independent phrases; but these independent heads remain separate morphemes within the newly derived constituent. An example of merger is the operation that combines Tns with the main verb in Italian. The syntax provides the hierarchical structure in (8a). Merger joins the node Tns with the verbal head node as shown in (8b):

(8) a.

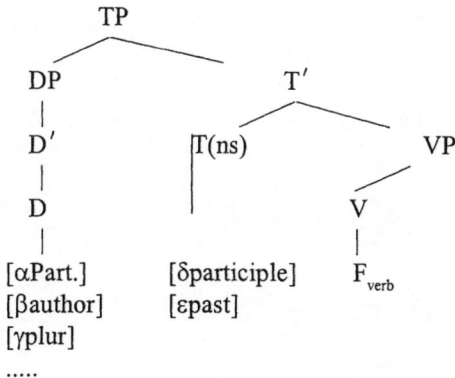

b.

```
                          TP
                    ┌──────────────┐
            DP                    T'
            |                     |
            D'                    VP
            |                    ╱
            D                   V
            |                  ╱╲
         [αPart.]          V      Tns
         [βauthor]         |       |
         [γplur]          F_verb  [δparticiple]
                                  [εpast]

          .....
```

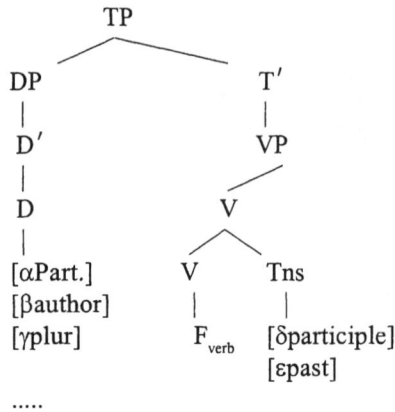

Another operation that plays an important role in our analysis is Morpheme insertion. As proposed by Halle and Marantz (1993), morphemes may be inserted in morphological structure to meet universal and/or language-specific well-formedness conditions. In many languages—for example, Italian, Russian, Latin, but not English and Hebrew—word stems must have a theme suffix, which has no syntactic or semantic role. It is natural to assume that such affixes are introduced by the rules of the morphology. By placing them in this part of the grammar, one accounts for their lack of effect in the syntax or at LF. A theme suffix /-a/ appears in the verbal stem of the imperfect /parla-v-a/ in (5a), as noticed before (see Harris 1975, 1987, 1997 on thematic vowels in the verbal morphology of Spanish which is identical to that of Italian under this respect).

Italian, English, Latin, and Russian are alike, however, in that they require a subject agreement morpheme for well-formed finite verbs. Following Halle and Marantz (1993), we could say that, like the theme suffix, agreement morphemes are added to heads in the morphology in accordance to language particular requirements about what constitutes a morphologically well-formed word in a given language. The insertion of the agreement morpheme onto which appropriate features of the subject have been copied transforms tree (8b) into tree (9). In (9), all Φ-features of the subject NP—person, gender, and number—are copied onto a special AGR node that is inserted as a sister of the Tense node.[4]

(9)

```
                              TP
                        ┌──────────┐
                       DP          T′
                        |          |
                       D′          VP
                        |          ┌────
                       D           V
                        |      ┌────────┐
                                V        Tns
                                |      ┌──────┐
                   [αPart.]   F_verb  Tns      Agr
                   [βauthor]          |        |
                   [γplur]       [δparticiple] [αPart.]
                                 [εpast]       [βauthor]
                   .....                       [γplur]
```

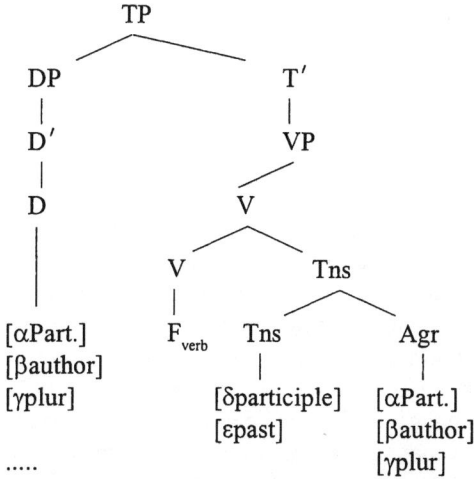

Tree (9) accounts for the morphological structures in (5b) and (5c). We have to account for (5a). Example (5a) is obtained by Fusion (Halle and Marantz 1993). Fusion takes two terminal nodes that are sisters under a single category node and fuses them into a single terminal node. Only one vocabulary item may now be inserted, an item that must have a subset of the morphosyntactic features of the fused node, including the features from both input terminal nodes. Unlike merger, fusion reduces the number of independent morphemes in a tree. Italian fuses the Agr head node with the sister Tns head node in the simple past as shown in (10):

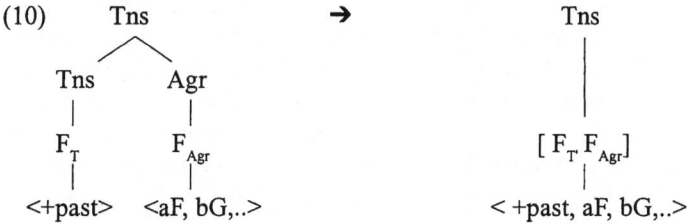

(10)
```
        Tns                    ➜               Tns
     ┌──────┐
    Tns    Agr                                  |
     |      |
    F_T    F_Agr                            [ F_T F_Agr ]
     |      |                                    |
  <+past>  <aF, bG,..>                    < +past, aF, bG,..>
```

By the operation of fusion, we obtain (6a).[5]

By fusion, we account for the difference between the Italian past tense in (5a) (see (12) for the full set of forms) and the Russian past tense in (11). As we know, Italian fuses the Tense and AGR features into a single morpheme in the past tense; in contrast, Russian always keeps Tense separate from AGR (examples from Halle 1997).

(11) a. nës- [l]   'carry' Past sgM
     b. nes-l- á   'carry' Past sgF
     c. nes-l- ó   'carry' Past sgN
     d. nes-l- í   'carry' Past pl

(12) a.   parl-a-i   'speak-Isg'
     b.   parl-a-sti   'speak-IIsg'
     c.   parl-ò   'speak IIIsg'
     d.   parl-a-mmo   'speak-Ipl'
     e.   parl-a-ste   'speak-IIpl'
     f.   parl-a-rono   'speak-IIIpl'

There is another difference, however, that needs to be accounted for. The two languages in fact differ with regard to the grammatical features that are signaled by the AGR morpheme. In Italian the exponent of the fused AGR/Tense represents the person and number features of the subject. In contrast, in Russian, the AGR exponent represents plural or gender.

In Distributed Morphology, the phonetic exponents of the different morphemes are listed in the Vocabulary. As illustrated in (14) and (15), each Vocabulary item pairs a phonological exponent with information about the grammatical context in which the exponent figures. The Vocabulary items constitute an essential part of speakers' knowledge of their language; this is knowledge that speakers must memorize item by item.

It was stated above that the Φ-features of the subject are copied onto the inserted AGR node. This should be true in all languages with subject-verb agreement and holds both for Italian and Russian. Thus, in both languages information about person, gender, and number of the subject is copied onto the AGR node. Not all of this information, however, is required for selecting the correct phonetic exponent: specifically, as already noted, in the Italian past tense forms we need information about number and person of the subject, but not about its gender, whereas in the Russian past tense forms we need information about number and gender, but not about person. This fact is reflected in the form of the Italian and Russian Vocabulary items: the Russian ones in (14) contain no information about the person of the subject (see Halle 1997 for more discussion), whereas those of Italian, shown in (15), contain no information about the gender of the subject (the features characterizing the different persons are those given in (13)):

(13)

	Isg.	IIsg.	IIIsg.	Ipl.	IIpl.	IIIpl.
[Author]	+	-	-	+	-	-
[Participant]	+	+	-	+	+	-
[Plural]	-	-	-	+	+	+

(14) a.   /i/ ↔ [+Pl] $_{Agr}$

           /a/ ↔ [+Fem] $_{Agr}$ in env. [+Past] $_{Tns}$ +____

           /o/ ↔ [+Neut] $_{Agr}$

           /Ø/ ↔ [ ] $_{Agr}$

     b.   /l/ ↔ [+past]

(15)   /-mmo/[6]   ↔   [+past, +author, +plural]$_{\text{Agr+Tns}}$

          /-ste/   ↔   [+past, +participant, +plural]$_{\text{Agr+Tns}}$

          /-sti/   ↔   [+past, +participant, -author]$_{\text{Agr+Tns}}$

          /-i/   ↔   [+past, +author]$_{\text{Agr+Tns}}$

          /-rono/   ↔   [+past, +plural]$_{\text{Agr+Tns}}$

          /-ò/   ↔   [+past]$_{\text{Agr+Tns}}$

The items in (14) and (15) are underspecified: none contains all the information that has been copied onto the AGR node. There is in fact no reason to provide all this information in the lexical items, because the function of the list is to insert the correct phonological exponent in each AGR node. What is important is to capture the distribution of the different lexical items in the most efficient way. We could thus assume that the principle in (16) governs feature assignments to lexical items:

(16)   For each lexical item I, the minimal set of features able to account for the maximal distribution of I is assigned to I.

As follows from (16), for insertion to take place only a subset of the features in the terminal node must be matched by the Vocabulary item. More formally, insertion of phonological exponents is governed by the Subset Principle (17) (from Halle 1997):

(17)   The phonological exponent of a Vocabulary item is inserted into a morpheme in the terminal string if the item matches all or a subset of the grammatical features specified in the terminal morpheme.

          Insertion does not take place if the Vocabulary item contains features not present in the morpheme. Where several Vocabulary items meet the conditions for insertion, the item matching the greatest number of features specified in the terminal morpheme must be chosen.

The Subset Principle (17) determines in part the order of precedence among Vocabulary items that, like the items in (14) and (15), compete for insertion into a given morpheme. Items that match more features take precedence over items that match fewer features. It is for this reason that the items in (14) and (15) and elsewhere are listed in the order of decreasing number of features that the items must match. [7] The last item of the list is what is called the "elsewhere" item, the item whose distribution—potential or actual—cannot be captured by any subset of the features relevant for the other items of the list. This item will be inserted when no other item of the list can be inserted. In the lists in (14) and (15), /Ø/ and /-ó/ are the elsewhere items. The prediction is that although they appear in (11) and (12) only with the function of SgMasc. or IIIsg, respectively, there could potentially be situations in which they express other combinations of features, if any other item of the list fails to be inserted as an ending, for some reason, in that situation. In the dialect of Livinallongo, we will see situations in which this actually occurs. It is assumed in Distributed Morphology that each list must contain an elsewhere item (see Harris 1993 for further discussion of this issue).

2. Analysis of the verbal morphology of the Livinallongo dialect

At this point we can start to deal with the peculiarities of the verbal paradigm in (1). The easiest set of forms are those appearing in the present indicative of the regular verb *sauté* 'to jump'. As mentioned above, these forms can be segmented as follows. We have the stem /*saut-*/, and the verbal endings /-e/, which appears in the first and second singular; /-a/, which appears in the third singular and plural; /-on/, which appears in the first plural; and /-ei/, which appears in the second plural. These endings are organized in the list in (18). I assume that /-e/ is the elsewhere item in this list.

(18)   /-on/   ↔   [+author, +plural]$_{AgrS}$

          /-ei/   ↔   [+participant, +plural]$_{AgrS}$

          /-a/   ↔   [-participant]$_{AgrS}$

          /-e/   ↔   [ ]$_{AgrS}$

I assume that, as in Italian, the present tense exponent is an unmarked null morpheme as in (19), the elsewhere case in the list. The other tense exponents appearing in (1) are also provided in (19). They will be discussed in more detail later:

(19)   /-s-/   ↔   [+subjunctive. +imperfect]$_{Tense}$

          /-b-/   ↔   [+subjunctive]$_{Tense}$

          /-v-/   ↔   [+imperfect]$_{tense}$

          /Ø/   ↔   [ ]$_{Tense}$

These lexical items are inserted in a hierarchically organized verbal structure which is the output of the morphological operations of merger and Theme and Agreement Insertion, as discussed above. It is given in (20):[8]

(20)

I am assuming that a theme vowel is also inserted in the indicative present of the regular verbs, as in the imperfect subjunctive and indicative of (1). This vowel is however deleted in the surface before vowel initial suffixes such as those in (18) by the readjustment rule in (21):

(21)   V   →   Ø/ [$_{Theme}$ ____] + [V

The need for this readjustment rule will be seen later.

The account proposed above assumes that Vocabulary items are inserted into the morphemes of a sentence only after morphological rules such as merger and insertion (or fusion) have had an opportunity to modify in various ways the feature complexes appearing in the morphemes. This procedure has been termed LATE INSERTION in the Distributed Morphology literature.

In the case of the auxiliary verbs *este* 'be' and *avej* 'have', we observe that the stem does not have the same exponent as in the case of the verb *sauté*, but has different exponents in different grammatical contexts. I follow Halle's (1997) analysis of the English copular verb *be*, which has a number of different stem alternants selected by different Tense-AGR morphemes. A first provisional analysis for the auxiliary verbs is provided in (22–23):

(22) a.   /si-/   ↔   [BE]$_{Root}$ / ____ + <+subjunctive, +present>

    b.   /s-/   ↔   [BE]$_{Root}$ / ____ + <+participant, +plural]

    c.   /s-/   ↔   [BE]$_{Root}$ / ____ + < +author>

    d.   /e-/   ↔   [BE]$_{Root}$

(23)   /a-/   ↔   [HAVE]$_{Root}$

According to this analysis, the stem has four different alternants for the verb BE (22), whereas only one for the verb HAVE (23). This analysis assumes that, although they are characterized by different stem alternants, the auxiliary verbal forms respect the word structure which characterizes the other regular verbs. Evidence for that is found in the plural forms *son* and *sei,* where we can recognize the ending /-on/ and /-ei/ which are found in the same persons of the regular verbs. This type of generalization must be captured, and thus leads to a segmentation /s-on/ and /s-ei/. The same is true for the plural forms *on* and *ei* of the present indicative of HAVE. Therefore the AgrS endings are those of the regular verb with the idiosyncratic additions (24c) and (24d) (to be revised below):

(24) a.   /-on/   ↔   [+author, +plural]$_{AgrS}$

    b.   /-ei/   ↔   [+participant, +plural]$_{AgrS}$

    c.   /-on/   ↔   [+author]$_{AgrS}$ / BE + ____ [+ind., +pres.]$_{Tns}$

    d.   /-s/   ↔   [+participant, -author]$_{AgrS}$ / AUX + ____

    e.   /-a/   ↔   [-participant]$_{AgrS}$

    f.   /-e/   ↔   [ ]$_{AgrS}$

By assuming the lexical items in (22–23) and (24), and the readjustment rule in (21), we can account for all the forms of the indicative present of BE and HAVE (cf. (25) and (26)):

(25) *este*

    s + on   →   son

    e + s   →   es

    e + e   → (21) → e

    s + on   →   son

    s + ei   →   sei

    e + e   → (21) → e

(26) *avej*

    a + e   → (21) → e

    a + s   →   as

    a + a   → (21) → a

    a + on   → (21) → on

    a + ei   → (21) → ei

    a + a   → (21) → a

If we consider the list in (22) more carefully, however, we find items that are homophonous. If we follow Halle (1997), this homophony should be eliminated. Besides, the hypothesis that the lexical items in (22b) and (22c) are homophonous is particularly problematic insofar as they are both inserted in terminal nodes which share the same feature [+participant]. A simpler alternative would be to replace them with the lexical item in (27b):

(27) a.   /si-/ ↔ $[BE]_{Root}$ / _____ + <+subjunctive>

    b.   /s-/   ↔ $[BE]_{Root}$ / _____ + <+participant>

    c.   /e-/   ↔ $[BE]_{Root}$

Given the more general formulation of the lexical item in (27b), we have to prevent the insertion of this lexical item in the II singular. In the literature on Distributed Morphology, a lexical item is prevented from being inserted in a given terminal node by deleting in this terminal node one of the features required in the lexical matching process (Halle and Marantz 1993, Halle 1997). This operation is called "impoverishment." In our case, we can prevent the insertion of the lexical item /-s/ in the terminal node of the II singular ([+participant, -author, -plural]) by deleting the feature [+participant]. The only other item that can be inserted in its place is the elsewhere stem allomorph /e-/ of (27), and we can thus account for the appearance of the allomorph /e-/ in place of /s-/ in the II singular of BE. There is a problem however. Given that lexical insertion is cyclic, and therefore applies inside out (Davis 1991), the stem allomorphs must be inserted before AgrS endings. Therefore if we want to adopt the preceding account of the appearance of elsewhere /-e/ as the stem allomorph in the II singular, we have to assume that the feature [+participant] of this person is deleted before the insertion of the AgrS endings. Observe now that the suffix /-s/ of the II singular ending in (24d) crucially requires

the feature [+participant] to be inserted. Given the preceding analysis, the suffix /
-s/ could not be inserted in this case, contrary to what actually happens.

To avoid this problem, I would like to propose a different formulation of
impoverishment. Different from what is currently assumed in the Distributed
Morphology literature, I would like to say that impoverishment does not involve
deletion of a given feature, but inhibition of this feature in the lexical insertion
process. I assume that when a feature is inhibited, it can no longer be used for the
matching purposes in a given insertion cycle. Therefore a lexical item specified
by that feature cannot be inserted in that cycle. However, given that it is not deleted,
this feature can be used in the matching process in a later insertion cycle. Thus a
lexical item characterized by it can be inserted. All cases of impoverishment found
in the literature can be easily captured by this modification.

Let us see how this works in the case under discussion. I propose that the
feature [+participant] in the feature bundle of the II singular is inhibited when the
stems are inserted in the present of BE (the inhibited feature is marked by an
asterisk):

(28)   *[+participant] [___, -author, -plural] in the stem insertion cycle

Thus the lexical item /s-/ cannot be inserted and the elsewhere item /-e/ in (27c)
takes its place. Observe, however, that this feature is not inhibited in the later
insertion cycles and thus can be used in the insertion of the suffix /-s/ in the AgrS
ending insertion cycle.

Let us consider the endings in (24) again at this point. In (24) I assumed that in
the case of BE the suffix /-on/ is simplified as in (24c) so that it can be directly
inserted in both the first singular and plural. This again creates homophony since
there is the other lexical item in (24a). There are two possible ways of eliminating
this homophony: (1) we can assume only the suffix in (24a) and have a special rule
that changes [!plural] into [+plural] in the case of the first person singular of BE;
or (2) we can assume only the suffix in (24c) but not restricted to BE, and have an
impoverishment rule applying to the first singular of all verbs but BE. The first
solution is obviously the most adequate one insofar as it characterizes the identity
between the I singular and plural of the present of BE as a special property that
must be memorized about this verb. As we will see, there is evidence for this
move. Thus I replace the list in (24) with that in (29) and assume the feature
change rule in (30):

(29) a.   /-on/ $\leftrightarrow$ [+author, +plural] $_{AgrS}$
     b.   /-ei/ $\leftrightarrow$ [+participant, +plural] $_{AgrS}$
     c.   /-s/ $\leftrightarrow$ [+participant, -author] $_{AgrS}$ / AUX + ____
     d.   /-a/ $\leftrightarrow$ [-participant] $_{AgrS}$
     e.   /-e/ $\leftrightarrow$ [ ] $_{AgrS}$

(30)   [-plural] $\rightarrow$ [+plural]/ BE + [____ , +author]

Observe also that the feature [−participant] must be inhibited in the case of the III singular and plural of BE to account for the appearance of elsewhere /-e/ in these forms:[9]

(31)   *[−participant]/BE + [+present] _____ in the AgrS insertion cycle

We can now proceed with the analysis of other verb forms, those of the subjunctive present of the regular verb sauté, repeated here in (32):

(32)   saute
              saute
              saute
              sautombe
              sauteibe
              saute

The syntactic structure in (20) predicts the presence of an exponent for mood/ tense (see note 7) before the AgrS exponent. An exponent characteristic of the subjunctive appears only in the I and II plural, but not in the expected position after the verbal stem, rather after the exponent for person/number. Before dealing with the position of this marker, we need to account for the absence of any mood marking in the singular and in the III plural. We can resort to impoverishment to obtain this. We can inhibit the subjunctive feature in the relevant persons and thus the elsewhere tense/mood exponent /-Ø-/ will be inserted as shown in (33):[10]

(33)

If we now consider the different AgrS endings, we can observe that the I and II singular are the same as the endings of the same persons in the indicative. However, in the III persons, instead of the /-a/ we find in the indicative, we find the unmarked ending /-e/. In this case we have to block the insertion of the relevant lexical items of the list in (29). This can again be obtained by impoverishment. We can simply say that the feature that is inhibited in the insertion cycle involving the lexical items in (29) is the feature [!participant]. Thus the lexical item [a] cannot be inserted in the terminal nodes in (33). The elsewhere case [-e] is inserted instead.

Consider now the I and II plural forms. We find a subjunctive marker only here. Absence of impoverishment could directly account for what happens in this case. A problem could be the unexpected position of the subjunctive suffix. Benincà has shown that the exponent /be/ of the subjunctive developed etymologically from the adverb BENE. Its verb-final position could therefore be expected from the historical point of view if it is assumed that in its development from BENE, the suffix /-be/ went through a stage in which it was an enclitic. The problem of its special position could be solved by assigning this suffix the requirement to be the last element of the phonological string, a requirement that would stem from its historical origin:

(34)   ] +be]##

However this solution appears problematic in light of the evident parallelism between the I and II plural of the present subjunctive and the same persons of the imperfect subjunctive and indicative: *sautonse, sauteise / sautonve, sauteive*. In the case of the latter forms, we know that the exponents /-se/ and /-ve/ which follow the person/number exponents are actually composite forms being formed by the suffixes [-s-] or [-v-] followed by an AgrS ending which alternates with [-a] in the III person. Now, the same analysis could be extended to the /-be/ of the subjunctive if we assume that the /-e/ that appears in all forms is simply the elsewhere AgrS suffix of (29). Under this analysis [-be] should be analyzed as a composite morpheme formed of a subjunctive suffix [-b-] followed by a person/number ending /-e/, in the same way as /-s-a/e/ and /-v-a/e/. This is the analysis assumed in the list in (19). By assuming it, a more general and regular segmentation of the verbal morphology of Livinallongo can be achieved. If this is correct, we would find three different exponents in the I and II plural endings, against the single exponent found in the other persons. How can we account for this tripartite exponence?

We can look for an answer to this problem in the corresponding forms of the imperfect subjunctive and indicative. The basic syntactic structure of the verb form I assume here is that in (20). This syntactic structure is respected in the singular of these forms and in the III plural. The lexical items for these two tenses are given in (19). Given (20), these two lexical items are attached to the verbal stem after the thematic vowel. The endings that we find here are those we find in the indicative present—that is, the endings of the list in (29). This is shown in (35) for the form *sautava* 'jump-3sgIMP-IND' (I focus on the imperfect indicative, but the same analysis could be extended to the imperfect subjunctive):

(35)

[/saut/<+Vb>]+[/a/ Thematic Vowel][/-v-/<+Imperf, +Ind>]+[/-a/ <IIIP, sg>]

As we know, the interesting forms are those we find in the first and second plural. In those forms the AgrS endings are found inside the Mood/Tense ending, in violation of the order expected from the structure in (20) (see (35)). In these forms, the string *sautavon* which would be expected given (20) and the other persons is split into a sequence which can be characterized as involving a first person plural indicative present /sauton/ + followed by imperfect marker/-v-/ and the unmarked ending /-e/. There is not only resequencing of morphemes, but also appearance of additional morphology—the suffix /e/. Cases involving the appearance of additional morphological material have been treated in the literature as involving the morphological operation of fission.

Noyer (1992) noticed a number of examples from the Afro-Asiatic languages and some Australian languages (Nungubuyu) which were characterized by the insertion of additional material beyond the lexical items which were expected in a given position. He also observed that this additional material was always identical with another Vocabulary item. For example, if the earliest item satisfying the Subset Condition was the suffix /-on/ and another item in the same list was /-e/, there were instances where both /on/ and /-e/ were inserted. Noyer accounted for these cases by proposing a special morphological operation he called "fission."

Halle (1997) has recently reformulated this morphological operation and proposed that it is a special modality of the lexical insertion procedure. In particular he proposes that morphemes subject to fission are especially marked as following an insertion procedure of their own. Usually vocabulary insertion comes to an end as the first item that satisfied the subset condition (17) is inserted into a morpheme. In the case of the morphemes subject to fission, however, after a first item is inserted, the insertion procedure does not stop as in the other cases. Simultaneously with insertion of the phonological exponent, instead a subsidiary morpheme is generated, into which are copied the features—if any such remain—that have not been matched in the first step. This subsidiary morpheme is then itself subject to Vocabulary insertion. Halle assumes that the insertion procedure stops at this point.

Let us see a possible analysis of the forms *sautonve* following this formulation of fission. First, we have to prevent insertion of the Mood/Tense suffix before the AgrS ending: we can do that by assuming that the first step in the derivation of this form is the application of fusion between Mood/Tense and AgrS nodes in the I and II plural. Lexical insertion will then apply to this fused Tense/AgrS node. In the insertion process, this fused node will be characterized by fission. A first round of lexical insertion will thus apply. The lexical item /-on/ can be inserted matching the features [+author, +plural]. At this point the features [+indicative, +imperfect] are still unmatched. Fission will create another morpheme containing these unmatched features. This morpheme is subject to lexical insertion. The exponent /-v-/ is thus inserted. Another application of fission will be needed at this point, however. It creates another morpheme containing still unmatched features or possibly no feature at all. The only exponent that could be inserted at this point would be the elsewhere exponent /-e/. This derivation is illustrated in (36) for this form:

(36)   After fusion applies:

/saut/ + [+ind, +imperf., +participant, +author, +plural] →

/saut/ + [/-on/ < [+author, +plural>] + [/-v/ <+ind. +imperf>]

    + [/-e/ <+participant>]

There are obvious problems with this account. The first problem involves the order of the different morphemes. There are no reasons for assuming that the suffix /-v-/ (or /-s-/ for imperfect subjunctive) must follow the AgrS suffix /-on-/. In all other forms of the paradigm, in fact, these suffixes precede the AgrS endings, and they thus must be characterized as attaching to the stem. It is unclear why in the fission procedure this subcategorization is changed and these markers are attached to a different element. A second related problem is that of the round-about use of fusion and fission. Fusion is needed to prevent insertion of the imperfect marker in its expected post-stem position. However, despite fission, the position in which this marker is inserted is still unaccounted for. A third problem is that in this analysis fission must apply twice, whereas in the Halle assumption fission may apply only once. Finally, there is the issue of why fission applies just in the I and II plural. There is no motivation for its application. It is just accidental.

Here I would like to propose an alternative formulation of fission to avoid these problems. I submit that fission is not just a modality of the lexical insertion procedure as assumed by Halle, but actually an operation on terminal features such as fusion and merger. In particular, I propose that fission is an instance of feature copying. Fission creates a copy of the feature bundle containing a given feature combination. Crucially, both the target of the copying and the copy belong to the same insertion cycle. Assuming that features can be matched only once in a given cycle, the features that are matched in the insertion of a lexical item are no longer available again for insertion in the fissioned complex. This reformulation of fission accounts for all of the cases analyzed in Halle (1997), as the interested reader can check.

In the cases under discussion, fission would be triggered by the feature combination [+imperfect, +participant, +plural]. The feature [+imperfect] is contained in the tense node; the feature [+participant, +plural] is in the AgrS node. Suppose that fission makes a copy not only of the given features, but also of directly dominating nodes. In this case, it will create a copy of both the Tense/Mood node and the AgrS node. Thus from the input in (37) it will create (38):

(37)

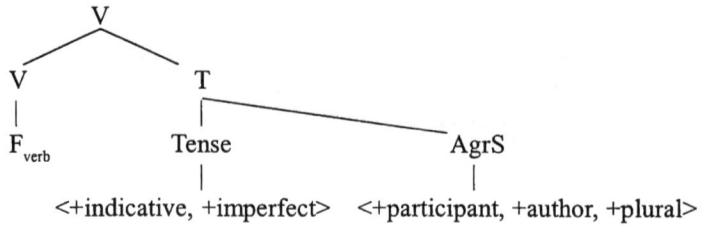

(38)

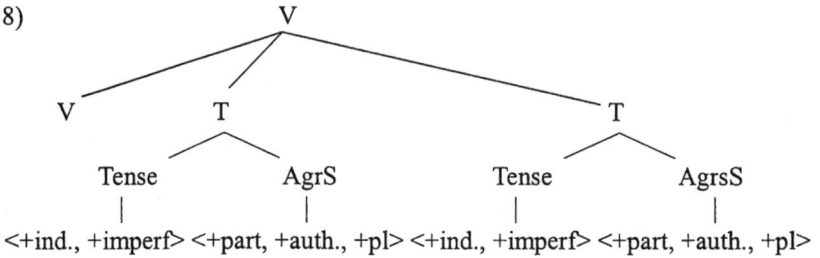

Insertion now applies to the fissioned complex. There are four possible insertion options:

(39)

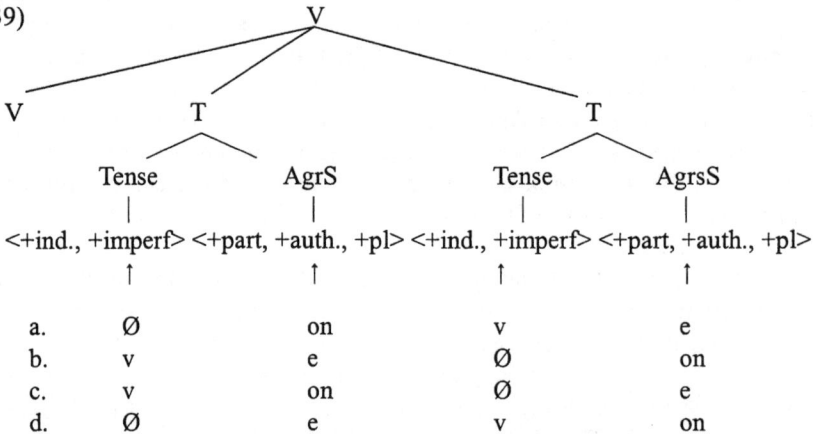

	Tense	AgrS	Tense	AgrsS
a.	Ø	on	v	e
b.	v	e	Ø	on
c.	v	on	Ø	e
d.	Ø	e	v	on

We have to eliminate three of the insertion modalities in (39). Options (39c) and (39d) can be eliminated if we assume that the application of fission is meant to eliminate a marked combination of exponents (see Calabrese 1998 for discussion of this issue). A combination of exponents α and β is marked when the nodes in which α and β are inserted are sister and α and β contain marked features. Let us suppose that the features [+imperfect], [+participant], [+plural] are marked. Thus the combination /v+on/ is marked in (39c) and (39d) insofar as /-v-/ contains the marked feature [+imperfect] and /on/ the marked features [+participant, +plural]. This combination is eliminated in (39a) and (39b), but not in (39c) and (39d). The idea is that by fission we create a sequence of unmarked first person plural present indicative and unmarked subjunctive imperfect. We now have to eliminate (39b). By requiring the unmarked indicative tense to be closer to the verbal stem, we obtain this result.

This account assumes that the structure provided by the syntax is identical in all persons of the imperfect indicative (or subjunctive). The only differences in the morphological realization of the different persons are the outcome of morphological operations. In the case of the I and II plural, in particular, they are the outcome of fission which in this case eliminates a marked combination of exponents, as defined above. Observe that there is cross-linguistic evidence that idiosyncratic exponents for the feature configuration [+Participant, +Plural] are avoided in many grammatical configurations (see Calabrese 1995 and note 11).[11] It is thus not strange to see that fission applies to this combination of features in this dialect.

We can now account for the forms we observe in the I and II plural of the subjunctive present of *sauté: sautombe* and *sauteibe*. Fission applies to the configuration where there is the marked combination [+subjunctive, +participant, +plural]. We thus obtain (41) from (40):

(40)

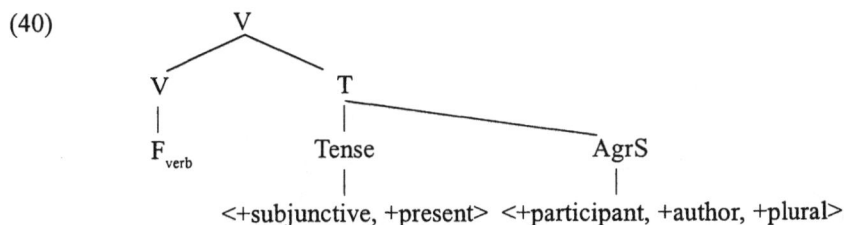

$$<\text{+subjunctive, +present}> \quad <\text{+participant, +author, +plural}>$$

(41)

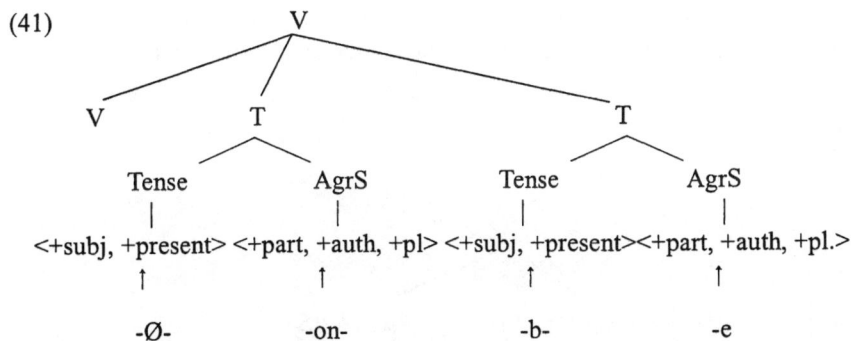

$$<\text{+subj, +present}> \quad <\text{+part, +auth, +pl}> \quad <\text{+subj, +present}> <\text{+part, +auth, +pl.}>$$

-Ø-   -on-   -b-   -e

Insertion as in the bottom line in (41) removes the idiosyncratic exponence for this marked configuration. The unmarked indicative present is inserted closer to the verbal stem. The subjunctive present marker /-b-/ in (1) is inserted in the rightmost tense position and the unmarked ending /-e-/ is inserted in the final AgrS position. An account for the forms *sautombe* and *sauteibe* is thus obtained.

Observe that the structural environment in which impoverishment—
[+subjunctive, +present]—applies is a subset of the structural environment in which
fission applies. If we assume that they are both operations on feature bundles,
fission in the I and II plural will bleed the more general impoverishment operation
by the elsewhere principle, insofar as the former is more specific than the latter.
This accounts for the absence of impoverishment in the I and II plural.

We can now discuss the different forms of the present subjunctive of the verb
BE. It is repeated in (42a), together with the imperfect indicative (42b) and
subjunctive (42c):

(42) a.	sombe	b.	sonse	c.	sonve
	siebe		ese		eve
	siebe		esa		eva
	sombe		sonse		sonve
	siebe		seise		seive
	siebe		esa		eva

I propose the following segmentation of the forms in (42a):

(43)   s + on+ b + e
         si + e + b + e
         si + e + b + e
         s + on+ b + e
         si + e + b + e
         si + e + b + e

Given the analysis I proposed for the subjunctive suffix /b-e/in the case of the
subjunctive present forms *sautombe/sauteibe*, I assume that fission applies to all
persons of the subjunctive present of BE as well to all persons of the subjunctive
present of HAVE. In the case of BE, fission of the input structure in (44) will give
(45):

(44)

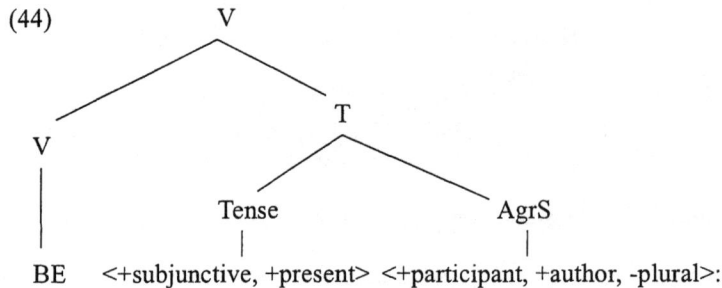

BE   <+subjunctive, +present> <+participant, +author, -plural>:

(45)

```
                              V
                    _____/_____
                   /                        \
                  /           T               T
          V      / \         / \            / \
          |     /   \       /   \          /   \
          |  Tense  AgrS  Tense  AgrS   Tense  AgrS
          |    |     |      |      |      |      |
```

BE <+subj,+present> <+part,+auth,+pl> <+subj,+present> <+part,+auth,+pl.>

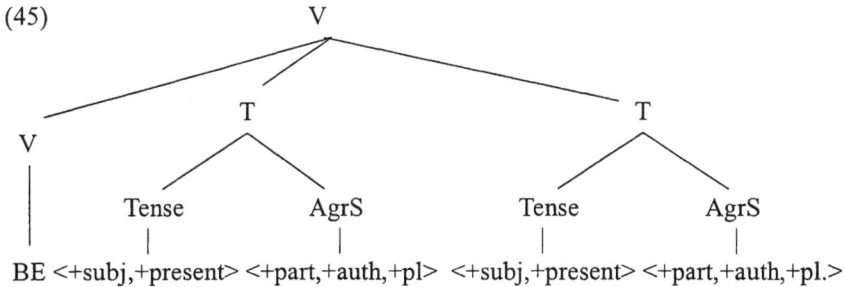

Let us focus on the stem for the moment. One of the peculiarities that needs to be accounted for is the distribution of a special stem allomorph which appears in the II and III singular and plural, but not in the I singular and plural, which instead display the same allomorph as in the present indicative. Given the list in (27) repeated in (47) the distribution of these items is easily accounted for if we assume impoverishment of the feature [+subjunctive] in the I singular and plural in the stem cycle (see (46)). By inhibiting this feature in this cycle, the lexical item /si-/ can no longer be inserted. In its -place the lexical item /s-/ of (47) can be inserted. Thus we have /s-on-b-e/.

(46)   *[+subjunctive]/ [_____ , +author] in the stem insertion cycle

(47)   /si-/   ↔   [BE]$_{Root}$ / _____ + <+subjunctive>
            /s-/   ↔   [BE]$_{Root}$ / _____ + <+participant>
            /e-/   ↔   [BE]$_{Root}$

Observe that the preceding treatment is evidence for the modification of impoverishment formulated earlier. We expect that inhibition of the feature [+subjunctive] in the stem cycle does not prevent this feature from playing an active role in later cycles. And in fact the feature [+subjunctive] plays a crucial role in the insertion of the lexical item [-b-] in later cycles after fission (e.g., s-on-b-e). In contrast, if impoverishment involved deletion, the feature [+subjunctive] would be removed from the terminal node and would not be there in later cycles, thus preventing the insertion of the subjunctive marker /-b-/.

To account for the shape of the different personal endings in (42a), the same impoverishment operations as in the indicative present need to be assumed. In addition, the feature [+participant] of the II plural needs to be inhibited. This accounts for why the elsewhere /-e-/ appears in all persons except the first. Finally, the presence of elsewhere /-e/ in final position is accounted for as discussed in *sautombe*.

We can now conclude the discussion of BE with an account of the imperfect subjunctive and indicative. For these tenses, I assume that fission applies only in the first and second plural as for the regular verb *sauté*. Crucially, however, the feature change in (30) repeated in (48) changes the first person singular into a first plural, as discussed earlier:

(48)   [–plural] → [+plural]/ [BE + ___ , +author]

After the feature change in (48) fission applies also in the first person singular. An account for the different forms of these tenses is thus readily obtained.

A few final observations on the verb HAVE. As for the present subjunctive of BE, I assume that there is fission in all persons of the present subjunctive of HAVE. A straightforward account is thus obtained for all persons—as shown in (49)—except for the II singular /abe/ where we should expect the ending /-e-/ in internal position *ebe:

(49)   a-e-b-e → (R.R. (21)) → ebe
              [—]
              a-a-b-e → (R.R. (21)) → abe
              a-on-b-e → (R.R. (21)) → onbe → (other rules) → ombe
              a-ei-b-e → (R.R. (21)) → eibe
              a-a-b-e → (R.R. (21)) → abe

A possible solution for the II singular is to assume that in this case the feature [+participant] is changed into [–participant] by rule (50); thus, the III person ending [-a] of (29) can be inserted:

(50)   [+participant] → [–participant]/ [___ , -author, HAVE]

As for the imperfect subjunctive and indicative, we have to assume that fission not only applies in the first and second plural, but crucially also in the first singular. This is to account for the form *ese* or *eve* instead of expected *ase* or *ave*.

An account for the complex system of verbal forms in (1) is thus obtained. The defining morphological feature of this verbal system is the presence of fission in the I and II plural for all verbs, in addition to fission in the present subjunctive of the auxiliary verbs.

In concluding this section, it is important to observe that the fact that a morphological rule such as (48), which accounts for the presence of the I singular forms *son, sombe, sonve, sonse*—or any of the other morphological rules proposed in the analysis developed above—is applied in the inflectional vocabulary of the dialect of Livinallongo does not imply that the speakers, or listeners, need in any way mentally "derive" the words they say, or hear, by means of such rules. What it does mean is that the generalizations they express belong to the regular morphological pattern of this dialect, while for example the I plural forms *se, *sebe, *seve and se, created by a hypothetical reversal of (48), would be irregular. The claim made is that someone who knows this dialect implicitly knows that morphological pattern and, under appropriate circumstances, will recognize the difference between regular and irregular forms, though he or she may not be able to verbalize the rules that underlie them.

3. Conclusion

In conclusion, we have seen that by adopting Distributed Morphology, we can obtain a successful account of the syntax/morphology interface we observe in the verbal morphology of the dialect of Livinallongo. In order to do that, however, we had reformulate the key operations of impoverishment and fission.

Notes

I dedicate this article to Paola Benincà who has been a great teacher and friend to me since my first days as a college student at the University of Padua. I am thankful to Morris Halle and William Snyder for comments on an earlier draft. The usual disclaimers apply.

1.   The subject clitics *t/te*, *l/el* and *i* occur in the II sg. and III sg. and pl., respectively. I am unable to find any clear generalization correlating the presence of the subject clitics to what happens in the endings, although the distinction between I sg. and pl., and II pl. (where the clitics are absent) vs. III sg. and pl., and II sg. (where the clitics are present) does play a role in the analysis of the endings. I am thus forced to focus only on what happens in the endings. The issue of how to account for the distribution of the subject clitics will be left to future research.

2.   The terminal nodes in the syntactic trees in (3) are composed of two parts, a string of phonemes and a complex of grammatical features. These terminal elements will be called "morphemes" and the term "phonological exponent" will designate the phoneme sequence in a morpheme. Not every morpheme need have a phonological exponent.

3.   See also Embick (2000) for important evidence in support of Distributed Morphology.

4.   The same structure can be obtained if we assume an underlying AgrS functional projection and merger applies to the AgrS head node.

5.   The asymmetry in the morphological expression between the Italian imperfect and past tenses in (5) is due to a number of phonological changes that historically affected the suffix [-v-] characterizing the Latin past tense in some conjugations. Thus, for example, in the case of III sg. in (5a), the suffix /-ò/ historically derives from the Latin formation /-a-v-it/ (/-a-/ = thematic vowel, /-v-/ = past tense suffix, /-it/ = III sg. ending) through an intermediate stage */aut/ after the deletion of the ending high vowel (see Tekavcic 1980:269)

If we consider the Italian verbal system from a synchronic point of view, however, there is no evidence that there is an underlying suffix /-v/u-/ in the III sg. of the past tense in this case, nor is there a synchronic phonological process fusing this suffix with the thematic vowels /-a-/, as happened historically. The available evidence simply shows that the lexical item inserted in the IIIsg. past is simply /-ò/, as proposed above.

The consideration of what happened historically, however, does throw a different light on the morphological process of fusion proposed in (10). One could in fact propose that morphological fusion is needed so that the syntactic structure can interface with the morphological peculiarities of Italian, which in this case are the outcomes of the phonological changes which affected the lexical items of this language. Due to its historical development, the Italian lexicon contains the lexical item /-ò/ which is idiosyncratic for the III sg. past. Morphological fusion applies as in (10) so that this lexical item can be inserted. Otherwise syntax and morphology would not converge in Chomsky's (1995) sense, and the syntactic structure would not be matched with appropriate phonological material.

6. The suffixal /-a-/ that appears in the forms in (12) is the thematic vowel which is deleted before vowel initial suffixes by the readjustment rule in (21). The I sg. is exceptional in this regard in not requiring the deletion of the thematic vowel.

7. Observe that underspecification of lexical items is not necessarily required. The same results obtained by underspecification could be obtained by assuming that lexical items are specified with all types of features, but that only a subset of them—those crucially used in lexical insertion, as determined by principle (16)—is specially marked (see Calabrese 1995) for more discussion of this issue).

8. Observe that I am assuming only a Tense terminal node. Other functional projections such as Aspect and Mood could be assumed from a syntactic and semantic point of view. If they are, I hypothesize that the operations of (1) Merger with the verbal head and (2) Fusion with the tense node eliminate them and lead to (20). See Harris (1994) for more discussion of the morphological structure of verbs in Spanish, which is similar to that of the other Romance languages in this respect.

9. I prefer this solution to a solution assuming the other lexical item in (i) since it would lead to homophony:

(i)   /e/   ↔   [-participant] BE ____

This solution may be the correct one, however, if we assume that BE belongs to a different conjugation class than HAVE.

10. A parallel situation occurs in Italian in the imperfect indicative of the verb *essere* 'to be'. As we can see in (i), the marker /-v-/ of the imperfect which is observed in the regular verb *parlavo* is absent in the singular and the III plural of the imperfect indicative of *essere*, but present in I and II plural:

(i)   a.   er-o   b.   parl-a-v-o
              er-i   parl-a-v-i
              er-a   parl-a-v-a
              er-a-v-amo   parl-a-v-amo
              er-a-v-ate   parl-a-v-ate
              er-ano   parl-a-v-ano

Impoverishment of the feature [+imperfect] can account for the asymmetry in the imperfect of *essere*.

A possible account of the asymmetry in (i) is the following: impoverishment in the imperfect creates irregularity. As we will see from later discussion (note 11), the combination of features [+participant, +plural] of the I and II plural is to be considered as marked. One can then propose that there is preference for a regular exponence in the case of exponents of marked morphological configurations. A principle of this type could block impoverishment in the I and II plural. The consequences of this idea on the analysis proposed later are unclear to me at this moment. This issue needs to be investigated further.

11. In my analysis a fundamental role is played by the configuration [+participant, +plural] characterizing I and II pl. I proposed that these two feature specifications are marked. The fission operation eliminates idiosyncratic exponents specified by these features in certain categories such as the imperfect subjunctive or indicatives. We should expect to find similar changes in other morphological categories. As a matter of fact, changes

affecting exponents of the I and II pl. are quite common in the Romance languages. In (i) I list some of these changes:

(i) a.   In the many Italian dialects, the exponent of the I Plural oblique clitic was replaced by the exponent of a locative.

b.   In the other Italian dialects, the exponent of the I Plural oblique clitic was replaced by the exponent of a partitive (< Latin INDE).

c.   In the Toscan dialect of Lucca, the exponent of the reflexive/impersonal clitic /si/ has also become the exponent of I Plural oblique clitic.

d.   In Toscan the I Plural subject is replaced by the reflexive/impersonal clitic /si/. The verb appears in the III Singular.

d.   In the Campidanese dialect of Sardinian, the exponent of the reflexive clitic /si/ has also become the exponent of I and II Plural.

e.   In many dialects, the I and II Plurals do not have a specific subject clitic. They appear either without clitic or with the same clitic appearing in the I Singular.

Reasons of space prevent me from providing an analysis of the changes in (i) (see Calabrese 1995 for discussion).

References

Baker, M. (1985) "The Mirror Principle and Morphosyntactic Explanation," *Linguistic Inquiry* 16:373–415.

Beninchà, P. (1996) "Agglutination and Inflection in Northern Italian Dialects," in C. Parodi, C. Quicoli, M. Saltarelli and M.L. Zubizarreta (eds.) *Aspects of Romance Linguistics: Selected Papers from the Linguistic Symposium on Romance Languages 24* (March 1994), pp. 59–72. Washington, D.C.: Georgetown University Press.

Beninchà, P. (1999) "Between Morphology and Syntax: On the Verbal Morphology of Some Alpine Dialects," Ms., University of Padua.

Calabrese, A. (1995) "Syncretism Phenomena in the Clitic Systems of Italian and Sardinian Dialects and the Notion of Morphological Change," in J. Beckman (ed.) *Proceedings of NELS* 25, pp. 151–173. Amherst, Mass.: Graduate Linguistic Student Association.

Calabrese, A. (1998) "Some Remarks on the Latin Case System and Its Development in Romance," in E. Treviño and J. Lema (eds.) *Theoretical Analysis of the Romance Languages*, pp. 71–126. Amsterdam: John Benjamins.

Chomsky, N. (1995) *The Minimalist Program*. Cambridge, Mass.: MIT Press.

Davis, R. (1991) "Allomorphy in Spanish." Ph.D. diss., University of North Carolina, Chapel Hill.

Embick, D. (2000) "The Morphosyntax of the Latin Perfect: Analytic and Synthetic Forms," *Linguistic Inquiry* 31(2):185–230.

Halle, M. (1997) "Distribute Morphology: Impoverishment and Fission," *MIT Working Papers in Linguistics* 30:425–449.

Halle, M. and A. Marantz (1994) "Some Key Features of Distributed Morphology," *MIT Working Papers in Linguistics* 21:275–288.

Harris, J. (1975) "Aspects of Spanish Verbal Morphology," in M. P. Hagiwara (ed.) *Studies in Romance Linguistics,* pp. 44–60. Ann Arbor: University of Michigan.

Harris, J. (1987) "The Accentual Patterns of Verb Paradigms in Spanish," *Natural Languages and Linguistic Theory* 5:61–90.

Harris, J. (1993) "Spanish Default Morphology." Ms., MIT.

Harris, J. (1994) "The Syntax-Phonology Mapping in Catalan and Spanish Clitics," *MIT Working Papers in Linguistics* 21:321–354.

Harris, J. (1997) "There Is No Imperative Paradigm in Spanish," in F. Martinez-Gil and A. Morales-Front (eds.), *Issues in the Phonology and Morphology of the Major Iberian Languages,* pp. 537–557. Washington, D.C.: Georgetown University Press.

Noyer, R. (1992) "Features, Positions, and Affixes in Autonomous Morphological Structure." Ph.D. diss., MIT.

Tekavcic, P. (1980) *Grammatica storica dell'italiano.* Vol. 2: *Morfo-sintassi* . Bologna: Il Mulino.

2

Motion Verbs as Functional Heads

Anna Cardinaletti and Giuliana Giusti

1. Introduction

In the dialect spoken in Marsala (Trapani, Sicily), motion verbs such as *iri* (go), *viniri* (come), and *passari* (pass) enter two different constructions: (1), which is parallel to the Italian control construction (cf. *Va a prendere il pane*) and (2), which has no Italian counterpart (cf. **Va a prende il pane*):

(1)   Va   a pigghiari u   pani.
             go-3s to fetch-INF the bread

(2)   Va   a pigghia u   pani.
             go-3s to fetch-3s the bread

In (1), the verb following the motion verb is infinitive. In (2), it is inflected for mood (indicative), for tense (present), and for agreement (3rd person singular). We call (1) the "infinitival construction" and (2) the "inflected construction." In this chapter, we show that the status of the motion verb is different in the two constructions and, in particular, that the motion verb in the inflected construction is a functional element, much like an auxiliary. We provide examples with the motion verb *iri* only, but all the properties we discuss hold for *viniri* and *passari* as well.[1]

We start by considering the connecting element *a*, which turns out to be different in the two constructions from both the synchronic and the diachronic point of view. We show that, although *a* in the inflected construction is derived from the Latin coordinative conjunction AC, this construction cannot be considered a coordination. In the rest of the chapter, we compare the motion verb in the inflected construction with auxiliary verbs and show that they behave alike with respect to a number of properties typical of functional elements. [2]

2. The connecting element *a*

In both (1) and (2) above, the connecting element *a* is adjacent to the verbal form *va* which ends with the same vowel. Since in fast speech only one (short) /a/ is pronounced, it is necessary to show that the connecting *a* actually occurs and motivate why only one sound appears.

Let us observe what happens when the verbal form does not end in /a/. In fast speech, if the final vowel of the verb cannot build a diphthong with /a/, it drops, as in (3a,b); if it can form a diphthong, it is preserved and realized as the first sound of the diphthong, as in (3c):

(3) a.   Va[japp]igghiari   u   pani.   (cf. Vajo a pigghiari ...)
          [I] go-1s to fetch-INF the bread

   a'.   Va[japp]igghio   u   pani.   (cf. Vajo a pigghio ...)
          [I] go-1s to fetch-1s   the bread

   b.   Van[napp]igghiari   u   pani.   (cf. Vanno a pigghiari ...)
          [they] go-3PL to fetch-INF the bread

   b'.   Van[napp]igghiano   u   pani.   (cf. Vanno a pigghiano ...)
          [they] go-3PL to fetch-3PL the bread

   c.   Va[japp]igghiari   u   pani.   (cf. Vai a pigghiari ...)
          [you] go-2s to fetch-INF the bread

   c'.   Va[japp]igghi   u   pani.   (cf. Vai a pigghi ...)
          [you] go-2s to fetch-2s the bread

Example (3) is sufficient evidence to claim that in (1) and (2) above, the single /a/ sound pronounced is the connecting element, while the final /a/ of the verb is dropped. Example (3) also shows that the connecting *a* triggers "Raddoppiamento sintattico" in both constructions.

The similar phonological properties, however, are not sufficient evidence to claim that *a* is one and the same element in the two constructions. It is clear from (4) that the two connecting *a*'s occur in different positions. In the infinitival construction, *a* can be preceded by a frequency adverb such as *sempre* (always), while in the inflected construction it must be adjacent to the motion verb:

(4) a.   Peppe va   (**sempre**) a pigghiari (**sempre**) u pani ne 'sta butia.
          Peppe go-3s (always) to fetch-INF (always) the bread in this shop

   b.   Peppe va   (*sempre) a pigghia (**sempre**) u pani   ne 'sta butia.
          Peppe go-3s (always)   to fetch-3s (always) the bread in   this shop

This means that in (4a) *a* occurs in a position which may be lower than the frequency adverb *sempre*, whereas in (4b) *a* occurs in a higher position.

Diachronic considerations also lead to the conclusion that the connecting element *a* is not the same element in the two constructions. According to Rohlfs

(1969: secs. 710, 761), in the infinitival construction, *a* derives from the Latin preposition AD; while in the inflected construction, *a* derives from the Latin coordinating conjunction AC.[3,4]

The inflected construction, however, cannot be considered a coordination from the synchronic point of view for a number of reasons. First, the coordinative conjunction in Marsalese is *e* (and), as in Italian. Second, the inflected construction does not behave as a coordination, since it is possible to extract a complement of the verb following the motion verb. We observe clitic extraction in (5a) (see section 6) and *wh*-extraction in (5b):[5]

(5) a. $\mathbf{U}_i$ vajo   a pigghio t_i.
         it$_{cl}$ go-1s to fetch-1s
         'I go and take it.'

    b.   **Cu soccu**$_i$ vai   a aggiusti a   machina t_i ?
         with what [do you] go-2s to fix-2s   the car?
         'What do you go and fix the car with?'

Both operations are impossible in a coordination. Example (6) shows that clitic climbing is not possible out of the second conjunct of a coordination, given the contrast between (6a) and (6b), while it is possible out of an embedded infinitival, as in (6c). Example (7)a shows that it is impossible to extract a *wh*-adjunct from a coordination. Example (7b) is a regular main clause with no conjunction, and (7c) shows that the same extraction is allowed from the embedded infinitival. Examples (6) and (7) give the Marsalese sentence first and then the Italian one:[6]

(6) a. * **U** vajo e   pigghio.   / *$\mathbf{Lo}$ vado e prendo.
         it$_{cl}$ go-1s and fetch-1s

    b.   Minni   vajo e **u** pigghio.   / Vado e **lo** prendo.
         REFL$_{cl}$LOC$_{cl}$ go-1s and it$_{cl}$ fetch-1s

    c.   **U**   vajo a pigghiari.   / **Lo** vado a prendere.
         [I] it$_{cl}$ go-1s to fetch-INF

(7) a. * Cu soccu   vai   e   aggiusti a machina?
           with what [do you] go-2s and fix-2s the car?

    a'. * Con che cosa   vai   e   ripari   la macchina?
           with what   [do you] go-2s and repair-2s   the car

    b.   Cu soccu   aggiusti a   machina?
          with what [do you] fix-2s   the car

    b'.   Con che cosa   ripari   la macchina?
          with what [do you] repair-2s   the car

    c.   Cu soccu   vai   a aggiustari a machina?
          with what [do you] go-2s to fix-INF   the car

c′.   Con che cosa   vai   a riparare   la macchina?
        with what [do you] go-2s to repair-INF the car

We conclude that from the point of view of extractions, the inflected construction in Marsalese does not behave as a coordination. It behaves parallel to the infinitival construction both in Marsalese and in Italian, in which the two verbs are clearly in a hierarchical configuration.

Two further observations against a coordination analysis concern the fixed order of the two verbs, (8a) vs. (8b), and the impossibility of other coordinating elements, (10a):

(8) a.   Vajo   a pigghio u   pani.
               go-1s to fetch-1s the bread

      b. * Pigghio u pani a vajo.
              fetch-1s the bread to go-1s

(9) a.   Minni   vajo   e   u   pigghio.   / Vado e lo prendo.
               REFL$_{cl}$LOC$_{cl}$ go-1s and it$_{cl}$ fetch-1s

      b.   U pigghio e   minni   vajo.   / Lo prendo e vado.
           it$_{cl}$ fetch-1s and REFL$_{cl}$LOC$_{cl}$ go-1s

(10)a. * U vajo   e   /o pigghio.
           it$_{cl}$ go-1s and / or fetch-1s

      b.   Minni   vajo   e   /o pigghio u pani.
           REFL$_{cl}$LOC$_{cl}$ go-1s and / or fetch-1s the bread

In (8) the motion verb obligatorily precedes the other verb, a restriction not found in ordinary coordinations such as (9). This order is expected under the hypothesis that the motion verb is an auxiliary-like verb, since in Marsalese auxiliaries always precede lexical verbs. In (10), we show that the inflected construction does not share the properties of a real coordination. The connecting element in the inflected construction in (10a) cannot be freely replaced by other coordinative elements, as opposed to the real coordination in (10b). (Two further arguments against the coordination analysis are given in notes 11 and 15 below.)

Before concluding this section, it is necessary to discuss another logical possibility—that is, that the motion verb and the subsequent verb are coordinated heads. In Romance, verbal heads can be coordinated under a special condition, namely, if they are morphologically related, as observed by Benincà and Cinque (1993). Consider the Italian examples in (11):

(11)a.   Lo leggo   e   rileggo.
           it$_{cl}$ read-1s and re-read-1s

      b. * Lo compro e   leggo.
           it$_{cl}$ buy-1s and read-1s

In (11a), the two verbs crucially share their object. The position of the clitic object to the left of the first verb suggests that the two verbs behave as a single head. This is not the case in (11b), where the verbs are morphologically unrelated, and head coordination is unallowed. Object sharing is thus excluded, and coordination must take place at a higher structural level, which implies the presence of two clitic pronouns: cf. *Lo compro e lo leggo* ([I] it$_{CL}$ buy and it$_{CL}$ read).

The inflected construction in (5a) above is only apparently similar to (11a). In (5a), the two verbs are not morphologically related. Differently from the head coordination in (11a), the inflected construction appears to be a property of a very restricted class of motion verbs, and there is no restriction with respect to the choice of the subsequent verb. Furthermore, the clitic pronoun in (5a) is not an argument of the motion verb, but only of the subsequent verb. In other words, the two verbs in the inflected construction never share any argument. We thus conclude that head coordination is not to be assumed in the inflected construction.[7]

In the following sections, we analyze the motion verb in the inflected construction in Marsalese compared to the infinitival construction. We show that the two constructions are different with respect to the position and the status of the motion verb. In the inflected construction, it is a functional verb,[8] and the main verb is the one following *a*, while in the infinitival construction it is a main verb which selects a control clause.[9]

The proposal that the inflected construction involves a functional motion verb is supported by the observation that in a whole set of phenomena (co-occurrence with adverbs and floating quantifiers, deficient morphological paradigm, lack of selectional properties, lack of co-occurrence with pleonastic clitic pronouns, and obligatory application of restructuring), it parallels functional verbs such as the auxiliaries *aviri* (have) and *stari* (stay) which form the present perfect and the progressive, respectively. This is the topic of the rest of the chapter.

3. The adjacency restriction

The morpheme *a* is the only element which can intervene between the two verbs in the inflected construction. While in the infinitival construction in (12), a floating quantifier (*tutti* 'all') can appear between the two verbal forms, in the inflected construction in (13), the quantifier must follow the lexical verb:

(12) a.   I   picciotti vanno tutti a pigghiari u pani ne 'sta butìa.
          the boys   go-3PL all to fetch-INF the bread in this shop

     b.   I   picciotti vanno a pigghiari tutti u pani ne 'sta butìa.
          the boys   go-3PL to fetch-INF all the bread in this shop

(13) a. * I   picciotti vanno tutti a pigghiano u pani ne 'sta butia.
          the boys   go-3PL all to fetch-3PL the bread in this shop

     b.   I   picciotti vanno a pigghiano tutti u pani ne 'sta butia.
          the boys   go-3PL to fetch-3PL all   the bread in this shop

The adjacency restriction exemplified in (13) suggests that here the motion verb does not head its own clause. If it did, nothing should prevent it from being followed by a floating quantifier, as is the case in (12).

The same point can be made on the basis of the distribution of frequency adverbs. Cf. *sempre* (always) in examples (4) above and *mai* (never) in (14)–(15) below:

(14) a. Un vajo mai a pigghiari u pani ne 'sta butìa.
         not go-1s never to fetch-INF the bread in this shop

     b. Un vajo a pigghiari mai u pani ne 'sta butìa.
         not go-1s to fetch-INF never the bread in this shop
         'I never go buy bread in this shop.'

(15) a. * Un vajo mai a pigghio u pani ne 'sta butìa.
         not go-1s never to fetch-1s the bread in   this shop

     b. Un vajo a pigghio mai   u pani ne 'sta butìa.
         not go-1s to fetch-1s never the bread in this shop
         'I never go buy bread in this shop.'

In the infinitival construction in (4)a and (14), there are two possible positions for the frequency adverb. This differentiates it from the inflected construction in (4b) and (15), where the frequency adverb can occupy only one position. Although the free occurrence of the adverb in (4)a and (14) is not necessarily evidence for a biclausal analysis of the infinitival construction, the fixed position of the adverb in (4b) and (15) can straightforwardly be captured by a monoclausal analysis of the inflected construction.

The adjacency restriction is also found with another functional verb—namely, the perfect auxiliary *aviri* (have). In the perfect tense, no element (such as the negative adverb *mai* 'never') can appear between the auxiliary and the past participle, as in (16):

(16) a. * Un ci   hajo mai   stato.
         not there_{cl} have never been

     b. Un ci   hajo stato mai.
         not there_{cl} have been never
         'I've never been there.'

Taking for granted that the auxiliary is a functional verb, we interpret the parallelism between (15) and (16), together with the contrast between (14) and (15), as compelling evidence that *iri* in the inflected construction is a functional verb. Since the motion verb precedes the finite lexical verb, which in turn precedes floating quantifiers and frequency adverbs, we assume that it occurs in a very high functional head, higher than the head to which the finite verb moves in Marsalese.

The structure we obtain is (17):

(17) [$_{FP}$ [motion verb [$_{FP}$ [*a* [$_{AgrSP}$ [lexical verb$_i$ [$_{FP}$ *mai*[... [$_{VP}$ [t$_i$]]]]]]]]]]]

4. Invariant morphological forms

Whereas in the infinitival construction the verb is always fully inflected, as shown in (18), the inflected construction allows for the motion verb to occur in the invariant form *va* in all persons except for the 1st and 2nd plural, as in (19):[10]

(18) a. (Eo) vajo /*va a pigghiari u pani.
        (I) go-1s/ go to fetch-INF the bread

     b. (Tu) vai   /*va a pigghiari u pani.
        (you) go-2s/ go to fetch-INF the bread

     c. (Iddu / Idda) va   a pigghiari u pani.
        (he / she)   go-3s to fetch-INF the bread

     d. (Niatri) emo   /*va a pigghiari u pani.
        (we) go-1PL / go to fetch-INF the bread

     e. (Viatri) ite   /*va a pigghiari u pani.
        (you) go-2PL / go to fetch-INF the bread

     f. (Iddi / Idde) vanno /*va a pigghiari u   pani.
        (they)   go-3PL / go to fetch-INF the bread

(19) a. (Eo) vajo   /va a pigghio u   pani.
        (I) go-1s/ go to fetch-1s the bread

     b. (Tu) vai   /va a pigghi u pani.
        (you) go-2s/ go to fetch-2s the bread

     c. (Iddu / Idda) va   a pigghia u pani.
        (he / she)   go-3s to fetch-3s the bread

     d. (Niatri) *emo   /*va a pigghiamo u   pani.
        (we) go-1PL / go to fetch-1PL the bread

     e. (Viatri) *ite   /*va a pigghiati u pani.
        (you) go-2PL / go to fetch-2PL the bread

     f. (Iddi / Idde) vanno / va a pigghiano u   pani.
        (they)   go-3PL / go to fetch-3PL the bread

The invariant form *va* is homophonous to the 3rd person singular, (19c), and can be seen as a reduction of the inflected forms *vajo*, *vai*, and *vanno*. This explains why this form is not possible in the 1st and 2nd person plural, which are built with a different allomorph of the verb *iri*, namely, *e-/i*: cf. *emo*, *ite* in (18d,e). For the ungrammaticality of the forms *emo/ite* in the inflected construction (19d,e), see section 7.

The property of displaying an invariant form cannot be reduced to the recoverability of tense and person features in the inflected construction, given that this option is also present with other functional verbs in Marsalese, such as the auxiliary verb *aviri* (have) and the aspectual verb *stari* (stay = be), which combine with a nonfinite form:

(20) a.   (Eo) un ci   hajo   / ha   stato mai.
           (I)   not there$_{cl}$ have-1s / have been never

     b.   (Tu) un ci   hai   / ha   stato mai.
           (you) not there$_{cl}$ have-2s / have been never

     c.   (Iddu / Idda) un ci   ha   stato mai.
           (he / she)   not there$_{cl}$ have-3s been never

(21) a.   (Eo) ci   stajo / sta enno.
           *(I) there$_{cl}$ stay-1s / stay go-*GER

     b.   (Tu) ci   stai / sta enno.
           *(you) there$_{cl}$ stay-2s / stay go-*GER

     c.   (Iddu / Idda) ci   sta   enno.
           *(he / she)   there$_{cl}$ stay-3s go-*GER
           'I'm / you're / he's / she's going there.'

Notice that parallel to motion verbs, the invariant form is homophonous to the 3rd person singular; but differently from motion verbs, these verbs only allow the invariant form in the singular.

In all the three cases, the invariant form is not allowed when the verb is lexical:

(22) a.   (Eo) ci   vajo / *va.
           (I)   there$_{cl}$ go-1s / go
           'I go there.'

     b.   (Eo) ci   hajo   /*ha na soro.
           (I) there$_{cl}$ have-1s / have a sister
           'I have a sister.'

     c.   (Eo) ci   stajo   /*sta.
           (I) there$_{cl}$ stay-1s / stay
           'I stay there.'

It is not the place here to establish exactly why some auxiliaries in Marsalese display the optional reduced forms. We can speculate that, contrary to lexical verbs which start in the V position and move to functional heads to check their features, auxiliaries are inserted into the relevant functional heads directly. For this reason, they may dispense with checking features which are realized lower in the structure. Assuming that auxiliaries may be higher than the person head could explain why they may lack person features. Whatever analysis of the invariant forms in Marsalese turns out to be correct, for our discussion it is relevant to notice that in the inflected construction and only in that construction the motion verb behaves parallel to auxiliaries.

5. Adjuncts and complements

In the infinitival construction, the motion verb can combine with and be immediately followed by adjuncts such as *c'a machina* (by car) as in (23a); but this is not possible for the motion verb in the inflected construction (23b):

(23) a.   Peppe va   a mangiari c'a machina.
         Peppe go-3s to eat-INF   by car
         'Peppe goes to eat by car.'

    b. * Peppe va   a mangia c'a machina.
          Peppe go-3s to eat-3s by car

This contrast supports the hypothesis that in the inflected construction, the motion verb is functional. Our prediction is that *iri* in the inflected construction should also not select a directional complement such as *a casa* (home). Consider (24):

(24)   Peppe va   a mangia a casa.
         Peppe go-3s to eat-3s *home / at home
         'Peppe goes to eat at home.'

In Marsalese (as in Italian) directional and locative complements are most often expressed by the same prepositions. *A casa* does not morphologically distinguish between motion and status. However, the glosses show that (24) is ungrammatical if *a casa* is understood as a directional complement, as expected, and grammatical if *a casa* is understood as a locative complement associated with *mangiari*.

In order to distinguish the two types of complements, we can use the lexical preposition *agghiri a* (toward), which is only directional. This preposition can be found in the VP headed by the motion verb in (25a), but cannot be found in the VP headed by *mangiari* (eat) in (25b):

(25) a.   Va   agghiri a casa a mangiari.
         go-3s toward to home to eat-INF
         'He goes toward home to eat.'

    b. * Va   a mangiari agghiri a casa.
         go-3s to eat-INF   toward to home

When the motion verb is functional, as in (26), it cannot select the directional PP:

(26) a.   * Va agghiri a casa a mangia.

    b. * Va   a mangia agghiri a casa.
         go-3s to eat-3s toward to home

In conclusion, the hypothesis that the motion verb in the inflected construction is functional also captures the fact that it shares with auxiliaries the property of not taking any kind of complements or adjuncts.

6. Pleonastic clitic pronouns

When *iri* is used as a main verb without other complements, it is always found together with two pleonastic clitic pronouns: a reflexive clitic (*mi, ti*, etc.) and the locative clitic *ni*, (27a). This complex form is also optionally found when the verb takes some complement(s), (27b,c):

(27) a.   Minni   vajo.
           $REFL_{cl}LOC_{cl}$ *go-1s*
           'I'm going away.'

     b.   (Minni)   vajo a casa.
           $REFL_{cl}LOC_{cl}$ *go-1s home*

     c.   (Minni)   vajo (a casa) c'a machina.
           $REFL_{cl}LOC_{cl}$ *go-1s (home) by car*
           'I'm going (home) by car.'

The optionality of the clitic cluster is also found in the infinitival construction, (28a), where the infinitival clause counts as a complement of the motion verb. On the contrary, no clitic can appear when the motion verb is used as a functional head in the inflected construction, (28b):[11]

(28) a.   (Minni)   vajo a mangiari a casa.
           $REFL_{cl}LOC_{cl}$ *go-1s to eat-INF home*

     b.   (*Minni)   vajo a mangio a casa.
           $REFL_{cl}LOC_{cl}$ *go-1s to eat-1s home*

The same contrast arises with lexical *stari*, which can co-occur with the same clitic cluster, and auxiliary *stari*, which cannot:

(29) a.   (Minni)   stajo   a casa.
           $REFL_{cl}LOC_{cl}$ *stay-1s at home*

     b.   (*Minni)   stajo   mangianno a casa.
           $REFL_{cl}LOC_{cl}$ *stay-1s eat-GER   at home*

Similarly, *aviri* must co-occur with the locative clitic *ci* when it is lexical and cannot when it is functional:[12]

(30) a.   Ci   hajo   na soro.
           $there_{cl}$ *have-1s a sister*

b.   (*Ci) hajo   mangiato a casa.
there$_{cl}$ have-1s eaten   at home

Pleonastic clitics are a subcase of selection. It is therefore expected that the conclusion reached in the previous section holds for this section as well, thereby confirming our hypothesis that the motion verb in the inflected construction is a functional verb.

7. Restructuring effects

"Restructuring" effects such as clitic climbing are optional, although preferred, in the infinitival construction in (31), as well as with modals in (32). They are obligatory in the inflected construction in (33), as well as with the two functional verbs *aviri* and *stari* discussed above, (34)–(35):[13, 14]

(31) a.   ? Vajo a pigghiàllo.
                go-1s to fetch-INF- it$_{cl}$

b.   U vajo a pigghiàri.
        it$_{cl}$ go-1s to fetch-INF
        'I go to fetch it.'

(32) a.   ? Pozzu pigghiàllo.
                can-1s fetch-INF- it$_{cl}$

b.   U pozzu pigghiàri.
        it$_{cl}$ can-1s fetch-INF
        'I can fetch it.'

(33) a.   * Vajo a pìgghiolo.
                go-1s to fetch-1s- it$_{cl}$

b.   U vajo a pigghio.
        it$_{cl}$ go-1s to fetch-1s
        'I go and fetch it.'

(34) a.   * Hajo   pigghiàtolo.
                have-1s fetch-PAST.PART- it$_{cl}$

b.   L'hajo   pigghiato.
        it$_{cl}$ have-1s fetch-PAST.PART
        'I have fetched it.'

(35) a.   * Stajo   pigghiànnolo.
                stay-1s fetch-GER- it$_{cl}$

b.   U stajo   pigghiànno.
        it$_{cl}$ stay-1s fetch-GER
        'I'm fetching it.'

Notice that the lexical verb in (33) is finite and could in principle attract a proclitic pronoun. However this is not the case. Clitic climbing puts the clitic pronoun in front of the highest verb—that is, the motion verb. Intermediate placing of the pronoun is ungrammatical in the inflected construction (36c), on a par with all other cases involving infinitival verbs, (36a,b,d,e):[15]

(36) a.   * Vajo a u pigghiàri.
         go-1s to it_{CL} fetch-INF

    b.   * Pozzu u pigghiàri.
         can-1s it_{CL} fetch-INF

    c.   * Vajo a u pigghio.
         go-1s to it_{CL} fetch-1s

    d.   * Hajo   u pigghiato.
         have-1s it_{CL} fetch-PAST.PART

    e.   * Stajo   u pigghiànno.
         stay-1s it_{CL} fetch-GER

The comparison with auxiliary verbs with respect to clitic climbing indicates once again that the inflected construction is a monoclausal structure, which implies that the motion verb is inserted in a functional head.

8. Tense, Mood, and Person restrictions

One final piece of evidence for the functional status of the motion verb in the inflected construction is the fact that this construction displays a number of inflectional restrictions which would be unexpected with a lexical verb.

While there is no tense restriction in the infinitival construction (37), the inflected construction is impossible in the past tense and in the imperfect. As shown in (38) and (39), respectively, any combination of forms is impossible:[16]

(37) a.   Ii / Ia   a pigghiari u pani.
         go-PAST-1s / go-IMPERF-1s to fetch-INF the bread

    b.   Isti / Ia   a pigghiari u pani.
         go-PAST-2s / go-IMPERF-2s to fetch-INF the bread

    c.   Iu / Ia   a pigghiari u pani.
         go-PAST-3s / go-IMPERF-3s to fetch-INF the bread

    d.   Emu / Ìamo   a pigghiari u pani.
         go-PAST-1PL / go-IMPERF-1PL to fetch-INF the bread

    e.   Istivu / Ìavu   a pigghiari u pani.
         go-PAST-2PL / go-IMPERF-2PL to fetch-INF the bread

f.   Ero / Ìano   a pigghiari u pani.
     go-PAST-3PL / go-IMPERF-3PL to fetch-INF the bread

(38) a. * Ii   a pigghiai   u pani.
         go-PAST-1s to fetch-PAST-1s the bread
         etc.

b.   * Ii   a pigghio u pani.
     go-PAST-1s to fetch-1s the bread
     etc.

c.   * Vajo /*Va a pigghiai   u pani.
     go-1s / go   to fetch-PAST-1s the bread
     etc.

(39) a. * Ia   a pigghiava   u pani.
         go-IMPERF-1s to fetch-IMPERF-1s the bread
         etc.

b.   * Ia   a pigghio   u pani.
     go-IMPERF-1s to fetch-PRES-1s   the bread
     etc.

c.   * Vajo /*Va a pigghiava   u pani.
     go-1s / go   to fetch-IMPERF-1s the bread
     etc.

Furthermore, the inflected construction cannot be found in the subjunctive (which is also the suppletive form for the conditional), while no such restriction is imposed on the infinitival construction:[17]

(40) a. Si tu tinn'issi a accattari u pani ne sta butìa, spinnissi chiù picca.
        if you REFL_cl LOC_cl go-SUBJ to buy-INF the bread in this shop, spend-SUBJ less
        'If you went to buy bread in this shop, you would spend less.'

b. * Si tu issi a accattassi u pani ne sta butìa, spinnissi chiù picca.
   if you go-SUBJ to buy-SUBJ the bread in this shop, [you] spend-SUBJ less

Finally, as shown in (41), there is no agreement restriction on the infinitival construction, while in the inflected construction the motion verb has a defective paradigm, (42). It can appear only in the 1st, 2nd and 3rd singular and 3rd plural; 1st and 2nd plural are excluded:[18]

(41) a.   Vajo a pigghiari u pani.
          go-1s to fetch   the bread

b.   Vai a pigghiari u pani.

c.   Va a pigghiari u pani.

    d.   Emo a pigghiari u pani.

    e.   Iti a pigghiari u pani.

    f.   Vanno a pigghiari u pani.

(42) a.   Vajo a pigghio u   pani.
          go-1s to fetch-1s the bread

    b.   Vai a pigghi u pani.

    c.   Va a pigghia u pani.

    d.   * Emo a pigghiamo u pani.

    e.   * Iti a pigghiati u pani.

    f.   Vanno a pigghiano u pani.

The verb *iri* has two allomorphs *e-/i-* and *va-*. The persons of the paradigm which are not allowed in the construction are all formed with *e-/i-*. This allomorph is also used to build the past and the imperfect tense and the subjunctive mood, which we have seen above to be ungrammatical in the inflected construction. These observations can be captured by a single generalization:[19]

(43)   Only those forms that contain the allomorph *va-* can instantiate the inflected construction.

A tentative way of accounting for (43) is to say that only the allomorph *va-* can be marked as functional in the lexicon. In this perspective, the Marsalese lexicon differentiates between a lexical motion verb *iri* which is realized with two allomorphs (*va-* and *e-/i-*), and a functional verb realized with *va-* only. The latter is inserted in a high functional head of the clause and shares many properties with auxiliaries.[20]

    The existence of two allomorphs cannot be taken as specific of the pattern of the verb *iri*. Two allomorphs are also found overtly for the verb *viniri*, which has the allomorph *ven-* for 1st, 2nd, 3rd singular and 3rd plural persons of the present indicative and the allomorph *vin-* for 1st and 2nd plural of the present indicative and for all persons of other tenses and moods. The fact that the other verb entering the construction *passari* does not display an overt differentiation in its morphological pattern does not necessarily imply that this verb does not have two homophonous allomorphs. We assume that in Marsalese (but, for example, not in the Southern dialects mentioned in note 18) only the allomorphs which realize 1st, 2nd, 3rd singular and 3rd plural are listed in the lexicon as functional verbs entering the inflected construction.

       All things considered, allomorphy cannot be taken as the ultimate cause of the inflection restrictions. On the contrary, it must be the result of some general property of the verbal inflectional system which interacts with syntactic principles. Discussion on this very general issue goes beyond the scope of the present chapter and must be left for future research.

9. Conclusions

We have suggested that a motion verb can be a functional verb. We have based our conclusion on the analysis of the inflected construction found in Marsalese, where a motion verb combines with an inflected verb. Since the motion verb precedes the inflected verb (introduced by the connecting element *a*) which, in turn, precedes floating quantifiers and frequency adverbs, it must be inserted in a very high functional head in the clause tree. The exact position of this functional head in the structure remains to be established, as well as a full analysis of the nature and distribution of the connecting element *a*.

We have observed that the inflected construction is only possible with one allomorph of the motion verbs entering the construction. This excludes from the inflected construction all tenses, moods, and persons which do not utilize this allomorph. We have suggested that only this allomorph can be marked in the lexicon as a functional head of this kind. In this way, we have tried to capture the intricate system of restrictions on tense, mood, and person inflection displayed by the inflected construction.

Notes

This fragment of dialectal syntax has taken inspiration from the pioneering work by Paola Benincà, who was one of the first scholars to apply a theoretical approach to research in the domain of Italian dialectology.

We thank Giuliana's in-law family in Marsala for data. We are particularly indebted with Giuseppe Rallo (Giuliana's husband) as our invaluable informant for his patience in providing us with judgements at any minute and for his new interest in language architecture along with his old love for garden architecture. We would also like to thank Paola Benincà, Guglielmo Cinque, and Michal Starke for their usual availability in discussion; Lori Repetti for her phonological advice; Anna Thornton for her morphological advice; and the audiences of the "Quarta giornata italo-americana di dialettologia" held in Padua on June 9, 1998, and of the "XXV Incontro di Grammatica Generativa" held in Siena on February 25–27, 1999, for comments and criticism.

1. For example:

(i)   Vene   / Passa   a pigghiari u   pani.
        come-3s / come-by-3s to fetch-INF the bread
(ii)   Vene   / Passa   a pigghia u   pani.
        come-3s / come-by-3s to fetch-3s the bread

2. All the examples in the chapter are main clauses. Notice, however, that both constructions can be found in embedded clauses:

(i) a.   Mi   disse chi va   a pigghiari u pani.
          to-me told that go-3s to fetch-INF the bread

b.   Mi   disse chi va   a pigghia u   pani.
       to-me told   that go-3s to fetch-3s the bread

This excludes any analysis built on the root vs. embedded distinction.

3.   This is shown by some related dialects; cf., e.g., Calabrese in (i), in which the connecting element of the inflected construction is the same as the coordinative conjunction (from Rohlfs 1969:164):

(i)   Sutta a la te   finestra vegnu   **e**   staju.
            under the your window come-1s and stay-1s

A parallel case can be made for English in (ii) and Swedish in (iii):

(ii)   Come **and** talk to me!
(iii)   Hans prövar **och** läser.
            Hans try-PRS and read-PRS

4   Since in both cases the Latin form has a final consonant, we take, following Chierchia (1986:29), that the underlying form of both *a*'s contains a coda. This is why both trigger "raddoppiamento Sintattico," as noted in the text.

5.   Even in the cases mentioned in note 3 (in which the coordinating conjunction appears as the connecting element between the motion verb and the subsequent verb), there are reasons to believe that we are not dealing with a real coordination. This has been claimed for English by Carden and Pesetsky (1977) and the references quoted there, and for Swedish by Wiklund (1996).

6.   The Marsalese version of (6b) has to contain the pleonastic clitic cluster *minni* for the independent reason to be mentioned in section 5. Crucially, the fact that *minni* and *u* cannot form a clitic cluster cannot be the reason for the ungrammaticality of (6a), since the Italian sentence displays the same degree of deviance.

7.   The lack of object sharing also excludes that the inflected construction is parallel to serial verb constructions. See Baker (1989) and Collins (1997) for recent discussions.

8.   Motion verbs have already been analyzed as functional verbs in the literature, as in the English construction in (i) (see Jaeggli and Hyams 1993 and the references quoted there):

(i)   I go talk to him every day.

However, the restrictions displayed by the phenomenon dealt with here are different from those found in English. For lack of space, we will not discuss those differences here.

9.   As a matter of fact, nothing in our proposal forces us to this conclusion. A possible alternative, which is compatible with our approach, is that the motion verb can be a functional head in the infinitival construction as well. It is also not excluded that the infinitival construction is ambiguous between a monoclausal and a biclausal analysis (see Cinque, chapter 3 of this volume, for a recent analysis of Italian along these lines). This is never the case with the inflected construction.

Whatever the correct analysis of the infinitival construction turns out to be, the motion verb must be in a position different from the one it occupies in the inflected construction, given that frequency adverbs and floating quantifiers appear in a different position in the two constructions; cf. (4), (12)–(13), and (14)–(15). The same should be said with reference to the infinitival *a*, which must be lower than the *a* occurring in the inflected construction. This is compatible with the observation in section 2. that they are diachronically different. A final decision on these matters is beyond the scope of this chapter.

10. Among motion verbs, the property of displaying an invariant form is restricted to the verb *iri*.

11. The ungrammaticality of (28b) with the clitic cluster can be taken as a further argument against a coordination analysis of the inflected construction. If (28b) were a coordination, the motion verb would be a main verb with no argument and should therefore occur with the clitic cluster, as it does in (27a). Thus, (28b) contrasts with the coordination in (6b), where *minni* is obligatory as in (27a).

12. Sentence (30b) is acceptable with the clitic if it is a right dislocation structure, where *ci* anticipates the right-dislocated PP *a casa*. But this is irrelevant to our argument.

13. Long NP-movement, another restructuring effect, is possible in both constructions:

(i) a. E cassatedde si vanno a pigghiari.
        the pastries   SI go-3PL to take-INF
    b. E cassatedde si vanno a pigghiano.
        the pastries   SI go-3PL to take-3PL

In these cases NP-movement can also be procrastinated to LF, as shown by the possibility of postverbal agreeing subjects in (ii):

(ii) a. Si vanno a pigghiari e cassatedde.
     b. Si vanno a pigghiano e cassatedde.

14. Notice that the Italian counterparts of (35) are both grammatical:

(i) a. Sto   prendendolo.
        stay-1s fetch-GER-it$_\alpha$
    b. Lo sto   prendendo.
        it$_\alpha$ stay-1s fetch-GER

The contrast between (i)a and (35a) in the text suggests that the status of this functional verb is different in the two languages: in Italian, *stare* behaves more like a modal verb, allowing optional clitic climbing, whereas in Marsalese *stari* behaves just like an auxiliary, requiring obligatory clitic climbing. The exact derivation of clitic placement is beyond the scope of this chapter.

15. The inflected construction (36c) should be compared with the coordination (6b). The different placement of the clitic pronoun in the two cases can be used as a further argument against a coordination analysis of the inflected construction.

16. Future forms do not exist in this dialect. Present tense is used instead.

17. Present subjunctive cannot be tested since it is not found in Marsalese.

18. In other dialects, the tense and agreement restrictions are not operative. Rohlfs (1969:166) quotes a sentence from a collection of fairy tales told by Pitré in a Sicilian dialect where it is possible to have the inflected construction in the past tense (notice that the presence of clitic climbing makes sure that we are dealing with an inflected construction):

(i)   Idda si   iju   a curcau.
             she herself went-3s to laid-3s
             'She went to sleep.'

As for the agreement restriction, Kunert (1997:173) finds the construction with the imperative 1st person plural in the Occitan dialect spoken in Guardia Piemontese in Calabria:

(ii)   Jammu ssettamu.
             go-1PL sit-1PL
             'Let's go and sit down.'

19. This generalization correctly captures the fact that the inflected construction is possible in the imperative singular but impossible in the imperative plural:

(i)   Va   pigghia   u   pani!
             go-IMP-2s fetch-IMP-2s the bread
(ii)   * Iti   pigghiati   u   pani!
             go-IMP-2PL fetch-IMP-2PL the bread

Since the imperative displays a number of different restrictions, such as the lack of the connecting element *a*, we will not deal with it in this chapter for reasons of space.

According to the generalization in (43), the inflected construction should be impossible with the infinitive. This is possibly the case. However, it is indistinguishable from the infinitival construction, which is expectedly allowed:

(iii)   Vogghiu iri   a pigghiari u pani.
             want-1s go-INF to fetch-INF the bread

20. Our proposal is still compatible with the hypothesis that the motion verb occurring with the infinitival in Italian is also functional (see Cinque, chapter 3 of this volume). In note 8, we hinted at the fact that the two motion verbs are in different positions in the structure. This amounts to saying that they realize different features and are inserted in different functional heads. If this is so, the two instances of the motion verb should be listed separately in the lexicon. The lexical entry for the motion verb that appears in the inflected construction in Marsalese only contains the root *va-*, while both the lexical verb and the functional verb which enters the infinitival construction would have the two allomorphs: *va* and *e-/i-*.

References

Baker, M. (1989) "Object Sharing and Projection in Serial Verb Constructions," *Linguistic Inquiry* 20(4):513–553.

Benincà, P. and G. Cinque (1993) "Su alcune differenze tra enclisi e proclisi," *Omaggio a Gianfranco Folena*, pp. 2313–2326. Padua: Editoriale Programma.

Carden, G. and D. Pesetsky (1977) "Double-Verb Constructions, Markedness, and a Fake Co-ordination," in W. A. Beach, et al. (eds.) *Papers from the Thirteenth Regional Meeting of the Chicago Linguistic Society*, pp. 82–92. University of Chicago.

Chierchia, G. (1986) "Length, Syllabification and the Phonological Cycle in Italian," *Journal of Italian Linguistics* 8(1):5–33.

Cinque, G. (this volume) "The Interaction of Passive, Causative, and Restructuring in Romance."

Collins, C. (1997) "Agreement Sharing in Serial Verb Constructions," *Linguistic Inquiry* 28(3):461–497.

Jaeggli, O. and N. Hyams (1993) "On the Independence and Interdependence of Syntactic and Morphological Properties: English Aspectual *come* and *go*," *Natural Language and Linguistic Theory* 11:313–346.

Kunert, H. P. (1997) "L'infinitif dans l'Occitan de Guardia Piemontese," *Revue des Langues Romanes* 101(1):167–175.

Rohlfs, G. (1969) *Grammatica storica della lingua italiana e dei suoi dialetti*, vol. 3: *Sintassi e formazione delle parole*. Turin: Einaudi.

Wiklund, A. (1996) "Pseudocoordination is Subordination," *Working Papers in Scandinavian Syntax* 58:29–54.

3

The Interaction of Passive, Causative, and "Restructuring" in Romance

Guglielmo Cinque

In what follows, I want to show how the hierarchy of functional projections investigated in Cinque (1999) provides an unforeseen solution to a puzzle of Romance syntax: the selective application of passive to verbs triggering "restructuring" (or "clause reduction").[1]

1. The puzzle

As Aissen and Perlmutter (1983:390ff) observed, in "clause reduction" contexts the object of the embedded verb should quite generally become the subject of the matrix verb when the latter is passivized. This is indeed the case in Spanish, with such verbs as *terminar* and *acabar* 'finish' (cf. (1) and (2), their (P32) and (P33)), but is, unexpectedly, not possible with the majority of "clause reduction" triggers (see, for example, (3) and (4), their (P36) and (P37)):

(1) a.   Los obreros están terminando de pintar estas paredes.
           'The workers are finishing painting these walls.'

     b.   Estas paredes están siendo terminadas de pintar (por los obreros).
           (Lit.) These walls are being finished to paint (by the workers).

(2) a.   Los obreros acabaron de pintar las casas ayer.
           'The workers finished painting the houses yesterday.'

     b.   Las casas fueron acabadas de pintar (por los obreros) ayer.
           (Lit.) The houses were finished to paint (by the workers) yesterday.

(3) a.   Trataron de pintar las paredes ayer.
           'They tried to paint the walls yesterday.'

b.   *Las paredes fueron tratadas de pintar ayer.
       (Lit.) The walls were tried to paint yesterday.

(4) a.   Quieren cortar esta madera
           'They want to cut this wood.'

    b.   *Esta madera es querida cortar
           (Lit.) This wood is wanted to cut.

This is all the more surprising as the embedded object has no difficulty in becoming the matrix subject in the corresponding "se-passives." See (5):

(5) a.   Las paredes se trataron de pintar ayer
           the walls   se *tried*   *to   paint yesterday*
           (Lit.) The walls were tried to paint yesterday.

    b.   Esta madera se   quiere cortar
           this wood   se *wants to cut*
           (Lit.) This wood is wanted to cut.

Aissen and Perlmutter (1983:391f) further observe that "[t]he subclass of Clause Union triggers that allow passives like (1b) and (2b) seems to be roughly the class that specifies the end point of an action. We have no explanation for this, which we assume to be a language-particular fact that needs to be stated in the grammar of Spanish. Thus we assume that there are languages in which Passive in Clause Union structures is not limited to a small subclass of Clause Union triggers."

This limitation to verbs marking the end point of a process (and to few other verb classes, as we shall see) is not a quirk of Spanish syntax, however, but holds in Italian, Portuguese, Catalan, and various northeastern Italian dialects (I conjecture, in fact, throughout Romance). Its general character thus calls for a principled explanation, and I want to suggest that this resides in the position that the Voice head occupies in the hierarchy of functional projections relative to the modal and the different aspectual heads.[2]

Before getting to that, consider the situation of Italian (and, more briefly, that of other Romance varieties). As shown in (6), indeed very few restructuring verb classes in Italian allow for the "long passive" seen in (1) and (2):[3]

(6) a.   *Mi è stato voluto dare (da Gianni).   (Rizzi 1976:31)
           (Lit.) It was wanted to give to me (by G.).
           (cf. Gianni me lo ha voluto dare. 'G. it wanted to give to me.')

    b.   *È stata dovuta riscrivere.   (Burzio 1986:374)
           (Lit.) It was had to rewrite.
           (cf. L'ha dovuta riscrivere. 'He it had to rewrite.')

    c.   *Non fu più potuto rivedere.   (Burzio 1986:374)
           (Lit.) It was no longer been able to see again.
           (cf. Non lo potè più rivedere. 'He it could no longer see.')

d.   *Era desiderato conoscere da tutti.
      (Lit.) It was desired to meet by everybody.
      (cf. Tutti lo desideravano conoscere. 'Everybody him desired to
         meet.')

e.   *Non era usato dire da nessuno.
      (Lit.) It was not used to say by anybody.
      (cf. Nessuno lo usava dire. 'Nobody it used to say.')

f.   *Fu cercato/tentato di aggiustare (da Gianni).
      (Lit.) It was tried to mend (by G.).
      (cf. Lo cercò/tentò di aggiustare Gianni. 'It tried to mend G.')

g.   *Fu provato ad aggiustare (da Gianni).
      (Lit.) It was tried to mend (by G.).
      (cf. Lo provò ad aggiustare Gianni. 'It tried to mend G.')

h.   *Non era osato fare da nessuno.
      (Lit.) It was not dared to do by anybody.
      (cf. Nessuno lo osava fare. 'Nobody it dared to do.')

i.   *Non fu saputo tradurre da nessuno.
      (Lit.) It wasn't known to translate by anybody.
      (cf. Nessuno lo seppe tradurre. 'Nobody it could translate.')

l.   *Non fu saputo come fare (da nessuno).
      (Lit.) It wasn't known how to do (by anybody).
      (cf. (?)Non lo sapeva come fare. 'It he didn't know how to do.')

m.   *Era teso a fare da tutti
      (Lit.) It was tended to do by everybody.
      (cf. (?)Tutti lo tendevano a fare. 'Everybody it tended to do.')

n.   *Fu smesso/cessato di vedere.
      (Lit.) It was stopped/quit seeing.
      (cf. Lo smisero/(??)cessarono di vedere. 'It they stopped/quit
         seeing.')

o.   *Non fu riuscito a vedere da nessuno.
      (Lit.) It wasn't managed to see by anybody.
      (cf. Nessuno lo riuscì a vedere. 'Nobody him managed to see.')

p.   *Era stato comprando.
      (Lit.) It had been buying.
      (cf. Lo stavano comprando. 'They it were buying.')

q.   *Era stato per comprare.
      (Lit.) It had been about to buy.
      (cf. Lo stavano per comprare. 'They it were about to buy.')

r.   *Fu ripreso a fare da tutti.
      (Lit.) It was resumed to do by everybody.
      (cf. Lo ripresero a fare tutti 'Everybody it resumed to do.')

s.   *Fu finito per accettare da tutti.
      (Lit.) It was ended up accepting by everybody.
      (cf. Lo finì per accettare 'He it ended up accepting.')

t.   ??Fu continuato/seguitato a fare nonostante la loro opposizione.
      (Lit.) It was continued/kept on doing their opposition
         notwithstanding.
      (cf. Lo continuarono/seguitarono a fare. 'They continued/kept on
         doing.')

u.   La casa fu finita di costruire il mese scorso.
      (= (116b) of Van Tiel-Di Maio 1978:97)
      (Lit.) The house was finished building the last month.
      (cf. La finì di costruire il mese scorso 'He it finished building.')

v.   Quelle case furono iniziate/?cominciate a costruire negli anni '20.
      (Lit.) Those houses were started to build in the '20s.
      (cf. Le iniziarono/cominciarono a costruire negli anni '20. 'They
         them started to build in the '20s.')

z.   Sarete passati a prendere più tardi.[4]
      (Lit.) You (pl.) will be passed to fetch later.
      (cf. Vi passeremo a prendere più tardi. 'We you will pass to fetch
         later.')

w.   Furono mandati a prendere a casa.[5]
      (Lit.) They were sent to fetch at home.
      (cf. Li mandarono a prendere. 'They them sent to fetch.')

Comparable data are found in Portuguese. *Acabar* 'finish', *começar* 'begin', and
mandar 'send' can be passivized in restructuring contexts (see (7a–c)), but neither
modals nor other aspectual verbs can (see (8a–d)):[6]

(7) a.   As casas foram acabadas de construir em 1950.
          'The houses were finished building in 1950.'

    b.   ?As casas foram começadas a construir em 1950.
          'The houses were begun to build in 1950.'

    c.   As crianças foram mandadas alcançar à estação.
          'The children were sent to fetch at the station.'

(8) a.   *As casas foram podidas/devidas/queridas demolir só recentemente.
          'The houses were could/should/wanted to pull down only recently.'

b.   ???As casas foram continuadas a construir durante essa epoca.
       'The houses were continued to build during this period.'

c.   *As casas foram tentadas demolir muitas vezes.
       'The houses were tried to pull down many times.'

d.   *As casas foram finalmente tratadas demolir.
       'The houses were finally managed to pull down.'

Similarly, in Catalan, "restructuring" FINISH and BEGIN verbs can be passivized (*Aquestes parets han estat acabades de pintar pels obrers* 'these walls have been finished painting by the workers'; *Aquestes cases van ser començades a construir el 1950* 'these houses were begun to build in 1950'), but neither modals (*Els documents van ser poguts aprovar* 'the documents were been able to approve') nor other aspectual verbs can (Lluïsa Gràcia, p.c.).[7] Analogous facts hold in Paduan (Paola Benincà, p.c.) and Venetian (Cecilia Poletto, p.c.).

2. A solution to the puzzle

Why should only *finire* 'finish', *iniziare* 'begin', and (some of) the motion verbs be passivizable, whereas all other "restructuring" verbs resist passivization? What do the former verbs have in common which distinguishes them from the latter?

An answer to these questions appears to come from the relative position of the distinct clausal functional heads in the hierarchy proposed in Cinque (1999), at least if we accept the idea that the restructuring use of a verb is nothing other than its generation in the semantically corresponding functional head (rather than in a lexical VP).[8]

Modal functional heads, and the majority of aspectual functional heads appear to be higher than the (Active/Passive) Voice head (see Cinque 1999, chapter 4 and appendix 2, for a cross-linguistic survey). One instance of completive aspect ('terminate a process at its natural ending point', 'finish') is, however, crucially lower than Voice (see the discussion in Cinque 1999, sec. 4.26, and note 10 below)

If, following current assumptions, we assume that for a verb to be passivized it must raise to Voice°, either overtly or covertly, to pick up passive morphology (alternatively, to check the features of its passive morphology), it follows that only those verbs which are generated lower than Voice° will be passivizable. In other words, only the lexical verb, head of VP, and restructuring FINISH verbs, which can be licensed in the completive aspect head lower than Voice°, will be able to be passivized. All "functional" verbs licensed in heads higher than Voice° (such as the modals and the majority of aspectual verbs in their restructuring use) will be unable to bear passive morphology, as lowering is excluded.[9]

This almost accounts for the pattern in (6). What is left out is the possibility of passivizing motion verbs and BEGIN verbs. The latter case is particularly problematic as Inceptive aspect ('begin doing something') appears to be higher than (heads higher than) Voice° in several languages documented in Cinque (1999, appendix

2): for example, in the Niger-Congo language Kako, in the Eskimo language Aleut, in the Papuan language Tauya, and in the Amerind language Ika.

The position of Inceptive aspect (and that of Conative and of "Success" (or Frustrative) aspects), as well as the position of the functional head corresponding to motion verbs, were not systematically investigated in Cinque (1999).

At least for the case of motion verbs, there is some evidence that the functional head in which their restructuring use is licensed is lower than Voice°.

A number of Australian and African languages possess a verbal affix (rendered as 'go and . . .', sometimes called "andative" or "distantive"), which signals that "a distance is traversed before the action is done" (Fagerli 1994:35). See also Evans (1995:311), and Dixon (1977:219ff), where these affixes are called "coming/going aspectual affixes." The West African language Fulfulde offers direct evidence that the functional head corresponding to this affix is lower than Voice°. The "distantive" suffix in this language is a derivational suffix, closer to the verb stem than the suffix expressing Voice, which is a portemanteau inflectional suffix also marking aspect and polarity distinctions (Fagerli 1994:35):[10]

(9)   Bingel soof-oy-i.
        child wet-DIST-Voice/Aspect/Polarity
        'The child went and urinated.'

Extrapolating from Fulfulde, motion verbs (in their restructuring use) are thus compatible with passivization. This leaves us with BEGIN-type verbs, which also allow passivization (6v) although they shouldn't, as the available evidence appears to show that Inceptive aspect is higher than Voice.

Here, I would like to follow a suggestion of Paola Beninca's (p.c.), which seems to offer a principled solution to the problem. She notes that parallel to the pair of Terminative aspect (which marks the termination of an unbounded, or bounded, process at an arbitrary point: 'stop'/'quit'/'cease') and Completive aspect (which marks the termination of a bounded process at its natural end point: 'finish'), one could posit the existence of two distinct Inceptive aspects: one marking the beginning of an unbounded, or bounded, process at an arbitrary point (e.g., *start to shiver* or *start to sing the aria* [from some arbitrary point]); the other marking the beginning of a bounded process at its natural starting point (e.g., *begin building the house*).

Now, just as Terminative aspect is higher than Voice, and (one type of) Completive aspect is lower than Voice, so one could hypothesize that the former Inceptive aspect is higher, and the latter lower, than Voice. This implies that the BEGIN-type verbs which can be passivized should only be of the bounded/natural-starting-point kind (as only this kind of Inceptive aspect is lower than Voice).

Indeed, there is some evidence bearing out this prediction, and thus supporting Beninca's conjecture. While passivization of *iniziare/cominciare* is possible in (6v) or (10a), which constitute bounded processes (with a natural starting point), it becomes impossible if the process is turned into an unbounded one, say, by having a bare plural DP subject, as in (10b):[11]

(10) a.   Furono iniziate/?cominciate a costruire solo due case.
            (Lit.) Were begun to build only two houses.

     b.   *Furono iniziate/cominciate a costruire case.
            (Lit.) Were started to build houses.

Conversely (given this line of analysis), we expect that all the restructuring verbs
which *cannot* passivize (as they are in heads higher than Voice°) should be able to
embed a passive, whereas the restructuring verbs which *can* passivize (as they are
located lower than Voice°) should not be able to embed a passive.

    These predictions appear to be largely confirmed, too. The verbs in (6a–s)
indeed can embed a passive (see (11a–s)), whereas those in (6t–w) cannot, except
for *continuare, finire*, and *iniziare/cominciare*, to which I return:

(11) a.   Gianni gli voleva essere presentato.
            G. to-him wanted to be introduced

     b.   Gianni gli doveva essere presentato.
            G. to-him had to be introduced

     c.   G. non gli poteva esser presentato.
            G. not to-him could be introduced

     d.   Gianni ne desiderava essere informato.
            G. of-it desired to be informed

     e.   Non gli solevano essere presentati.
            (they) not to-him used to be introduced

     f.   ?Gli cercò/tentò di esser presentato.
            to-him (he) tried to be introduced

     g.   Gli provò ad esser presentato.
            to-him (he) tried to be introduced

     h.   Non gli osava essere presentato.
            not to-him (she) dared to be introduced

     i.   Ne sapeva essere affascinato.
            from-it (he) was able to be fascinated

     l.   Non gli sapeva come essere presentato.
            not to-him (he) knew how to be introduced

     m.   Ne tendeva ad essere affascinato.
            from-it (she) tended to be fascinated

     n.   Gli smise di essere indicato come la persona più adatta.
            to-him (he) stopped being indicated as the most suitable person

     o.   Ne riuscì ad essere informata prima di noi.
            of-it (she) managed to be informed before us

p.   Ne stava venendo ottenebrato anche lui.
     from-it was being clouded over even him

q.   Gli stava per essere presentata.
     to-him (she) was about to be introduced

r.   Vi riprese ad esser ammesso.
     there he resumed to be admitted

s.   Gli finiranno per essere concessi tutti i prestiti.
     to-him will end up being granted all the loans

t.   Ne continuò/seguitò ad essere affascinato.
     from-it (he) continued/kept on being fascinated

u.   Gli finirono di essere concessi prestiti.
     to-him finished to be granted loans

v.   Gli cominciarono/?iniziarono ad esser inflitte delle punizioni.
     to-him began to be inflicted punishments

z.   *Gli passò ad esser presentato uno straniero.[12]
     to-him passed to be introduced a foreigner

w.   *Gli mandarono ad esser presentato uno straniero.
     to-him they sent to be introduced a foreigner

The problem raised by the well-formedness of (11t–v) disappears if we consider the fact that a Continuative, an Inceptive, and a Completive aspect head is also present to the left of Voice° (Cinque 1999, chapter 4).[13]

3. An extension to causatives

Along similar lines, the fact that causative verbs in Italian can be passivized (cf. *Gli fu fatto leggere* (Lit.) To-him it was made read), but cannot embed a passive (**Farò essere invitati tutti* (Lit.) I will make to be invited all—see Rizzi 1976:31f; Radford 1977:226; Burzio 1986:280f, among others) can now be seen as a consequence of the fact that the Causative functional head is lower than the Voice head.[14]

This is confirmed by the fixed order of causative and passive suffixes (V-CAUS-PASS) in those languages which have, like the Romance languages, Baker's type 1 causatives (namely, those which change the subject of an embedded transitive verb into an oblique object, rather than a direct object—Baker 1988:162ff).

If so, it is also to be expected that those restructuring verbs which are licensed in heads higher than Voice° will, a fortiori, be unable to embed under a causative verb (as this is lower than Voice). This expectation is also fulfilled. See (12) (and Burzio 1981:587):

(12) a.   *La feci voler leggere a tutti.
(Lit.) It (I) made want to read to everybody.
'I made everybody want to read it.'

b.   *Lo faranno dover ammettere anche a Gianni.
(Lit.) It (they) will make have to admit to G. too.
'They will make G. too have to admit it.'

c.   *Lo farò poter leggere a tutti.
(Lit.) It (I) will make be able to read to everybody.
'I will make everybody be able to read it.'

d.   *La farà desiderare di incontrare a tutti.
(Lit.) Her (he) will make desire to meet to everybody.
'He will make everybody desire to meet her.'

e.   *Lo faceva sempre usar fare alle sue amiche.
(Lit.) It (she) made always use to do to her friends.
'She always made her friends use to do it.'

f.   *La farò cercare/tentare di incontrare a Gianni.
(Lit.) Her I will make try to meet to G.
'I will have G. try to meet her.'

g.   *La farò provare ad incontrare a Gianni.
(Lit.) Her I will make try to meet to G.
'I will have G. try to meet her.'

i.   *Glielo faremo saper tradurre.
(Lit.) To-him it (we) will make be able to translate.
'We will have him be able to translate it.'

l.   *Glielo farò saper come fare.
(Lit.) To-him it (I) will make know how to do.
'I will make him know how to do it.'

m.   *Lo facevano tendere a fare a tutti.
(Lit.) It (they) made tend to do to everybody.
'They used to have everybody tend to do it.'

n.   *Fallo smettere di importunare anche a Gianni.
(Lit.) Make him stop pestering to G. too.
'Make G. too stop pestering him.'

o.   *La fecero riuscire ad aggiustare anche a Maria.
(Lit.) It (they) made manage to fix even to M.
'They made even M. manage to fix it.'

p.   *Lo faremo star facendo anche a Gianni.
       (Lit.) It (we) will make be doing even to G.
       'We will have even G. be doing it.'

q.   *Glielo feci star per comprare.
       (Lit.) To-him it (I) made be about to buy.
       'I had him be about to buy it.'

r.   *La fecero riprendere a interpretare a Gianni.
       (Lit.) It (they) made resume to interpret to G.
       'They had G. resume interpreting it.'

s.   *Lo faranno finire per comprare anche a Gianni.
       (Lit.) It (they) will make end up buying even to G.
       'They will have even G. end up buying it.'

t.   (?)?Glielo fece continuare a costruire.   (Burzio 1981:591)
       (Lit.) To-him it (he) made continue building.
       'He had him continue building it.'

While (12t) is somewhat intermediate (possibly suggesting the presence of some type of Continuative aspect head below Causative°, and Voice°—see also note 3 here on the marginal possibility of passivizing *continuare*, noted by Burzio), the embedding under *fare* of *finire/terminare, iniziare/cominciare,* and *passare/mandare/andare* in their restructuring use, are perfectly grammatical (cf. (13)). This suggests that the corresponding functional heads are also lower than Causative°, not just lower than Voice°.[15]

(13) a.   La fecero finire/terminare di costruire a Gianni.
          (Lit.) It (they) made finish/terminate to build to G.
          'They had G. finish/terminate building it.'

     b.   Gliela fecero iniziare/cominciare a costruire.
          (Lit.) To-him it (they) made initiate/begin to build.
          'They had him begin to build it.'

     c.   Gliela fecero passare a prendere alle cinque.
          (Lit.) To-him it (they) made pass to fetch at 5 o'clock.
          'They made him pass and fetch it at 5 o'clock.'

     d.   Ce lo fecero andare a prendere subito.[16]
          (Lit.) To-us it (they) made go to fetch immediately.
          'They made us go and fetch it immediately.'

     e.   Glielo fecero mandare a prendere subito.
          (Lit.) To-him it (they) made send to fetch immediately.
          'They made him send to fetch immediately.'

Conversely, causatives should be possible under the restructuring verbs in (12), but not under those in (13), as the former are higher and the latter lower than the causative head. The first prediction is correct (see (14)). As to the second prediction, it cannot be tested with *finire/terminare* and *iniziare/cominciare*, which can also be licensed in heads higher than Causative°, as we have seen, but it can be tested with motion verbs, and it appears confirmed. See (15):

(14) a. Gliela volevo far vedere.
         (Lit.) To-him it (I) wanted to make see.
         'I wanted to have him see it.'

     b. Gliela dovevo far vedere.
         (Lit.) To-him it (I) had to make see.
         'I had to make him see it.'

     c. Non gliela potrò far vedere.
         (Lit.) Not to-him it (I) will be able to make see.
         'I will not be able to have him see it.'

     d. Gliela desideravo far conoscere.
         (Lit.) To-him her I desired to make meet.
         'I desired to have him meet her.'

     e. Gliela usavano far guidare d'estate.
         (Lit.) To-him it (they) used to make drive in the summer.
         'They used to have him drive it in the summer.'

     f. Gliela cercarono/tentarono di far guidare.
         (Lit.) To-him it (they) tried to make drive.
         'They tried to have him drive it.'

     g. Gliela provarono a far guidare.
         (Lit.) To-him it (they) tried to make drive.
         'They tried to have him drive it.'

     i. Gliela sapremo far tradurre.
         (Lit.) To-him it (we) will be able to make translate.
         'We will be able to have him translate it.'

     l. Gliela sapremo come far tradurre.
         (Lit.) To-him it (we) will know how to make translate.
         'We will know how to have him translate it.'

     m. Gliela tenderebbero a far portare sempre.
         (Lit.) To-him it (they) would tend to make carry always.
         'They would tend to have him always carry.'

n. Glielo smise di far leggere.
(Lit.) To-him it (he) stopped to make read.
'He stopped to have him read it.'

o. Glielo riuscii a far vedere.
(Lit.) To-him it (I) managed to make see.
'I managed to have him see it.'

p. Gliela stava facendo firmare.
(Lit.) To-him it (he) was making sign.
'He was having him sign it.'

q. Gliela stava per far firmare.
(Lit.) To-him it (he) was about to make sign.
'He was about to make him sign it.'

r. Gliela riprese a far vedere.
(Lit.) To-him it (he) resumed to make see.
'He resumed to make him see it.'

s. Gliela finì per far comprare.
(Lit.) To-him it (he) ended up making buy.
'He ended up making/letting him buy it.'

t. Glielo continuò a far vedere.
(Lit.) To-him it (he) continued to make see.
'He continued to let him see it.'

(15) a. *La sono passata a far firmare a Gianni.
(Cf. Sono passato a farla firmare a G.)
(Lit.) It (I) have passed to make sign to G.
'I have passed and make G. sign it.'

b. *Gli siamo andati a far firmare la lettera.
(Cf. Siamo andati a fargli firmare la lettera.)
(Lit.) To-him (we) went to make sign the letter.
'We went and make him sign the letter.'

c. *Mandaglielo a far prendere.
(Cf. ?Manda a farglielo prendere.)
(Lit.) Send to-him it to make fetch.
'Send to make him fetch it.'

The order of functional heads for which evidence was discussed here is thus the following:[17]

(16)   ...Voice° > Perception° > Causative° > $\text{Asp}_{\text{inceptive(II)}}$/ ($\text{Asp}_{\text{continuative(II)}}$)
        > Andative° > $\text{Asp}_{\text{completive(II)}}$

The dots are meant to cover such aspects as Predispositional ('tend to'), Terminative, Conative, Success/Frustrative ('(not) manage to'), Continuative(I), Inceptive(I), Completive(I), Progressive, Prospective ('to be about to'), and others (Cinque 1999), whose relative order remains in part to be determined.[18]

Notes

I am indebted to Manuela Ambar, Paola Benincà, Anna Cardinaletti, Giuliana Giusti, Lluïsa Gràcia, Cecilia Poletto, and Eduardo Raposo for comments and judgements; especially to Paola, for suggesting to me an ingenious solution to an ordering paradox involving the inceptive aspect head.

1.   Although cast in different frameworks, Rizzi's (1976, 1978) "Restructuring" hypothesis and Aissen and Perlmutter's (1976, 1983) "Clause Reduction/Union" hypothesis share the idea that modal, aspectual, and motion verbs in Romance, when followed by a sentential complement, may be affected by a process which turns the biclausal structure into a monoclausal one. For present concerns, I will consider the two hypotheses as identical. Alternative analyses such as Kayne's (1989), and others mentioned there, are also equivalent, as far as I can see, with respect to the problem addressed here.

2.   If correct, the account to be proposed must be valid beyond Romance, to which my discussion here is confined.

3.   In Rizzi (1976:31) it is stated that "the output of verb raising but not that of restructuring can undergo the passive transformation" [my translation], *cominciare* 'begin' being a partial exception (cf. his n. 21) in that it can be passivized (marginally) in certain contexts (*?Questa chiesa fu cominciata a costruire nel 1525* '(Lit.) This church was begun to build in 1525'), though not in others (**Questo articolo sarà cominciato a leggere domani* '(Lit.) This article will be begun to read tomorrow').

Also according to Burzio "matrix passives with restructuring are at best unsystematic" (1981:689) and "impossible with exceptions with restructuring" (1986:382). He suggests that the impossibility of such cases as (6a) is due, in his analysis (pro$_i$ mi è stato voluto [$_{VP}$dare t$_i$] [$_s$PRO ___]), to the fact that PRO lacks an antecedent; but he says he has "no precise answer" as to why the case with *cominciare* "differ[s] from the *volere* case . . . with respect to the possibility of interpreting the embedded subject PRO" (1986:378).

In addition to *cominciare* 'begin', mentioned in Rizzi (1976, n. 21), Burzio takes *continuare* 'continue' to marginally allow passivization (*?Il palazzo fu continuato a costruire per ordine del principe* '(Lit.) the palace was continued to build at the order of the prince'—1981:591; *?(?)L'affitto fu continuato a pagare fino alla fine dell'anno* '(Lit.) The rent was continued to pay till the end of the year'—1986:376). I find such cases somewhat harder than those with *cominciare*.

4.   The restructuring use of this motion verb is very restricted. It is only possible (in either the active or passive form) with *prendere* 'fetch', *salutare* 'greet', and perhaps a couple of other verbs. Nonetheless, to the extent that it is possible in the active it appears to be possible in the corresponding "long passive."

Similar remarks hold for *mandare* (see (6w)), the causative of *andare* 'go'. As to *andare* itself in its restructuring use, although considered ungrammatical in Burzio (1986:374), it appears (marginally) possible in certain contexts (for some speakers): *(?)I libri saranno andati a prendere entro domani* 'The books will be gone to fetch by tomorrow'; ?*I malati furono andati a prendere a casa* '(Lit.) The ill were gone to fetch at home'). Also see (13d) and note 16 here.

5. *Mandare* 'send' also enters a "complement object deletion" construction (Fiengo and Lasnik 1974): *Mandarono la macchina a riparare* '(Lit.) they sent the car to fix'. Cliticization or passivization of the object (*La mandarono a riparare* 'They it sent to fix'; *Fu mandata a riparare* 'It was sent to fix') yields a word order identical to that formed by "clitic climbing" or "long passive" with the restructuring use of *mandare* (see (6w), for which no 'Complement Object Deletion' interpretation is possible: **Mandarono i bambini a prendere a casa* 'They sent the children to fetch home').

6. I thank Manuela Ambar, Manuel Gonçalves Simões, and Eduardo Raposo for sharing with me their intuitions, which were remarkably consistent.

7. For Gràcia, however, motion verbs are very hard to passivize.

8. This means that only verbs whose meaning closely corresponds to the functional meaning of a certain functional head can have the restructuring option. I refer to Cinque (in preparation) for arguments in favor of this interpretation of "restructuring."

9. That the cause of the ungrammaticality of (6a–s) is in the passive morphology rather than in the DP-movement component of the construction is confirmed by the fact, noted above, that the corresponding "*si*-passives" (which involve the DP-movement component of passive, but no passive morphology) are all grammatical.

10. Incidentally, Completive aspect, in Fula/Fulfulde, is also a derivational suffix closer to the verb stem than both the Andative and Voice suffixes. See Fagerli (1994:53). Fula/Fulfulde thus gives evidence for the (partial) relative order of heads shown in (i):

(i) ... Voice° ... >... Andative° ...>... $Asp_{completive}$... (V)

11. Positing an Inceptive aspect for unbounded processes (higher than Voice) distinct from an Inceptive aspect for bounded ones (lower than Voice) may also make sense of the preference for *iniziare* 'initiate' vs. *cominciare* 'begin' in the passivization cases. Although both are possible with either Inceptive aspect, *iniziare* is slightly more natural for marking the natural starting point of a bounded process (something which has an *inizio* 'a proper starting point'). So, for example, while *ha cominciato a cantare l'aria* 'he started to sing the aria' is equally appropriate whether someone started singing the aria from the beginning or from the middle, the preferred interpretation of *ha iniziato a cantare l'aria* is definitely the former situation.

12. Burzio (1981:611f) also notes the "difficulty" with cases such as *Gianni gli andrà ad esser presentato* 'G. to-him will go to be introduced', for which he has "no precise account."

13. *Finire* 'finish', in Italian, can apparently also be licensed in the head of Terminative aspect (which signals termination of a process at an arbitrary, rather than at the natural, end point), a usage which is not available to *finish* in English, as Richard Kayne pointed out to me (p.c.). Cf. *Finì di piovere* vs. **It finished raining*. On the marginal acceptability of *finish* in the quasi-accomplishment interpretation of activities (?*John finished working for the day*), see Binnick (1991:176).

14. As Italian, French, and Spanish do not allow causatives to embed passives (Kayne 1975:251ff; Zubizarreta 1985:282: **Pierre a fait être lu(s) ces passages*; **Pedro hizo ser leido(s) esos pasajes* '(Lit.) P. made be read these passages'); which suggests that in these languages, too, the causative head is lower than Voice. However, the fact that (contrary to Italian) their causatives cannot be passivized either (Kayne 1975:244ff; Zubizarreta 1985:268: **La maison a été faite construire; *La casa fue hecha construir* '(Lit.) the

house was made to build') remains to be understood. Note that there is no semantic ban on having passive under the scope of a causative verb, as shown by such sentences as *Ho fatto sì che fosse invitato* 'I made it so that he be invited', or by the *faire-par* construction in Romance (Kayne 1975). The only ban is on the embedded verb bearing passive morphology (ultimately, a consequence, in the present analysis, of the unavailability of lowering). Perception verbs can also enter the causative construction, but , to judge from the contrast in (i), they appear to correspond to a head higher than Causative° as they can embed , but cannot be embedded under, causatives (note that *vedere*, qua lexical verb, can embed under *fare*: *gliel'ho fatta vedere* 'I made him see it'):

(i)   a.   Gliel'ho vista far cadere. 'I saw him make it fall.'
      b.   * Gliel'ho fatta veder cadere. 'I made him see it fall.'

The contrast in (ii) suggests that this head is still lower than Voice°:

(ii) a.   Gli fu vista cadere addosso. 'She was seen to fall on him.'
      b.   * Gliel'ho vista esser presentata. 'I saw her be introduced to him.'

15. Interestingly, in Aissen's (1977) investigation of clause reduction under causatives in Spanish all the examples are with *empezar* 'begin', except one with *tratar* 'try': (i) *Al niño le dejaron tratar de hacer los deberes solo* 'They let the boy try to do his homework alone'. While the Italian analogue of *empezar*, *cominciare* can also embed under causatives, as seen above, *cercare, tentare, provare* 'try' cannot. Should (i) really turn out to be possible in Spanish, an interference could be involved with Exceptional Case Marking (admitted by *dejar* 'let'), perhaps with *leismo* (as in *Le hice correr* 'I made him run').

16. Although, as noted, the passive of *andare* in its restructuring use (?*Furono andati a prendere a casa* 'they were gone to fetch at home') is somewhat marginal, and is judged impossible by Burzio, he nonetheless cites as only slightly marginal a sentence like (i); which gives evidence for the location of the corresponding functional head below Causative° and Voice° even in his Italian:

(i)   ?Il libro fu fatto andare a prendere a Giovanni. (Burzio 1981:580)
      "The book was made go to fetch to G."

17. The evidence for locating the Andative head below the Inceptive(II) and Continuative(II) aspect heads comes from the following contrasts:

(i)   a.   Lo comincio ad andare a vedere domani.
           it I begin to go and see tomorrow
      b.   * Lo vado a cominciare a vedere domani.
           it I go and begin to see tomorrow
(ii) a.   Lo continuò ad andare a vedere tutti i giorni.
           it he continued to go and see every day
      b.   * Lo andò a continuare a vedere l'anno scorso.
           it he went and continued to see last year

The well-formedness of both (iiia) and (iiib) suggests, instead, that the Andative head is higher than the lower Completive aspect head and lower than the higher one:

(iii) a.   Lo finisco di andare a leggere domani.
            it I finish to go and read tomorrow
      b.   Lo vado a finire di leggere domani.
            it I go and finish reading tomorrow

18. Perhaps, grammatical function changing heads such as Causative should not be completely assimilated to "grammatical" functional heads of the mood, modality, tense, and aspect kind. The former, but not the latter, besides operating on the lexical verb's arguments, can apparently freely iterate (cf. (i)), and appear to be able to enter partially different orderings within and across languages. For example, the causative suffix is inside the distantive suffix in Fulfulde (cf. Fagerli 1994:53), which suggests that the Causative head is lower than the Andative head in this language, differently from Italian.

(i) a.   Taroo ga Ziroo ni Itiroo o aruk-ase-sase-ta
          T. NOM   Z. DAT   I. ACC   walk-CAUS-CAUS-PAST
          'T.had Z. make I. walk' (Japanese; Shibatani 1976:244)
    b.   A   daay-n-in-i   Yero bingel e wuro na
          You far-CAUS-CAUS-VOICE/ASP/POL Y.   child from town Q
          'Did you make Y. take the child out of town?' (Fulfulde; Fagerli 1994:42)
    c.   Gliela faremo far riparare
          To-him it (we) will make make fix
          'We will make him have it fixed' (Italian)

References

Aissen, J. (1977) "The Interaction of Clause Reduction and Causative Clause Union in Spanish," *Proceedings of the 7th Meeting of the North East Linguistic Society*, pp. 1–17.

Aissen, J. and D. Perlmutter (1976) "Clause Reduction in Spanish," *Proceedings of the Second Annual Meeting of the Berkeley Linguistics Society*, pp. 1–30. Berkeley: Berkeley Linguistics Society.

Aissen, J. and D. Perlmutter (1983) Postscript to republication of "Clause Reduction in Spanish," in D. Perlmutter (ed.) *Studies in Relational Grammar* 1, pp. 383–396. Chicago: University of Chicago Press.

Baker, M. (1988) *Incorporation: A Theory of Grammatical Function Changing*. Chicago: University of Chicago Press.

Binnick, R. I. (1991) *Time and the Verb: A Guide to Tense and Aspect*. New York: Oxford University Press.

Burzio, L. (1981) *Intransitive Verbs and Italian Auxiliaries*. Ph.D. diss., MIT.

Burzio, L. (1986) *Italian Syntax: A Government-Binding Approach*. Dordrecht: Reidel.

Cinque, G. (1999) *Adverbs and Functional Heads: A Cross-Linguistic Perspective*. New York: Oxford University Press.

Cinque, G. (in preparation) "Restructuring and Clause Structure."

Dixon, R. M. W. (1977) *A Grammar of Yidin*. Cambridge: Cambridge University Press.

Evans, N. D. (1995) *A Grammar of Kayardild*. Berlin: Mouton de Gruyter.

Fagerli, O. T. (1994) *Verbal Derivations in Fulfulde* (Issue 21 of *University of Trondheim Working Papers in Linguistics*). Cand. Philol. diss., University of Trondheim.

Fiengo, R. and H. Lasnik (1974) "Complement Object Deletion," *Linguistic Inquiry* 5:535–571.

Kayne, R. (1975) *French Syntax.* Cambridge, Mass.: MIT Press.

Kayne, R. (1989) "Null Subjects and Clitic Climbing," in O. Jaeggli and K. Safir (eds.) *The Null Subject Parameter*, pp. 239–261. Dordrecht: Kluwer.

Radford, A. (1977) *Italian Syntax: Transformational and Relational Grammar.* Cambridge: Cambridge University Press.

Rizzi, L. (1976) "Ristrutturazione," *Rivista di Grammatica Generativa* 1:1–54.

Rizzi, L. (1978) "A Restructuring Rule in Italian Syntax," in S. J. Keyser (ed.) *Recent Transformational Studies in European Languages*, pp. 113–158. Cambridge, Mass.: MIT Press.

Shibatani, M. (1976) "Causativization," in M. Shibatani (ed.) *Japanese Generative Grammar (Syntax and Semantics*, vol. 5), pp. 239–294. New York: Academic Press.

Van Tiel-Di Maio, M. F. (1978) "Sur le phénomène dit du déplacement 'long' des clitiques et, en particulier, sur le constructions causatives," *Journal of Italian Linguistics* 3(2):73–136.

Zubizarreta, M. L. (1985) "The Relation between Morphophonology and Morphosyntax: The Case of Romance Causatives," *Linguistic Inquiry* 16:247–289.

4

Aspects of the Syntax and Semantics of *ne*

Diana Cresti

1. Introduction

Consider the following Italian sentence:

(1)   Martina   ne   ha   presi   due.
        *Martina   **ne**   has   taken   two*
        'Martina took two of them.'

The clitic *ne* in (1) is sometimes called a "partitive" clitic because it is associated with a DP that appears to be partitive in meaning, as suggested by the English translation of (1). Several Romance languages besides Standard Italian have this kind of clitic (cf. Catalan *en*, French *en*, Paduan *ge-ne*), and some Germanic languages use the word for 'there' in the same manner, as shown below:

(2) a.   Ik   heb   er   sommige   gelezen.   (Dutch)
         *I   have   **there**   some   read*
         'I read some of them.'

    b.   ... da   Valère   der   viere   geeten   eet.   (West Flemish)
         *that   Valère   **there**   four   eaten   has*
         '...that Valère ate four of them.'

The syntactic properties of these elements have been recently studied by various authors;[1] the basic line of analysis is that *ne*-cliticization, and the corresponding process in the Germanic languages, is a form of subextraction from DP (or from QP; see Cardinaletti and Giusti 1992). According to this analysis, (1) would be assigned a structure like (3a), and (2b), for instance, would have a structure like (3b).

(3) a.   Martina *ne$_i$* ha presi [$_{DP}$ due *e$_i$*].
     b.   ... da Valère *der$_i$* [$_{DP}$ viere *e$_i$*] geeten eet.

In this kind of structure *e$_i$* appears to stand in for something like 'of them'. But despite the apparent partitive meaning of this element, one finds that a DP associated with *ne* (hereafter referred to as *ne*-DP) can occur in environments where a partitive DP is barred. In particular, a *ne*-DP can occur in positions which are subject to a definiteness restriction, such as the postcopular position of existential *there be . . .* sentences. This fact suggests that at least some *ne*-DPs, unlike true partitive DPs, are weak in the sense of Milsark (1977). On the other hand, it can be argued that some *ne*-DPs do have a true partitive reading, since strong determiners like *most* can be stranded by *ne*-cliticization.

In this chapter I argue that (a) indefinite DPs can be treated as unambiguous and (b) some of the properties of existential sentences are derived from simple syntactic requirements like the need to maintain a c-command relation between a trace and its antecedent (hence *there* as a scope blocker). In Section 2 I illustrate some morphological aspects of Paduan *ge-ne* constructions which suggest that (i) *there*-type elements and *ne*-type clitics are related and (ii) both *there/ci* and *ne* originate inside the complement of V. In Section 3 I look at data from Italian, West Flemish, and English which support the hypothesis that *there* and *ne* are morphologically related. In Section 3 I explore some semantic properties of *ne/ (d)er* which show that *ne*-DPs are often ambiguous between a weak reading and a strong (partitive) reading. In Section 4 I show that all these aspects of *ne*, *(d)er*, and *there* can be brought together under a surprisingly simple set of assumptions: (a) treatment of all indefinite DPs in the spirit of Heim (1982), but with modifications of the kind proposed in Cresti (1995b), and (b) an analysis of *ne* as an oblique form of *there*. In Section 5 I present some new data that, to my knowledge, have not been discussed in any of the work done on *ne*. In particular, the data show that (i) *ne*-DPs can take scope within the constituent marked by the s-structure position of *ne*; (ii) this constituent does not include the subject position; (iii) there is some evidence that even postcopular DPs of *there* sentences take scope—though their scope is also blocked by the surface position of *there*; (iv) scope reconstruction for *ne*-DPs is obligatory when these elements have undergone *wh*-movement out of their base position—a situation that has been already observed in *there* constructions with the postcopular DP.

2. The Relationship between *ne* and *there*

2.1 Evidence from Paduan

Before entering into considerations about the general behavior of *ne/(d)er*-DPs, I would like to show, based on one particular language, that the similarities between Romance *ne/en* and Germanic *(d)er* are more than coincidental. A potential obstacle to a unified analysis of *ne* and *(d)er* is that these elements are distinct on a language internal basis. In other words, all languages that have *ne/en* also have a word for 'there' which is morphologically distinct from *ne/en*. My hypothesis that *ne* is an oblique version of *there* suggests that the main difference between these two elements is morphological; indeed, in this subsection we will see evidence that there exist forms of *ne* that overtly involve *there* morphology. This evidence comes from some northern Italian languages, where *ne*-type clitics and *there*-type clitics are very intimately related—in the sense that one of the two clitics requires the presence of the other at all times. In Paduan, for instance, *ne* can never appear without *ge* 'there'.

First I illustrate the general behavior of Paduan sentences containing *ne*. This clitic has the same function as Italian *ne*, with which it shares a good number of syntactic properties; the main difference pertains to its interaction with the expletive *ge* 'there'. *Ge* is in many respects similar to the Italian existential clitic *ci*: in canonical existential constructions, it appears immediately to the left of the tensed verb (as in (4a)), and if the postcopular DP is split by *ne*-cliticization, *ge* must immediately precede *ne* (as in (4b)).

(4) a. *Ge*   ze   do   studenti. (Paduan)
         there   are   two   students

   b. *Ge*   n-è   do.
         *there   **ne**-are   two*

Paduan *ge*, like its counterpart *ci* in Italian, can be assumed to be a clitic (see Burzio 1986). It is plausible to assume that *ge* in existential sentences like those in (4) is related to something in subject position,[2] though, strictly speaking, this element cannot be considered a subject clitic.[3] It must be noted, however, that *ge*, just like *ci*, cannot occur in (or be related to) the subject position of a clause which is not strictly existential in meaning. Sentences formed with a transitive or even an unergative predicate, but with a *there*-type element occurring in subject position, are found in several Germanic languages (e.g., Vikner 1990). In Paduan such constructions are uniformly impossible (cf. (d) examples below). However, when "partitive" *ne* occurs in a sentence, the presence of *Ge* is obligatory:[4]

(5) a. Ze   rivà   do   studenti.
         are   arrived   two   students

   b. Ge   n-è   rivà   do.
         *there   **ne**-are   arrived   two*

   c. * N-è rivà do.
   d. * Ge ze rivà do.

(6) a. Ga   telefonà   do   student.
         have   phoned   two   students

   b. ± Ge   n-a   telefonà   do.[5]
         *there   **ne**-have phoned   two*

   c.   * N-a telefonà do.
   d.   * Ge ga telefonà do.

(7) a.   Go   magnà   do pomi.
            I-have   *eaten*   *two apples*

   b.   Ge   n-o   magnà   do.
            there   *ne-I-have* *eaten*   *two*

   c.   * N-o magnà do.
   d.   * Ge go magnà do.

The (b) sentences above have the same meaning as the corresponding *ne*-constructions in Italian (which would have the form (c)). So despite the fact that *Ge* in pure existential constructions like (4) may in one way or another be related to whatever is in subject position, there is reason to doubt that there is any such relation in (5b)–(7b). All evidence indicates that *Ge* and *ne* are intrinsically linked in these constructions, since neither one can occur without the other. Since *ne* is an object clitic,[6] I believe it would be counterintuitive to say that this element is (necessarily) associated with the SpecIP position in (5)–(7).

The claim that *ge* (or an associated expletive pro) is not in SpecIP (or SpecAgr$_S$P) is evidenced by the fact that an overt subject may occur in that position, followed by *ge*. In (8a) the subject is a full DP, which can be dislocated and doubled by a pronoun, as seen in (8b). Both these options are available with the *ge-ne* variant in (8c), suggesting that there can't be an expletive pro in SpecIP for *ge* to be coindexed with.

(8) a.   La Luisa ga   comprà do libri.
            the Luisa has bought two books

   b.   La Luisa ʟa ga comprà do libri.
            the Luisa she has bought two books

   c.   La Luisa (ʟa) ɢe   n-a   comprà do.
            *the Luisa (she) there **ne**-has bought two*

In addition, the sequence *ge-ne-V*$_{[+Tns]}$ cannot be broken up by any lexical item, including other clitics:[7]

(9)   Te   - ge - n- o   dà   uno.
          you$_{DAT}$- *there* -**ne** - *have given one*
          'I gave you one (of them).'

Furthermore, *ge-ne* moves as a unit in V-to-C constructions, as would be expected with regular object clitics:

(10)a.   Quanti   studenti ze rivà?
            how-many students are arrived

b.   Quanti   ge   n-è   rivà?
      *how-many there **ne**-are arrived*

(11) a.   Quanti   pomi   ga-lo   magnà?
          how-many apples has-he   eaten

b.   Quanti   ge   n-a-lo   magnà?
      *how-many there **ne**-has-he eaten*

c.   Quanti   libri   gè-to   comprà?
      how-many books have-you bought

d.   Quanti   ge   n-è-to   comprà?
      *how-many there **ne**-have-you bought*

The sentences in (11), in particular, show that *ge* patterns with object clitics, as opposed to subject clitics (as *lo* in (11a–b) and *to* in (11c–d)), in remaining to the left of the tensed auxiliary, rather than to its right. Additionally, in restructuring contexts *ge* may be found in the embedded clause, specifically attached to *ne* when this element is enclitic to the lower verb:

(12) a.   El   vorìa   tore   dieze   libri.
          he   would-want take   ten   books

b.   El   ge   ne   vorìa   tore   dieze.
      *he   there **ne** would-want take   ten*

c.   El   vorìa   tor-ge-ne   dieze.
      *he   would-want take-there-**ne** ten*

(13) a.   Quanti   libri   vu-to   tore?
          how-many books want-you take

b.   Quanti   ge   ne   vu-to   tore?
      *how-many there **ne** want-you take*

c.   Quanti   vu-to   tor-ge-ne?
      *how-many want-you take-there-**ne***

In light of the above facts, it is reasonable to assume that the *ge-ne* cluster is composed of two object clitics which presumably originate in the same object DP. In the following section I illustrate a proposal to the effect that *ge/ci* in existential sentences originate in a local configuration with their associate DP, and in subsequent sections I propose that these elements, as well as *(ge)-ne* and *(d)er* in non-existential sentences, all originate inside the DP.

2.2 Ne *pro-PP and oblique demonstrative* there

Aside from the "partitive" *ne/der*-DPs discussed in the previous sections, there are several other situations in which the clitic *ne* or *der* appears; in these cases the clitic is related to an oblique element or to the object of a PP. One subclass of these cases includes various arguments or relational modifiers of N:

(14) a.   Gianni   ha   mangiato   ogni   parte   del   pollo.   (Italian)
           Gianni   has eaten   every part   of-the chicken
           'Gianni has eaten every part of the chicken .'

    b.   Gianni   ne   ha   mangiata   ogni   parte.
           *Gianni   **ne**   has eaten   every part*

(15) a.   ... dan-k   ieder stikste van da   kieken   ip-geeten   een.   (WF)
           that-I   every part   of   the   chicken   up-eaten   have
           '... that I have eaten every part of the chicken.'

    b.   ... dan-k der   ieder stikske   van   ip-geeten   een.
           *that-I **there** every part   **of**   up-eaten   have*

At first sight, the examples in (14) would seem quite similar to the partitive *ne*-DPs discussed above. There are several differences, however. First, the object DPs in (14b)–(15b) have a true head N (usually meaning 'part' or 'piece' or 'content'). In Italian, this head triggers morphological agreement on the main verb; so, for instance, in (14b) *mangiat-a* agrees with the feminine singular *parte*, rather than, say, the masculine singular *pollo*. Second, this kind of clitic can leave behind a Det corresponding to a universal quantifier, unlike the *ne/der*-DPs discussed in the previous sections. Finally, the "source" of *ne/der* is structurally a PP, as evidenced by the fact that in WF the preposition is actually visible in the position immediately preceding the gap (cf. (15b)). Other DP-internal obliques (usually arguments of N) can be cliticized in this way:

(16) a.   Maria   ne   conosce   l'autore. (Italian)
           *Maria   **ne**   knows   the author*
           'Maria knows its author.'

    b.   ... dan-k   der   den schrijver   van kennen. (WF)
           *that-I   **there** the author   **of** know*
           '... that I know its author.'

(17) a.   Maria   ne   conosce   il   padre. (Italian)
           *Maria   **ne**   knows   the father*
           'Maria knows her/his father.'

    b.   ... dan-k   der   den zeune   van   kennen. (WF)
           *that-I   **there** the son   **of**   know*
           '...that I know her/his son.'

Note that in all these cases the PP related to *ne/der* is morphologically genitive. By this I mean that all DP-internal phrases which allow this kind of cliticization can be expressed as PPs headed by a preposition corresponding to English 'of'. There no obvious semantic connection between these PPs, only a morphological one.

The other subclass of *ne/der*-PPs is represented by arguments of V. This class is morphologically more heterogeneous than the DP-internal PPs, and here we see that *der* is more productive than *ne*.

(18) a. ... da Valère der gisteren tegen geklaapt eet.
         that Valère **there** *yesterday* **against** *talked has*
         '... that Valère talked about it yesterday.'

    b.   ... da Valère der gisteren binnen geweest eet.
         that Valère **there** *yesterday* **in** *been has*
         '... that Valère was (in) there yesterday.'

    c.   ... da Valère der nie wilt in goan.
         that Valère **there** *not wants* **in** *go*
         '... that Valère doesn't want to go in there.'

    d.   ... da Valère der nie wilt ut kommen.
         that Valère **there** *not wants* **out** *come*
         '... that Valère doesn't want to come out of there.'

(19) a. Gianni ne ha parlato ieri.   **ne** ≈ 'of'/about this thing
         Gianni **ne** *has spoken yesterday*
         'Gianni has spoken about it yesterday.'

    b.   * Gianni ne è stato ieri.   **ne** ≈ in/at this location
         Gianni **ne** *has been yesterday*

    c.   * Gianni non ne vuole andare.   **ne** ≈ to this location
         Gianni not **ne** *wants to-go*

    d.   Gianni non ne vuole uscire.   **ne** ≈ from this location
         Gianni not **ne** *wants to-go-out*
         'Gianni doesn't want to come out of there.'

Descriptively, WF *der* can be extracted from several morphologically different kinds of PPs; the presence of the stranded preposition in some sense seems to allow for the recovery of the type of oblique argument involved. On the other hand, Italian *ne* is never associated with a stranded preposition and only occurs when the PP is headed by *di* 'of' or, in some cases, by *da* 'from'. In general, then, *ne* seems to be "genitive"[8] in character. This fact becomes evident when we observe that the reason for the ungrammaticality of (19b–c) is simply due to the fact that the wrong kind of clitic is used. In such sentences the appropriate locative clitic is *ci* 'there':

(20) a. Gianni c'è stato ieri.
         Gianni **there-has** *been yesterday*
         'Gianni has been there yesterday.'

b.   Gianni   non ci   vuole   andare.
        *Gianni   not **there**   wants   to-go*
        'Gianni doesn't want to go there.'

It seems, then, that Italian is very much like WF in these cases; locative *ci* in (20) is not associated with a preposition because these locative elements don't always require a preposition (cf. *Gianni è stato lì.* 'Gianni has been there'), and in this sense they behave like their English translations. Other locatives, however, do require an overt preposition, which might then be expected to show up even when *ci*-cliticization is present. In these cases the preposition is stranded, just as we have seen with the WF examples of (18):

(21) a.   Maria   è   montata   sul   cavallo.
          Maria   has climbed   on-the   horse

     b.   Maria   ci   è   montata   sopra.
          *Maria   **there** has climbed   upon*

Hence it becomes increasingly apparent that this kind of cliticization indeed has uniform properties across these languages. Given these facts, I believe that we would be missing a generalization if we were to maintain that *ne*-cliticization is unrelated to cliticization out of a nongenitive PP. A better description of these facts could be as follows: if a PP is genitive, then its clitic counterpart surfaces as *ne*, while if the PP is not genitive the clitic surfaces as *ci*.[9] To account for these patterns, I propose that *ne*-cliticization involves incorporation into P (or, more in general, into a genitive head), while *der/ci*-cliticization doesn't. This entails the claim that *there/der/ci* is a DP, and, in fact, a D. In the case of *ne*, this element incorporates (or adjoins) into a genitive head as a D before cliticizing onto the tensed main verb; this is illustrated in (22).

(22)   Morphosyntactic derivation of *(ge-)ne*

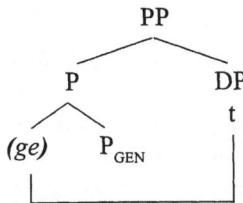

Paduan could be taken to be the most transparent example of this: the result of *GE* adjoining to a genitive head (which could plausibly be *ne* itself, at least in this language) is the unit *GE-ne*.

For the case of *der*, I follow the analysis of Haegeman (1993) who, in the spirit of van Riemsdijk (1978), proposes that *der* raises—as a maximal projection—to the specifier of PP before cliticizing higher up. This analysis was originally motivated by the observation that prepositions in Dutch and WF exhibit agreement with *(d)er* when it precedes these elements:

(23) a.　　vu　wadde　(WF)
　　　　　for　what

　　b.　　vur　eur
　　　　　for　her

　　c.　　der-vueren
　　　　　***there**-for(e)*

Quite reasonably, cases like (23c) ought to be assimilated to the general case of Spec-Head agreement, hence the DP *der* is in the specifier of its PP in (23c).[10] This is illustrated in (24).

(24)　　　Spec-Head agreement with *(d)er*

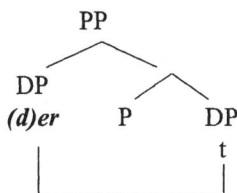

```
              PP
          /        \
       DP              \
      (d)er     P        DP
        |                 t
        |_____|
```

The structure in (24) is then the first step in *(d)er*-cliticization. One could also imagine that (24) is the correct structure for the Italian cases of locative *ci*-cliticization like (21b); furthermore, English also seems to have this process, though it is not quite as productive as in Dutch or WF:

(25) a.　　He spoke thereof.　　　　"of that/this topic"
　　b.　　the father thereof　　　　"of that/this person"
　　c.　　Therefore, ...　　　　　　"for that/this reason"
　　d.　　..., thereby ...　　　　　　"by (means of) this"
　　e.　　Therein lies the secret.　　"in that location"

3. Anaphoric properties of *ne*-DPs

3.1 Not all ne-DPs are partitive

Just like with other (nominal) clitics, the presence of *ne* indicates that the associated DP is an anaphoric element whose interpretation requires that we be able to retrieve an antecedent for it; the antecedent, then, will provide us with the appropriate interpretation for (the gap in) the *ne*-DP. Therefore, in order to establish whether a *ne*-DP can have a partitive interpretation, we need to examine what kinds of elements can serve as antecedents for it. This way we can construct an appropriate paraphrase for the *ne*-DP in question and examine this full constituent to verify whether we have a true partitive.

　　According to Jackendoff (1977:111), a true partitive is taken to be a DP of the form [Det_1 of [Det_2 common noun]], where Det_2 is definite (i.e., a definite article, a demonstrative, or a possessive). Semantically, the DP headed by Det_1

"picks out" subsets (or subgroups) of the set (group) denoted by [Det$_2$ common noun]. For instance, the DP meaning [*two of the boys*] picks out subsets of cardinality two of the set [*the boys*] (see appendix). This fact will be useful in the discussion that follows.

The first idea that comes to mind, in regard to how we should interpret a *ne*-DP, is suggested by the translations of (1) and (2). Suppose the gap associated with *ne* should be reconstructed as a constituent containing a plural (anaphoric) pronoun. In other words:

(26)   *ne$_i$* ... [Det *e$_i$*]   →   ... [Det *of them*]

Notice that this move does not force us to interpret a *ne*-DP as necessarily partitive. Wilkinson (1992) examines English DPs of the form [Det *of them*] and shows that in some cases these are not true partitives. She notes that these constituents can appear in the postcopular position of *there be* . . . sentences, unlike true partitives:

(27)   Late homework assignments are impossible to grade, and
    a.   there are many of them.
    b.   * there are many of the late homework assignments.

If the DP *many of them* in (27a) were a true partitive, we should be able to paraphrase *them* as *the late homework assignments,* as in (27b). But (27b) is ungrammatical and (27a) isn't; and, if we look more closely, the two continuations of (27) are not even synonymous, since (27a) simply means *there are many late homework assignments*. Wilkinson argues that when the antecedent of a plural pronoun is a kind denoting bare plural, as is the case with the subject of (27), what the pronoun "picks up" is not a referring expression but rather a kind. Thus the antecedent for this pronoun should be something which makes the appropriate kind salient: in the case at hand, this could be the set of all things which have the property of being late homework assignments. Depending on how one analyzes kind-denoting DPs, one could obtain the appropriate meaning by simply copying a common noun (phrase) denotation from the antecedent DP into the place of *of them* in (27a).

(28)   there are many [of them]   →   there are many [late homework
            assignments]

Note that no partitive reading arises in these cases: the *of them* component of the DP seems to have no meaningful structure of its own, being simply a kind of (genitive-marked) anaphoric element. Wilkinson proposes that all (plural) pronouns which have kind denoting bare plurals as antecedents are common noun (phrase) (CN-) anaphors. She further suggests that French *en* should be treated as a CN-anaphor as well:

(29)   Les rhinoceros sont   mes animaux   favoris,   mais ...
            the rhinos   are   my animals   favorites   but ...

a. J'en   ai   vu   peu   en   Afrique.
    I-en have seen few   in   Africa

b. * J'ai   vu   peu   d'entre eux   en   Afrique.
    I-have seen few   among   them in   Africa

Since the expression *d'entre eux* in French is necessarily understood as partitive, (29b) is not allowed as a continuation of (29), where the intended antecedent of *eux* (viz. *les rhinoceros*) is kind denoting. Example (29a), however, is perfectly ok, and means "I have seen few rhinos in Africa," a case closely parallel to (27a).

On the other hand, *en*-DPs in French, and *ne*-DPs in Italian, do not require a kind-denoting DP as an antecedent.[11] In fact, these kinds of anaphors do not even require a plural DP as an antecedent, as we will see shortly. Furthermore, in the case of English (27a), the element *of them* must be anaphoric to the entire descriptive part of its antecedent DP—viz. late homework assignments, and not, for instance, homework assignments. This is not necessarily the case with *en/ne*-DPs. These facts are illustrated by the following example from Italian:

(30)   Maria   ha   un cappello verde ed io ne   ho   [due *e* rossi].
       *Maria   has a   hat   green and I   **ne** have two   red*
       'Maria has a green hat and I have two red ones.'

The second conjunct in (30) can be paraphrased as *io ho due cappelli rossi*, 'I have two red hats'. An appropriate paraphrase for (30) *cannot* be "Maria has a green hat and I have two of them (which are red)". The *ne*-DP in the second conjunct is clearly not a partitive, and it isn't kind-referring, either (although we cannot conclude from this that kinds are irrelevant to the analysis of these DPs; see later). Its antecedent is simply 'hat-', a constituent not marked for number. The most appropriate English paraphrase for (30) involves what is called a *ones*-anaphor. Wilkinson gives a French example similar to (30), translating it with a *ones*-anaphor as well. I believe that this is the closest kind of anaphor to the Romance *ne*-DP. In English, a *ones*-anaphor can stand in for a variety of subconstituents of a DP, in the same way as a *ne*-DPs can:

(31)   Gianni ha   comprato una grande foto di   Venezia, ...
       Gianni has bought   a   large   photo of   Venice

a. e   Mario ne   ha comprata una   piccola.
    *and Mario **ne** has bought   one   small*

b. e   Mario ne   ha comprata una   di Firenze.
    *and Mario **ne** has bought   one   of Florence*

(32)   I told two silly stories about overnight train rides, ...
a.   and John told a long one.
b.   and John told one about getting stuck in traffic.

The gap related to *ne* in (31a) can mean 'photograph' or 'photograph of Venice', and in (31b) it can mean 'photograph' or 'large photograph'. Similarly, *one* in (32a) can mean either 'story' or 'story about overnight train rides'; in (32b) it can mean either 'story' or 'silly story'. Thus minimally the copying operation must involve the denotation of the nominal head of the antecedent DP, but it may also involve any larger subconstituent of the antecedent DP, up to but not including the head D. Clearly, then, this kind of anaphor does not involve a relation of coreference with its antecedent, nor does it involve binding of individual variables or constructing definite descriptions, which may contribute to a partitive interpretation; in this respect these DPs are thus similar to those in Wilkinson's examples discussed above. On the other hand, the case of *ne*-DPs and *ones*-anaphors differs from Wilkinson's examples in that it doesn't typically involve kind-denoting antecedents. The copying rule involved might simply be a syntactic operation, perhaps similar to whatever operations are assumed to be operative in cases of VP ellipsis.[12]

This latter hypothesis is supported by another fact about these anaphors. From the examples below we see that the copied material can contain pronouns, which can be anaphoric to a DP in the first conjunct or to one in the same clause as the copied pronoun, giving rise to ambiguities due to "strict" and "sloppy" patterns of coreference inside the gap:

(33)   Io   racconto una storia sulla mia   infanzia,
        I   tell   a   story about my   childhood

        poi   ne racconti   una tu,
        then ne tell   one you

        poi   ne racconta una lei, ...
        then ne tells   one she

(34)   I tell a story about my childhood, and then you tell one,
        and then she tells one ...

Here the sentences can be understood in two ways: either that each person tells a story about their own childhood ("sloppy" coreference), or that everybody tells a story about the speaker's childhood ("strict" coreference). I believe this ambiguity is not present with the cases discussed by Wilkinson.[13] I take this fact to support an analysis of weak *ne*-DPs in terms of an LF-syntax copying rule.

3.2 Interpretive constraints on strong ne-DPs

We have seen that at least some *ne*-DPs are not partitive. Now I will consider cases of *ne*-DPs which *do* get partitive readings. The existence of these strong *ne*-DPs is evidenced by the fact that some strong determiners can be stranded by *ne*-cliticization. For reasons that are not clear to me at this moment, in all languages I've seen that have this process a Det corresponding to a universal quantifier cannot be stranded.[14] Nevertheless, we see that other strong Dets like the word for 'most', or other proportional Dets (such as 'the best half', 'the 5% most intelligent', etc.), or Dets like Dutch *sommige* 'sóme/certain' are allowed. In these cases a partitive reading is obligatory. This is illustrated in (35):

(35)   Ieri   ho   comprato un chilo di farina;
         yesterday I-have bought   a   kilo of flour

         ne ho   usata [la maggior parte *e*] per fare il   pane.
         ne *I-have used the greater part   to   make the bread*

The *ne*-DP above can only be interpreted as *la maggior parte de-il chilo di farina che ho comprato ieri* 'most of the kilo of flour that I bought yesterday'. This paraphrase suggests that these anaphors should be analyzed either by means of an E-type approach (see Evans 1977) or by some form of (dynamic) variable binding. According to the E-type strategy, the meaning of the *ne*-DP in (35) can be retrieved by copying the content of the first conjunct as a relative clause headed by the DP *(un) chilo di farina* into the position of the empty category inside the *ne*-DP,[15] essentially resulting in the paraphrase above. With respect to the example in (35), this would appear to be the correct result.

However, there is reason to believe that an E-type analysis of partitive *ne*-DPs will not work out, for at least two reasons. First, strong *ne*-DPs do not typically have an indefinite DP as an antecedent. There is general agreement in the literature that the E-type analysis is not appropriate for pronouns with definite antecedents, and the arguments made there can easily be reproduced for the cases considered here. Second, there are cases where the antecedent of a *ne*-DP is in a c-command relation to it. In these cases an E-type approach would not be applicable for technical reasons alone.[16]

What is interesting here is that strong *ne*-DPs do not seem to have a place in conventional Binding Theory. What we find is that the gap in a strong *ne*-DP behaves like an R-expression in some cases and as a pronominal in others. So, for instance, the following example is ungrammatical:

(36) a.   * [Gianni e Mario]$_i$ mi hanno chiesto di riceverne [uno *e*$_i$]
           'Gianni and Mario asked me to receive-**ne** one

           prima delle undici.
           before eleven o'clock.'

     b.   * [Gianni e Mario] mi chiesero di ricevere
          * '[Gianni and Mario] asked me to receive

           uno di-[Gianni e Mario/questi ragazzi].
           one of [Gianni and Mario/these guys].'

     c.   [Gianni e Mario]$_i$ mi chiesero di ricevere uno di loro$_i$ ...
           '[Gianni and Mario]$_i$ asked me to receive one of them$_i$ ...'

If we substitute an R-expression or a demonstrative for the gap in (36a) we get exactly the same degree of ungrammaticality (under the intended coreferential reading), as illustrated in (36b). But if we were to substitute a pronoun, as in (36c), we would get a perfectly grammatical sentence. Thus the gap in the *ne*-DP cannot be [+pronominal], or we would have no explanation for the Principle C effect in (36a). This fact is parallel to similar sentences in English involving a *ones*-anaphor which is understood as partitive:

(37)   * [John and Mary]$_i$ asked me to meet [one e_i].

On the other hand, if we were to establish that the gap in a *ne*-DP (or, for that matter, in a *ones*-anaphor) is an R-expression, we would not be able to explain why sentences like (38)–(39) are ok.[17, 18]

(38)   [Quei lamponi]$_i$ sembravano così buoni che ho deciso
            'Those raspberries seemed so good that I-have decided

            di comprarne uno/la maggior parte e_i.
            to buy-**ne** one/the greater part.'

(39)   [Those watermelons]$_i$ seemed so juicy that I just had to get one e_i.

In both cases, some c-command relation must be at stake in order to rule out sentences like *They$_i$ seemed so juicy that I just had to get one of [those watermelons]$_i$ as Principle C violations. Clearly the anaphoric properties of partitive *ne*-DPs are rather complex and need a closer look than is provided here.

At any rate, what we know about partitives in general is that they are certainly anaphoric. When their antecedent is not to be found in the same sentence, we can say that they are discourse anaphors—that is, they are D-linked in the sense of Pesetsky (1987); this is also equivalent to saying that they are presuppositional in the sense of Strawson. This is the most straightforward sense in which an indefinite DP can be considered strong. Thus strong *ne*-DPs can be analyzed as involving a [+definite] gap which is most appropriately treated, I believe, in the way that Heim (1982) analyzes definite DPs (recall that the E-type analysis of these gaps would not be appropriate in cases where the strong *ne*-DP is c-commanded by its antecedent). The next section is devoted in part to further discussion of these issues.

It is important to note that, with the exception of *ne*-DPs headed by strong determiners (which are always interpreted as true partitives), any *ne*-DP is in principle ambiguous between a weak and a strong reading. We should then expect most constructions containing this kind of DP to be at least two-ways ambiguous due to this fact.[19] And, indeed, this is what we find. Consider the example below:

(40) a.   Ci   sono   molti film   stasera   in   TV,
            there are   many   movies this evening on   TV

            ma io   ne   ho   già   visti [due e].
            but I ne   have already seen   two

b. ... io ho già visto due film.
    '... I already saw two movies.'

c. ... io ho già visto due dei film che sono in TV stasera/
    '... I already saw two of the movies that are on TV tonight/

    due di quei film.
    two of those movies.'

In (40a) the second conjunct can be interpreted as in (40b), where the *ne*-DP simply means 'two movies'; under this reading, the speaker is basically making a statement about movie-watching, not about any particular movies which happen to be on TV that evening. Or we can have a reading as in (40c), where the *ne*-DP is a true partitive, and the movies in question are indeed two of the movies made salient in the first conjunct.

In Dutch and West Flemish, a *(d)er*-DP is also potentially ambiguous in this way, although the well-known properties associated with scrambling in these languages (Diesing 1992) conspire to limit this ambiguity:

(41) a. ... da Valère **der** vandoage a **viere** geeten eet. (WEAK)
         ... *that Valère* ***there*** *today* *already* ***four*** *eaten* *has*
         '... that Valère ate four of them yesterday.'

b. ... da Valère der vandoage **viere** a geeten eet. (STRONG)

c. ... da Valère der **viere** vandoage a geeten eet. (STRONG)

In the West Flemish example above, the only case where the *der*-DP is interpreted as weak is (41a), where the stranded element *viere* 'four' appears to the right of both adverbs *vandoage* 'today' and *a* 'already', indicating that the DP is not scrambled. In the other two cases, *viere* appears to the left of one or both adverbs, indicating that the *der*-DP is scrambled: in these cases, the only possible interpretation for this DP is a strong one. Thus with cardinal determiners, the potential ambiguity can be eliminated if there is a way to tell whether or not the DP is scrambled.

When a determiner which forces a strong reading is present, we see that the *der*-DP must be scrambled:

(42) a. ... da Valère **der** **tmeeste** gisteren geeten eet.
         ... *that Valère* ***there*** ***most*** *yesterday* *eaten* *has*
         '... that Valère ate most of them yesterday.'

b. ... da Valère **der** gisteren **tmeeste** geeten eet.
    ... *that Valère* ***there*** *yesterday* ***mostly*** *eaten* *has*
    '... that Valère ate of them mostly yesterday.'

The West Flemish word *tmeeste* has one interpretation as the determiner 'most' and one as the adverb 'mostly'. In (42a) the former interpretation is possible. The presence of the temporal adverbial to the right of *tmeeste* indicates that the object has been scrambled outside of VP. Here the determiner *tmeeste* is stranded by *der*-

cliticization, and only a true partitive reading is possible. In (42b) only the latter interpretation is possible for *tmeeste*; this word cannot be interpreted as a determiner, in this case, but only as a VP modifier. Of course, *der* in (42b) is still associated with a DP, but one with a zero determiner; this means that the *der*-DP may be interpreted inside VP, and thus receive a weak interpretation.

As mentioned above, these facts are consistent with the observations of Diesing (1992), who proposes that strong indefinite DPs are quantifiers which presuppose their descriptive content and are interpreted outside of VP, while weak indefinites are not quantifiers or presuppositional, and are interpreted inside VP. This same idea can be found in Moro (1991, 1993) with respect to the case of existential *there*-sentences. In Cresti (1995b), I argued that all indefinite DPs are non-quantificational; hence even a strong indefinite may receive its quantificational force from existential closure (perhaps at the text level). Therefore the strength or weakness of an indefinite DP is not a consequence of ambiguity in the determiner, but rather of the accessibility (in terms of presupposition projection) of contextual material to elements that are topic marked in the sense of von Fintel (1994). In the case of a true partitive, the definite "inner" DP is clearly D-linked; thus by definition it is a topic. And since topic marking of an XP (in this particular sense) appears to be correlated in many languages with the XP being outside of VP at the syntactic level that feeds the interpretive component (or with what Manfred Krifka identifies as the "focus field"), my proposal shares some basic predictions with the Diesing/Moro-style analysis, but without assuming a costly ambiguity for indefinite DPs.

In what follows, I describe in some detail what I assume to be the syntax and semantics of *ne*-DPs; subsequently, I show how some new and perhaps surprising patterns exhibited by these DPs are also predicted by my analysis.

4. *Ne* and scope

We have seen that in principle any *ne*-DP (headed by an indefinite Det) is ambiguous between a weak reading and a strong reading. In particular, the gap in the *ne*-DP can be anaphoric in two ways: (a) it can be a CN anaphor, in which case the DP gets a weak interpretation; or (b) it can be the [+definite] constituent of a partitive DP (as per Jackendoff's 1977 definition), which correlates with a strong interpretation of the DP.

Recall that my earlier observations about the morphosyntax of *ne* and *der* led me to posit in section 2.2 that these elements are part of a PP constituent (see structures (22) and (24)). This conclusion, however, needs to be reconciled with the facts concerning the interpretation of weak *ne*-DPs, which seem to indicate that the *ne*-gap is more naturally analyzed as a nominal category (see also the discussion in Rizzi 1982). I will suggest that these two sets of assumptions are not only compatible, but in fact we should expect this kind of morphological patterning—at least in languages that don't have overt partitive case. I will thus analyze both weak and strong *ne*-gaps as essentially corresponding to NP gaps.

To illustrate the basics of this proposal, consider a variant of (40) above, where the *ne*-DP is ambiguous between a weak and a strong reading:

(43)   Stasera ci sono tre film: *Psycho, Amarcord,* e *Satyricon*; ma ...
         tonight there are three films

  a.   ... Io ne ho già visti due ___.
  b.   I have already seen [$_{DP}$ two films].
  c.   I have already seen [$_{DP}$ two of those films / them].

The structures I assume for the DPs in (43b) and (43c) are given in (44a) and (44b), respectively:

(44) a.   Weak *ne*-DP   b.   Strong *ne*-DP

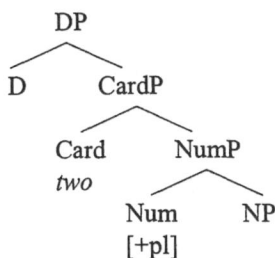
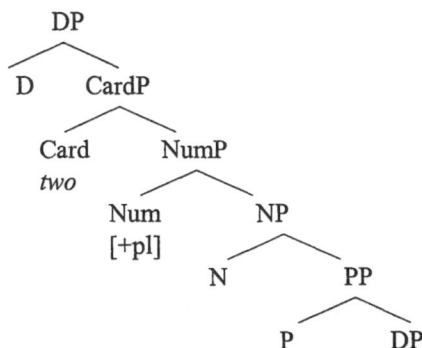

The only phonetically overt element in the DPs in (44a) and (44b), of course, is the numeral *two*. I have opted to analyze it as heading its own "Cardinality" phrase, based in part on the assumption that cardinality words are not true determiners (see appendix) and in part on the observation that because numerals are not interchangeable with regular adjectives, they should not be allowed to occur in standard adjective positions. In the case of *ne*-DPs this distinction is rather important, since—as we have seen—*ne*-cliticization may or may not leave behind adjectival elements, but it must always leave behind a numeral.[20] The presence of a Number (or "plurality") phrase projection separate from NP reflects the fact that, as we saw in section 3.1, the gap associated with *ne* is underspecified for number, thus it should not include number information. The assumption that NumP is a separate projection from CardP reflects my tentative conclusion from other work that semantic plurality and syntactic/morphological plurality must be treated as independent aspects of grammar.[21]

The NP node in both (44a) and (44b) does not dominate any overt material; furthermore, at least in the case of (44a), the NP constituent is the largest possible site for the anaphor—since, as we saw, the [+plural] feature in Num° is already not anaphoric. Thus in principle the NP ought to correspond to the anaphor in question; but the weak/strong ambiguity of *ne*-DPs compels us to say something more.

Semantically, the available antecedent for the gap in (43b) is the predicate **film′**, which I assume is underspecified for number; this predicate is naturally located at the NP node of (44a). The antecedent for the gap in (43c) is the maximal "extensional" set (or group) of contextually salient movies, [*those films/ them*] in (43c), which I represent as $\{P, A, S\}$; this antecedent is not naturally located at the NP node, which under standard assumptions should be a predicate. The set $\{P, A, S\}$ is best analyzed as a DP. In (44b), the DP in question is the one dominated by the PP complement of N. The N head itself is not phonetically realized, as we would expect with regular partitive constructions; but it has a semantic function, which is to create a predicate out of the group entity $\{P, A, S\}$—hence the Π 'part-of' operator in its translation (see Appendix). The interpretation of (44a) and (44b) is then computed on LFs roughly equivalent to the following:

(45) a.   Weak *ne*-DP   b.   Strong *ne*-DP

			DP				DP	
		D	CardP			D	CardP	
			Card NumP				Card NumP	
				Num NP				Num NP
				[+pl]				[+pl] N PP
								P_GEN DP

	D	Card	NumP(NP)	D	Card	Num	N	P	DP
a1.	Ø	two	films						
a2	δ	[*two*]	**film′**						
b1.				Ø	two	Ø		of	those films
b2.				δ	[*two*]	$\lambda z \lambda x[x\Pi z]$	Ø		$\{P, A, S\}$

In (45a) the DP we need is essentially the object DP of (43b), as indicated in (45a1). Given the similar behaviors of the gap in weak *ne*-DPs and that in VP ellipsis, it seems plausible that whatever analysis of the latter turns out to be correct (viz., either copying of the appropriate constituent into the gap, or deletion of material under "identity" of some kind) may also apply to the former. In (45a2) I give the semantic values for the constituents of the DP (see appendix for details). Whenever a constituent is "invisible" at a certain level, I marked it with a 'Ø' on the corresponding line. Depending on one's theory, the [+plural] feature on Num° is either a purely formal feature that is not visible at the PF and LF interfaces, or is essentially limited to carrying plural morphology (whether or not it is visible, say, at PF).

In (45b) the DP we need is something like the object DP of (43c), as shown in (45b1). Having rejected an E-type analysis of strong *ne*-DPs, I propose to treat the element that I paraphrased as 'those films/them' as a "familiar discourse referent" in the spirit of Heim (1982). In the case at hand, I have assumed that this discourse referent corresponds to the group {*P*, *A*, *S*}, though one must keep in mind that this "referential" treatment of partitives is overly simplified would need to be complicated somewhat to extend the analysis to partitives in embedded contexts.[22] The semantic values of the constituents in (45b) is shown in (45b2). Note that the semantics does not "see" Num° or the genitive P°. The element responsible for creating the predicate we need—the predicate that is true of any entity just in case it is a subset/subgroup of {*P*, *A*, *S*}—is the head noun (see appendix). The genitive P°, then, also has a purely morphological role, as we would expect with arguments of N in the languages we're looking at.

I must stress, at this point, that (45a1–b1) do not actually represent the morphology of *ne* (or *der*). This may be easier to see with (45b), since I have already observed that the anaphor in question does not seem to behave either like a name or like a pronoun; thus the anaphor is not literally the DP *those films* or the DP *them*. As argued earlier, what the morphology/syntax sees is an element more like *there* (or Italian *ci*, Paduan *ge*, West Flemish *der*). If this element is a head, as in the case of Italian and Paduan, this head will incorporate into the genitive P° in the manner indicated in section 2.2, yielding *ne* or *ge-ne*; this process is completely compatible, I believe, with most current assumptions about cliticization—including the possibility that the NP (or even the NumP) may move along for licensing of object agreement.

In the case of (45a), and of weak *ne*-DPs in general, it may not be so obvious that there is a genitive P° with a sister DP to analyze as I just did, but there are some indications that some variant of this account can be constructed.

One possibility is that any NP node correlates with genitive morphology simply by virtue of the fact that its head is inherently associated with genitive marking on its arguments. This case marking will only "take over" the NP when this element is extracted from its DP by cliticization or other means. As a mere descriptive generalization, this statement seems satisfactory: it is regularly observed in many languages that whenever a subconstituent of a DP—usually something that looks like an NP—is separated from the DP, some sort of case marker or preposition often shows up. In Italian, in particular, this preposition is what I have called a P_{GEN}. In fact, *ne*-cliticization itself exhibits this behavior. Consider the following variant of (43):

(46)   Stasera ci sono tre film: *PSYCHO*, *AMARCORD*, e *SATYRICON*; ma ...

   a.   ... Io ne ho già visti due, di film.
   b.   ... Io ne ho già visti due, di quei film.

The right-peripheral element *di film/di quei film* seems to have the function of "filling in" the content of the *ne*-gap in contexts which may require such information. This element will disambiguate a *ne*-DP which may otherwise be read as either weak or strong. In the strong case (46b) we basically see something like (45b1), where *di quei film* can be analyzed as corresponding to the embedded PP of (45).[23] In the weak case (46a) we have a situation that is more difficult to account for; of course, the string *di film* would appear to be a PP, but the lack of a determiner seems to suggest that the P° does not have a DP sister: all we have is the bare noun *film*. The next question then is: What is the status of this element?

One possibility is that *di film* is indeed a PP, and that *film* is, after all, a DP. In Italian, bare nouns usually cannot be full DPs, though the class of "exceptions" to this observation is significant enough to have been the object of a fair amount of research (see in particular Benincà 1980 and Longobardi 1994). Most recently, Chierchia (1998) has suggested that bare nouns may denote (names of) kinds. If this is correct, then a bare noun in an argument position of a V or P can be analyzed as a true argument of the V or P whenever it can be interpreted as kind-denoting, since names of kinds are of semantic type *e*—the type of arguments. For the sake of uniformity, I will assume that these arguments are DPs. To be sure, if we consider our current object of inquiry from a semantic perspective, we cannot say that a bare noun like *film* is a "true argument" of the P *di*, since this latter element is by hypothesis invisible to the semantics. However, because the PP *di film* ultimately "belongs" inside the NP in a structure like (44a), the kind-denoting DP *film* is really a true argument of what now can be analyzed as a (phonetically) empty N head of the NP. In other words, the weak case (44a) could actually be analyzed according to a structure similar to the one in the strong case (44b), thus accounting for the identical morphology of weak and strong *ne*-DP. In the semantics, however, the difference remains clear: first, the DP *film* is not D-linked, as is the case with a definite DP; second, the N head in this case does not host a semantic 'part-of' operator, as in the case of true partitives. Since, by hypothesis, the argument of this N is a kind and the NP is a predicate, the N must be interpreted as an operator that takes kinds and yields predicates; an appropriate operator for this purpose is Chierchia's ^{U} ('up') function.

To recapitulate, then, the analysis of weak *ne*-DP remains essentially as in (45a) (repeated below), but is further articulated to include these latest assumptions. In (47a2) the expression FILM is a kind-level individual, so that ^{U}FILM = **film'**. Given the translation assigned to N in (47), the larger DP in this structure has the same interpretation as its counterpart in (45).

If (47) is the correct analysis of *ne*-DP, then the morphological derivation in (22) will apply here in the same way as it does in the case of the strong *ne*-DP (45b).

An important consequence of treating *ne* as an oblique form of *there* is that we expect not only that some of the morphological properties of *there* will carry over to *ne*, but that some of its semantic properties may carry over as well. In particular, English *there* appears to be a scope blocker, in the sense that its associate DP cannot take scope in or above the position occupied by *there*. Although it is far from established why this should be the case—and, in fact, it is often assumed that a DP associated with *there* simply cannot take scope—there are some intriguing new facts which suggest that *there* and *ne* behave similarly in this respect. Keep in mind that I am analyzing all indefinites as nonquantificational, thus subject to existential closure in various places (at least at VP and Text levels). For plural indefinites, there will also be a distributive operator which can give the appearance of scope, and which may or may not be at the same location as the existential closure operator. In the appendix I illustrate the details of this mechanism. This might help in evaluating the facts to be presented in the next section.

5. *There*, *ne*, and Scope

According to my analysis of *ne* as an oblique counterpart of *there*, we might expect this element to restrict scope-taking possibilities of its associated DP like *there* does. Specifically, if the clitic *ne* is located in INFL (=Agr$_s$), we might expect that a *ne*-DP will not take scope above this position. First, I present data which show that a strong *ne*-DP can indeed take scope. Consider the examples in (48):

(48) a.   Ho risolto due problemi in un'ora; per gli altri ci ho messo di più.
          'I solved two problems in an hour; for the others it took me longer.'

    b.   Ne ho risolti due in un'ora; per gli altri ci ho messo di più.
          '*ne* I solved two in an hour; for the others it took me longer.'

In (48a) the indefinite *due problemi* can be understood as taking scope over the temporal adverbial *in un'ora*. The relevant reading can be paraphrased as follows: there are two problems, each of which is such that it took me an hour to solve it; and there are others for which it took me longer. The continuation is meant to bring out the wide scope reading of the indefinite, which is usually not the preferred option. Sentence (48b), where the indefinite is cliticized with *ne*, also allows a wide scope reading of the *ne*-DP.

Now, it is reasonable to assume that the adverbial in (48) is a VP-modifier, or in any case is attached lower than IP. If this is correct, then the pattern above is correctly predicted to be possible. But there is strong evidence that shows that a *ne*-DP cannot take scope over the SpecIP position. This evidence comes from the interaction of a *ne*-DP with negative elements. Consider the following two sets of sentences:[24]

(49) a.   Gianni non ha risolto molti problemi.
            'Gianni didn't solve many problems.'

     b.   Gianni non ne ha risolti molti.
            *Gianni not **ne** has solved many*

(50) a.   Nessuno ha risolto molti problemi.
            nobody has solved many problems

     b. # Nessuno ne ha risolti molti.
            *nobody **ne** has solved many*

The sentences in (49) are ambiguous with respect to the relative scope between the indefinite and the negative element *non*. Example (49a), for instance, allows for a reading in which the indefinite *molti problemi* takes scope over *non*. This reading will be true in a situation where there are many problems that Gianni didn't solve—even if there are also many others that he did solve. Under the opposite scope configuration, (49a) could be paraphrased as 'It is not the case that Gianni solved many problems.' Clearly this reading is false in the situation described; thus the wide scope reading of the indefinite exists as a distinct reading of (49a). Example (49b), where the *ne*-DP can be interpreted as 'many problems' or as 'many of the problems', shares this very same wide scope reading of the *ne*-DP. So we can assume that whatever is responsible for the scope of the *ne*-DP can be located above the position where negation is interpreted.[25] Now, (50a) is also fully ambiguous: it can mean either that nobody is such that she or he solved many problems (i.e., everyone solved few problems), indicating that *nessuno* is taking scope over *molti problemi*; or it can mean that there are many problems that weren't solved by anybody—though there could be one or more people who solved many other problems. This is the wide scope reading of *molti problemi*, which is also truth-conditionally distinct from the wide-scope-of-*nessuno* reading. Assuming that *nessuno* is interpreted in subject position,[26] the reading where *molti problemi* takes wide scope requires its scope-taking operator to be above the subject position. In (50b) this latter reading is absent (indicated by the '#' before the example). The sentence can only mean that there is nobody who solved many problems (or many of the problems); this leads me to conclude that a *ne*-DP cannot take scope above the subject position, as might be expected given my analysis of *ne*-DPs as related to DPs associated with *there*.

In the case of *there*, the idea that this element blocks the scope of its associate is fairly well accepted. To recast this observation in terms of the analysis I propose, this would mean that existential closure at the text level is not possible for the postcopular indefinite, presumably due to the blocking effect of *there*. This could be because *there* itself might be a binder of its associate DP; or there might be something more subtle involved, resulting in the impossibility of any potential binder above the position of *there* to "see" the variable in the postcopular DP. This latter hypothesis, though less explicit, may be preferable in light of the following facts. Consider the sentences below (from Moro 1993):

(51) a.   There are exactly two things on every student's mind (e.g., grades and parties).
  b. .   There are many books in every bookstore.

Both (51a) and (51b) appear to be genuinely ambiguous. The parenthetical in 51a) is intended to bring out a reading where *exactly two things* takes scope over *every student's mind*; under this reading, (51a) can be true if the issue of grades is on every student's mind, as well as the issue of parties. If we ignore the parenthetical, (51a) can be understood with the DP *exactly two things* taking narrow scope with respect to the locative; this reading would be true in a situation where all students' minds are occupied with exactly two issues, though not necessarily the same two issues for every given student. Similarly, (51b) can be understood as a statement about a certain large number of books that can be found in every bookstore (the scope here being *many books > every bookstore*); or it could be a statement about how every bookstore contains a large number of books (*every bookstore > many books*). Given the assumptions from section 4 plus the observation that *there* blocks scope of higher operators, we may assume that the two readings of (51b), for instance, may have roughly the following LFs:

(52) a. $\exists$ [$_{IP}$ there $\exists$ [$_{VP}$ be [$_{SC}$ [$_{DP}$ many books] [$_{PP}$ in [$_{DP}$ every bookstore]]]]]
  b. $\exists$ [$_{IP}$ there[$_{DP}$ every bookstore]$_2$ $\exists$ [$_{VP}$ be [$_{SC}$ [$_{DP}$ many books] [$_{PP}$ in t_2]]]]

The notation '||' is intended to depict the "blocking" effect of *there*. Note that even with one existential operator determining the scope of the indefinite, we can derive the two scope configurations (where (52a) corresponds to *many books > every bookstore*, and (52b) corresponds to *every bookstore > many books*), as long as the locative can be interpreted either in situ (see appendix) or in a position c-commanding the VP-level $\exists$. The structures given in (52) are simplified versions of those proposed in Cresti and Tortora (2000).

In the case of the examples in (51) it is not obvious that the text-level $\exists$ is not responsible for the ambiguity observed. To see that this kind of scope-blocking is real, we need to look at different kinds of facts. To this end, I will discuss one clear set of cases which show that even if *there*-DPs can take scope, this scope must be narrowly constrained. Before moving on to those cases, however, I will illustrate how the analysis sketched above can be extended to the facts in (49)–(50), as long as we assume that *ne* shares the scope-blocking properties of *there*.

For reasons that will become clear shortly, I will assume a modified version of Diesing's original idea that "VP-level" existential closure is always located right above VP. Several authors have observed that this $\exists$-operator might sometimes be located higher up in a clause, depending perhaps on topic/focus articulation. In the case of examples (49)–(50), the facts seem to indicate that this operator, under some readings, might be located higher than NegP. Let us see, then, what LFs are predicted in accordance with these assumptions. In all of the following examples,

the (i) LF corresponds to the wide scope reading of the indefinite/*ne*-DP, and the
(ii) LF corresponds to its narrow reading.

(53) a.   Gianni non ha risolto molti problemi. (ambiguous)
         'Gianni didn't solve many problems.'

     i. $\exists$ [$_{\text{IP}}$ Gianni non ha $\exists$ [$_{\text{NegP}}$ t_{non} [$_{\text{VP}}$ risolto [$_{\text{DP}}$ molti problemi]]]]

     or $\exists$ [$_{\text{IP}}$ Gianni non ha $\exists$ [$_{\text{NegP}}$ t_{non} [$_{\text{VP}}$ risolto [$_{\text{DP}}$ molti problemi]]]]

     ii. $\exists$ [$_{\text{IP}}$ Gianni non ha [$_{\text{NegP}}$ t_{non} $\exists$ [$_{\text{VP}}$ risolto [$_{\text{DP}}$ molti problemi]]]]

   b.   Gianni non ne ha risolti molti. (ambiguous)
         *Gianni not **ne** has solved many*

     i. $\exists$ [$_{\text{IP}}$ Gianni non **ne** ha $\exists$ [$_{\text{NegP}}$ t_{non} [$_{\text{VP}}$ risolti [$_{\text{DP}}$ molti t_{ne}]]]]

     ii. $\exists$ [$_{\text{IP}}$ Gianni non **ne** ha [$_{\text{NegP}}$ t_{non} $\exists$ [$_{\text{VP}}$ risolti [$_{\text{DP}}$ molti t_{ne}]]]]

(54) a.   Nessuno ha risolto molti problemi. (ambiguous)
         'Nobody has solved many problems.'

     i. $\exists$ [$_{\text{IP}}$ Nessuno ha $\exists$ [$_{\text{VP}}$ risolto [$_{\text{DP}}$ molti problemi]]]

     ii. $\exists$ [$_{\text{IP}}$ Nessuno ha $\exists$ [$_{\text{VP}}$ risolto [$_{\text{DP}}$ molti problemi]]]

   b.   # Nessuno ne ha risolti molti. (nonambiguous)
         *nobody **ne** has solved many*

     ii. $\exists$ [$_{\text{IP}}$ Nessuno **ne** ha $\exists$ [$_{\text{VP}}$ risolti [$_{\text{DP}}$ molti t_{ne}]]]

In all of (53a), (53b), and (54a) there are possible LFs corresponding to wide
scope readings of the indefinite/*ne*-DP, while in (54b) a wide scope reading is
predicted not to be available due to the assumption that *ne* blocks text-level
existential closure. Note that the text-level $\exists$ is also unavailable in (53b), though
the possibility that $\exists$-closure may occur above NegP—an option which is irrelevant
to the case of (54b)—allows for the wide scope interpretation of the *ne*-DP in that
case.

     Returning now to the discussion of *there* as a scope blocker in English, I will
present some data where wide scope should be expected due to *wh*-movement of
how-many-phrases, which are standardly assumed to contain an indefinite (see,
e.g., Higginbotham 1993). Typically, a *how-many* phrase will exhibit secondary

scopal interactions independent of the scope of the *wh*-operator, which lead to ambiguities of the kind illustrated below:

(55)   How many people do you need to meet tomorrow?

   a.   For what n: there are n people x such that you need to meet x tomorrow.

   b.   For what n: you need to meet n people tomorrow.

The rough paraphrases in (55a) and (55b) show that there is an indefinite component of *how many people* (viz. the higher order variable [n people]) which can take scope above the verb *need*—thus above the embedded IP *PRO to meet t tomorrow* (55a) or below *need* (55b). Now, it was noticed by Heim (1987) that wide scope interpretations of *wh*-phrases are barred in cases where the *wh*-element is extracted from the postcopular position of a *there be* . . . construction. Thus in a case like (56) the only acceptable reading is the (b) reading:

(56)   How many people do you need there to be at the meeting (tomorrow)?

   a.   * For what n: there are n people x such that you need there to be x at the meeting.

   b.   For what n: you need there to be n people at the meeting.

Heim suggested that the definiteness restriction in *there be* . . . constructions can be understood as a restriction against the occurrence of individual variables in the position of the indefinite. This essentially means that the scope of an extracted quantifier (in the present case, the [n people] part of the *how many*-phrase) must be reconstructed below *there*.

These observations about the scope-blocking properties of *there* and *ne* lead to the prediction that if a construction containing *there* or *ne* is embedded in an environment which forces a wider scope than is allowed by these elements, extraction of the *there*- or *ne*-associate will result in ungrammaticality. It appears that such an environment is provided by weak islands. In Cresti (1995a), I argued that the restrictions imposed on the extraction of elements out of weak islands cannot be formulated in purely syntactic terms (e.g., Relativized Minimality); rather, the appropriate generalization seems to be that only individual variables can occur inside these environments. Hence semantic reconstruction in general is not allowed inside these islands—scope reconstruction being a particular subcase of this constraint (see also Longobardi 1987; Frampton 1990; Rullman 1993). Therefore we expect that cases where a constituent is extracted out of a *there be* . . . clause and across a weak island will be uniformly impossible, since the two environments are mutually incompatible. This prediction is entirely borne out:

(57) a1.   How many fish are there in the lake?

   a2.   * How many fish do you wonder whether there are in the lake?

b1.   What kind of fish is there in the lake?
b2. * What kind of fish do you wonder whether there is in the lake?

c1.   What is there in Austin?
c2. * What do you wonder whether there is in Austin?

The same pattern can be seen with extraction of a *ne*-DP out of a weak island:

(58) a.   Quanti   libri   gè-to   dito   che te poi tore? (Paduan)
           how-many books have-you   said   that you can take

     b.   Quanti   gè-to   dito   che te   ge   ne poi tore?
           *how-many have-you said   that you   there **ne** can take*

(59) a.   Quanti   libri   gè-to   domandà se te   podarìsi tore?
           how-many books have-you   asked   if you could   take

     b. * Quanti   gè-to   domandà se te ge   ne   podarìsi tore?
           *how-many have-you   asked   if you there **ne** could   take*

(60) a.   Quanti libri hai detto che puoi prendere?(Italian)
           'How-many books did you say that you can take?'

     b.   Quanti hai detto che ne puoi prendere?
           'How-many did you say that (you) **ne** can take?'

(61) a.   Quanti   libri   hai   chiesto se puoi   prendere?
           how-many books did you ask   if you can take

     b. * Quant   hai   chiesto se   ne puoi prendere?
           *how-many did you ask   if (you) **ne** can   take*

The questions in (58) and (60) are all grammatical. But (58a)–(60a) are ambiguous in a way that (58b)–(60b) cannot be. The (a) sentences can mean 'For what n: there are n books x such that you said you can take x', where [n books] is taking scope over the matrix verb; or they can mean 'For what n: you said you can take n books,' where what is asked for is a number of unspecified books. However, (58b)–(60b)—where the *wh*-phrase is a *(ge-)ne*-DP—only allow this latter reading, where [n books] is taking narrow scope with respect to the matrix verb. This is predicted by the analysis of *ne*-DPs that I propose, since the scope of [n books], according to this analysis, is restricted by the s-structure/LF position of *ne* in the way illustrated above. Now, if we look at the sentences in (59a)–(61a), we note that the ambiguity present in (58a)–(60a) is gone: the *wh*-island forces the wide scope reading of [n books] in all cases. Similarly, this reading should be forced in (59b)–(61b); but as we have seen, since the extracted DP is a *(ge-)ne*-DP, this wide scope reading is not allowed. Hence these sentences are ungrammatical.

6. Conclusion

In this work I have tried to show that the various kinds of *ne* clitics can be derived by the same morphological process involving incorporation into a preposition which I have called P_{GEN}. Although, to my knowledge, *ne* does not appear to be historically connected with genitive case, it may be the case that certain syntactic processes are correlated with a reduction in morphological differentiation—for example, cliticization of the PPs in (19a–d) yields *ne* in a way perhaps similar to cliticization of both datives and benefactives, which yields a dative clitic. Another interesting case that could shed light on this putative morphological reduction is the phenomenon called genitive-of-negation. Finnish, which has a comparatively rich case system, appears to have a "partitive-of-negation" construction, which seems to have very similar properties to those commonly observed with Russian genitive-of-negation constructions. Unfortunately, my very limited knowledge of these facts does not allow me to draw any solid conclusions from this observation.

In any case, my analysis of the morphology of *ne* has lead me to an even stronger claim: that *ne* is an oblique variant of *ci* 'there'. I have tried to show that this connection is not merely a morphological one, as highlighted by the Paduan, Dutch, and West Flemish facts, but also a semantic one. This claim is supported by the facts discussed in section 5, where I argue that both *there* and *(ge-)ne-* are scope blockers for their associate DPs. The main semantic difference between a *ne*-DP and a DP associated with *there* is that the latter is subject to the Definiteness Restriction while the former is not. This difference might be related to all the facts pertaining to "thematic" subjects not being interpreted in SpecIP, as is the case with *there*-DPs in English, but also with *(d)er*-DPs in Dutch and West Flemish. Thus compare the widely known observation that Dutch subjects must be interpreted as weak when *er* is in SpecIP, with the facts noted here in section 3.2 that *(d)er*-DPs (where the DP is not a subject) are not subject to a Definiteness Restriction (modulo scrambling).

Appendix

In this chapter assume a treatment of (upward monotone) indefinites of the kind proposed in Cresti (1995b), where indefinite DPs have denotations of type $\langle\langle e, t\rangle, t\rangle$ (derived from a possibly empty D of type $\langle\langle e, t\rangle, \langle\langle e, t\rangle, t\rangle\rangle$) but lack a quantifier; furthermore, numerals or words like *many* are treated as cardinality predicates which, in this chapter, are considered to head their own projection, CardP. Note that plural indefinites are treated as inherently collective:

(A1) a.   *a book*   → $\lambda P[\textbf{book}'(x) \ \& \ P(x)]$
     b.   *three books* → $\lambda P[\textbf{three}'(x) \ \& \textbf{books}'(x) \ \& \ P(x)]$

The quantificational force of an indefinite is thus always obtained by means of the free variable in it (e.g., x in (A1a) and x in (A1b)) ending up bound by a c-commanding operator—typically a $\exists$-operator in the cases we consider here. The weak/strong distinction is derived via an independent process of topic marking, which has the effect of making the indefinite description presuppositional.

Another feature of this analysis is that indefinites and quantifiers can be interpreted in situ by means of a process that I have called 'theta-grid saturation' by which a verb (or other predicates) is supplied by the lexicon with its θ-roles already inserted in the form of "dummy" variables; these predicates thus are of type t, and due to the saturation mechanism depicted in (A2) they can combine with arguments of type e or $\langle\langle e, t\rangle, t\rangle$:

(A2)   Bob read a book.   → $\exists x[\textbf{book}'(x) \& \textbf{read}'(\textbf{Bob}, x)]$

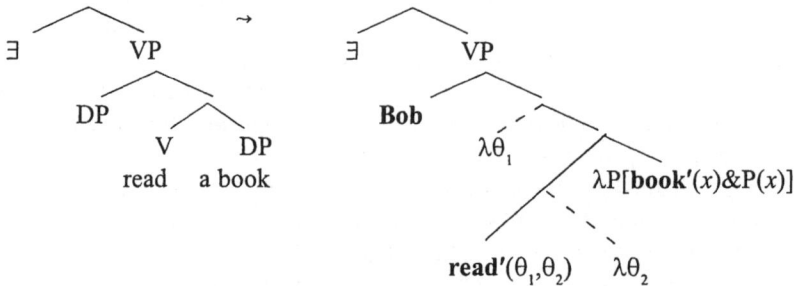

This technique can also be applied within small clauses as in the example in (52), with the proviso that the DP *many books* may be interpreted distributively or collectively (though the example here corresponds to a collective interpretation):

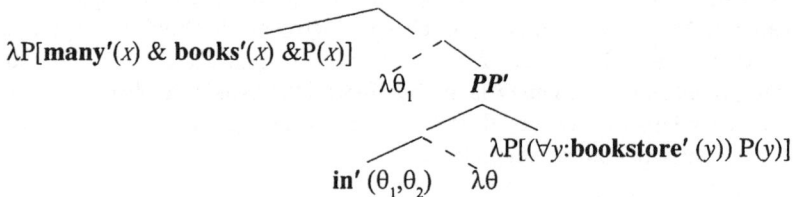

Below I derive the complete denotations for the *ne*-DPs discussed in section 4. As mentioned there, I assume the heads Num and P to be "invisible" to the semantics; thus the computation of the meanings for (45a) and (45b) can be performed on the simplified LFs in (A3).

(A3) a.   Weak *ne*-DP (45a)   b.   Strong *ne*-DP (45b)

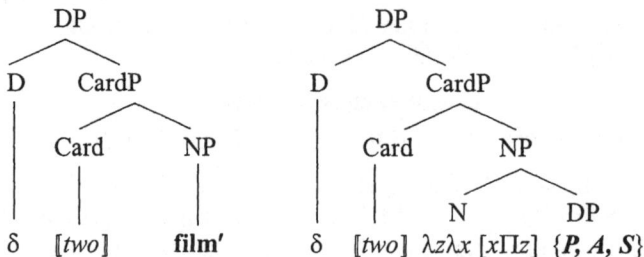

As mentioned above, the D in these structures is responsible for the DP's semantic type; this node is thus translated as $\delta = \lambda Q \lambda P[Q(x) \& P(x)]$. The numeral adds a cardinality predicate to the denotation of its sister node, thus $two = \lambda P \lambda x$ [**two'**(x) & $P(x)$].

From the discussion in sections 3.1 and 4 I concluded that the predicate **film'** is semantically underspecified for singular or plural; I will assume, then, that **film'** is a join semilattice which contains both singular and plural individuals as its members. For simplicity we can think of this as the powerset of the set of films, minus the empty set. Thus all members of the predicate **film'** are represented as sets, with singular (atomic) individuals being the singletons. The DP in (A3a) is thus interpreted as the plural (collective) indefinite *two films*:

[(A3a)] $= \delta ([two] (\textbf{film'})) = \lambda P[\textbf{two'}(x) \& \textbf{film'}(x) \& P(x)]$

The meaning obtained above is essentially the same that Diesing (1992) assumes for weak indefinites. On the other hand, the partitive DP in (A3b), which Diesing would assume has its own quantificational force, is interpreted here by means of the same determiner meaning used in (A3a), namely δ; thus strong DPs are also subject to existential closure—an operation which, as we have seen, I take to be available in places higher than VP. The strength of the DP, then, is a result of (possibly) wider scope and of the presence of a presuppositional element in the DP. In the case of partitives, the definite DP inside the partitive is this presuppositional element.[27] The (phonetically) empty N in (A3b) is interpreted as the source of a part-whole relation, which I take to be Link's (1987) individual-part-of operator, Π. I will assume for simplicity that this corresponds to a subsethood operator—that is, for any a, b: $a \Pi b := a \subseteq b$. Thus we have:

[(A3b)] $= \delta ([two] (\lambda z \lambda x [x \Pi z] (\{\textbf{P}, \textbf{A}, \textbf{S}\}))) = \delta ([two] (\lambda x [x \subseteq \{\textbf{P}, \textbf{A}, \textbf{S}\}]))$
$= \lambda P[\textbf{two'}(x) \& X \subseteq \{\textbf{P}, \textbf{A}, \textbf{S}\} \& P(X)]$

To recapitulate, then, [(A3a)] turns out to be the non-D-linked indefinite *two films*; [(A3b)], on the other hand, is a true partitive—indicated by the $X \subseteq \{\textbf{P}, \textbf{A}, \textbf{S}\}$ component, where $\{\textbf{P}, \textbf{A}, \textbf{S}\}$ is the definite which I paraphrased as 'those films'. Because definites are presuppositional, this *ne*-DP is interpreted as strong.

As for the possibility that [(A3a)] could be derived from a structure like (47a), where the *ne*-anaphor is hypothesized to be a kind rather than a predicate, the interpretation is supplemented as follows. The anaphor itself is a Carlsonian kind-level individual, FILM. The predicate **film'** is then derived from the kind FILM by means of an appropriate operator, which I have assumed here to be Chierchia's (1998) '^{U}'. This operator applies to a kind-level individual and creates the corresponding predicate: ^{U}FILM = **film'**. Note that—although this is not explicit here—a predicate obtained by these means may turn out to be empty in a given world or situation (see Chierchia 1998). Hence this operation does not introduce a presuppositional element any more than the "underived" nominal predicate does.[28] As illustrated below, I assume that the empty N has the role of introducing the ^{U}-operator.

(A4)   Alternative derivation of weak *ne*-DP (47a)

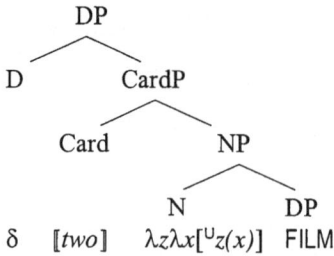

```
              DP
           /      \
          D        CardP
                  /      \
              Card        NP
                        /      \
                      N         DP
              δ   [two]   λzλx[ᵁz(x)]  FILM
```

The derivation of the meaning of (A4) is then straightforward:

$$[(A4)] = δ ([two] (λzλx [ᵁz(x)] (FILM))) = δ ([two] (λx [ᵁFILM(x)]))$$

$$= δ ([two] (λx [\textbf{film}'(x)])) = λP[\textbf{two}'(x) \& \textbf{film}'(x) \& P(x)] = [(A3a)]$$

Notes

I would like to thank Paola Benincà for her invaluable input on the data and on earlier versions of the analysis presented here. I also thank Liliane Haegeman, Andrea Moro, Orin Percus, and Luigi Rizzi for their insightful comments and criticisms at various stages of this work.

1.   See, among others, Burzio (1986), Cinque (1991), Cardinaletti and Giusti (1992) for Standard Italian; Pollock (1986) for French; Rigau (1991) for Catalan.

2.   This relation, however, will turn out to be a predicate-argument relation, rather than a coreference or movement relation. See section 3 for further discussion of this issue.

3.   This can be seen by the fact that, although Paduan has subject clitics (such as *to* in (ii) below), existential *Ge* does not pattern with such elements in V-to-C constructions:

(i) a.   Cosa   ge   ze ? (ii) a.   Ge   si-to ?   c.   * Si-to- Ge ?
            what there is   *there are-you*
            'What is there?'   ' Are you there?'
     b.   * Cosa ze- ge ?   b.   * Si- ge-to ?

Note, incidentally, that (iia) is an apparent violation of the definiteness restriction on DPs occurring in postcopular position of existential sentences. Facts similar to this will be discussed in section 3.

4.   Cecilia Poletto (p.c.) informs me that in the dialects of Conegliano and Verona one finds the mirror image of this pattern: expletive *Ge* requires the presence of *ne*. Although I won't have anything to say about these dialects, I believe the analysis I propose for *there* and *ne* can shed light on these facts as well. What I would say is that *ne* in these cases is the overt reflex of a genitive case marker inside the postcopular DP. These facts are strongly suggestive of Belletti's (1988) original analysis of postverbal DPs in existentials and unaccusatives.

5.   The '±' sign indicates dialectal variation in the grammaticality judgement for this sentence. There is a significant number of speakers who accept *ne*-cliticization out of the subject of unergative predicates. For all speakers, however, both (6c) and (6d) are utterly ungrammatical.

6. Notice that for all speakers, including those who accept (6b), *ne*-cliticization out of a transitive subject is absolutely unacceptable:

(i) a. Do studenti ga   magnà   kei pomi.
         two students have eaten   those apples
     b. * Do ge   ne ga   magnà   kei pomi.
         two there ne have eaten   those apples
     c. * Ge ne ga magnà do kei pomi.
     d. * Ge ne ga magnà kei pomi do.

7. While it is generally the case that adding a third clitic to a *Ge-ne* cluster causes *Ge* to be dropped, examples like (9) are judged to be quite acceptable by some speakers. For those who would drop *Ge* even in (9) it is still true, in any case, that (9) is more acceptable than an equivalent sentence with a different ordering of the three clitics, as shown below:

(i) a. ? Te-ge-n-o dà uno.   (=(9))
     b. * Ge-te-n-o dà uno.
     c. * Ge-ne-t-o dà uno.

8. I use the word "genitive" for what I claim is the case marking on this clitic, though one should not take this too literally. I could have made up a new name for this particular case marker, say "genitive1," but I prefer to leave this slight inaccuracy untouched for the sake of simplicity.

9. In nonstandard varieties of Italian, we find that even datives and benefactives can cliticize with *ci*, for instance:

(i) a. Ci   ho   fatto una torta con   le candeline.
         there   I-have made   a   cake   with the candles
         'I made a cake with candles for her/him.'
     b. Ci   ho   dato   una grossa mancia.
         there   I-have given a   large   tip
         'I gave her/him a big tip.'

These are quite marginal in standard Italian, but they get better when the dative/benefactive is [-human]. This fact seems connected with the binding facts discussed in note 17.

10. Liliane Haegeman (p.c.) speculates that there could be an AgrP dominating PP in these cases. This would be perfectly compatible with my analysis of *der*-cliticization. Since nothing in this chapter hinges on this distinction, I will maintain the simpler version of the structure, which highlights the basics of the current proposal.

11. It turns out that even English DPs of the form [Det *of them*] may behave as CN-anaphors when their antecedent is not kind-denoting. Thus, as pointed out to me by Irene Heim (p.c.), the DP *few friends* in (i) below is not kind-denoting, while the DP *many of them* simply means 'many friends'—that is, it is interpreted as a CN-anaphor and not as a partitive DP.

(i)   John has few friends, but Mary has many of them.

Wilkinson (1992) does not consider examples such as (i) since her discussion concentrates on the analysis of bare plurals.

12. Of course, if this analogy turns out to be correct, and if there is good reason to believe that VP ellipsis is best analyzed as involving deletion (rather than copying), then the *ne/ones* anaphors might also be analyzed by means of a deletion rule. I am not sure what the consequences of such an approach would be, but presently I don't see any serious problem with this idea.

13. So a sentence like (i), for those who accept it, can only mean 'Don't tell too many (generic) childhood stories'.

(i)   ? Stories about one's childhood are fun. Don't tell too many of them, though.

14. Italian has a form of *ne* which leaves behind a head *parte* 'part', and which allows universal quantifiers to head the *ne*-DP. These cases, however, can be shown to be systematically different from the *ne*-DPs discussed here. The reason I group *la maggior parte* with strong *ne* is that this element acts as if it had no internal structure: for instance, as Luigi Rizzi (p.c.) points out, it does not require verbal agreement with *parte*, as these other *ne*-DPs do.

15. See Heim (1990) for a possible way of achieving this by means of an LF transformation.

16. Of course, one could assume that some *ne*-DPs (as the one in (35)) can receive an E-type analysis, while others (like the one in (38)) can be handled by means of a bound-variable approach. After all, this eclectic treatment is assumed to be applicable to (nondeictic) pronouns. I would prefer, for the time being, to assume a uniform analysis of strong *ne*-DPs—at least until some really stringent evidence comes along that forces me to change this assumption.

17. There might be some influence on the part of certain features like [±human] or [±animate], since a sentence like (i) seems better than (37) but worse than (39).

(i)   ?? [Those watermelons]$_i$ inspired me to buy one e_i

18. For the case of a weak *ne*-DP, there are both syntactic and semantic reasons to believe that the gap is not a pronoun: the gap contains no D°, which is assumed to be the original site of pronouns (an idea that goes back to Postal 1969) and of reference (see Longobardi 1994). So it's unclear what one could say about sentences like (i.a) (from Gennaro Chierchia, p.c.):

(i) a.   Uno studente che ho incontrato in corridoio mi ha annunciato che
          'A student that I encountered in the hallway announced to me that
          ne sarebbe venuto un altro a trovarmi in ufficio tra cinque minuti.
          ne would come another to my office in five minutes.'
    b.   Uno studente mi ha annunciato che sarebbe venuto un altro studente.
          'A student announced to me that another student would come.'

The Binding Theory seems irrelevant in this case, since there is really no coreference to speak of. Although compare (i.a) with the marginal status of (ii) below, which is intended to potentially bring out a Principle B violation:

(ii)   ?? Gli studenti ne hanno visitato uno/un altro.
           the students **ne** *have*   *visited* *one/another*

19. Rigau (1991) had already noticed this ambiguity with Catalan *en*, which is like Italian *ne*.

20. I should mention here that Link (1987) had already suggested that noun phrases should contain a separate "number" or cardinality projection to accommodate numerals.

21. I certainly cannot do full justice to this claim here, but I will provide one small piece of evidence in favor of it. Consider the examples in (i) and (ii) below:

(i) a.   Less than two letters have arrived.
     b.   * Less than two letter has arrived.
(ii) a.   At most one letter has arrived.
     b.   * At most one letters have arrived.

While (i.a) and (ii.a) are truth-conditionally equivalent, the former requires plural morphology while the latter requires singular morphology (even within the DP!). This is plausibly due to agreement with the numeral alone, though the semantics of *less than two* and *at most one* must be essentially the same. Note that if we assume that the numeral alone heads its own projection (e.g., the CardP in (44a–b)), we may account for the number agreement in the DP by means of some form of head-head relation (perhaps head movement) between Num° and Card°. The semantics would then independently construct cardinality predicates with the modifiers *less than* and *at most*, respectively. These facts would be more difficult to explain if one were to assume, for instance, that the modified numerals *less than two* and *at most one* are located in the specifier of Num°.

22. For instance, in (i) the intended antecedent of *them*—namely *his friends*—is naturally interpreted as the maximal group consisting of John's friends, but in (ii) there is no such referent, because the pronoun *his* is bound by *every boy*.

(i)   John asked his friends if he could help one of them.
(ii)   Every boy asked his friends if he could help one of them.

23. It is possible that *di quei film* might be a constituent larger than a PP. Given the structure in (45b), another option is that this element is an NP.

24. Thanks to Luigi Rizzi for providing these examples.

25. Here we should assume that the movement of *non* is undone at LF, or that (the base position of) the head of NegP is responsible for semantic negation.

26. It is not impossible to interpret subjects in SpecVP, though I don't think this can happen in Italian, perhaps due to the availability of free inversion. In the case of *nessuno*, in particular, there might be problems with negative concord if we were to assume that this DP can be reconstructed from the SpecIP position to a position below Neg.

27. See Cresti (1995b) for a theory of presupposition projection consistent with the assumptions made here for strong indefinites.

28. A number of authors have argued that kinds are presuppositional. The notion of presupposition, however, needs to be clarified, in particular with respect to the weak/ strong distinction. I will assume the following. When a DP argument of a verb (or other clausal predicate) is interpreted as a kind-level individual, the meaning of that DP is assumed to be similar to that of a name. In this sense, we can say that the DP is referential; therefore a sentence containing such DP presupposes that the kind in question exists, just like a sentence containing the name *Bob* presupposes that an individual named "Bob" exists (in any context where this sentence is uttered).

Now, one popular view of what it means for a quantificational DP to be presuppositional is that its restriction must not be empty. This notion can be extended to DPs that are not inherently quantificational as a requirement that the entire descriptive content of these DPs (hence the denotations of the NPs inside them) be nonempty. Since I am claiming that indefinites are uniformly nonquantificational, my version of a presuppositional indefinite will conform with this latter requirement. This kind of indefinite, then, is what I identify as strong, whereas an indefinite that does not have this kind of presupposition is what I identify as weak. Under these assumptions, then, the *ne*-DP in (A4) is weak, since the kind FILM is not in a position to be interpreted like a name, but rather is used to create the (possibly empty) predicate **film′**.

References

Belletti, A. (1988) "The Case of Unaccusatives," *Linguistic Inquiry* 19:1–34.

Benincà, P. (1980) "Nomi senza Articolo," *Rivista di Grammatica Generativa* 5:51–63.

Burzio, L. (1986) *Italian Syntax*. Dordrecht: Reidel.

Cardinaletti, A. and G. Giusti (1992) *"Partitive ne and the QP Hypothesis: A Case Study."* Ms., Università di Venezia.

Cinque, G. (1991) "Lo statuto categoriale del *ne* Partitivo," *Saggi di Linguistica e di Letteratura in Memoria di Paolo Zolli*. Padua: Ed. Antenore.

Chierchia, G. (1998) "Reference to Kinds across Languages," *Natural Language Semantics* 6:339–405.

Cresti, D. (1995a) "Extraction and Reconstruction," *Natural Language Semantics* 3:79–122.

Cresti, D. (1995b) "Indefinite Topics." Ph.D. diss., MIT.

Cresti, D., and C. Tortora (2000) "Aspects of Locative Doubling and Resultative Predication," in S. Chang, L. Liaw, and J. Ruppenhofer (eds.), *Proceedings of the 25th Annual Meeting of the Berkeley Linguistics Society* (BLS25), pp. 62–73. Berkeley: Berkeley Linguistics Society.

Diesing, M. (1992) *Indefinites*. Cambridge, Mass.: MIT Press.

Evans, G. (1977) "Pronouns, Quantifiers, and Relative Clauses," *Canadian Journal of Philosophy* 7:467–536.

Frampton, J. (1990) "The Fine Structure of Wh-Movement and the Proper Formulation of the ECP." Ms., Northeastern University.

Haegeman, L. (1993) "The Development of the Indefinite Pronouns in the West Flemish Dialect." Ms., Université de Genève.

Heim, I. (1982) *"The Semantics of Definite and Indefinite Noun Phrases."* Ph.D. diss., University of Massachusetts, Amherst.

Heim, I. (1987) "Where Does the Definiteness Restriction Apply? Evidence from the Definiteness of Variables," in E. Reuland and A. ter Meulen (eds.) *The Representation of (In)definiteness*, pp. 21–42. Cambridge, Mass.: MIT Press.

Heim, I. (1990) "E-Type Pronouns and Donkey Anaphora," *Linguistics and Philosophy* 13:137–177.

Higginbotham, J. (1993) "Interrogatives," in K. Hale and S. J. Keyser (eds.) *The View from Building 20: Essays in Linguistics in Honor of Sylvain Bromberger*, pp. 195–227. Cambridge, Mass.: MIT Press.

Jackendoff, R. (1977) *X′ Syntax: A Study of Phrase Structure*. Cambridge, Mass.: MIT Press.

Link, G. (1987) "Generalized Quantifiers and Plurals," in P. Gärdenfors (ed.) *Generalized Quantifiers*. Dordrecht: Reidel.

Longobardi, G. (1987) "Extraction from NP and the Proper Notion of Head Government," in A. Giorgi and G. Longobardi (eds.) *The Syntax of Noun Phrases*. Cambridge: Cambridge University Press.

Longobardi, G. (1994) "Reference and Proper Names: A Theory of N-movement in Syntax and Logical Form," *Linguistic Inquiry* 25:609–665.

Milsark, G. (1977) "Toward an Explanation of Certain Peculiarities in the Existential Construction in English," *Linguistic Analysis* 3:1–29.

Moro, A. (1991) "The Raising of Predicates: Copula, Expletives and Existence," *MIT Working Papers in Linguistics* 15. Cambridge, Mass.: MIT.

Moro, A. (1993) "The Raising of Predicates: Predicative Nominals and the Theory of Clausal Structure." Ph.D. diss., Istituto Universitario Lingue Moderne, Milan.

Pesetsky, D. (1987) "*Wh*-in-situ: Movement and Unselective Binding," in E. Reuland and A. ter Meulen (eds.) *The Representation of (In)definiteness*, pp. 98–129. Cambridge, Mass.: MIT Press.

Pollock, J.-Y. (1986) "Sur la syntaxe de *en* et le paramètre du sujet nul," *La Grammaire Modulaire*. Paris: Éd. de Minuit.

Postal, P. (1969) "On So-Called 'Pronouns' in English," in D. Reibel and S. Schane (eds.) *Modern Studies in English*. Englewood Cliffs, NJ: Prentice Hall.

Rigau, G. (1991) "On the Functional Properties of Agr," *Catalan Working Papers in Linguistics 1991*. Universitat Autònoma de Barcelona.

Rizzi, L. (1982) *Issues in Italian Syntax*. Dordrecht: Foris.

Rullman, H. (1993) "Scope Ambiguities in *How Many*-Questions." Paper presented at the 1993 Linguistic Society of America meeting, Los Angeles.

van Riemsdijk, H. (1978) *A Case Study in Syntactic Markedness*. Dordrecht: Foris.

Vikner, S. (1990) "Verb Movement and the Licensing of NP-positions in the Germanic Languages." Ph.D. diss., Université de Genève.

von Fintel, K. (1994) "Restrictions on Quantifier Domains." Ph.D. diss., University of Massachusetts, Amherst.

Wilkinson, K. (1992) "Bare Plurals, Plural Pronouns and the Partitive Constraint." Ms., Ben Gurion University of the Negev.

5

Person Morphemes and Reflexives in Italian, French, and Related Languages

Richard S. Kayne

1. Introduction

Helke (1973), Pica (1987), Iatridou (1988), Safir (1996) and others have emphasized the importance of the internal structure of reflexives of the English *himself* type and the Italian *se stesso* type. In this article, I would like to extend that line of thought to the apparently monomorphemic non-clitic reflexives found in French and Italian (and many other European languages). More specifically, I will argue that French *soi* and Italian *sé* are themselves bimorphemic and that each subcomponent makes a distinct syntactic contribution.

I will simultaneously argue that *soi* and *sé* form a natural class with (French) *moi/toi* and (Italian) *me/te*, the first and second person singular non-clitic pronouns. In all of these, there is a consonantal person morpheme *m-*, *t-*, or *s-* that is followed by a morpheme *-oi* (in French) or *-é* (in Italian) having the property 'singular'.[1]

The person morphemes *m-/t-/s-* themselves are arguably not intrinsically 'singular'. This is certainly true of reflexive *s-*, and perhaps even of *m-* and *t-*, as we will see later.

2. *m-* and *t-*

2.1 French possessives

Let us begin with French possessives. When the possessor is first or second person singular and the noun plural, we have:

(1)   mes tables ('my tables')
(2)   tes tables ('your tables')

Compare these with the corresponding definite article:

(3)   les tables ('the tables')

The definite article with feminine singular nouns beginning with a consonant is also very similar to the corresponding first and second person singular possessives:

(4)   ma table ('my table')
(5)   ta table ('your table')
(6)   la table ('the table')

It is natural to take these paradigms to indicate that possessive *mes* and *tes* should be analyzed as *m-/t-+-es*, where *m-* and *t-* are the first and second singular person morphemes and *-es* represents agreement with the plurality of *tables*.[2] The definite article *les* will then be analyzed as *l-* plus the same *-es*.

The possessives in (4) and (5) are then *m-/t-+-a*, with *m-* and *t-* again the person morphemes, and *-a* agreement with the feminine singular *table*. In (6), the definite article is the same *l-* as in (3) plus the *-a* of (4) and (5).

It is quite clear in these cases that the person morphemes are just the consonants *m-* and *t-*. With a masculine singular noun, things are a bit more complex:

(7)   mon livre ('my book')
(8)   ton livre ('your book')
(9)   le livre ('the book')

Comparing (7) and (8), we see that the person morphemes *m-* and *t-* are followed by a morpheme *-on* that does not appear with the definite article.[3] This *-on* is specific to possessives. A variant of it, *-ien*, occurs with possessives when there is no overt noun (in which case the possessive is preceded by the definite article):[4]

(10)   le mien ('the mine')
(11)   le tien ('the your(s)')

These examples have the understood noun as masculine singular. When the understood noun is feminine singular, we have:

(12)   la mienne
(13)   la tienne

and when the understood noun is plural (masculine/feminine):

(14)   les miens/les miennes
(15)   les tiens/les tiennes

The possessives forms in (10)–(15) are composed of the person morpheme *m-/t-* plus *-ien* plus an agreement ending sensitive to the gender and number of the phonetically unrealized noun.

In light of (10)–(15) and (7)–(8), I will take (1)–(2) and (4)–(5) to also contain a possessive morpheme (i.e., an abstract counterpart of *-on/-ien*), so all the possessive forms will consist of 'person morpheme + possessive morpheme + agreement'.[5]

2.2 French nonpossessives

The person morphemes *m-* and *t-* occur as preverbal clitics:

(16)   Jean m'invite. ('J. me invites')
(17)   Jean t'invite. ('J. you invites')

When the verb begins with a consonant, there is an orthographic *-e* (a schwa that is sometimes not pronounced):

(18)   Jean me voit. ('J. me sees')
(19)   Jean te voit. ('J. you sees')

I will not take this *-e* to be a separate morpheme but, rather, to be epenthetic, so that the clitic is syntactically always just *m-/t-*.[6]

The epenthetic character of this *-e* may underlie the fact that it cannot appear postverbally in positive imperatives, where it might be expected to:

(20)   * Invite-me! ('invite me')
(21)   * Invite-te! ('invite you(rself)')

This could not be attributed to final stress falling on the *-e*, since these examples contrast with (22), which does have a final stressed *-e*:

(22)   Invite-le! ('invite him')

The *-e* of *le* must then not be epenthetic. It must rather be a masculine (singular) word marker (in Harris's 1991 sense), so that *le* here is bimorphemic.[7]

The *-e* of *le* in (22) is thus parallel to the feminine singular *-a* of:

(23)   Invite-la! ('invite her')

In having *-a*, the third person accusative clitic of (23) is just like the definite article in (6) and (12)/(13). Both are *l-+-a*. The claim that the *-e* of (18)/(19) is distinct from that of (22) is therefore supported by the fact that there is no clitic in *-a* for *m-* and *t-*:

(24)   * Jean ma voit.
(25)   * Jean ta voit.

I will return below (cf. (77)) to this property of *m-/t-*.

The way in which French expresses (20) is:[8]

(26)   Invite-moi! ('invite me')

and similarly for (21) (changing the verb to make it more natural):

(27)   Couche-toi! ('lie-down you(rself) = lie down')

The *moi* and *toi* (pronounced /-wa/) found here are identical to the form of these pronouns found in non-clitic environments, for example:

(28)   Jean parle de moi. ('J. speaks of me')
(29)   Jean pense à toi. ('J. thinks of you')

(30)   Moi, j'aime cela. ('me, I like that')
(31)   Toi, tu aimes cela. ('you, you like that')

Thinking of Haiman's (1980, 215) analysis of pronouns in Hua and of the basic fact that *m-* and *t-* are person morphemes, I will take these to be bimorphemic— that is, to be *m-/t-+oi*.[9]

In conclusion so far, *m-* and *t-* are person morphemes that in French sometimes occur with *-oi*, sometimes with a possessive morpheme, as in section 2.1, and sometimes alone, as in (16)–(19).

2.3 Italian

The Italian counterparts of (28) and (29) are:

(32)   Gianni parla di me.
(33)   Gianni pensa a te.

In the spirit of the preceding discussion, I take these non-clitic *me* and *te* in Italian to be bimorphemic—that is, to be *m-/t-+-é* (see note 1). The clitic counterparts are (when no other clitic follows) *mi* and *ti*, as in:

(34)   Gianni mi vede. ('G. me sees')
(35)   Gianni ti vede. ('G. you sees')

I will take the vowel /i/ to be epenthetic, as suggested by Benincà (1998, note 11).

These object clitics take the form *me/te* when followed by another clitic (of a certain type):[10]

(36)   Gianni me lo dice. ('G. me it says')
(37)   Gianni te lo dice. ('G. you it says')

I take this alternation not to reflect any change in the syntactic status of the object clitic: since in (34)/(35) it is monomorphemic—that is, *m-/t-* with an epenthetic vowel—then it is in (36)/(37), too. The person morphemes in question are *m-* and *t-* in Italian, just as in French.

Italian possessives, while different from French in some interesting respects, also fit well with the idea that the person morphemes for first and second singular are *m-* and *t-*. Italian possessives co-occur for the most part with an article. Thus the Italian equivalents of (4) and (5) above are:

(38)   la mia tavola ('the my table')
(39)   la tua tavola ('the your table')

The final *-a* in each word is the feminine singular word marker. Its presence in *mia* and *tua* reflects agreement with the gender (and number) of the noun *tavola*.[11]

I take the fact that (38) has an *-i-* where (39) has a *-u-* to be an irregularity that is compatible with the analysis of *mia* and *tua* as trimorphemic, that is, as *m-i-a* and *t-u-a*. This is supported (looking ahead a bit) by:

(40)   la sua tavola ('the his/her table')

with the same -u-, but with s- instead of t-. Much as in the discussion of French above in section 2.1, I take this -i/u- to be a possessive morpheme. Again, the person morpheme is just m-/t- (or s-).

2.4 m-/t- and number

It is uncontroversial to say that French and Italian m- and t- are specified for person (first and second, respectively).[12] It is equally clear that they are not specified for gender. Somewhat less clear is their status with respect to number.

To say that they are singular is natural and perhaps correct. But it is worth pointing out a (cross-dialectal) way in which their singularity seems less rigid than their person feature. What I have in mind is the fact that in some Italian dialects the clitic form of m- can in some (accusative, more than dative) contexts also be first person plural. Thus in Milanese, as described by Nicoli (1983: 142, 146, 150, 358), the following are possible:[13]

(41)   El me véd nun. ('he me sees us' = 'He sees us.')
(42)   La vegnarà a toeumm. ('she will-come to get-me' = 'She will come
          to get us.')[14]

With the same initial n- as that of non-clitic nun in (41), Milanese also allows ne as a first person plural clitic:

(43)   La ne dà... ('she us gives...')

In other words, Milanese has both n- and m- as object clitics for first person plural (again, I take the vowel of ne and me in (43) and (41) to be epenthetic).

Now me is also the (only) object clitic for first person singular:

(44)   El me véd nò. ('he me sees not')

Thus it seems that in Milanese, m- is to be characterized as first person, without rigid specification for number.

Something rather similar is found in various French dialects, in the case of the subject clitic je, which in standard French is first person singular.[15] In these dialects, (the equivalent of) je can occur in the first person in both singular and plural (with differing verb forms). The following is from the dialect described by Fougeu-Fontaine (1986:52):[16]

(45)   J èm. ('I love')
(46)   J èmô. ('I love-1pl' = 'we love')

In these dialects, then, j- seems to be first person, without specification for number.

We can now note an asymmetry between person and number, as far as m-/j- is concerned. Although in certain dialects, the specification for singular can be suspended, so that m- or j-, depending on the dialect, becomes compatible with both singular and plural, there does not seem to be any dialect that drops the specification for first person (which would have yielded, for example, neutralization between first and second person).

It may be, then, that these morphemes are fundamentally specified for (first) person, but not fundamentally specified for singular. In the languages (and contexts) in which *m-* or its variant *j-* is incompatible with plural, that must be a secondary effect.[17]

The phenomena discussed in this section, where *m-* or *j-* is compatible with plural, have involved object or subject clitics. I do not know of any Romance language/dialect in which something comparable is found with a non-clitic pronoun:

(47)   Hanno visto me. ('they-have seen me')
(48)   Ils ont parlé de moi. ('they have spoken of me')

In these two Italian and French examples, non-clitic *me* and *moi* are strictly singular. Assume that this holds across all of Romance without exception. The question then is: Why should there be such a difference between clitic pronouns (in which first person *m-/j-* can sometimes be neutralized for number) and non-clitic pronouns (in which, by hypothesis, first person *m-(/j-)* cannot be so neutralized)?

I would like to suggest that this difference is due to the bimorphemic character of the non-clitic first person pronouns in (47)/(48) (and in their counterparts in other Romance languages) vs. the monomorphemic character of the corresponding clitics. The non-clitic forms are composed of *m-* combined with another morpheme (*-oi* in French and *-é* in Italian; see note 1). The corresponding clitics are, on the other hand, monomorphemic, i.e. *m-* plus at most an epenthetic vowel. The reason that the non-clitics always remain singular is that their second morpheme *-oi/-é/* is always itself specified for singular.[18] (This property of *-oi/-é* will play an important role in the discussion of reflexives below).

2.5 n-/v- *in French*

In French, first and second person plural are associated with the consonantal morphemes *n-* and *v-*.[19] The possessive forms with a singular noun (there is no visible agreement with the gender of that noun) are:

(49)   nôtre livre ('our book')
(50)   vôtre livre ('your book')

With a covert noun, there is a change in vowel:

(51)   le nôtre ('the ours')
(52)   le vôtre ('the yours')

If the noun is plural:

(53)   nos livres ('our books')
(54)   vos livres ('your books')

If the noun is plural and covert:

(55)   les nôtres
(56)   les vôtres

The subject clitic forms for first and second plural are *nous/vous*, and the object clitic forms are the same:

(57)   Nous partons. ('we leave')
(58)   Vous partez. ('you leave')
(59)   Jean nous voit. ('J. us sees')
(60)   Jean vous voit. ('J. you sees')

These are furthermore the same as the non-clitic forms:

(61)   Jean parle de nous. ('J. speaks of us')
(62)   Jean parle de vous. ('J. speaks of you')

In each of the above pairs, the first person plural form in *n*- is identical to the second person plural form in *v*-, except for the *n*- vs. *v*- difference itself.

This makes it plausible to take consonantal *n*- and *v*- to be first and second person plural morphemes. As in the case of *m*- and *t*-, each is specified for person and indifferent to gender. Number-wise, they seem to be less flexible than *m*- (perhaps because plural is more "marked" than singular).

If *n*- and *v*- are separate morphemes, the question arises as to the status of the other parts of the words containing them. The *-ous* of (57)–(62) might be decomposable into a plural *-s*[20] and a morpheme *-ou*-, perhaps the plural counterpart of the singular *-oi* of (48). (The *-s* of *nos/vos/nôtres/vôtres* in (53)–(56), on the other hand, almost certainly reflects agreement with the possessed noun, rather than the plurality of the first/second person itself.) The other pieces are better understood, I think, by switching back to Italian.

7. Italian n- *and* v-

First person plural *n*- in Italian fails to appear in the object clitic, which is instead *ci*.[21] Apart from that irregularity, *n*- parallels the second person plural *v*-. The non-clitic forms corresponding to French (61)/(62) are:

(63)   Gianni parla di noi.
(64)   Gianni parla di voi.

The final *-i* is plausibly the final plural *-i* found in all three words of a DP like:[22]

(65)   i ragazzi tristi ('the boys sad')

in which case the *-o-* of *noi/voi* would have the same status as the *-ou-* of the French examples.[23]

The feminine plural of the definite article and of many nouns and adjectives ends in *-e*:

(66)   le ragazze tristi ('the girls sad')
(67)   le ragazze piccole ('the girls small')

Noi and *voi* cannot end in *-e*. They retain their *-i* ending no matter what their referent:

(68)   * noe/* voe

This is in all probability part of the more general fact, to which I will return below, that first and second person pronouns in French and Italian never inflect for gender.

The possessive forms with *n-* and *v-* in Italian are illustrated by:

(69)   la nostra tavola ('the our table')
(70)   la vostra tavola ('the your table')

The final *-as* are the feminine singular word marker. The *-o-* is probably that of *noi/voi*, the *-s* an irregular (for Italian) plural morpheme. The *-tr-* might be a possessive morpheme like the *-i* and *-u* of (38)–(40), or it might be a reduced form of the root *altr-* ('other'),[24] in which case the possessive morpheme in (69)/(70) would be null.

2.7 m-/t- vs. l-

In preceding sections, I have claimed that *m-* and *t-* (and similarly *n-* and *v-*) are person morphemes that sometimes occur alone, as, for example, when they are object clitics (though there may be an epenthetic vowel). Sometimes they occur in combination with other morphemes, as in the case of non-clitic pronouns (and also possessives). To call these morphemes first and second person (singular and plural) raises by itself no severe problems.[25] But a question arises as to the term "third person."

Benveniste (1966) argued that what is standardly called third person is best thought of as "non-person." Some third person pronouns are illustrated for Italian in:

(71)   Gianni la vede. ('G. her sees')
(72)   Gianni vede lei. ('G. sees her')

These are the feminine singular forms, clitic *la* and non-clitic *lei*. The question can be phrased as follows: Do *la, lei* and the other third person pronouns form a natural class with the first and second person pronouns discussed so far?

I think that Benveniste was right and that the answer to this question is negative. If so, then the term "third person pronoun" should be abandoned. I will (try to) use the term "determiner pronoun" instead, thinking of Postal (1966) and later work that grew out of his.[26] The term "determiner pronoun" is straightforwardly appealing for French since the accusative "third person" clitics (*le, la, les*) are identical in form to the definite article:

(73)   Jean le/la/les voit. ('J. him-or-it/her-or-it/them sees')

(74)   le livre, la table, les livres ('the book, the table, the books')

In Italian, the accusative clitics can likewise be paired with corresponding definite articles (although one form of the definite article (*il*) cannot appear as a clitic, and the clitic *li* corresponds only partially to the definite article *i*):[27]

(75)   Gianni lo/la/li/le vede.
(76)   lo zio, la tavola, i ragazzi, le ragazze ('the uncle, the table, the boys, the girls')

All the object clitics of (73) and (75) begin with an *l*-. So do the "third person" dative clitics of French (*lui*(3sg), *leur*(3pl)) and two of the three dative forms in Italian (*gli*(3msg/3pl), *le*(3fsg), *loro*(3pl)). The non-clitic "third person" pronouns also show an *l*- for the most part. French has *lui*(3msg), *elle*(3fsg), *eux*(3mpl), *elles*(3fpl). Italian has *lui*(3msg), *lei*(3fsg), *loro*(3pl).

Is this *l*- to be grouped with *m*- and *t*- (and *n*- and *v*-)? Four specific reasons to think that it should not be (i.e., to think that Benveniste was right) are the following: First, the singular accusative *l*-clitics in French and Italian always have a word marker reflecting gender, as seen in French *le, la* and in Italian *lo, la*.[28] There is no corresponding gender distinction with first or second person, e.g., in French:

(77)   Jean me/*ma voit. ('J. me sees')

The clitic *me* serves for both male and female speakers; there is no feminine object clitic **ma* (and similarly for *te*, **ta*).[29]

French dative clitics do not show a gender distinction, but Italian dative clitics do (*gli* 'msg' vs. *le* 'fsg'); again, there is no gender distinction in the first or second person. In the non-clitic forms, French distinguishes *lui* (msg) from *elle* (fsg) (*lui* vs. *lei* in Italian). Neither language shows any gender distinction in the first or second person non-clitic pronouns. There is thus a consistent difference between the determiner pronouns in *l*-, which often show gender distinctions, and the first and second person forms in *m*- and *t*-, which do not.

Second, the determiner pronouns in *l*- often express plural by adding the usual plural morpheme. This is true for French accusative clitic *les*, non-clitic *elles* (fpl) and subject clitics *ils* (mpl) and *elles* (fpl), as well as for the Italian accusative clitics *li* (mpl) and *le* (fpl).[30] But *m*- and *t*- have the notable property that they never combine with plural morphemes to express first or second person plural:[31]

(78)   * Jean mes/tes voit. (French)[32]
(79)   * Jean parle de mous/tous. (French)
(80)   * Gianni ha parlato di mei/tei. (Italian)

Third, *l*- never combines with the possessive morpheme that can show gender agreement with the head noun. Thus alongside (7)/(8), repeated here as (81)/(82), one might expect to find (83) (with the meaning 'his/her book'):

(81)   mon livre ('my book')
(82)   ton livre ('your book')
(83)   * lon livre

The same is true of the covert noun cases of, for example, (12) and (13), repeated here, which have no counterpart with *l*-:

(84)   la mienne ('the mine')
(85)   la tienne ('the yours')
(86)   * la lienne

Similarly, Italian has, corresponding to (38)/(39), repeated here, no form in *l*-:[33]

(87)   la mia tavola ('the my table')
(88)   la tua tavola ('the your table')
(89)   * la lia/lua tavola

Fourth, in some Italian dialects, *m*- and *t*- act differently from *l*- with respect to accusative clitic doubling. For Trentino, Gatti (1990, 195n) has pointed out:[34]

(90)   I me vede mi. ('they me see me')
(91)   I te vede ti. ('they you see you')
(92)   I la vede. (*?ela) ('they her see her')

Nonclitic *mi/ti* can co-occur in Trentino with clitic *me/te*, but non-clitic *ela* cannot co-occur with clitic *la*.[35]

It seems clear, then, that *m*- and *t*- belong to a natural class that does not include *l*- (although it does include reflexive *s*-, as we will see below).

As far as the clitic doubling facts of (90)–(92) are concerned, I think the difference in behavior seen there can be at least in part related to an Italian fact noted by Benincà (1993:272): if the direct object of a psych verb is preposed (without there being a clitic double present), that direct object can be preceded by the preposition *a* if the direct object is first or second person:[36]

(93)   A me preoccupa il viaggio. ('to me worries the trip')

This *a* recalls the *a* that is found more widely in Spanish. The fact pointed out by Benincà can be interpreted as indicating that the appearance of this *a* with direct objects is favored by the object being first or second person.

For a number of speakers, at least in the north of Italy, this predilection of direct object *a* for first and second person is seen even with non-psych-verbs:[37]

(94)   A me mi hanno visto. ('to me me they-have seen')
(95)   ??A lui lo hanno visto. ('to him him they-have seen')

The contrast seen in (90)–(92) can be linked to these if the doubling construction of (90)–(92) contains an unpronounced *a*.

That an unpronounced *a* may well be present in (90)–(92) is suggested by the fact that some North Italian dialects (e.g., Paduan and Venetian) allow sentences like:[38]

(96)   Ghe lo dago Giorgio. ('him$_{dat}$ it I-give George')

The proposal, then, is that (90)–(92) must have a similarly unpronounced *a*, which, like its overt counterpart in (93)–(95), is favored by first or second person.

As to why this *a* should be favored by first and second person, there may be a link to Sardinian, as characterized by Jones (1993, secs. 2.2.6, 5.1; 1996).[39] The Sardinian accusative *a* is basically limited to appearing before proper names and (some) pronouns.[40] Jones's proposal is essentially that Sardinian *a* is required before all accusatives that lack a determiner position. (Indefinites of various kinds are assumed to have a null determiner.) Those pronouns which take *a* are NPs. Those that do not are DPs. In the spirit of Jones's proposal, it may be that Italian *a* favors first and second person pronouns because those are not DPs, whereas Italian third person pronouns are DPs.[41]

If the locus of word markers is D, as suggested by Uriagereka (1995: note 4), then the absence of a feminine form for first and second persons seen in (77) would also follow from their non-DP status.

The general conclusion of this section, then, is that *l-* is separate from *m-* and *t-* (and *n-* and *v-*). This seems quite solid and leads the way to consideration of reflexive *s-*.

3. *s-*

3.1 Reflexive s-

Virtually everything that we have taken into account so far points to the conclusion that there is a reflexive morpheme *s-* that patterns strongly with *m-* and *t-* (rather than with *l-*).[42]

In French, alongside object clitic *m'/t'* (before vowels—cf. (16)/(17)), we have reflexive *s'*:

(97)   Jean m'invite. ('J. me invites')
(98)   Jean t'invite. ('J. you invites')
(99)   Jean s'invite. ('J. refl. invites')

Before consonants:

(100)   Jean me voit. ('J. me sees')
(101)   Jean te voit. ('J. you sees')
(102)   Jean se voit. ('J. refl. sees')

There is no feminine form:

(103)   * Jean ma voit.
(104)   * Jean ta voit.
(105)   * Marie sa voit.

And no plural in -*s*:[43]

(106)   * Jean mes voit.

(107)   * Jean tes voit.
(108)   * Jean et Marie ses voit. ('J. and M. refl.pl. see')

The non-clitic forms are entirely parallel in form (cf. (28)/(29)):

(109)   Quand on parle de moi,... ('when one speaks of me...')
(110)   Quand on parle de toi,... ('...of you')
(111)   Quand on parle de soi,... ('...of refl.')

This parallelism is found in Italian, too:[44]

(112)   Parla di me. ('he-speaks of me')
(113)   Parla di te. ('...of you')
(114)   Parla di sé. ('...of refl.')

None of these allow a plural morpheme to be added (see (80)):

(115)   * Parla di mei.
(116)   * Parla di tei.
(117)   * Parlano di sei. ('they-speak of refl.pl.')

The parallelism in form carries over to the object clitics:

(118)   Gianni mi vede. ('G. me sees')
(119)   Gianni ti vede. ('G. you sees')
(120)   Gianni si vede. ('G. refl. sees')

including to the vowel change dependent on a following clitic, as mentioned above ((36)/(37)):

(121)   Gianni me lo dice. ('G. me it says')
(122)   Gianni te lo dice. ('G. you it says')
(123)   Gianni se lo dice. ('G. refl. it says')

Furthermore, the doubling facts of (90)–(92) group *se* with *me/te*, rather than with the determiner clitics. Thus in Paduan:

(124)   El me ga visto mi. ('he me has seen me')[45]
(125)   El te ga visto ti. ('he you has seen you')
(126)   El se ga visto lu. ('he refl. has seen him')
(127)   * I lo ga visto lu. ('they him have seen him')

The contrast between these last two examples shows that the earlier discussion of (90)–(92) was incomplete, since it attributed the deviance of (92) and now (127) to properties of the doubled non-clitic pronoun, which is the same *lu* in the grammatical (126). It may be that in the reflexive clitic example (126) no (unpronounced) *a* is needed (as opposed to the non-reflexive examples), for reasons having to do with the unaccusative-like status of reflexive clitic sentences.[46] Alternatively, or in addition, the contrast between (126) and (127) may indicate that the choice of clitic itself plays a direct role in determining the acceptability of doubling, with the D-clitic *lo* somehow making doubling more difficult to achieve (in these dialects—see note 34) than the non-D-clitic *se*.

I note in passing that the doubling parallel between *me/te* and *se* extends to the intriguing case of doubling in the 'neg...*che*' construction.[47] In Paduan, one has:

(128)   Nol me vede che mi. ('neg he me sees than/but me' =
           'he sees only me')

Burzio (1991: 90n) gives a comparable example with *se* for Piedmontese:

(129)   Giuanin a s guarda mac chiel. ('G. he refl. watches only him')

I conclude that reflexive *s-* forms a natural class with the person morphemes *m-* and *t-*.

3.2 *Reflexive* s- *and number.*

It would be natural to think, in light of the following Italian examples, that *s-* is neutral with respect to number:

(130)   Gianni s'invita. ('G. refl. invites')
(131)   Gianni e Maria s'invitano. ('G. and M. refl. invite')

And in fact it is perfectly true that reflexive clitics in Italian (and French) occur productively with both singular and plural antecedents. (When the antecedent is plural, a reciprocal interpretation is also possible.)

However, if we turn to Italian non-clitic *sé*, we find an asymmetry:

(132)   Il ragazzo ha parlato di sé. ('the boy has spoken of refl.')
(133)   ? I ragazzi hanno parlato di sé. ('the boys have...')

With a plural antecedent, *sé* is somewhat less good than with a singular antecedent, on the whole.[48] (I have found one speaker for whom (133) is impossible.)

That *sé* should tilt toward the singular is not entirely surprising, given its resemblance to non-clitic *me* and *te*. In particular, all three should be analyzed as X+*é*, where X is *m-*, *t-*, or *s-* and *-é* is a morpheme (see note 1) whose properties will be discussed next. (Important also is the fact that this resemblance does not extend to the plural *noi* and *voi*.)

The obvious proposal, now, is that the tilt toward singular seen with *sé* (as opposed to the clitic *si*, which is neutral between singular and plural) is to be attributed to the morpheme *-é* that *sé* has in common with non-clitic *me* and *te* (and that clitic *si* lacks).[49] In other words, it is *-é* itself that is singular.

This would seem to lead us to expect (133) to be sharply unacceptable, which is not the case. My hypothesis is the following:

(134)   *Sé* can have a plural antecedent only via the intermediary of
           a(n abstract) distributor.[50]

           As for the question where that abstract distributor is (in, for example, (133)), consider the following fact brought to my attention by Luigi Rizzi: namely, that a plural antecedent for *sé* is unacceptable if the antecedent is "long-distance." An example would be:[51]

(135) ? Il ragazzo mi ha convinto a parlare di sé.
         ('the boy me has convinced to speak of refl.=him')

(136) * I ragazzi mi hanno convinto a parlare di sé. ('the boys...')

The fact that (136) is worse than (135) suggests that the abstract distributor needed in (136) must be "local" with respect to both *sé* and the antecedent of *sé*.[52] Representing it as *DB*, this gives for (133):

(137) I ragazzi hanno parlato *DB* di sé.

But given the double locality requirement, there is no satisfactory position available in the long-distance case (136):

(138) * i ragazzi mi$_i$ hanno convinto a PRO$_i$ parlare *DB* di sé
(139) * i ragazzi mi$_i$ hanno convinto *DB* a PRO$_i$ parlare di sé

In (138), *DB* is too far from the antecedent *i ragazzi* (cf. the general locality requirement on floated quantifiers; Sportiche 1988). In (139), *DB* is too far from *sé* itself.

The conclusion that the *-é* of *sé* is singular (and that it therefore can never have a non-distributed plural antecedent) is supported by the fact that *sé* cannot be a reciprocal (as opposed again to the monomorphemic clitic *si*). Thus the contrast between (131) and (133) is mirrored by the (sharper) contrast (in interpretation) between:

(140) Loro si amano. ('they refl. love')
(141) ? Loro parlano di sé. ('they speak of refl.')

Whereas the first of these has a natural reciprocal interpretation (in addition to the reflexive one), the second is not possible as a reciprocal. The reason is that *sé*, because it contains *-é*, prohibits its antecedent from being a non-distributed plural. But a non-distributed plural antecedent is precisely what a reciprocal needs:[53]

(142) They're (*each) in love with one another.

In conclusion, the singularity of *-é* has significant effects in the case of *sé*, much as it did in the case of non-clitic *me* (cf. the discussion of (47) above).

3.3 Further restrictions on -é

To take non-clitic *me/te/sé* to form a natural class in Italian, representable as *m-/t-/s-* + *é* seems correct, yet there is clearly a difference that has so far been set aside, namely, that the antecedent of *sé* can be a full DP, whereas the antecedent of *me/te* cannot be.[54] Assume not only that this restriction on the antecedent of *me/te* is a fact about *m-/t-* but that it carries over to *-é* itself. Then Italian must be analyzed as containing a small discrepancy between the *-é* of *me/te* and the *-é* of *sé* (which are otherwise identical). That is, the *-é* of *sé* must be allowed to waive the antecedent restriction which it might otherwise be expected to take over from the *-é* of *me/te*.

Italian is evidently capable of bearing the burden of this discrepancy. French is not. The French counterpart of *sé* is non-clitic *soi* (cf. non-clitic first/second person *moi/toi*). The antecedent of *soi* generally cannot be a full DP:[55]

(143)   Quand on parle de soi,... ('when one speaks of refl.')
(144)   Chacun a parlé de soi. ('each has spoken of refl.')
(145)   * Ce linguiste a parlé de soi. ('that linguist...')

For Jean-Yves Pollock, there is a clear contrast between (145) and (146):

(146)   A ce colloque, chaque linguiste a parlé de soi
         ('at that conference, each linguist...')

There is also a contrast between the following:

(147)   * Tous les linguistes parlent de soi. ('all the linguists speak of refl.')
(148)   Tout linguiste parle de soi. ('every linguist...')

Thinking of Szabolcsi (1994) and Bartos (2001), it may be that *chaque linguiste* and *tout linguiste* differ from *ce linguiste* and *tous les linguistes* in that the former pair lack a DP projection. If so, then the precise requirement on the antecedent of *soi*, namely that it lack a DP projection, in fact falls together with the basic requirement on the antecedents of *moi* and *toi*, if first and second persons lack a DP projection, as discussed earlier ((text to) note 41).

I therefore take French *-oi* to be broadly consistent across *m-*, *t-*, and *s-* as far as choice of antecedent is concerned. Put another way, the restrictions on the antecedent of *soi* are now seen to be a property of its subcomponent *-oi*.

Since French clitic *se* lacks *-oi*, it is not surprising, either, that *se* (which just has an epenthetic vowel, when it has one at all) shows none of the restrictions to which *soi* is subject.

From this perspective, one might wonder if there is still not a discrepancy in French (smaller than in Italian) between *moi/toi* and *soi* concerning antecedents. Although *-oi* in all three cases has the property of needing an antecedent that is not a full DP, the antecedent taken by *moi/toi* is very particular and not narrowly extendable to the antecedents of *soi*. If we again associate the antecedent of *moi/toi* not only with *m-/t-* but also with *-oi*, the discrepancy in question is of interest to the present discussion.

French evidently tolerates this small discrepancy. But Piedmontese and various other North Italian dialects arguably do not.[56] They have a clitic in *s-*, but no non-clitic in *s-*. It may be that these dialects do not allow their counterpart of French *-oi* or Italian *-é* to be generalized from *m-/t-* to *s-* at all, for reasons having to do with uniformity of antecedent.

3.4 A restriction on reflexive s-

The preceding section considered certain restrictions on non-clitic *s*-forms in French and Italian and related dialects. Those restrictions were not shared by the corresponding clitic forms. There is, on the other hand, one class of restrictions that is common to all instances of French and Italian *s*-, both clitic and non-clitic, having to do with the person feature of the antecedent.[57] In neither language can the antecedent be first or second person, as in Italian:

(149)   * Tu s'inviti. ('you refl. invite')
(150)   * Io parlo di sé. ('I speak of refl.')

Taking *m-/t-/s-* to be strongly parallel, *m-* to be first person and *t-* to be second person, it would be natural to say that *s-* is itself neither first nor second person and therefore does not admit an antecedent that is. This would suffice for French and Italian, but not in general, as shown by various North Italian dialects that are less restrictive than French and Italian. For example, Nicoli (1983:151–152) gives:[58]

(151)   Nun se lavom. ('we refl. wash')

The question how to understand this kind of variation within Romance is complicated by the fact that some dialects sometimes allow sentences like:[59]

(152)   Mi a ma sa lavi i man. ('me *a* me refl. wash the hands' = 'I wash my hands')

Mi here is a (nonclitic) subject pronoun and *a* is a subject clitic.[60] Though there is only one other argument with 'wash' apart from the direct object *i man*, there are two further object clitics *ma* and *sa*.

How best to allow for this kind of "doubling" (*ma* and *sa* together when we would expect just one of them) is not yet clear.[61] But the existence of (152) raises the possibility that in sentences like (151) the relation between *s-* and the first or second person subject is mediated by an abstract counterpart of the *ma* of (152).[62] If so, then it might be feasible to take *s-* never to directly have a first or second person antecedent. In (152) (and (151)), it would be *ma* that has *mi* as antecedent. *Sa* would itself not have *mi* as antecedent, though it would be in a (quasi-)doubling relation with first person *ma*.

3.5 Reflexive s- *and Condition B*

First and second person pronouns are standardly assumed to fall under Condition B of the Binding Theory:

(153)   * I photographed me exactly twice yesterday.
(154)   * Why did you photograph you only twice yesterday?

If I have been correct in emphasizing the systematic parallels between *m-/t-* and *s-*, we would expect *s*-forms to be subject to Condition B, too.[63] In the case of clitic *s-*, it looks as if the expectation is not met, since the following (Italian) sentence is perfectly acceptable:

(155)   Gianni si fotografa. ('G. refl. photographs')

On the other hand, the same holds of clitic *m-/t-*:

(156)   Io mi fotografo. ('I me ...')
(157)   Tu ti fotografi. ('you you ...')

Examples (156)/(157) show that there is no discrepancy here among *m-/t-/s-*.[64]

Non-clitic *sé* does, however, display what I take to be clear Condition B effects. We can see this by taking, first, the following three sentences:

(158)   Gianni ha parlato di me. ('G. has spoken of me')
(159)   Gianni ha parlato di te. ('...of you')
(160)   Gianni ha parlato di sé. ('...of refl.')

All three are acceptable. Consider now the direct object counterparts of these:

(161)   Gianni ha fotografato me. ('G. has photographed me')
(162)   Gianni ha fotografato te. ('...you')
(163)   ??Gianni ha fotografato sé. ('...refl.')

The contrast between (163) and (160), which was pointed out by Giorgi (1984:328), varies in sharpness depending on the speaker. Judgments on (163) range from somewhat marginal to fully unacceptable. Giorgi correctly attributed the contrast to the presence of the preposition in (160). I would like to propose, now, that the deviance of (163) is to be interpreted as a Condition B effect (that can be neutralized by a preposition).[65]

I note in passing that the plural counterpart of (163) is sharply impossible:

(164)   * I ragazzi hanno fotografato sé. ('the boys have...')

The reason is that (164) combines the Condition B violation seen in (163) with the reluctance of *sé* to admit a plural antecedent seen in (133). More precisely, *sé* can have a plural antecedent only via the intermediary of a distributor, as stated in (134). The fact that (164) is appreciably less acceptable than (133) (with plural antecedent and preposition preceding *sé*) suggests that the required distributor is facilitated by the preposition (which perhaps provides a Spec position for the distributor that is unavailable in (164)).[66]

Returning to the contrast between (160) and (163), the idea that the preposition is playing a crucial role is suggested by the following judgments of Giuseppe Longobardi's: For him (160) itself is only acceptable in an "elegant" stylistic register. In his colloquial Italian, he has (with coreference):

(165)   Gianni ha parlato di lui. ('G. has spoken of him')

But he accepts (and prefers) *sé* when the subject is *ciascuno dei ragazzi*:

(166)   Ciascuno dei ragazzi ha parlato di sé.
          ('each of-the boys has spoken of refl.')

In other words, his colloquial Italian is (substantially) like French (see (text to) note 55). What is of primary importance here, though, is that he finds a sharp contrast between (165) and the following, which is impossible with coreference:[67]

(167)   * Gianni$_i$ ha fotografato lui$_i$.

Thus, the importance of the preposition seems clear.[68] (In the framework of Chomsky 1986, one might take the PP to be capable, in Italian and French, but not English, of counting as governing category for a pronoun[69]).

   Given the contrast between (167) and (165), and the fact that the former is certainly to be considered a Condition B violation, it is virtually certain that (163) should be considered a (weaker) Condition B violation, too. In which case, s- is visible to Condition B just as are m- and t-.

3.6 Pronominal s-

Italian (and French) have in possessives a pronominal s-:

(168)   Io ho visto la sua tavola. ('I have seen the his/her table')

This s- is clearly not reflexive.[70] The question is whether this s- is closer to the l- of determiner pronouns or to the reflexive s-. One consideration has to do with the absence of l- is comparable possessives: *la lua tavola (cf. (89) above). If this absence is not accidental (it might be related to facts about compounding—a pick-me-up vs. *a pick-him-up[71]), then the s- of (168) cannot have too much in common with l-.

   A second consideration has to do with the distribution within Romance of such pronominal s-. Apart from possessives, where it is commonly found, pronominal s- is found in non-clitic (non-possessive) forms in some dialects. Thus:

(169)   Qu'ei se que parlo. ('that it's him that speaks')
(170)   Ca ve de se. ('that comes from him')
(171)   I fau coqui per se. ('I do this for him')
(172)   I pèr sè ke d e travalò. ('it's for him that I have worked')

The first three are from the Limousin dialect studied by Chabaneau (1874:453), the last from the Savoie dialect studied by Ratel (1958:31).[72] In both of these dialects, this pronominal use of se seems to be limited to (some) non-clitic environments. In fact, with the one exception to be discussed shortly, pronominal s- seems never to occur as an object clitic.[73]

   Taken together with the point of the previous paragraph, this suggests that the s- of (168–172) is, first, not at all a variant of l- and, second, that it is in fact the same s- as the reflexive one. Put another way, s- is not intrinsically specialized as anaphoric.[74] It is primarily anaphoric in Romance but can also be pronominal.

The absence of any clitic pronominal *s*-, combined with my earlier proposals concerning the difference between (monomorphemic) clitics and (bimorphemic) non-clitics (in the case of *m-/t-/s-*) leads me to the more specific proposal that *s*- can be pronominal (non-anaphoric) only by virtue of amalgamating with a second morpheme, either *-é*, as in (169)/(172), or *-u*, as in possessives (or their counterparts in other Romance languages). (In effect, then, these morphemes *-é/-u* can be pronominal, at least in (168)–(172)).[75]

The antecedent of *se/sé* in the dialects illustrated in (168)/(172) seems to be limited to singular. Similarly, the antecedent of *su*- in (168) is necessarily singular. Thus, these pronominal instances of *s*- have the same bias toward singular that we saw in the case of reflexive nonclitic *s*- in section 3.2. This supports the idea that the two are basically the same *s*-,[76] in that both, when they combine with another morpheme, are restricted to combining with morphemes (*-é/-u*) that are inherently singular.[77]

3.7 A further question

The bias toward singular found with non-clitic *sé* was attributed in section 3.2 to a property of the morpheme *-é* with which *s*- combines. In a similar way, the singular bias of *su*- could be attributed to a property of the possessive morpheme *-u-*. The contrast with clitics in *s*-, which show no bias toward singular in either Italian or French, was attributed to the fact that those clitics are monomorphemic, so that if *s*- itself is neutral with respect to number, the contrast follows. There are, on the other hand, some dialects that seem to show some bias toward singular even in their reflexive clitics.

For example, Lepelley (1974:113) gives clitic *s*- for dative reflexive singular and plural and for accusative reflexive singular, but not for accusative reflexive plural.[78] Thus, it may be that in that dialect *s*- itself is not entirely neutral with respect to number. Alternatively, it might be that the accusative reflexive in question is bimorphemic, contrary to those of Italian and French.[79]

3.8 Morphology and anaphora

The main points that I have argued in this article are that non-clitic reflexive *sé* and *soi* in Italian and French are to be analyzed as *s*- + *-é/oi* and that, to a substantial extent, this *s*- patterns with first and second person *m*- and *t*-. These claims bear on Burzio's (1991) proposal concerning the relation between morphology and anaphora. Burzio proposed that the morphological poverty (lack of Φ-features) of forms in *s*- implied their anaphoric status.

However, if I am correct, the fact that *s*- cannot combine with number morphology (cf. (108), (117)) is a property shared by *m*- and *t*- (cf. (106)/(107)) and (115)/(116)). Consequently, incompatibility with number morphology cannot be a sufficient condition for anaphoric status.

Similarly, gender morphology cannot combine either with s- (cf. (105)) or with m- and t- (cf. (103)/(104)). Thus, incompatibility with gender morphology cannot be a sufficient condition for anaphoric status, either.[80]

On the other hand, if we set aside complex reflexives of the English type (see Jayaseelan 1996 and Safir 1996 for recent discussion), then it still might be the case, in the spirit of Burzio's approach, that lack of number (and perhaps gender— see note 80) is a necessary condition for anaphoric status.[81]

This might account for the fact that s- has no plural counterpart in the way that n- and v- are plural counterparts to m- and t- (cf. (49)–(70) above). Thus no Romance language, to my knowledge, has, for example, a z- that would be the plural counterpart of s-:

(173)   Il ragazzo si fotografa. ('the boy refl. photographs')
(174)   * I ragazzi zi fotografano. ('the boys refl.pl...')

(Related to this is the fact discussed above (cf. (132)–(142)) that sé is singular— that the morpheme -é with which s- combines to form a nonclitic is singular.)

Jayaseelan (1996, note 11) suggests that it might be only the person feature whose absence implies anaphoric status. If we take s- to be a person morpheme lacking specification for first or second person (cf. above and the 0-person (distinct from non-person) of Kayne (1993:16)),[82] the question is, is that sufficient to imply anaphoric status? If I am correct in taking some non-clitic s- forms to be non-anaphoric (cf. (168–172)), then the answer is, not exactly. The status of s- with respect to person may imply anaphoric status, but only in those (clitic) cases where s- combines with no other morpheme.

Notes

To Paola, whose inspired work has made dialect syntax indispensable.

1.   Italian writes sé with an accent and me/te without one. This is a purely orthographic differencethe vowel in all these nonclitic forms is the same (an open /e/). When referring to the vocalic morpheme by itself, I will use -é.
     French second singular toi and related forms with t- are restricted to "familiar"; second singular polite uses the plural vous and related forms in v-, some discussion of which can be found below.

2.   Cf. Haegeman (1993:63) on West Flemish pronouns and Picabia (1997) on the consonantal noun class morphemes of the Bantu language of Grande Comore. It is possible that -es itself is composed of two morphemes, with the -e- corresponding to Harris's (1991) word marker and the -s to number; on the status of number in French, see Tranel (1981:chap. 6) and Bernstein (1991).

3.   This -on also appears with feminine singular nouns beginning with a vowel:

(i)   mon intuition, ton intuition

4.   For further details, cf. Kayne (1975:sec. 2.20).

5. It should be emphasized here that the agreement in question is with the head noun (which may be covert) and not with the possessor itself. For example, the difference between (4) and (7) (*ma table* vs. *mon livre*) with respect to the form of the possessive (*ma* vs. *mon*) depends solely on the gender of the noun and is entirely independent of whether the speaker is male or female.

6. On treating (some) schwas as epenthetic in French phonology, see Tranel (1981:chap. 8) and references cited there.

7. It should be noted that the usual French masc. sg. WM is 0, as it in fact probably is in:

(i)   Marie l'invite. ('M. him invites')

Alternatively, (i) has an *-e* that has been deleted phonologically.

Morin (1979:310) notes that the *-e* of *le* in (22) is a front rounded vowel, rather than a schwa. Examples (20)/(21) are impossible with that pronunciation, too.

The *l-* of (i) can also correspond to 'her'—i.e. to *la*—with the fem. sg. WM *-a* of *la* failing to appear, just as in (ii) with the definite article:

(ii)   l'amie ('the friend (fem.)')

8. Bare *m-* (and *t-*) can appear postverbally when followed by the clitic *en*:

(i)   Donne-m'en! ('give me (some)of-it')

Possible in certain varieties of French is:

(ii)   Donne-moi-z-en!

For interesting discussion, see Rooryck (1992) and Morin (1979). Also Chenal (1986:360).

9. *M-* is replaced by (monomorphemic) *j-* in the subject clitic form, as seen in (30).

10. The oft stated view that *mi/ti* gives way to *me/te* in the presence of an immediately following clitic beginning with a sonorant cannot be completely right, given (i) (acceptable to some speakers):

(i)   Me ce ne vorranno due. ('me there of-them they-will-want two' =
             'I will need two (of them)')

11. As in French, this agreement morpheme does not and cannot reflect the gender of the speaker or hearer.

Many Italian dialects have the equivalent of 'la mi/tu tavola', with no agreement on the prenominal possessive—cf., for example, Mattesini (1976:190) and Pelliciardi (1977:70).

12. Further analysis of the notions "first person" and "second person" is certainly warranted, thinking, for example, of:

(i)   I don't like you, said John to Bill.

For relevant discussion, see Postal (1970:494), Nadahalli (1998) and Bevington (1998). Note also (with a matrix subject interpreted as "first person"):

(ii)   The person who is talking to you wants you to give him/*me some money.

13. See also the dialects studied by Lurà (1990:160) and Spiess (1976:206).

14. The double *mm* is an orthographic convention indicating a preceding short vowel, not a doubled consonant—see Nicoli (1983:49).

15. See note 9.

16. See Butler (1962:39, 42), Chauveau (1984:190), Ditchy (1977:21), Gesner (1979:17), Hervé (1973:51), Maze (1969:41, 66, 83, 85) (who notes that *je* cannot invert, and that *nous* can appear with inversion), Rouffiange (1983:115), Vey (1978:186), Villefranche (1978:24), Féral (1986:68, 73–75), Hauchard (1994:137), and Hull (1988).

17. See Harris's (1997:40) proposal that *m-* "loses out" to the more highly specified *n-* The details of Milanese will require further work.

18. See (78–80).

19. See the second paragraph of note 1.

20. See Harris (1997:39) on Spanish.

21. The second person plural object clitic *vi* may be synchronically parallel in a regular way to *mi* and *ti*, as in (34)/(35); alternatively, it may be more like *ci*. See Corver and Delfitto (1993:21).

22. This *-i* is normally incompatible with the word marker *-o* that appears in the singular:

(i)   ragazzo ('boy')
(ii)   ragazzi/*ragazzoi

The two do co-occur in possessive forms:

(iii)   i tuoi ragazzi ('the your boys')
(iv)   i suoi ragazzi ('the his/her boys')

This suggests that *-i* is a pure number morpheme that normally causes the word marker not to be pronounced. See Kihm (1997) on Wolof.

23. Note that the two morpheme *-oi* sequence in Italian *noi/voi* is pronounced approximately as written, as opposed to the single morpheme *-oi* of French *moi/toi*, pronounced /wa/.

24. Cf. Spanish *nosotros, vosotros* ('we others/you others' = non-clitic 'we/you'), and similarly in many Italian dialects.

25. See, however, note 12.

26. Cf. also Hale (1973).

27. Cardinaletti and Starke (1994:n.65) note that these discrepancies might indicate that clitics have more structure than determiners.

28. In the plural, Italian *li, le* shows a gender distinction, but French *les* does not. Thus, the contrast with the first and second person plural (which never show gender—see (68)) is a shade less striking than in the singular. I take the gender distinction in Spanish *nosotros, nosotras* to be a property of *otros, otras* ('others') and not a property of *nos*.

The word marker can fail to appear in some cases in both French (cf. note 7) and Italian.

29. Recall that possessive *ma, ta* in French are composed of *m-, t-* plus a word marker *-a* that reflects agreement with the head noun only—cf. the discussion of (4)–(6) above.

30. The *-s* of the French forms is only pronounced in certain syntactic environments (cf. note 2). Plural *-s* on determiner pronouns is particularly robust in Spanish, which has accusative clitic *los, las*, dative clitic *les*, and nonclitic *ellos, ellas*; Spanish supports the text discussion that follows, in that it does not allow plural *-s* to combine with *m-* or *t-*.

31. This appears to contrast with Cantonese, in which *deih* is added to *ngóh* (I) to yield *ngóhdeih* (we) (and similarly for second person), as described by Matthews and Yip (1994:79). It may be that in Cantonese and comparable languages, the plural morpheme in question is not a plural in the sense of French or Italian but, rather, something more like 'and company' (cf. Matthews and Yip (p.83)), thinking of Taljaard et al.'s (1991:12) characterization of Siswati (prefixal) *bo-*; for recent discussion, see Cheng and Sybesma (1999).

Malagasy *-re-* appears in the second person, but not in the first person, according to Zribi-Hertz and Mbolatianavalona (1997:245).

32. The *-s* of French possessive *mes, tes* does not express plurality of first or second person, but is rather an agreement morpheme reflecting the plurality of the head noun— cf. the discussion of (1–3) above.

Italian does have:

(i)   Gianni mi/ti vede. ('G. me/you(sg) sees')

But the *-i* here is not the plural morpheme, and the interpretation is not plural. On this *-i*, see the discussion of (34)/(35) above.

Some Walloon (cf. Remacle (1952:243)) has a form *tès-ôtes*—cf. notes 2, 24, and 31, especially Tranel's (1981:211) suggestion that plural /z/ in French might be a prefix on a plural noun or adjective.

33. Italian does have (without gender agreement):

(i)   la loro tavola ('the their table')

This *-or(o)* that combines with *l-* here must have a sharply different status from the *-on/- ien/-i/-u* of (81–89); *-or(o)* could be a Case/number ending, but not a possessive morpheme.

34. See Burzio (1989) on Piedmontese. This contrast seems to hold for Paduan, too, as I have learned from discussions with Paola Benincà; cf. Benincà (1983: note 8). On the other hand, it seems to be absent from the dialects studied by Nicoli (1983:144, 359), Pelliciardi (1977:93), Vassere (1993:97, 102), Spiess (1976:209), and Salvioni (1975:31).

35. And similarly for the other *l*-pronouns. The absence of a comma before the non-clitic object pronoun in Gatti's (1990) examples indicates that the doubling in question is non-dislocation doubling.

The text discussion does not imply that *l*-pronouns have nothing in common with *me/ te/sé*. In particular, they all (as opposed to full DPs) require or allow *di* with certain prepositions:

(i)   contro di me/te/sé/lui ('against of me/you/refl./him')

(ii)   contro il professore ('against the professor')

On this, cf. Rizzi (1988:522).

36. With a doubled clitic preceding the psych verb, *a* would not be limited to the first or second person; see also Belletti and Rizzi (1988: note 27).

37. Conversely (for Raffaella Zanuttini) (i) is very marginal, while (ii) is fine and (iii) intermediate:

(i)   ??? Me, mi hanno visto.
(ii)   Lui, lo hanno visto.
(iii)   ? Noi, ci hanno visto.

This construction is compatible with past participle agreement:

(iv)   A me mi hanno vista.

The combination of past participle agreement with the presence of *a* (also found in Occitan and Gascon; Miremont (1976:55) and Rohlfs (1977)) is not expected by Uriagereka (1995, note 70). See note 45. Anna Cardinaletti (p.c.) points out that in Central and Southern dialects (95) is possible in addition to (94).

38. Clitic doubling with datives is usually obligatory in the North Italian dialects; see Vanelli (1998:134).

On the fact that clitic doubling is more prevalent with datives than with accusatives, note Pollock's (1983:97) observation that dative clitic resumptives in French relatives (perhaps with an abstract dative *à*) are more possible than accusative. Paola Benincà points out (p.c.) that Friulian has clitic doubling of the (90) sort, but lacks the *a*-less (96).

39. Jones (1993:202) observes that dative clitic doubling with a postverbal *a* is limited in Sardinian to first and second person pronouns. Whether this restriction can be integrated with the others under discussion remains to be seen.

There also appear to exist cases of a preposition *a* preceding subject pronouns; see Tuaillon (1988:295), Baptista (1997:241).

40. See Marcellesi (1986) on Corsican.

41. Although Sardinian accusative and dative clitics have *l-*, it is notable that the third person non-clitic pronouns that take *a* (*isse, issa, issos, issas*) (which for Jones are NPs) do not, although they are presumably related to the Sardinian definite article (*su, sa, sos, sas*), and perhaps to the (close to addressee) demonstratives *cussu, -a, -os, -as* (Jones (1993:34)).

Probably relevant, too, is the contrast (also found in French) between Sardinian *nois átteros* ('we others'), *vois átteros* ('you others'), and the impossible **issos átteros* ('they others'); see Jones (1993:208).

For relevant discussion, see also Uriagereka (1995, sec. 4).

There may be a further link between the non-DP status of first and second person pronouns and their failure to trigger Hungarian object agreement; see Bartos (to appear).

On the special status of first and second person with respect to auxiliary selection, see Kayne (1993), and on the probably closely related person split with respect to ergativity, see Mahajan (1994), Nash (1997), and Manzini and Savoia (1998).

42. See Milner (1978) on Latin and Montaut (1997:125) on Dravidian.

43. Recall that the vowel in object clitics is in general epenthetic. There is also no:

(i)   * Jean ms invite.
(ii)   * Jean ts invite.
(iii)   * Jean et Marie ss invite.

44. Recall that the *e/é* difference is just orthographic (see note 1 above).

45. Here, however (see note 37 above), past participle agreement (which is normally optional with first and second person in Paduan) does not go well with doubling:

(i)   ?? El me ga vista mi.

Note that the auxiliary in (126) is 'have' (rather than 'be'); see Kayne (1993) and references cited there.

46. See Bouchard (1984:68), Kayne (1986).

47. On which, see Azoulay-Vicente (1985).

In Paduan (and Venetian), at least, the doubling seen in (128) and (124)/(125) is obligatory, in the sense that removing the clitic would make the sentences ungrammatical. (The same is true of (126), though there for a different reason, thinking of (167) below.) This suggests that Paduan direct object non-clitic *mi* and *ti* are obligatorily preceded by an abstract *a*, in which case the need for the clitic may be linkable to the obligatoriness of dative clitic doubling (see note 38).

48. Lidia Lonzi tells me that for her *sé* with a plural antecedent is better in control structures such as (i):

(i)   Ho invitato i ragazzi a parlare di sé.
             ('I-have invited the boys to speak of refl.')

See perhaps the discussion of Longobardi's judgements below.

Probably related to (132) vs. (133) is a fact pointed out by Cordin (1988:596)—namely, that a nonreflexive (nonclitic) pronoun can be a direct object coreferential with the subject in certain contexts, but only when the pronoun is plural:

(ii)   Vestivano di pelli loro e le loro donne.
             ('they-dressed in furs them and the their wives')

49. Cf. Cardinaletti and Starke's (1994) idea (contested by Zribi-Hertz 1998) that the extra structure associated with non-clitic 'third person' pronouns, as compared with their clitic counterparts, is responsible for the non-clitics' (relative) incompatibility with inanimate antecedents.

50. See Heim et al. (1991). Example (134) carries over to French *soi*—cf. Kayne (1975:chap. 5, note 4)—although in French the distributor may have to be overt.

Whether the plural uses of *m-/j-* in (41–42) and (45–46) involve an abstract distributor is left an open question.

51. This fact is masked in the Italian of those who (unlike Giorgi 1984) accept no long-distance reflexives at all.

It may be that (136) improves if *i ragazzi* is replaced by a coordination of singulars.

52. See also perhaps the locality effect pointed out by Burzio (1986:199):

(i)   They gave John a dollar each.
(ii)   * They want John to give me a dollar each.

Malagasy *izy/azy* looks similar to Italian *sé* in that, as discussed by Zribi-Hertz and Mbolatianavalona (1997:253), it allows a plural antecedent (and in their terms is a bound variable—p. 255) only under restricted conditions. Why the restrictions are less severe than with *sé* remains to be investigated.

53. Note that *all* and *both* (the latter for some speakers) are not necessarily distributors; see Dougherty (1970; 1971).

An interesting complication arises when we take into account:

(i)   Loro parlano di se stessi.

Here *sé* is accompanied by *stessi* ('same') (note that the accent on the *-é* is not used here). (On *stess-*, cf. Safir 1996, whose (p. 567) discussion of reciprocals suggests the potential relevance of (163) below.) *Stessi* is *stess-* plus the masculine plural *-i*. (With appropriate antecedents, there are also *stesso, stessa, stesse*.) Example (i) remains impossible as a reciprocal, like (141) and (133). But unlike those two, (i) is fully acceptable; that is, there is no longer a problem with a plural antecedent (and a reflexive reading). It may be that the presence of plural *stessi* facilitates the licensing of a DB.

The singularity of *-é* in Italian is mirrored by the singularity of the *-eg* of Faroese *seg*, to judge by Barnes's (1994:212) example:

(ii)   Tey nokta seg sekan ('they deny refl. guilty')

with the adjective *sekan* in the accusative masculine singular agreeing with *seg* (and not with the plural *tey*).

54. See, however, note 12.

55. Cf. Kayne (1975:sec. 5.1) and Legendre (1997:56). For Anne Zribi-Hertz (144) is not possible in spoken French (nor is (146) or (148)), as opposed to (143).

56. Cf. Burzio (1991:91); also the dialects described by Ditchy (1977:22), Francard (1980:209), and Remacle (1952:223), among others.

57. Impersonal and middle *s-* (cf. Cinque 1988) fall outside the scope of this article.

58. The first person plural non-reflexive object clitic in Milanese is *ne* (Nicoli 1983:149). Similarly, the Veneto and Friuli dialects discussed by Vanelli (1998:122) have *se* for first plural reflexive, but *ne* and *nus*, respectively, for first plural non-reflexive. See also Blinkenberg (1948:96), Remacle (1952:224), and, on Catalan, Picallo (1994:279).

59. Example from Spiess (1976:207). See also Nicoli (1983:152), Lurà (1990:161), Vassere (1993:35, 48), and Salvioni (1975:33).

Note that the *-a* of *ma* and *sa* in (152) is not a gender marker and in all probability corresponds to no separate morpheme.

60. On this *a*, see Poletto (1993; 1995; 1998).

61. For proposals concerning a perhaps comparable phenomenon in Catalan, see Bonet (1991) and Harris (1997:43).

62. If so, the question arises whether some comparable abstract doubling is present in Slavic languages.

A related question is whether anything comparable to (152) could exist with a non-clitic *s*-form.

63. Much as Riny Huybregts suggested in Pisa in 1979 for Dutch *zich*. For recent discussion, see Jayaseelan (1996; 1998), among others.

64. On the question why there is no Condition B effect here (or in (126) or (129), with

s' doubling an *l*-pronoun), see note 82; also Kayne (1986) and McGinnis (1998).
    65. Fully acceptable, on the other hand, is:

(i)   Gianni ha fotografato se stesso. ('...refl. same')

Here there is no Condition B effect, probably much as in English *John photographed his
children*, with the phrase *his children* (and similarly *se stesso*) counting as the phrase
within which the pronoun *his/sé* has successfully failed to be bound. See Chomsky (1986),
Kayne (1991).
    The fact that (163) is not fully unacceptable to all speakers is perhaps to be attributed
to the possibility of an abstract *stesso*, in turn perhaps related to the fact that the object
pronouns in (161)/(162) are contrastive. Alternatively, Jayaseelan (1996:notes 9 and 18)
emphasizes a similarity between the Malayalam counterpart of *sé* and first and second
person pronouns. A third possibility would be to look for some relevant property of *-é*
that distinguishes it from the (different) morphemes that combine with *l-*.
    66. See perhaps Kayne (1975:sec. 5.3) and Belletti (1982) on French and Italian
(nonclitic) reciprocals.
    67. The contrast between (165) and (167) holds, too, for Guglielmo Cinque and for
Cecilia Poletto. Anna Cardinaletti accepts though:

(i)   Gianni è così egoista: ha fotografato LUI, non noi.
(ii)   Gianni è così egoista: ha fotografato solo lui.

    68. For those speakers who reject (165) (and accept (160)), such as Burzio (1991:90),
the effect of the preposition must be limited to the case of *sé*. Burzio (note 6) argues
against the relevance of the preposition on the basis of (i) (from Zribi-Hertz 1980):

(i)   Victor n'aime que lui. ('V neg loves but him')

Kupferman (1986) has shown, however, that this example, although acceptable, is not
typical and that the direct object/prepositional object distinction is significant (datives
pattern with direct objects; see also Authier and Reed 1992:309). Burzio's example given
in (129) above is important, but is probably to be interpreted as showing that a doubled
pronoun can receive special treatment; see note 64.
    The presence of a preposition seems to matter, too, for overlapping reference. Thus,
(ii) seems better than (iii):

(ii)   ? Avete votato per te. ('you$_{pl}$-have voted for you$_{sg}$')
(iii)   * Avete scelto te. ('you$_{pl}$-have chosen you$_{sg}$')

    69. See Kupferman (1986:493).
    70. Some possessive *s-* may be reflexive; see Kayne (1975:chap. 2, note 154) on French.
    71. See Postal (1988).
    That the *s-* of (168) has more in common with *m-* and *t-* than with *l-* has been seen by
Nash (1997, note 9).
    72. See Bonnaud (1974:29). Note that the demonstratives in (170)/(171) have a different

consonant from *se*; in Ratel's (1958:35–37) dialect, demonstratives are vowel-initial (initial *c-* was lost). Thus, it is not likely that these *se* are demonstratives.

Vey (1978:191) seems to indicate that a form *set* can still be used for *lui* ('him') in the Limousin, Perigord, and Auvergne regions, but only as the object of a preposition or after *être* ('be'), a distribution which suggests that it is not a demonstrative.

73. French prenominal possessives, although clitic-like in a number of respects (cf. Kayne 1975:sec. 2.20), are bimorphemic (not even counting the agreement ending—cf. (text to) note 5), whereas first and second person and reflexive clitics are monomorphemic, which is the heart of the matter.

The non-standard Spanish use of clitic *se* for non-reflexive second plural *os* mentioned by Picallo (1994:280) might have *os*—>*se* via dropping of the *o*- plus an epenthetic *-e*, as suggested by Jones's (1993:213) discussion of Campidanese. That is, this *se* might just be the plural *-s* of *os*, and may be unrelated to the person morpheme *s-* that aligns with *m-* and *t-*.

Somewhat similarly, the Spanish spurious *se* (cf. Perlmutter 1971:chap. 2) recently discussed by Harris (1997:43–50) might not contain the *s-* of *m-/t-/s-* but, rather, be an (expletive) locative parallel to that found in Sardinian (Jones 1993:220):

(i)   Bi l'appo datu. ('loc. it I-have given' = 'I gave it to him/her/them')

The impossibility of plural *-s* in Spanish (ii) could reflect the incompatibility of locatives with plural, as in (iii):

(ii)   Yo se(*s) lo doy. ('I *se*(+pl.) it give' = 'I give it to him/her/them.')
(iii)   * I went theres.

Harris discusses varieties of Spanish that allow (iv) to be interpreted as having a singular direct object and a plural indirect object:

(iv)   Yo se los doy. ('I refl. it+pl. give')

Here the *-s* apparently belonging to accusative *los* actually reflects the plurality of the dative argument.

Assume that (i) and (ii) have a phonetically unrealized dative clitic. Then a plausible proposal is that (iv) has a plural dative clitic realized only as (plural) *-s* (rather than as the full form *les*). This will carry over to the parallel Sardinian case, from Jones (1993:220):

(v)   Narrabilos! ('tell+loc.+it+pl.' = 'Tell it to them.')

From this perspective, both (iv) and (v) have three clitics, in the order locative-accusative-dative.

In a proper subset of the preceding varieties, Harris notes, one can have *no-los* for an expected *nos-lo* ('us-it'). Perhaps the *-s* of this *no-los* is an instance of number agreement in a position lower than that of the first person clitic.

That there is more syntax going on in (ii) and (iv) than meets the eye is also suggested by Roca's (1992:sec. 2.10) observation that spurious *se* has a blocking effect on any binding from above of an immediately following accusative (human) clitic.

74. This recalls the fact that clitic *m-/t-*, while normally pronominal, can also act as anaphoric, in (156)/(157)—cf. note 82 below.

I am not following Burzio's (1991) attempt (cf. Reinhart 1983) to reduce Condition B to a "by-product" of Condition A. That attempt takes as its starting point the existence of reflexives. Alternatively, one can take the existence of reflexives as something in need of explanation and try to explain it as a "by-product' of Condition B (whose independence is suggested by the phenomenon of overlapping reference—see note 68). The whole question is beyond the scope of this article.

75. I am leaving open the question how this amalgamation takes place, that is, what the internal structure is. For relevant discussion, see Rouveret (1991:364ff), Haegeman (1993: 62ff), Cardinaletti and Starke (1994:sec. 6), and Zribi-Hertz and Mbolatianavalona (1997).

76. See Picallo (1994:280).

77. Why exactly s- has this property (which it shares with m- and t- —cf. the discussion of (47)/(48) above) remains to be understood.

Although French is like Italian with respect to (168) allowing only a singular antecedent, northern Italy has many dialects whose possessive s- can have either a singular or a plural antecedent. It may be that in sentences where the antecedent of possessive s- is plural, an abstract distributor is involved—cf. note 50 above. Similarly for Spanish and Catalan; see Picallo (1994) (whose translation (p. 281, (48a)) makes it look as if Italian su- could have a plural antecedent).

I know of no Romance language having any s-form, whether pronominal or anaphoric, that takes only a plural antecedent.

A special case is the reciprocal $s'ente$ (=s-+'between/among') found in the Gallo dialect of French. The following are from Chauveau (1984:203):

(i)   I s'ente taient mordus. ('they refl.+betw. were bitten' =
         'They had bitten each other.')
(ii)   On s'ente lë passët. ('one refl.+betw. it passed' =
         'we were passing it back and forth to each other.')

78. The coreferential clitic in the accusative plural is in l- (and is identical in form to the "third person" dative plural clitic). See in part Cochet (1933, 37); also Barras (1979:9), Coppens (1959:58), Page (1985:108), Reymond and Bossard (1982:82).

79. That would leave open the possibility that a related dialect could have an otherwise similar pronominal s-form (which would be more like a "weak pronoun" in the sense of Cardinaletti and Starke 1994).

80. Although m- and t- cannot combine directly with a feminine word marker, as seen in (i), they can, in some Romance languages, sometimes trigger past participle agreement, as seen in (ii):

(i)   * Gianni ma vede. ('G. me-fem. sees')
(ii)   Gianni mi ha vista. ('G. me has seen-fem.')

(At least) in such cases, m- and t- presumably do have a gender feature, even though it cannot be spelled out on the pronoun itself.

S- can occur with past participle agreement, too:

(iii)   Maria si è vista. ('M. refl. is seen')

Whether this requires s- to have a gender feature here is less clear than for m- in (ii), since the source of -a might be *Maria*; for relevant discussion, see Kayne (1993).

Note that none of *m-/t-/s-* have suppletive variants for feminine, either.

81. We would also have to set aside Malayalam *taan*—see Jayaseelan (1996). On the potential importance of number for argument status/independent reference, see Rizzi (1986:543), Kihm (1997), and Zribi-Hertz and Mbolatianavalona (1997). Rouveret (1997:195) argues that number is not sufficient for independent reference.

For me, the number of the pronominal part of the English reflexive need not match the number of *self*:

(i)   If someone buys themself a new car,...
(ii)   (?) We should each get ourself a new car.

82. This difference in feature content between *s-* and *m-/t-* arguably allows *m-* and *t-*, but not *s-*, to be ordinary object clitics linked only to object position; see (text to) note 46. (In all probability, that in turn plays a role in various instances of special behavior of *s-*.) If *m-* and *t-* in reflexive clitic contexts are not ordinary object clitics, but rather more like *s-*, then sentences like (i) may not interact with Condition B in any simple way:

(i)   Je me vois. ('I me see')

References

Authier, J.-M. and L. Reed (1992) "On the Syntactic Status of French Affected Datives," *The Linguistic Review* 9:295–311.

Baptista, M. (1997) "The Morpho-Syntax of Nominal and Verbal Categories in Capeverdean Creole." Ph.D. diss., Harvard University.

Barnes, M. P. with E. Weyhe (1994) "Faroese," in E. König and J. van der Auwera (eds.) *The Germanic Languages*, pp. 190–218. London: Routledge.

Barras, C. (1979) *Etude d'un patois Couètsou*. Mémoire de licence, University of Fribourg, Switzerland.

Bartos, H. (2001) "Object Agreement in Hungarian—A Case for Minimalism," in G. Alexandrova and O. Arnaudova (eds) *The Minimalist Parameter*, pp. 311–324. Amsterdam: John Benjamins.

Belletti, A. (1982) "On the Anaphoric Status of the Reciprocal Construction in Italian," *The Linguistic Review* 2:101–138.

Belletti, A. and L. Rizzi (1988) "Psych-Verbs and θ-Theory," *Natural Language and Linguistic Theory* 6:291–352.

Benincà, P. (1983) "Il clitico a nel dialetto padovano," *Scritti linguistici in onore di G. B. Pellegrini*, pp. 25–35. Pisa: Pacini. Reprinted in Benincà (1994).

Benincà, P. (1993) "Sintassi," in A.Sobrero (ed.), *L'Italiano: le Strutture, la Variazione*, pp. 247–290. Bari: Laterza.

Benincà, P. (1994) *La variazione sintattica. Studi di dialettologia romanza*. Bologna: Il Mulino.

Benincà, P. (1996) "Agglutination and Inflection in Northern Italian Dialects," in C. Parodi, C. Quicoli, M. Saltarelli and M.L. Zubizarreta (eds.) *Aspects of Romance Linguistics*, pp. 59–72. Washington, D.C.: Georgetown University Press.

Benincà, P. (1998) "Between Morphology and Syntax. On the Verbal Morphology of some Alpine Dialects." Ms., University of Padua (earlier version appeared as Benincà (1996)).

Benveniste, E. (1966) *Problèmes de linguistique générale*. Paris: Gallimard.

Bernstein, J. (1991) "DP's in French and Walloon: Evidence for Parametric Variation in Nominal Head Movement," *Probus* 3:101–126.

Bevington, B. (1998) "Indexical Expressions: Syntax and Context." Ph.D diss., Graduate Center, City University of New York.

Blinkenberg, A. (1948) *Le patois de Beuil* (Acta Jutlandica. Aarsskrift for Aarhus Universitet 20(3) (H34)). Copenhagen: Ejnar Munksgaard.

Bonet, E. (1991) "Morphology after Syntax: Pronominal Clitics in Romance Languages." Ph. D. diss., MIT.

Bonnaud, P. (1974) *Nouvelle grammaire auvergnate*. Clermont-Ferrand: Cercle d'Auvergne.

Bouchard, D. (1984) *On the Content of Empty Categories*. Dordrecht: Foris.

Burzio, L. (1986) *Italian Syntax: A Government-Binding Approach*. Dordrecht: Reidel.

Burzio, L. (1989) "Work in Progress." Ms., Harvard University.

Burzio, L. (1991) "The Morphological Basis of Anaphora," *Journal of Linguistics* 27:81–105.

Butler, A. S. G. (1962) *Les parlers dialectaux et populaires dans l'oeuvre de Guy de Maupassant* (Publications romanes et françaises 72). Geneva: Droz and Paris: Minard.

Cardinaletti, A. and M. Starke (1994) "The Typology of Structural Deficiency. On the Three Grammatical Classes," *Working Papers in Linguistics* 4:41–109. University of Venice.

Chabaneau, C. (1874) "Grammaire limousine (suite)," *Revue des Langues Romanes* 5:171–196, 435–481.

Chauveau, J.-P. (1984) *Le gallo: une présentation* (Studi n. 27, Vol. 2). Faculté des Lettres de Brest, Université de Bretagne Occidentale (Section de Celtique).

Chenal, A. (1986) *Le franco-provençale valdôtain*. Aoste: Musumeci.

Cheng, L.L.-S. and R. Sybesma (1999) "Bare and Not-So-Bare Nouns and the Structure of NP," *Linguistic Inquiry* 30:509–542.

Chomsky, N. (1986) *Knowledge of Language*. New York: Praeger.

Cinque, G. (1988) "On *Si* Constructions and the Theory of *Arb*," *Linguistic Inquiry* 19:521–581.

Cochet, E. (1933) *Le patois de Gondecourt (nord)*. Paris: E. Droz.

Coppens, J. (1959) *Grammaire aclote: Parler populaire de Nivelles*. Fédération wallonne du Brabant.

Cordin, P. (1988) "I pronomi riflessivi," in L. Renzi (ed.) *Grande grammatica italiana di consultazione*, vol. 14: *La frase. I sintagmi nominale e preposizionale*, pp. 593–603. Bologna: Il Mulino.

Corver, N. and D. Delfitto (1993) "Feature Asymmetry and the Nature of Pronoun Movement," *OTS Working Papers*. Research Institute for Language and Speech, University of Utrecht.

Ditchy, J. K. (1977) *Les acadiens louisianais et leur parler*. Geneva: Slatkine Reprints. (Paris: Droz (1932)).

Dougherty, R. C. (1970) "A Grammar of Coordinate Conjoined Structures: I," *Language* 46:850–898.

Dougherty, R. C. (1971) "A Grammar of Coordinate Conjoined Structures: II," *Language* 47:298–339.

Féral, R. (1986) *Le patois de Saussey*. Fontaine lès Dijon: Association Bourguignonne de Dialectologie et d'Onomastique.

Fougeu-Fontaine, M. (1986) *Le patois de Chaumont Le Bois*. Fontaine lès Dijon: Association Bourguignonne de Dialectologie et d'Onomastique.

Francard, M. (1980) *Le parler de Tenneville: Introduction à l'étude linguistique des parlers wallo-lorrains* (Bibliothèque des Cahiers de l'Institut de Linguistique de Louvain-19). Louvain-la-Neuve: Cabay.

Gatti, T. (1990) "Confronto tra fenomeni sintattici nell'italiano e nel dialetto trentino: participio passato, accordo e ausiliari." Tesi di laurea, University of Trento.

Gesner, B.E. (1979) *Etude morphosyntaxique du parler acadien de la Baie Sainte-Marie, Nouvelle-Ecosse (Canada)*. (Publication B-85). Québec: Centre International de Recherche sur le Bilinguisme.

Giorgi, A. (1984) "Toward a Theory of Long Distance Anaphors: A GB Approach," *The Linguistic Review* 3:307–361.

Haegeman, L. (1993) "The Morphology and Distribution of Object Clitics in West Flemish," *Studia Linguistica* 47:57–94.

Haiman, J. (1980) *HUA: A Papuan Language of the Eastern Highlands of New Guinea*. Amsterdam: John Benjamins.

Hale, K. (1973) "Person Marking in Walbiri," in S. R. Anderson and P. Kiparsky (eds.) *A Festschrift for Morris Halle*, pp. 308–344. New York: Holt, Rinehart and Winston.

Harris, J. (1997) "Morphologie autonome et pronoms clitiques en catalan et en espagnol," in A. Zribi-Hertz (ed.) *Les Pronoms. Morphologie, syntaxe et typologie*, pp. 35–55. Saint-Denis: Presses Universitaires de Vincennes.

Harris, J. W. (1991) "The Exponence of Gender in Spanish," *Linguistic Inquiry* 22:27–62.

Hauchard, V. (1994) *Vie et parler traditionnels dans le canton de Condé-sur-Noireau, Calvados*. Caen/Condé-sur-Noireau: Presses Universitaires de Caen, Charles Corlet.

Heim, I., H. Lasnik and R. May (1991) "Reciprocity and Plurality," *Linguistic Inquiry* 22:63–101.

Helke, M. (1973) "On Reflexives in English," *Linguistics* 106:5–23.

Hervé, B. (1973) *Le parler de Plouguenast*. Mémoire de Maîtrise, University of Haute Bretagne.

Hull, A. (1988) "The First Person Plural Form: Je Parlons," *The French Review* 62:242–247.

Iatridou, S. (1988) "Clitics, Anaphors, and a Problem of Coindexation," *Linguistic Inquiry* 19:698–703.

Jayaseelan, K. A. (1996) "Anaphors as Pronouns," *Studia Linguistica* 50:207–255.

Jayaseelan, K. A. (1998) "Blocking Effects and the Syntax of Malayalam *Taan*," in R. Singh (ed.) *The Yearbook of South Asian Languages and Linguistics*, pp. 11–27. New Dehli: Sage.

Jones, M. A. (1993) *Sardinian Syntax*. London: Routledge.

Jones, M. A. (1996) "The Pronoun~Determiner Debate: Evidence from Sardinian and Repercussions for French." Paper presented at 26th Linguistic Symposium on Romance Languages, Mexico City.

Kayne, R. S. (1975) *French Syntax: The Transformational Cycle.* Cambridge, Mass: MIT Press.

Kayne, R. S. (1986) "Thematic and Case-Assigning Properties of Past Participles." Abstract of paper presented at the Princeton Workshop on Comparative Grammar.

Kayne, R. S. (1993) "Toward a Modular Theory of Auxiliary Selection," *Studia Linguistica* 47:3–31.

Kayne, R. S. (1991) "Romance Clitics, Verb movement, and PRO," *Linguistic Inquiry* 2:647–686.

Kihm, A. (1997) "Wolof Noun Phrase Structure: Implications for the Position of Gender and the Merger vs. Fusion Contrast." Ms., CNRS-LACITO.

Kupferman, L. (1986) "Le pronom réfléchi non-clitique existe-t-il en français?" in D. Kremer (ed.) *Actes du 19e Congrès de Linguistique et de Philologie Romanes,* vol. 2, pp. 485–494. Tübingen: Max Niemeyer.

Legendre, G. (1997) "Secondary Predication and Functional Projections in French," *Natural Language and Linguistic Theory* 15:43–87.

Lepelley, R. (1974) *Le parler normand du Val de Saire (Manche)* (Cahiers des Annales de Normandie N° 7). Caen: Musée de Normandie.

Lurà, F. (1990) *Il dialetto del Mendrisiotto,* 3rd ed. Mendrisio-Chiasso: Edizioni Unione di Banche Svizzere.

Mahajan, A. (1994) "The Ergativity Parameter: *have-be* Alternation, Word Order and Split Ergativity," in M. Gonzalez (ed.) *Proceedings of NELS,* 24. University of Massachusetts, Amherst: GLSA.

Manzini, M. R. and L. Savoia (1998) "Clitics and Auxiliary Choice in Italian Dialects: Their Relevance for the Person Ergativity Split," *Recherches Linguistiques de Vincennes* 27:115–138.

Marcellesi, J.-B. (1986) "Le 'complément d'object direct' en corse: *à* + SN de GV, 0 + SN de GV," *Morphosyntaxe des langues romanes,* pp. 127–138 (Actes du XVIIe Congrès International de Linguistique et Philologie Romanes, vol. n° 4). Aix-en-Provence: Université de Provence.

Mattesini, E. (1976) "Tre microsistemi morfologici del dialetto di Borgo Sansepolcro (Arezzo)," *Problemi di morfosintassi dialettale,* pp. 177–202. Pisa: Pacini.

Matthews, S. and V. Yip (1994) *Cantonese: A Comprehensive Grammar.* London: Routledge.

Maze, C. (1969) *Etude sur le langage de la banlieue du Havre.* Geneva: Slatkine Reprints. (1903).

McGinnis, M. J. (1998) "Locality in A-movement." Ph.D. diss., MIT.

Milner, J.-C. (1978) "Le système du réfléchi en latin," *Langages* 50:73–86.

Miremont, P. (1976) *La syntaxe occitane du Périgord.* Cuers.

Montaut, A. (1997) "Les pronoms personnels, emphatiques et réfléchis dans les langues indiennes," in A. Zribi-Hertz (ed.) *Les Pronoms: Morphologie, syntaxe et typologie,* pp. 101–128. Saint-Denis: Presses Universitaires de Vincennes.

Morin, Y.-C. (1979) "More Remarks on French Clitic Order," *Linguistic Analysis* 5:293–312.

Nadahalli, J. (1998) "Aspects of Kannada Grammar." Ph.D. diss., New York University.

Nash, L. (1997) "La partition personnelle dans les langues ergatives," in Zribi-Hertz (ed.) *Les Pronoms. Morphologie, syntaxe et typologie,* pp. 129–149. Saint-Denis: Presses Universitaires de Vincennes.

Nicoli, L. (1983) *Grammatica milanese.* Busto Arsizio: Bramante Editrice.

Page, L. (1985) *Le patois fribourgeois,* 2nd ed. Fribourg: La Sarine.

Pelliciardi, F. (1977) *Grammatica del dialetto romagnolo*. Ravenna: Longo.

Perlmutter, D. (1971) *Deep and Surface Structure Constraints in Syntax*. New York: Holt, Rinehart and Winston.

Picabia, L. (1997) "Les traits du pronom-accord en grand-comorien," in Zribi-Hertz (ed.) *Les Pronoms: Morphologie, syntaxe et typologie*, pp. 151–179. Saint-Denis: Presses Universitaires de Vincennes.

Pica, P. (1987) "On the Nature of the Reflexivization Cycle," *Proceedings of NELS*, 17: 483–499. University of Massachusetts, Amherst: GLSA.

Picallo, M.C. (1994) "Catalan Possessive Pronouns: The Avoid Pronoun Principle Revisited," *Natural Language and Linguistic Theory* 12:259–299.

Poletto, C. (1993) *La sintassi del soggetto nei dialetti italiani settentrionali*, (Quaderni Patavini di Linguistica. Monografie 12). Padua: Unipress.

Poletto, C. (1995) "Split Agr and Subject Clitics in the Northern Italian Dialects," *GLOW Newsletter*, 34.

Poletto, C. (1998) "The higher functional field in the Northern Italian dialects." Ms., University of Padua/CNR.

Pollock, J.-Y. (1983) "Sur quelques propriétés des phrases copulatives en français," *Langue Française* 58:89–125.

Postal, P. M. (1970) "On Coreferential Complement Subject Deletion," *Linguistic Inquiry* 1:439–500.

Postal, P. M. (1966) "On So-Called 'Pronouns' in English," in F. P. Dineen (ed.) *Report of the Seventeenth Annual Roundtable Meeting on Linguistics and Language Studies*, pp. 177–206. Washington, D.C.: Georgetown University Press.

Postal, P.M. (1988) "Anaphoric Islands," in E. Schiller, B. Need, D. Varley, and W. H. Eilfort (eds.) *The Best of CLS: A Selection of Out-of-Print Papers from 1968 to 1975*, pp. 67–94. Chicago Linguistic Society.

Ratel, V. (1958) *Morphologie du patois de Saint-Martin-la-Porte* (Savoie) (Publications de l'Institut de Linguistique Romane de Lyon, 13). Paris: Les Belles Lettres.

Reinhart, T. (1983) *Anaphora and Semantic Interpretation*. London: Croom Helm.

Remacle, L. (1952) *Syntaxe du parler wallon de la Gleize*, vol. 1, Bibliothèque de la Faculté de Philosophie et Lettres de l'Université de Liège, Fas. 126. Paris: Les Belles Lettres.

Reymond, J. and M. Bossard (1982) *Le patois vaudois: Grammaire et vocabulaire*, 3rd ed. Lausanne: Payot.

Rizzi, L. (1986) "Null Objects in Italian and the Theory of *pro*," *Linguistic Inquiry* 17:501–557.

Rizzi, L. (1988) "Il sintagma preposizionale," in L. Renzi (ed.) *Grande grammatica italiana di consultazione. Vol. 1. La frase: I sintagmi nominale e preposizionale*, pp. 507–531. Bologna: Il Mulino.

Roca, F. (1992) *On the Licensing of Pronominal Clitics: The Properties of Object Clitics in Spanish and Catalan*. Universitat Autònoma de Barcelona: Treball de Recerca.

Rohlfs, G. (1977) *Le gascon. Etudes de philologie pyrénéenne*. Tübingen: Max Niemeyer.

Rooryck, J. (1992) "Romance Enclitic Ordering and Universal Grammar," *The Linguistic Review* 9:219–250.

Rouffiange, R. (1983) *Le patois et le français rural de Magny-Lès-Aubigny (Côte-d'Or)*. Fontaine lès Dijon: Association Bourguignonne de Dialectologie et d'Onomastique.

Rouveret, A. (1991) "Functional Categories and Agreement," *The Linguistic Review* 8:353–387.

Rouveret, A. (1997) "Les pronoms personnels du gallois: Structure interne et syntaxe," in Zribi-Hertz (ed.) *Les Pronoms: Morphologie, syntaxe et typologie*, pp. 181–212. Saint-Denis: Presses Universitaires de Vincennes.

Safir, K. (1996) "Semantic Atoms of Anaphora," *Natural Language and Linguistic Theory* 14:545–589.

Salvioni, C. (1975) "Fonetica e morfologia del dialetto milanese," *L'Italia Dialettale* 38:1–46.

Spiess, F. (1976) "Di un'innovazione morfologica nel sistema dei pronomi personali oggetto del dialetto della Collina d'Oro," *Problemi di morfosintassi dialettale*, pp. 203–212. Pisa: Pacini.

Sportiche, D. (1988) "A Theory of Floating Quantifiers and Its Corollaries for Constituent Structure," *Linguistic Inquiry* 19:425–449.

Szabolcsi, A. (1994) "The Noun Phrase," in F. Kiefer and K. É. Kiss (eds.) *The Syntactic Structure of Hungarian*. San Diego: Academic Press.

Taljaard, P. C., J. N. Khumalo and S. E. Bosch (1991) *Handbook of Siswati*. Pretoria: J.L. van Schaik.

Tranel, B. (1981) *Concreteness in Generative Phonology. Evidence from French*. Berkeley: University of California Press.

Tuaillon, G. (1988) "Le français régional: Formes de recontre," in G. Vermes (ed.) *Vingtcinq communautés linguistiques de la France*, pp. 291–300. Paris: L'Harmattan.

Uriagereka, J. (1995) "Aspects of the Syntax of Clitic Placement in Western Romance," *Linguistic Inquiry* 26:79–123.

Vanelli, L. (1998) *I dialetti italiani settentrionali nel panorama romanzo. Studi di sintassi e morfologia*. Rome: Bulzoni.

Vassere, S. (1993) *Sintassi formale e dialettologia. I pronomi clitici nel luganese*. Milan: FrancoAngeli.

Vey, E. (1978) *Le dialecte de Saint-Etienne au XVIIᵉ siècle*. Marseille: Laffitte Reprints. (Paris (1911)).

Villefranche, J.-M. (1978) *Essai de grammaire du patois lyonnais*. Geneva: Slatkine Reprints. (Bourg (1891)).

Zribi-Hertz, A. (1980) "Coréférences et pronoms réfléchis: Notes sur le contraste *lui/lui-même* en français," *Lingvisticae Investigationes* 4:131–179.

Zribi-Hertz, A. (1998) "Les pronoms forts du français sont-ils [+animés]? Spécification morphologique et spécification sémantique," Ms., University of Paris.

Zribi-Hertz, A. and L. Mbolatianavalona (1997) "De la structure à la référence: Les pronoms du malgache," in A. Zribi-Hertz (ed.) *Les Pronoms: Morphologie, syntaxe et typologie*, pp. 231–266. Saint-Denis: Presses Universitaires de Vincennes.

6

On Some Differences between Exclamative and Interrogative Wh-Phrases in Bellunese: Further Evidence for a Split-CP Hypothesis

Nicola Munaro

1. Introduction

In this chapter I analyze comparatively the distributional properties of different classes of *wh*-phrases in main exclamative and interrogative sentences in a north-eastern Italian variety spoken in the northern area of the Veneto region, which will be referred to for simplicity as *Bellunese.*

Differently from what happens in main interrogatives, where some classes of *wh*-phrases appear in situ, in main exclamatives all *wh*-phrases appear, in this dialect, invariably in sentence initial position; in order to account for this difference in the distribution of *wh*-phrases and in particular for the obligatoriness of overt movement in exclamative contexts, it will be proposed that *wh*-phrases appearing in initial position occupy a different structural position in interrogatives and in exclamatives.

More precisely, following a proposal put forth by Benincà (1996), who analyzes the syntactic properties of exclamative sentences in Paduan, it will be argued that in *Bellunese wh*-phrases in main exclamatives raise to the specifier position of a functional projection of the CP system which is structurally higher than the one occupied in interrogative sentences.

This assumption provides further support to the hypothesis that the highest functional portion of sentence structure, generically labeled as CP, consists of different layers of projections, each of which is characterized by specific features.

2. The distribution of *wh*-phrases in interrogatives

As discussed extensively in Munaro (1997), the distribution of *wh*-phrases in main interrogatives in the northern Veneto dialects can be accounted for based on a requirement concerning the identification of the (nominal) head of the *wh*-phrase: a sufficient identification of the (empty) category constituting the head of the phrase determines the occurrence of the phrase itself in initial position— that is, its raising in overt syntax to a functional specifier position. When the head of the *wh*-phrase is not sufficiently identified, the constituent fails to undergo syntactic movement and appears in situ; it is connected at the interpretive level with an abstract *wh*-operator licensed in the specifier of the functional projection whose head is occupied by the inflected verb, which is endowed in interrogative contexts with specific inflectional features (as shown by the presence of inversion between verb and enclitic pronominal subject).

In Bellunese we can distinguish three classes of *wh*-phrases with respect to their distribution in a main interrogative sentence.

The class of *wh*-phrases appearing in initial position comprises the phrases consisting of the *wh*-modifiers *che/quant* followed by a phonetically realized nominal head (or by a phonetically unrealized nominal head which is identified through sufficiently specific inherent features) and the *wh*-element *cossa*, analyzed as a nominal head which has diachronically developed into an interrogative operator (as argued in Munaro 1998a):

(1) a.   *Quanti libri* à-tu ledést?
         'How many books have you read?'

   b.   *De che question* avé-o parlà?
         'About which problem have you spoken?'

   c.   *Cossa* à-lo comprà?
         'What has he bought?'

The second class of *wh*-phrases is constituted by the interrogative elements *qual* and *quant* when used pronominally—that is, not followed by a phonetically realized nominal head; these *wh*-elements can appear optionally in initial position or in situ:

(2) a.   *Quanti* ghén'à-tu vist?

   b.   Ghen'à-tu vist *quanti*?
         'How many of them have you seen?'

(3) a.   *Qual* avé-o ciot?

   b.   Avé-o ciot *qual*?
         'Which one have you taken?'

This optionality has been traced back in Munaro (1997) (and 1998b) to the *d-linking* properties of these *wh*-elements, hence, ultimately, to the potentially ambiguous identification of the empty category constituting the nominal head. More precisely, in the case of occurrence in situ the identification takes place crucially through reference to an antecedent in the discourse, while in the case of movement the nominal head of the *wh*-phrase is identified with a *pro*, that is, with an empty pronominal category endowed with independent reference.

The class of *wh*-phrases which occur invariably in argumental position comprises the interrogative elements *chi* and *che* and some interrogative adverbs:

(4) a.   É-lo *chi* che te à ciamà?
           'Who called you?'

     b.   À-li catà *che*?
           'What have they found?'

     c.   Sé-tu 'ndàt *andé*?
           'Where have you gone?'

It has been proposed that the *wh*-elements belonging to this class, whose nominal head is presumably occupied by a not (sufficiently) identified empty category, head a QP which is internal to the extended nominal projection; owing to their structural properties, these phrases fulfill a requirement of categorial and structural parallelism with the abstract *wh*-operator licensed by the raising of the inflected verb to the relevant functional head position, and can therefore undergo a process of matching with it at the interpretive level.[1]

3. The structure of main *wh*-exclamatives

In her description of exclamative sentences in Italian, Benincà (1995) observes that the function of the exclamative sentence is to characterize as "unexpected" the propositional content of a given utterance. The attitude of astonishment expressed by the speaker who utters an exclamative sentence can either concern the whole event described by it or refer to a single constituent; in this latter case we have a so called *wh*-exclamative sentence.

Benincà further points out that the relation between exclamative sentences focalized on a constituent and *wh*-interrogative sentences is quite complex, not only because the introductory elements are very often the same (that is, *wh*-phrases) and occupy in both cases the initial position, but also because sometimes interrogatives can have the "illocutive" strength of exclamatives. Given the possibility of expressing conjectures on the plausibility of the possible answer, the interrogative sentence can be used pragmatically as an exclamative.

In light of this remark, a given sentence having the same syntactic properties as an interrogative will be considered here as an instance of exclamative if it can be answered by a rhetorical answer—that is, if it conveys a hint at the speaker's mental attitude toward the expected answer: namely, that the event, the object, or the quality referred to is worth noticing.

Let's consider now the distribution of different classes of *wh*-phrases in main exclamatives in Bellunese. As one can see from the examples reported in (5) and (6), exclamative *wh*-phrases containing a nominal head (introduced either by the invariable determiner *che* or by the determiner *quant-* agreeing in gender and number with the noun) can be followed either by the verb displaying inversion with the enclitic pronominal subject or by the complementizer. The only difference consists in the fact that when the *wh*-phrase is introduced by the determiner *che* and is followed by the verb (as in (5a)), no adjectival modifier can intervene between the *wh*-element and the nominal head:

(5) a.   *Che (*bela/*bruta) casa se à-lo fat?!*

    b.   *Che (bela/bruta) casa che'l se à fat!*
        'What a (beautiful/horrible) house he has built for himself!'

(6) a.   *Quanti (bei) libri à-lo ledést?!*

    b.   *Quanti (bei) libri che l'à ledést!*
        'How many (beautiful) books he has read!'[2]

Despite the seeming equivalence, though, there is a different interpretive implication in the examples in (a) and in those in (b). While the examples in (b) are neutral, that is, have no particular implication concerning the speaker's opinion about the event referred to (beside the fact that the event is worth pointing out, as noted above)—the examples in (a) imply that the event described is judged negatively by the speaker, who expresses a sort of reproachful dismay about it. So, while (5a) implies that the speaker thinks that the person referred to has built for himself a very strange or uncomfortable house he dislikes, (5b) has no particular implication, as shown by the fact that both a positive and a negative adjective can intervene between *che* and the noun. Similarly, differently from (6b), the example reported in (6a) without the adjective implies that he read either too many or too few books, while the presence of the (semantically positive) adjective *bei* presupposes an ironical or critical attitude of the speaker (who implies either that the person referred to read hardly any interesting books or that that person wrongly thinks he has read many interesting books).

As pointed out for Paduan by Benincà (1996), a peculiar syntactic behavior is displayed by the adverb *quant(o)*, which can modify either an adjective on which the exclamation focuses or the predicate. If it modifies an adjective, which always originates from a predicative structure, inversion is obligatory, as one can see from the contrast between (7a) and (7b):

(7) a.   *Quant alt é-lo deventà?!*

    b. * *Quant alt che l'é deventà!*
        'How tall he has become!'

When *quant* modifies the verb, one can find either the structure with inversion between verb and subject clitic or the structure with the complementizer and without inversion (as exemplified in (12b–c) below).

The pattern reported in (7) has to be contrasted with the exclamatives focusing on an adjectival predicate introduced by *che*, which don't admit inversion but require on the contrary the presence of the complementizer:[3]

(8) a.   * *Che alt* é-lo deventà?!

   b.   *Che alt* che l'é deventà!
      'How tall he has become!'

The contrast in grammaticality reported in (8) mirrors the one reported in (5) above, which seems to indicate that an exclamative *wh*-phrase introduced by the *wh*-element *che* followed by an adjective (followed, in turn, by a noun) obligatorily requires the presence of the complementizer and is therefore incompatible with inversion between inflected verb and enclitic pronominal subject; as can be seen in (5a), this restriction doesn't hold for the cases in which *che* is followed only by a nominal head.[4]

As anticipated above, even with the right intonational pattern, in Bellunese the exclamative interpretation of a sentence containing a *wh*-phrase in situ is excluded, as the hearer is in this case unequivocally induced to give a nonrhetorical answer: that is, to provide the questioner with additional information previously unavailable to him.

The exclamative reading is by far more natural if the same class of *wh*-phrases appears in initial position; with bare *wh*-elements we have two options, as the *wh*-phrase can be followed either by the finite verb marked with the interrogative inflectional morphology (that is, inversion between verb and subject clitic pronoun), or by the complementizer *che* followed, in turn, by the verb inflected according to the assertive paradigm, as shown, respectively, in the examples in (b) and (c):

(9) a.   ??Ghen'à-tu comprà *quanti*?!

   b.   *Quanti* ghen'à-tu comprà?!

   c.   *Quanti* che te ghen'à comprà!
      'How many you have bought!'

(10) a.   ??À-tu invidà *chi*?!

   b.   *Chi* à-tu invidà?!

   c.   *Chi* che te à invidà!
      'Whom you have invited!'

(11) a.   ??Sié-o 'ndadi *andé*?!

   b.   *Andé* sié-o 'ndadi?!

   c.   *Andé* che sié 'ndadi!
      'Where you have gone!'

(12) a.   ??Avé-o laorà *quant*?!

   b.   *Quant* avé-o laorà?!

c.   *Quant* che avé laorà!
      'How hard you have worked!'

Again, the examples in (b), differently from the ones in (c), convey the particular reading described above and are therefore adequate and acceptable as exclamatives in a situation in which the speaker evaluates, respectively, as excessive the amount of objects bought, inopportune the invitation of that particular person, unexpectedly far or dangerous the place and overconscientious the people referred to.

4. The relative order of exclamative, left dislocated, and interrogative phrases

Considering the reciprocal order of constituents situated at the left periphery of the sentence, Benincà (1996) establishes for Italian and Paduan a relative order in which the exclamative phrase is followed by the left dislocated phrase which is followed, in turn, by the interrogative phrase. The relevant contrast is the one between (13a) and (13b), which shows that an exclamative *wh*-phrase, but not an interrogative one, can precede a left dislocated constituent:[5]

(13) a.   A to sorela, *che libro* vorissi-to regalarghe?
          'To your sister, which book would you like to give as a gift?'

     b.   *Che bel libro*, a to sorela, che i ghe ga regalà!
          'What a nice book, to your sister, they have given as a gift!'

Benincà takes these data as evidence that the *wh*-phrase of the exclamative sentence moves to a position which is structurally higher than the one occupied by the corresponding interrogative phrase.

Let's see now how the presence of a dislocated constituent interacts with the distribution of exclamative *wh*-phrases in Bellunese, considering first the class of *wh*-phrases consisting of the determiners *che/quant* followed by (an adjective and) a nominal head. In this case a constituent can appear in a right dislocated position (however, this kind of structure, exemplified in (14a), may be derived under Kayne's (1994) antisymmetric approach), between the *wh*-phrase and the complementizer (as in (14b)), and, marginally, in initial position as well—that is, in a left dislocated position preceding the *wh*-phrase (as in (14c)):

(14) a.   *Che/Quanti bèi vestiti* che la à comprà, to sorèla!

     b.   *Che/Quanti bèi vestiti*, to sorèla, che la à comprà!

     c.   ? To sorèla, *che/quanti bèi vestiti* che la à comprà!
          'Your sister, how (many) beautiful dresses, your sister, (she) has bought, your sister!'

If we compare this pattern with the corresponding interrogatives in which the complementizer doesn't appear and inversion between the verb and the subject clitic takes place, we see that the two structures in which the constituent is right or left dislocated (reported in (15a) and (15c), respectively), are again grammatical, but the one in which the constituent appears between the *wh*-phrase and the inflected verb (exemplified in (15b)) is clearly ungrammatical:

(15) a.   *Che/quanti libri* avéo comprà, ieri?

   b. * *Che/quanti libri*, ieri, avéo comprà?

   c.   Ieri, *che/quanti libri* avéo comprà?
         'Yesterday, what/how many books, yesterday, have you bought, yesterday?'

Differently from what we have seen in (14) above, in this case the *wh*-phrase cannot be separated from the verbal head, which can be interpreted as evidence for the fact that in interrogatives the structural relation between the two elements is closer than in exclamatives (possibly one of spec-head agreement).

Let's consider now the other class of phrases, namely those consisting of a bare *wh*-element; these admit in exclamative contexts both the structure with complementizer and the one with inversion. The only completely grammatical structure is the one in which the dislocated phrase appears at the right periphery of the sentence (examples in (16a) and (17a)), while if it appears left dislocated, as in (16c) and (17c), the sentence is still acceptable but slightly deviant. The only completely ungrammatical structure is the one in which the constituent follows the *wh*-phrase and precedes the complementizer (as can be seen from the examples in (16b) and (17b)):

(16) a.   *A chi* che l'é 'ndat a dirghela, sta roba!

   b. * *A chi*, sta roba, che l'é 'ndat a dirghela!

   c. ? Sta roba, *a chi* che l'é 'ndat a dirghela!
         'To whom he has told this thing!'

(17) a.   *Quant* che avé laorà, par sta festa!

   b. * *Quant*, par sta festa, che avé laorà!

   c. ? Par sta festa, *quant* che avé laorà!
         'How hard you have worked for this party!'

Under the crucial assumption that the position occupied by the left dislocated constituent is the same in all of these structures, the impossibility for a constituent to intervene between an exclamative *wh*-phrase and the complementizer can be taken as evidence that the *wh*-element occupies the specifier position of a maximal projection whose head is occupied by the complementizer; this specifier position must be lower than the one occupied by complex exclamative *wh*-phrases, which, as we have seen above, can be separated from the complementizer by an intervening constituent; on the other hand, such position must be higher than the one occupied by interrogative *wh*-phrases appearing in sentence initial position, which must be followed by the verbal head and can't be followed by the complementizer.[6]

If this interpretation of the data is correct, the internal structure of the *wh*-phrase appearing in exclamative sentences indeed plays a role in the position of the phrase itself, as it does in main questions; we can assume that, while a bare *wh*-element has to enter a *spec-head* configuration with the complementizer (hence cannot be separated from it by intervening material), a complex *wh*-phrase still retains the possibility of raising further to a higher specifier position.

5. A tentative account of the data

The data that have been analyzed in the previous sections confirm the correctness of Benincà's analysis: that is, the hypothesis that in main exclamative sentences the *wh*-phrase occupies a higher structural position than in main interrogatives.

More precisely, we are led to distinguish at least three different layers of structure inside this CP-area, a hypothesis which is compatible with many recent works about the CP-system (among which we mention Rizzi 1998 and, for the Northern Italian dialects, Poletto 2000).

The lowest projection, Int(errogative) P(hrase), activated already in main interrogative sentences, is the one whose head is occupied by the inflected verb onto which the pronominal subject encliticizes; in questions containing *wh*-phrases in situ the presence of a specific interrogative inflectional morphology on the verbal head licenses in the corresponding specifier an abstract *wh*-operator which is connected at the interpretive level with the *wh*-element in situ, so that this can escape overt movement; in the case of complex interrogative *wh*-phrases, structurally and categorially incompatible with such operator, we have overt raising of the *wh*-constituent to the specifier position of the functional projection whose head is occupied by the inflected verb.

We have then a second projection Excl(amative) P(hrase), which we assume to be activated only in exclamative sentences, whose specifier hosts exclamative *wh*-phrases consisting of a bare *wh*-element and whose head is occupied by the complementizer *che*; above this projection, we have to postulate the presence of at least a third projection whose specifier is occupied in exclamatives by complex *wh*-phrases (formed by a determiner and a nominal or adjectival head) and whose head is possibly empty.[7]

If this formalization of the data is correct, the functional structure of this part of the sentence should then be represented as follows:

(18)   XP
              ╱‾‾‾‾‾‾‾╲
     complex *excl-wh*   X′
                        ╱‾‾‾╲
                    X°   ExclCP
                         ╱‾‾‾‾╲
                 bare *excl-wh*   Excl′
                               ╱‾‾‾╲
                           Excl°   IntCP
                           che   ╱‾‾‾╲
                  complex *int-wh*/*wh*Op   Int′
                                       ╱‾‾‾╲
                                   Int°   ...
                              V°+ subject clitic

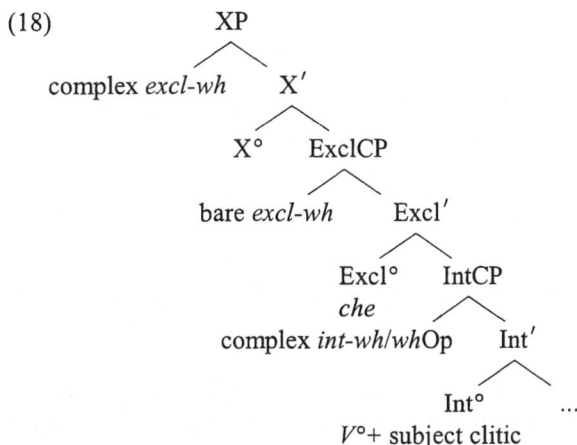

The fact that in exclamatives the complementizer can (and sometimes must) be phonetically realized can be interpreted as evidence for the fact that the higher raising of the exclamative *wh*-phrase activates a functional projection which is not activated in main interrogatives, where the complementizer never appears.[8]

As for the impossibility for *wh*-phrases to appear in situ in main exclamative sentences, I propose that the interpretive strategy exploiting an abstract *wh*-operator—hence the occurrence of bare *wh*-elements in argumental position—is excluded in exclamative contexts just because the inflected verb doesn't move so high as to reach the head position of the relevant functional projection (which can be optionally filled by the complementizer *che*). Hence, the impossibility for the verbal head to license an abstract (exclamative) *wh*-operator in the relevant specifier position and the obligatory overt raising of exclamative *wh*-phrases to that position.

Note that a further argument for assuming that *wh*-phrases occupy a higher structural position in exclamatives than in interrogatives comes from the particular reading described above which is associated to the structure with inversion— namely, the reading implying a negative attitude of the speaker toward the event, the object or the quality on which the sentence focuses. I suggest that in this case the inflected verb, raised to Int°, still retains the faculty of licensing from this position an abstract *wh*-operator in the corresponding specifier position and that such operator, intervening structurally between the exclamative *wh*-phrase and its trace, creates a minimality effect which deletes the neutral exclamative interpretation and forces, for some reason, that particular reading. Under the hypothesis that exclamative *wh*-phrases occupy the lower specifier, we would have no way to account for the interpretive contrast noted. When the complementizer is realized, no abstract operator is present, hence no minimality effect is induced and the interpretation is the ordinary one.[9]

6. Summary

Following a proposal put forth by Benincà (1996) for Paduan, I have tried to show that a comparative analysis of the distribution of *wh*-phrases in main interrogative and in main exclamative sentences in Bellunese provides suggestive evidence that in exclamatives the *wh*-phrases appearing in initial position occupy, within the CP area, a specifier position which is structurally higher than the one occupied in interrogatives.

The data discussed here strengthen the hypothesis proposed in the last years according to which the structural area covered by the CP layer should be extended and subdivided into different functional projections, each of which devoted to a specific function.

We have also seen that the assumption that exclamative *wh*-phrases raise to a position higher than the one occupied by interrogative *wh*-phrases can account both for the lack of *wh*-in situ in exclamatives and for a particular interpretive implication associated to *wh*-exclamatives with inversion.

Moreover, the data suggest a further distinction concerning the distribution of complex vs bare *wh*-phrases in exclamatives; it seems that in *Bellunese* complex *wh*-phrases raise to a position which is even higher than the one occupied by bare *wh*-elements, thus confirming the relevance, also in exclamative contexts, of the internal structure of a constituent in determining its distribution.

Notes

This chapter is dedicated to Paola Benincà, who kindly accepted the (probably not so pleasant) role of supervisor of my Ph.D. thesis and provided interesting comments and suggestions on various parts of it, thereby (implicitly) communicating to me the clear awareness that what I was doing was worth pursuing. Her attitudes constantly remind us of the fact that we should behave as thinking and feeling human beings long before acting as thinking and feeling linguists.

Following a hypothesis put forth by her, I develop here some ideas and observations that have been dealt with rather concisely in my Ph.D. thesis.

1. The functional projection containing the relevant head position is labeled in Munaro (1997) *TypeP* and is connected to the determination of the sentential type to which a given utterance belongs. In main interrogative sentences the relevant feature of the head Type° is checked by the enclitic subject pronoun which is assumed to be generated there. In Munaro (1997) I also put forth an hypothesis to account for a peculiar prosodic property found in interrogatives containing *wh*-elements in situ, to the effect that other arguments of the predicate have to appear in a dislocated position. I also examined the distributional properties of *wh*-phrases in different contexts of subordination: in indirect questions (where they invariably occupy the initial position), in cases of extraction from complement clauses (where their distribution mirrors exactly that found in main interrogatives), and in the particular syntactic configurations defined *island conditions* (inside which these *wh*-phrases cannot appear).

2. Benincà (1996) points out that, if the noun is not accompanied by an adjective, the structure of these exclamative sentences corresponds to that of an indirect interrogative;

according to her, the analogy is confirmed by the fact that in both cases there is no inversion between verb and clitic subject, and a nominal subject cannot appear between complementizer and verb:

(i)   a.   *Quanti libri* che (??Mario) à ledést Mario!
       b.   (No so) *quanti libri* che (??Mario) à ledést Mario
               '(I don't know) how many books Mario has read.'

Hence, as Benincà notes, although the intonation of an exclamative is very different from the one of an interrogative, the properties concerning the order of the elements different from the *wh*-phrase seem to be similar, as shown by the fact that other possible arguments of the verb are indeed preferably emarginated to the right and their clitic copies are not obligatory.

3. A contrast in grammaticality similar to the one reported in (8) is attested with the *wh*-element *cossa*, which in exclamative contexts can assume the meaning of *how much*; in this case it has to be followed by the complementizer and the alternative structure with inversion is ungrammatical:

(i)   a.   *Cossa* ghe piàze-lo, al gelato!
       b.   *Cossa* che 'l ghe piàze, al gelato!
               'How much he likes ice cream!'

Note however that when it has the meaning of *why cossa* always requires inversion between verb and subject clitic, which may be due to the fact that the *wh*-element *why* doesn't admit an exclamative interpretation, but only an interrogative one:

(ii)   a.   *Cossa* sé-tu 'ndat a parlar con quel là (par far *che*)!
       b.   *Cossa* che te sé 'ndat a parlar con quel là!
               '*What* have you gone to speak with that one (to do *what*)!' =
                                    'Why have you gone...'

As one can see from the example in (iia), the introductory *wh*-element *cossa* can be optionally resumed by the phrase *par far che* which appears in argumental position. The possibility of resumption by a *wh*-element in situ is available also when *cossa* is used in exclamatives with its primary meaning of *what*, but, crucially, only when the *wh*-phrase is followed by the verb inflected in the interrogative form, and not when it is followed by the complementizer:

(iii) a.   *Cossa* sé-tu 'ndat a comprar *che*!
       b.   *Cossa* che te sé 'ndat a comprar *che*!
               '*What* have you gone to buy *what*!' = 'what the hell have you bought!'

The ungrammaticality of (iiib) can be seen as a further argument in favor of the hypothesis (put forth in Munaro 1997 and 1998b) that the possibility for some *wh*-elements to appear in situ in main interrogatives is crucially tied to the presence of inversion between verb and subject clitic—that is, to the raising of the verbal head to a specific structural position.

4. In order to explain the contrast between (7) and (8), Benincà (1996) suggests that exclamative sentences introduced by *quant-* which are compatible with the inversion between

inflected verb and subject clitic (like the ones in (12b) and (7a)) are actually, from the syntactic point of view, interrogative structures whose exclamative interpretation is determined pragmatically by contextual factors. In particular, for the example in (7a) we can assume an internal structure of the adjectival phrase like the one proposed by Zamparelli (1996), where the measure phrase occupies the specifier position, a *Deg(ree) Phrase*, which selects as its complement an adjectival phrase in whose head is generated the adjective; this raises, through the head Deg°, to the head Agr° of the projection AgrP which selects DegP; AgrP is in turn selected by a QP in whose head are generated agreementless adverbial modifiers (like *molto, tanto, poco, così, più*). Zamparelli attributes the presence of a *default positive amount* reading in examples like (7a)—that is, the speaker's presupposition that the person referred to is tall to a remarkable extent—to the *default* interpretation at LF of an empty operator in Deg°. Note that, beside the ungrammaticality of (7b), it is also impossible to have the alternative version in which only *quant* moves to the initial position, while the adjective remains in predicative position, or the version with the whole adjectival phrase in situ:

(i)   a.   *$\widetilde{Quant}$ é-lo (deventà) *alt*?!
        b.   *É-lo (deventà) *alt quant*?!
                'How tall he has become!'

Both of these structures are instead perfectly grammatical in the interrogative interpretation.

5. Based on the following contrast, Benincà shows that in the main interrogative sentence the *wh*-phrase follows obligatorily a left dislocated constituent:

(i)   a.   *A *chi*, to sorela, ghe la ga-li presentà?
        b.   To sorela, *a chi* ghe la ga-li presentà?
                'tell me to whom, your sister, to whom have they introduced'

Concerning the position of the complementizer *che*, Benincà also suggests that in Paduan the complementizer that appears in exclamative sentences is the same as the one which is lexicalized in indirect questions; this is shown by the fact that both in main exclamatives (as in (13b)) and in indirect questions (as shown in the following examples) the complementizer has to follow the dislocated constituent and the *wh*-phrase:

(ii)   a.   *Dime *a chi* (che) to sorela (che) i ghe la ga presentà.
        b.   Dime to sorela *a chi* che i ghe la ga presentà.
                'tell me to whom, your sister, to whom they have introduced'

According to Benincà, another piece of evidence in favor of this hypothesis is represented by the fact that in both cases *che* is in complementary distribution with inversion: if inversion is interpreted as leftward movement of the verb, the incompatibility of such a movement with the complementizer can be accounted for, assuming that *che* occupies the same position in both cases.

6. Further evidence in favor of the hypothesis that (bare) exclamative *wh*-phrases occupy a specifier position higher than the one occupied by interrogative *wh*-phrases and have a looser structural relation to the verbal head comes from the contrast in grammaticality between the examples in (a) and the ones in (b):

(i)   a.   *_Quante òlte/quant_, to fradèl, à-lo proà?!
                ?_Quante òlte/quant_, anca to fradèl, no à-lo proà?!
                'How many times/how long, (also) your brother, (not) has he tried?!'
(ii)   b.   *_Quanta roba/quant_, senza pagar, avé-o magnà?
                ?_Quanta roba/quant_, senza pagar, no avé-o magnà?!
                'How much (stuff), without paying, (not) have you eaten?!'

The examples in (a), where a constituent intervenes between the interrogative _wh_-phrase and the verb, are completely ungrammatical, while the ones in (b), where the sentence, hence the _wh_-phrase, has an exclamative interpretation, are almost acceptable. The exclamative reading of the examples in (b) is determined by the presence of the negative marker _no_, which is in this case an instance of _expletive negation_, whose distribution and interpretive import in exclamatives has been described by Benincà (1996); more recently, Portner and Zanuttini (1996, 1997) claim that the clitic negative marker _no_ which appears in both exclamatives and interrogatives in Paduan, in addition to contributing the ordinary meaning of negation, triggers a characteristic scalar implicature to the effect that an exclamative sentence like the one reported in (iii) implicates that he told him all sorts of unexpected things and that whatever he didn't tell him must be so unlikely or implausible that it hardly deserves consideration:

(iii)   _Cossa_ no ghe dise-lo!
                'What he's telling him!'

So, despite the fact that _no_ is here semantically a true negation, by implicating that only the lowest-ranked proposition is true, the sentence indicates that he is telling him almost everything, thus masking the negative force of _no_. Portner and Zanuttini also provide a syntactic representation of exclamatives, arguing that they contain two levels of CP-structure, the higher of which contains an exclamative operator, while the head of the lower CP projection may be filled by a complementizer, by the cluster formed by negation and verb, or by a generic operator; in exclamatives the _wh_-phrase occurs in the higher specifier in the syntax (leaving room for another phrase in the lower specifier), while in questions the _wh_-phrase occupies the lower specifier and the verb raises to the corresponding head position.

7. I would like to suggest, without arguing for it, that complex exclamative _wh_-phrases are in fact left dislocated; evidence that complex constituents, differently from simple ones, are amenable to an analysis in terms of dislocation is provided by Rizzi (1998) concerning the possibility of left dislocating (complex vs. simple) negative quantifiers in Italian (as exemplified in (i) and by Ordóñez 1996) concerning the obligatoriness of inversion with (complex vs simple) _wh_-phrases in Spanish (as shown in (ii)):

(i)   a.   _Nessuno di questi ragazzi_ lo conosco veramente bene.
                'no one of these boys (I) cl-know really well'
        b.   *_Nessuno_ l'ho visto.
                'no one (I) cl-have seen'
(ii)   a.   _En qué lugar_ tus amigos se divorciaron?
        b.   *_Donde_ tus amigos se divorciaron?
                'in which place/where your friends got divorced'

These data provide further support to our hypothesis that the internal structure of a constituent may play a major role in determining its distribution; more generally, these contrasts reveal that language, hence grammar, is probably more structure-sensitive than is usually assumed, even in the generative framework.

8. The hypothesis that the verbal head displaying inversion heads the projection whose specifier hosts interrogative *wh*-phrases while the complementizer heads the one whose specifier hosts exclamative *wh*-phrases (that is, the implicit assumption that while inversion is intrinsically tied to an interrogative reading, the presence of the complementizer marks the exclamative reading) gains support from a recent proposal put forth by Portner and Zanuttini (1998). Analyzing Paduan, they investigate the relevance of the interaction between the elements occupying the specifier and the head of a CP projection in determining the clause type. They observe that when the *wh*-phrase contains a noun, the presence of the complementizer *che* in C° gives rise to an exclamative, regardless of whether the *wh*-word is *che* or *quanto*, while inversion always gives rise to a question (as shown, respectively, in (i) and (ii)):

(i)   a.   [*Che libro*] [*che*] te lezi!
             'What a book you are reading!'
      b.   [*Quanto late*] [*che*] te ghè comprà!
             'How much milk you bought!'
(ii) a.   [*Che libro*] [*lezi-to*]?
             'What book are you reading?'
      b.   [*Quanto late*] [*ghe-to*] comprà?
             'how much milk did you buy?'

When the *wh*-element is followed by an adjective, *quanto* is associated with a question and so is incompatible with the complementizer *che*, which marks an exclamative; on the contrary, the *wh*-word *che*, being associated with an exclamative, is incompatible with inversion, which marks a question; so, when the *wh*-phrase is introduced by *che*, the presence of the complementizer yields an exclamative, while inversion gives rise to ungrammaticality:

(iii) a.   [*Che bravo*] [*che*] te si!
       b.   *[*Che bravo*] [*si-to*]!
             'How good you are!'

With *quanto*, the overt complementizer in ungrammatical, while inversion yields a question:

(iv)   a.   *[*Quanto belo*] [*che*] te si!
       b.   [*Quanto belo*] [*si-to*]?
             'How beautiful are you?'

Concerning examples involving the negative morpheme *no* and inversion in C°, Portner and Zanuttini (1998) propose that the clause type is determined in this case by the lexical material hosted in the specifier position.

It remains to be seen whether a sentence like (iv.b) can be considered as a question from the interpretive/pragmatic point of view as well. As pointed out by Benincà (1995), the possible coincidence of the linguistic act and the identity of the relevant lexical elements makes it sometimes very difficult to distinguish clearly between the exclamative and the interrogative clausal type; an intermediate position is occupied, according to Benincà, by so-called "rhetorical questions" whose ambiguity can be eliminated in the spoken language through different intonation (which decreases constantly in the exclamative reading, while in the interrogative one the flat intonational curve undergoes a sudden lowering after the last stressed syllable).

9. I assume here that the inflected verb raises to the same head position in main interrogatives and exclamatives; under this assumption, following Benincà's claim that exclamatives with inversion have to be analyzed syntactically as interrogatives, one could propose that the class of *wh*-phrases appearing in situ in interrogatives selects the exclamative reading by raising to the specifier position corresponding to the head occupied by the inflected verb (the same specifier position that we assume to be occupied by the abstract *wh*-operator in interrogatives). I discard this alternative interpretation of the data which, besides being conceptually less attractive, doesn't account either for the fact that we never have *wh*-phrases in situ in main exclamatives or for the particular reading associated with the structure with inversion between verb and subject clitic pronoun.

References

Benincà, P. (1995) "Il tipo esclamativo," in L. Renzi, G. Salvi, and A. Cardinaletti (eds.) *Grande grammatica di consultazione*, vol. 3, pp. 127–152. Bologna: Il Mulino.

Benincà, P. (1996) "La struttura della frase esclamativa alla luce del dialetto padovano," in P. Benincà, G. Cinque, T. De Mauro, and N. Vincent (eds.) *Italiano e dialetti nel tempo. Saggi di grammatica per Giulio C. Lepschy*, pp. 23–43. Rome: Bulzoni.

Kayne, R. S. (1994) *The Antisymmetry of Syntax*. Cambridge, Mass.: MIT Press.

Munaro, N. (1997) "Proprietà strutturali e distribuzionali dei sintagmi interrogativi in alcuni dialetti italiani settentrionali." Ph.D. thesis, University of Padua.

Munaro, N. (1998a) "L'evoluzione del sintagma interrogativo *che cosa* nei dialetti veneti settentrionali," in P. Ramat and E. Roma (eds.) *Sintassi storica: Atti del XXX Congresso Internazionale della SLI*, pp. 267–292. Rome: Bulzoni.

Munaro, N. (1998b) "*Wh*-in situ in the Northern Italian Dialects," in O. Fullana and F. Roca (eds.) *Studies on the Syntax of Central Romance Languages*, pp.189–212. Col.leció 'Diversitas' 5: Universitat de Girona.

Ordóñez, F. (1996) "The Inversion Construction in Interrogatives in Spanish and Catalan," Ms., Graduate Center, City University of New York.

Poletto, C. (2000) *The Higher Functional Field: Evidence from the Northern Italian Dialects*. New York: Oxford University Press.

Portner, P. and R. Zanuttini (1996) "The Syntax and Semantics of Scalar Negation: Evidence from Paduan," in K. Kusumoto (ed.) *Proceedings of NELS* 26:257–271. University of Massachusetts, Amherst : GLSA.

Portner, P. and R. Zanuttini (1997) "Negation and the Structure of Exclamatives," talk given at the University of Padua.

Portner, P. and R. Zanuttini (1998) "The Interdependence of Specifier and Head of CP," talk given at the University of Padua.

Rizzi, L. (1998) "The Fine Structure of the Left Periphery," in P. Benincà and G. Salvi (eds.) *Romance Syntax*, pp. 112–158 (Budapest Studies in Romance Linguistics). Budapest: L. Eötvös University.

Zamparelli, R. (1996) "The Syntax and Semantics of Adjectives and Measure Phrases," talk given at the *XXII Incontro di Grammatica Generativa* (Bergamo, February 22–24 1996).

7

Cosa ch'a l'é sta storia?
The Interaction of Pragmatics and Syntax in the Development of WH-Interrogatives with Overt Complementizer in Piedmontese

Mair Parry

1. Introduction

Data from the *Atlante Sintattico dell'Italia Settentrionale* analyzed in Poletto and Vanelli (1995) reveal that in a number of northern Italian dialect areas, partial or WH-interrogatives are introduced by the complementizer *che* in addition to the WH-phrase (henceforth [WH+*che*]), as in the above quotation from a nineteenth century play in Piedmontese (*Cichin-a*, p. 20). *ASIS* questionnaire replies show the phenomenon occurring in both main and subordinate clauses in Piedmontese, Swiss-Lombard dialects of the Lugano area (but not Locarno); some Alpine Lombard varieties; and some Romagnolo, Veneto, and Friulian varieties; but only in subordinate clauses in Trentino and not at all in most Ligurian, Emilian, and Lombard dialects. The fact that *che* is a subordinating complementizer[1] and that [WH+*che*] is not found anywhere in main interrogatives exclusively, suggests to the authors that such structures emerged in main clauses as "copies" of the subordinating constructions: "sembra dunque che la presenza dei due introduttori anche nelle interrogative indipendenti sia un caso di 'copia della struttura delle subordinate" (Poletto and Vanelli 1995:152, 157). A diachronic study of interrogatives and a detailed analysis of [WH+*che*] were outside the scope of their excellent overview of interrogative structures in northern Italian dialects, especially since more detailed data than those available were required.

In an attempt to shed some light on the development and spread of [Wh+*che*] structures in one of the areas most affected by the phenomenon, namely Piedmontese, this study examines their distribution and use in selected texts dating from the period of expansion (late eighteenth and nineteenth centuries). It considers their emergence in both main and subordinate clauses and examines in particular the hypothesis that the use of [WH+*che*] in the former is simply an extension of use in the latter. Section 2 describes the range of interrogative structures available in today's dialects; section 3 presents the diachronic data, which are discussed in section 4. Here it will be shown that the "extra" *che* is first attested not in subordinate clauses but in exclamative constructions, whose binary informational structure is highlighted by the use of *che* as a foregrounding device. It is argued that as a result of semantic, syntactic, and morphological links between exclamatives on the one hand and interrogative and relative clauses on the other, such exclamatives contributed to the spread of *che* to interrogatives. Section 5 offers a brief syntactic explanation in support of this diachronic interpretation, and the conclusion follows in section 6.

2. WH-interrogatives in modern Piedmontese

WH-interrogatives present a presupposition involving a variable (x) whose value is sought through the interrogative pronoun.[2] In Piedmontese, as in many other languages, questions that focus on a particular constituent place the interrogative or WH-phrase in clause initial position.[3]

2.1 Main clauses

Three different construction types, however, are commonly found in root interrogatives, their distribution depending on the particular variety of Piedmontese (Parry 1997):

1. WH-phrase followed by declarative order of subject clitic – verb (henceforth [WH+verb]):

(1)   Chi   a   parla?   (Brero and Bertodatti 1988:73)
         who   3scl   speaks
         'Who speaks?'

(2)   Dont   a   ven   cost'uva?   (ibid. 81)
         from-where   3scl   comes   this grape
         'Where do these grapes come from?'

2. WH-phrase followed by "inversion" of verb and subject clitic pronoun[4] [WH+inv.]:

(3) Rueglio:

         Chi   mängg-lo   sì?
         who   eats-3$_{scl}$ here
         'Who eats here?'

(4) Rueglio:

> Co   ha-l   dì   Marco?
> *what   has-3sg.$_{scl}$ said   Marco*
> 'What has Marco said?'

In standard, literary, Piedmontese based on the dialect of Turin, and in certain other conservative varieties a subject pronoun appears proclitically as well as enclitically:

(5)   Còs   a   fan-lo, lor?   (Brero and Bertodatti 1988:73)
             what 3$_{scl}$ do-3$_{scl}$, they
             'What do they do?'

(6) Mondovì:

> Landa   i   deuv-le   indé?
> *where 1$_{scl}$ must-1sg. go?*
> 'Where must I go?'

   3. WH-phrase+*che* followed by declarative word order [WH+*che*]:

(7)   Còsa   **ch'**it   veule?   (Brero and Bertodatti 1988:82)
             what that-2sg.$_{scl}$ want?
             'What do you want?'

(8)   Chi   **ch'**a-i   ven?   (ibid. 82)
             who   that-there comes?
             'Who is coming?'

(9) Agliano:

> Perché **ch'**i   veuro parlete?
> *why   that-3pl.$_{scl}$ wish to-speak-to-you?'*
> 'Why do they wish to speak to you?'

   4. The logical possibility WH-phrase+*che* followed by inversion
      (WH+*che*+inv.) is not normally found but is sporadically attested in
      the province of Turin:

(10)   Còsa   **ch'**it   **l'has-to**   fàit?   (ASIS)
             what that-2sg.$_{scl}$ scl have-2sg.$_{scl}$ done
             'What have you done?'

(11)   Anté   **ch'**a   **va-lo?**   (Poletto and Vanelli 1995:153)
             where that-3$_{scl}$ goes-3$_{scl}$
             'Where is he going?'

This combination appears to contravene a general prohibition on inversion in the presence of an overt complementizer (Radford 1988:416; Roberts 1997:37–38). Within generative theory this ban is seen to derive from the fact that a complementizer blocks the movement of the verb to its "inverted" position, precisely that of the complementizer.[5]

In addition to the above three "basic" interrogative structures, clefting may be used with each type:

[WH+verb]
(12) Biellese:
> Chi a l'é ch'a l'ha nen giugà?
> 'Who is it that hasn't played?'

[WH+inv.]
(13) Rueglio:
> Quand é-lo ch'i l'eun vista?
> 'When was it we last saw her?'

[WH+che]
(14) Bajo Dora:
> Chi ch'a l'é ch'a l'ha mangià sì?
> 'Who is it who ate here?'

Clefting appears to be compulsory with some 'which' type interrogatives unusually formed from the distal demonstrative:

(15)   Cole   ch'a   son le   cite   ch'it   conòsse?
        those   that-3$_{scl}$ are the   girls   that-2sg.$_{scl}$ know
        'Which are the girls you know?'

The erstwhile demonstrative cannot be followed directly by the noun to which it refers, but with the verb 'to be' we have simply:

(16)   Col   ch'a   l'é   to   can?
        that that-3$_{scl}$ $_{scl}$is   your dog
        ' Which is your dog?'[6]

The modern dialects show the following distribution:

1. Preservation of [WH+inv.] (single enclitic pronoun) in a few conservative dialects, e.g. Rueglio.

2. [WH+inv.] (proclitic and enclitic pronouns) is also a relatively conservative structure— it is found in southern Piedmontese, e.g. Mondovì and also preserved in the literary standard.

3. [WH+che] characterizes most informal varieties.

4. [WH+verb] seems to be gaining ground, probably due to Italian influence.

The availability in the Piedmontese repertoire of more than one interrogative construction (e.g., in the standard and in the local variety) allows for pragmatic differentiation. For instance, in Oglianico the use of the traditional [WH+inv.] nowadays conveys surprise in contrast to the "normal" [WH+*che*]:

(17) Oglianico:

> Qué ch'et fè?
> *what that-2sg.$_{scl}$ do?*

(18) Oglianico:

> Qué   fè-të?[7]
> *what   do-2sg.$_{scl}$?*
> (+ surprise = 'What on earth are you doing?)

The spread of [WH+*che*] to root interrogatives may be seen as a way to avoid inversion (the more economical option since the unmarked word order is retained), but inversion may persist in yes-no interrogatives, which would otherwise have no explicit morphosyntactic interrogative marker—for example, in the dialects of Agliano and Oglianico.

2.2 Subordinate clauses

Less variation is found in WH-subordinate clauses since interrogative inversion is not available. Subordinate clauses may be introduced by a WH-phrase only [WH+verb]:

(19)   Am   piasrìa   savèj   **còsa** it   veule. (Brero 1976:204)
        3$_{scl}$-me should-please to know   what   2$_{scl}$ want

More usually, it may be introduced by a WH-phrase followed by the complementizer [WH+*che*]:

(20)   I'm   ciamo **còsa** ch'a   veussa.   (ibid. 204)
        1$_{scl}$ refl ask   what that-3$_{scl}$ wants

(21) Rueglio:

> Dimi   **chi** ch'a-i   ven-a staseira.
> *tell-me who   that-3$_{scl}$-loc comes tonight*

3. A diachronic analysis of WH-interrogatives

The three basic interrogative types described above represent different stages of development (Parry 1997), which do not correspond to the order in which they were exemplified in section 2. The type found in early Piedmontese texts is [WH+inv.] with single enclitic pronoun; the emergence of inverted structures with proclitic and enclitic subject pronouns dates from the end of the eighteenth century (in Turinese), as do [WH+*che*] structures, which preclude inversion; [WH+verb] may already be found in nineteenth century texts.[8] For the study of the emergence and diffusion of [WH+*che*], theatrical texts were selected for analysis, since direct exchanges between characters were likely to contain a higher proportion of questions than other literary genres. The texts span roughly a century, from the late eighteenth to the late nineteenth centuries, during which period there appear alternative interrogative structures in place of the traditional [WH+inv.]. Table 7.1 charts the gradual but definite establishment of [WH+*che*] in main clauses (the values relate to percentages of the total number of root interrogatives, rounded to the nearest half decimal).

There is a clear difference between the beginning and end of our period with regard to the respective frequency of [WH −*che*] and [WH+*che*]; the intervening years show a rather uneven rise until the 1880s in the use of the latter, but this is not unexpected when one takes into account the many variables involved (e.g., the plays are written by different authors, speaking different local dialects). The slow beginnings of the innovation, followed by rapid spread during the 1880s (and 1870s?), is typical of the S-curve model of linguistic change with its slow-quick-

TABLE 7.1 Establishment of [WH+*che*] in main clauses

Title of play + date	WH−*che*[9](%)	WH+*che*(%)	WH cleft(%)
Ël nodar onorà, 1774–1779	97	1.5	1.5
Le ridicole illusioni, c. 1800	83	2	15
La festa dla pignata, 1804	88	0	12
La Cichin-a 'd Moncalé, c. 1850	63.5	23.5	13
Guera o pas, 1859	67	22.5	10.5
Marioma Clarin, c. 1860	83	16	1
Le miserie 'd Monssù Travet, 1863	61	34	5
Un bacan spiritual, 1867	75	23.5	1.5
'L cotel, c. 1869	75	22	3
I fastidi d'un grand om, 1881	34	57.5	8.5
Ij mal nutrì, 1886	36.5	61.5	2

quick-slow progression. Also, the content, tone, and characters of the plays differ, so that it is possible that sociolinguistic and pragmatic variables such as different levels of formality or various types of presupposition or emotional involvement will govern the choice of structure. The possibility that pragmatic and discourse factors govern the type of interrogative structure used is of crucial concern for our investigation into the reasons for the change, since they may suggest refinements to the hypothesis that [WH+che] structures in main clauses, which do not normally contain overt complementizers, emerged simply as "copies" of subordinate structures.

The texts provide far fewer examples of embedded interrogatives, as may be seen in table 7.2, which also records the distribution of [WH+verb] and [WH+che] in the embedded clauses. Clefting, which involves particular focusing on the WH-element, is rare in subordinate clauses. The small number of tokens renders the calculation of percentages for the purposes of comparison unreliable, but one may note that, except in *Le miserie 'd Monssù Travet*, the incidence of the complementizer in embedded interrogatives appears not significantly higher than in main clauses, until the last decades (cf. table 7.1).

TABLE 7.2 Distribution of [WH+verb] and [WH+che] in embedded clauses

Title of play + date	Total Main	Total Sub.	Subord. WH+verb	Subord. WH+che	Subord. cleft
Ël nodar onorà, 1774-79	61	17	16 (94%)	1 (6%)	0
Le ridicole illusioni, c. 1800	100	14	12 (86%)	0	2 (14%)
La festa dla pignata, 1804	56	18	18 (100%)	0	0
La Cichin-a 'd M., c. 1850	47	3	2 (67%)	1 (33%)	0
Guera o pas, 1859	76	5	3 (60%)	2 (40%)	0
Marioma Clarin, c. 1860	99	12	9 (75%)	3 (25%)	0
Le miserie 'd M. T., 1863	168	28	1 (4%)	25 (89%)	2 (7%) +che
Un bacan spiritual, 1867	64	14	10 (71%)	4 (29%)	0
'L cotel, c. 1869	36	6	4 (67%)	2 (33%)	0
I fastidi d'un grand om, 1881	94	18	3 (17%)	15 (83%)	0
Ij mal nutrì, 1886	91	5	1 (20%)	4 (80%)	0

3.1 Exclamatives, absolute relatives, and adverbial subordinate clauses

Before proceeding to discuss the significance of the above statistics for the diffusion of [WH+*che*], let us consider briefly other relevant types of structures and functions—exclamatives, headless relatives, and adverbial subordinate clauses.

3.1.1 Exclamatives

Exclamatives that focus on one constituent rather than on the whole sentence are introduced by elements that have the same lexical form as interrogatives (*che, quant,* etc.) Modern informal Italian of the northern variety usually shows the complementizer *che* appearing after the focused nominal or adjective preceded by the sentence-initial modifier *che*:

(22)   Che stanco che sarà!
         'How tired (that) he must be!'

(23)   Che bravo professore che è!   (Benincà 1995:138)
         'What a good teacher (that) he is!'

Northern varieties may also insert *che* after phrases introduced by *quanto:*

(24)   Quanta fatica (che) ho fatto!   (ibid. 137–139)
         'What an effort (that) I've made!'

In the Paduan dialect the complementizer is compulsory in both contexts:

(25)   Che libro che te lezi!   (Benincà 1996:31)
         'What sort of book (that) you are reading!'

(26)   Quanti pomi che te ghe comprà!
         'How many apples (that) you have bought!'   (ibid.)

In Piedmontese the complementizer *che* already features in this context by the period under consideration, and it is significant that in an earlier play, *Il conte Pioletto*, (end seventeenth century, but not printed till 1784), exclamative WH-structures involving a NP may have an overt complementizer, whereas all WH interrogatives have the traditional form [WH+inv]:[10]

(27)   O, **ch'bel**   giovnôt, /
         oh, what fine   youth   /

         Cha   ven   da   nôstra ca!   (*Il conte Pioletto*, 14)
         that-3$_{scl}$ comes from our   house

(28)   **Quante**   cose, **ch'ij**   direu!   (ibid., 61)
         how-many   things that-1$_{scl}$ to him will-say

In our two earliest texts, in which the incidence of [WH+*che*] in root and embedded interrogatives is extremely low or non-existent, we find that exclamatives of the [*che, quant*+NP] type with an overt complementizer are as frequent as those without:

(29)   **Che** bel giovnet **ch'a** l'é!   (*Ël nodar onorà*, p. 88)
        'What (a) handsome young man (that) he is!'

(30)   **Che** brav òm **ch'a** l'é mai nòstr Curà 'd campagna! (*Le rid. ill.* p. 82)
        'What a fine fellow (that) our country parson is!'

(31)   **Quante** bele còse **ch'a** veul feme vëdde sur Cont!   (ibid., 57)
        'How many lovely things (that) you want to make me see, (sir) Count!'

In addition to WH-structures, our texts also display two other types of exclamative: the first, also found in *Il Conte Pioletto,* is formed by demonstratives (or personal pronouns deriving from a demonstrative) followed by *che*[11] introducing a sentential complement:

(32)   O   costa   si,   **ch'a** l'é   na brava fia.   (*Il conte Pioletto*, p. 56)
        *oh this-one yes that-3*_{scl scl}*is a good girl*
        'Oh, this one is a good girl!'

(33)   Chila **ch'a** 'l'é   fin-a!   (*Marioma Clarin*, p. 97)
        *she   that-3*_{scl scl} *is refined*
        '*You* (polite) really are refined!' (sarcasm)

(34)   Côl   **ch'a** l'é   un toch d'un aso!   (*I fastidi*, p. 148)
        *that (one) that3*_{scl scl} *is a bit of an ass*
        '*He* really is a bit of an ass!'

The second focalizes a NP which is followed by what seems to be a relative clause introduced by *che*:[12]

(35)   E   cola Brigida c'a l'é ancora nen tornà d'an piassa!   (Le Miserie,
        *and that B.   that-3*_{scl scl} *is still not returned from in square*   p. 59)
        'And (that) Brigida who has still not returned from the square!'

(36)   O   lò   ch'i   sent!   (*Un bacan spiritual*, p. 17)
        oh that that I hear
        'What's this I hear?' (surprise)

3.1.2 Relative clauses

The last form mentioned, *lò(n)*[13] *che,* is found today in several Piedmontese dialects (e.g., Agliano, Turin) in main clauses as an interrogative, meaning 'what?' However, it does not have that function in *Un bacan spiritual* (instead *cosa* (*che*) is used) or in the other plays, except in embedded interrogatives. Its origin is presumably the relative construction:

(37)   Sevo   lòn   ch'i   veuj   fé?   (*Ël nodar onorà*, p. 57)
          know-you   that   that-1$_{scl}$ wish (1sg.) to-do
          'Do you know what I wish to do?'

The use of *lò(n) che* in root interrogatives may thus derive from exclamative usage and/or embedded interrogatives.

This brings us to other relative forms which are formally identical to interrogatives—headless relatives; these also begin to show overt complementizers about the middle of the period under examination:

(38)   Chi   ch'a   dipend nen da   chila   (*Guera o pas*, p. 27)
          whoever   that-3$_{scl}$ depends neg from   you (polite)
          'Whoever is not dependent on you'

(39)   A chi   ch'a-j   pias   nen parèj (*Mar. Clarin* p. 100)
          for whoever that-3$_{scl}$ to-them pleases   neg thus
          'For whoever does not like this.'

3.1.3 Adverbial clauses

In modern Piedmontese varieties, conjunctions such as *quand* 'when', *com* 'as', and *mentre* 'while' are regularly followed by the subordinate complementizer *che*. Again, it is during the period examined here that *che* is generalized as a marker of subordination. In our two earliest texts, however, the phenomenon is not attested except in the case of causal *përché:*

(40)   Përché ch'i son bon patriòt   (*Le ridicole illusioni*, p. 47)[14]
          'Because I'm a good patriot.'

4. Discussion of the diachronic data

4.1 The "copying" or extension hypothesis

It will be recalled that the hypothesis that *che* in root interrogatives is an extension of its use in subordinate clauses rests on the fact that in none of the dialects represented in the *ASIS* data was [WH+*che*] found in main clauses unless it was also attested in subordinate clauses. The spread of *che* in embedded interrogative clauses is linked by Poletto and Vanelli (1995) to its generalization in other embedded clauses: adverbial clauses of time and cause introduced by conjunctions that originally had no *che* element, but which performed the double role of adverb and complementizer. From a functional point of view it can be argued that a tendency in informal discourse toward a separation of functions and a one-to-one matching of form and function caused the spread of the complementizer *che* as a general marker of subordination. This context then provided the model for the structure of main clauses. Support for their extension-to-main-clauses hypothesis is also found in the fact that the distribution of *che* among the WH-phrases in the various dialects and the mechanism by which it spreads in main clauses replicates that found in subordinate clauses. That is, in both types of clause an implicational hierarchy is identified: if the complementizer occurs with only one WH-phrase, this will be the [+human] pronoun *chi*.[16]

The extension hypothesis may explain interrogative forms deriving from demonstratives: *lò(n) che* 'what' and *col che* 'which' (see (37) and (15)–(16)), whose original function as "head + restrictive relative clause" could be reinterpreted as a subordinate interrogative:

(41)   Dime   lòn / col   ch'it   veule.
           tell me   that / that one that you want

Yet certain aspects of the diffusion of *che* in main interrogatives suggest that it does not depend solely on a mechanical extension from subordinates:

1. If the influence of subordinate or indirect interrogatives is the decisive factor, one might expect such structures to reveal from the start a far higher incidence of *che* than root interrogatives and also perhaps to occur more frequently in the plays analyzed. Instead, subordinate clauses lacking *che* are found in close proximity to main interrogatives with *che*, as in:

(42)   Costa l'e na bela landa! . . . 'S peullo saveisse còsa l'é sta storia . . .
           I veuj saveilo. **Còs ch'**a l'é sta malinconìa? Còsa ch'a son ste
           lacrime? (*La Cichin-a 'd Moncalé*, p. 11)
           'This is a fine story! . . . Can one know what it's all about . . . I want
           to know (it). What (that) is this melancholy? What (that) are
           these tears?'

2. The extension of the complementizer *che* from subordinate to main clause appears to contradict the very reason for the generalization of *che* in the subordinate clause—namely, as a marker of complementation or subordination. However, one could perhaps argue that, as in the case of Italian polite imperatives formed with the subjunctive, structures used for indirect questions (implying elliptical main verbs of doubt or command) came to be used in *particular pragmatic circumstances.*

3. The fact that the mechanism of the change appears identical—the process seems to affect initially, at least in the modern dialects (see n. 15), [+human] *chi* in main and subordinate clause does not necessarily confirm the extension hypothesis, since the association of *che* with one particular interrogative pronoun suggests that there is more to the spread of *che* thanexplicitly marking subordination.

It is thus worth investigating other factors that may have contributed to the emergence of *che* in root interrogatives.

4.2 A pragmatic approach

The Piedmontese diachronic data in section 3 suggest that other clause-types, closely related to interrogatives both structurally and semantically, may have contributed to the appearance of *che* in interrogatives.

4.2.1 Exclamatives

The first structures to show an overt complementizer in contexts where previously none appeared are exclamatives and interrogatives used as exclamatives. Already in *Il Conte Pioletto,* as we saw in (28), root exclamatives have lost the characteristic earlier inversion seen, for example, in farces by G. G. Alione (early sixteenth century and written in a Monferrino variety):

(43)   Quant   affan   eu-i   pôrtà   per vôi!   (Bottasso 1953:
        how much trouble have-1sg.$_{scl}$ carried for you   220, 600)
        'How much suffering have I endured for you!

(44)   Côm   sogn-i   mai reid an d'la schina!   (ibid., 55, 452)
        how   am-1sg.$_{scl}$ ever stiff in the back
        'How stiff my back is!

Compare the late-eighteenth-century structures:

(45)   quante   brute còse a-s   descreuvo!   (*Le rid. ill.,* p. 64)
        how many ugly things 3$_{scl}$-refl discover

(46)   Oidé   com a l'é   vej e   cataros!   (*Ël nodar onorà*, p. 29)
        oh dear, how   3$_{scl\ scl}$ is old and full of catarrh

Inversion appears not to have been a feature of exclamatives introduced by *che*+NP, which may be considered "true" exclamatives, as opposed to the above interrogative structures used for exclamative purposes in:

(47)   early-sixteenth-century, Alione

        Che   bella   prôvisiôn t'hai   fag.   (Bottasso 1953: 197, 584)
        what   fine   provision 2$_{scl}$ have made

In modern Paduan main clauses the lack of inversion distinguishes "true" exclamatives from interrogatives used for the illocutionary purpose of exclamation (Portner and Zanuttini 1998:18–21).[16] As far as WH-exclamatives are concerned, we have seen that in Piedmontese it is the *che/quanto* + NP structures which first witness the use of the complementizer (see (27)–(28)), so that in our plays, alongside the earlier type seen in (45) and (48):

(48)   Che   gòj sarà   la mia!   (*Ël nodar onorà* p. 38)
        what   joy will-be   the mine

We find:

(49)   quanti   past   **ch'** j'eu   mangiaje.   (*Le rid. ill.*, p. 44)
          how -many meals that-1$_{scl}$ have eaten there

(50)   Oh   che   gòj   **ch'a** l'é   la   mia!   (*Ël nodar onorà*, p. 85)
          oh   what   joy   that-3$_{scl\ scl}$ is   the   mine

Che/quanto+NP are structures that can be used as verbless or elliptical exclamatives, e.g. *Che goj! Che bel giovnet!*.[17] The appearance of the complementizer may thus be attributable to a tendency to add the presuppositional clause as an afterthought, thus making explicit the binary pragmatic structure of the exclamative: Focus – Presupposition.[18] The *che* clause "anchors" the focused constituent to the actual situation or to the previous discourse, a function typically associated with relative clauses (Fox and Thompson 1990), as in the exclamative type focalizing a non-WH NP; consider (35) and (51):

(51)   Oh quàder ch'am   gava   le   lacrime!   (*Le rid. ill.*, p. 71)
          oh picture that-3$_{scl}$ (from) me   draws the tears

Schachter (1973) argues that the striking structural similarities observed between cleft and relative constructions in many unrelated languages may be ascribed to a shared semantic/pragmatic property, that of foregrounding a part of the proposition.[19] This property is, of course, also shared by exclamatives and WH-interrogatives. It is noteworthy that in all the plays analyzed here [*che/quanto -che*] exclamatives focalize NPs only, although in modern northern Italian varieties exclamative *che* may modify a noun, adjective or adverb (Benincà 1995: 138–139). It is NPs that predominate in verbless exclamatives, so this apparent early restriction to NPs may well be due to the influence of the structure of relative clauses.[20]

4.2.2 Interrogative structures used for exclamation

Surprise or indignation at an unexpected turn of events may be expressed through polite, sarcastic, or irate querying of the "given" situation. If the value of the variable questioned (*x*) is already known, such interrogatives, often characterized by adverbs such as *mai* 'ever' or expletives such as *diao* 'devil', have the illocutionary force of an exclamation rather than a question seeking information:

(52)   Còsa dis-lo   mai!   (*Marioma Clarin*, p. 93)
          what   say-3$_{scl}$ ever
          'What ever are you (polite) saying?!'

But with increasing frequency in the plays examined, this type of exclamation contains an overt complementizer:

(53)   Oh! còsa **ch'i**   disi mai?   (*La Cichin-a 'd Moncalé*, p. 17)
         oh   what   that-2pl.$_{scl}$ say ever
         'Whatever are you saying?' (dismay and fear)

(54)   Ah! Còsa **ch'i**   dëscheurvo!   (ibid., 21)
         oh what   that-1sg.$_{scl}$ discover
         '*What* am I discovering?' (bewilderment and horror as realization
                                                               dawns)

(55)   Ò   bruta cativa! **Përché ch'it**   parli 'd meuiri?   (ibid., 6)
         oh   ugly wretch   why   that-2sg.$_{scl}$ speak of dying

In fact, all eleven [WH+*che*] interrogatives found in *La Cichin-a 'd Moncalé* are
of an exclamatory nature and, moreover, they are all introduced by either *còsa che*
(8) or *përché che* (3), i.e. (prep.) NP+*che*. On examining the three root [WH+*che*]
interrogatives found in the earlier plays, we discover that these, too, are exclamatory
structures containing a NP+*che*:

(56)   **Che ch'i**   son nen stà   mi?   (*Ël nodar onorà*, p. 68)
         what   that 1sg.$_{scl}$ am not been   me
         '*What* have I not been?'

(57)   **Përché ch'it**   has   col sabron?   (*Le ridicole illusioni*, p. 7)
         or-what that-2sg.$_{scl}$ have that sabre
         'Why have you got that sabre?'

         Giuradindonora!
         'For God's sake!'

(58)   **Còsa ch'it**   dije bestiassa?   (ibid., 58)
         what   that-2sg.$_{scl}$ say idiot
         'What are you saying, (you) idiot?'

Also significant is the fact that (56) and (58) are exclaiming about something
which has just been said, a situation rather similar to that of echo questions, which
show the subject clitic – verb order of declaratives and, significantly, the early
appearance of the complementizer:

(59) Cav.:   Dunque, Madama, cosa **pensla**   'd fé?   (*Guera o pas*, p. 28)
              So,   Madam,   what think-you to do?

     Mad.:   Cosa **ch'i penso**   'd fé?
              What that I think   to do?

Thus, our texts reveal that the first interrogatives with *che* show a similar pragmatic
function (expression of surprise) and a similar syntactic structure (NP+*che*) as the
"true" exclamatives examined above. Indeed, sequences such as the following
show how, before *che* becomes generalized, it is the traditional inversion structure
that occurs when an answer is expected, as in the following sequence:

(60)   **Cosa ch'a l'è**   sta scena?   (*Guera o pas*, p. 27)
         what   that-3$_{scl}$ $_{scl}$ is   this scene
         '*What*'s going on?' (rhetorical question)

         Chi ch'a l'a   ciamaje?
         who that-3$_{scl}$ $_{scl}$has called-3$_{IOcl}$?
         '*Who* called you?' (rhetorical question)

         Cosa **veulne** si   drinta?
         what want-$_{scl}$ here inside
         'What do you want in here?'

In the [WH+*che*] structures, as in canonical interrogatives, the WH phrase is moved to initial focus position but is assigned a particular prominence in view of its exclamative nature. Such foregrounding is achieved by means of *che*, following the already discussed model of exclamatives and relatives. A similar effect may be obtained by clefting:

(61)   Òh! Dio mio! **Cos'é-lo ch'**i dije?   (*Cichin-a 'd Moncalé*, p. 18)
         'Oh! My God! What is it that you're saying!' (exclamation of
              surprise and fear)

In fact, it has been suggested that [WH+*che*] interrogative structures are reduced forms of clefts, but given the parallels between them and exclamatives, the appearance of an overt complementizer seems to be structurally justified without having recourse to clefts as an intermediate stage. Instead, both clefts and [WH+*che*] can be considered alternative ways of achieving particular foregrounding in exclamations. Overuse and the law of diminishing returns can then lead to one being used to reinforce the other, for example, in emotional rhetorical questions:

(62)   E peui **chi ch'a l'é che** a l'avrìa tenù duvert 'l negossi..?   (*I fastidi,*
         'And then who (that) is it that would have kept   p. 157)
             the shop open ...?'

Support for the hypothesis that interrogative [WH+*che*] structures occur first in pragmatically marked contexts comes from another area of northern Italy: Poletto (1997:78–79) finds [WH+*che*] restricted in certain Friulian dialects to expressions of disappointment or surprise (a reaction therefore to a supposition), where the verb is in the subjunctive and the equivalent Italian sentence would contain *mai* 'ever' after the finite verb:

(63)   [du'la k a l   'vedi mi'tu:t   kel 'libri] (Friul.)
         where that3$_{scl}$ $_{scl}$have put   that book
         'Where on earth can he have put that book?'
         (It.: Dove avrà mai messo quel libro?)

4.2.3 Interrogative structures used for exclamation and eliciting information

The same structures can, of course, be used for emotional reactions which also seek enlightenment: these contain "real" questions since the value of x is actually not known. Individual sentences may be ambiguous between a question and an exclamation, but in context their function is usually clear:

(64)   **Cosa ch'i**   veule voi?   (*Marioma Clarin*, p. 88)
          what   that-2pl.$_{scl}$ *want   you*
          'What on earth do *you* want?' (surprise and annoyance)

(65)   **Chi   ch'a l'ha**   ciamalo   chiel?   (ibid., 126)
          who   that-3$_{scl\ scl}$ *has   called-3*$_{ocl}$ *you (polite)*
          'Who on earth called *you*?' (surprise and annoyance)

High frequency of use of pragmatically marked structures eventually leads to diminished impact (cf. the well-known case of reinforced negation and "Jespersen's cycle") and as the new forms replace the earlier structures, grammaticalization ensues.

4.2.4 Headless relatives

The structural parallelism with relative clauses has been noted on several occasions. In my corpus the first examples of *che* following a headless relative comes from *La Cichin-a:*

(66)   E   ch'a-i   ven-a **chi ch'a**   veul...   (*La Cichin-a*, p. 30)
          and that-3$_{scl}$ *loc come who that-3*$_{scl}$ *wants*
          'And let whoever wants to come, come...'

A tendency to substitute analytic for synthetic structures is characteristic of the colloquial language—as in the case of the adverbial subordinate clauses, the use of *che* here separates two functions previously combined in one form and could have been encouraged by the pattern found in synonymous "headed" relative constructions involving the distal demonstrative and *che,* e.g. *côl ch'a parla* 'that (one) who 3scl talks'. Such structures may well have encouraged the spread of *che* in interrogatives, given the semantic and formal overlapping of relative and interrogative pronouns. In a relative structure such as (67), it is not difficult to see a link with an understood question, 'Who will lose out?'

(67)   A la fin chi ch'a-j giontrà i saroma sempre noi.   (*Mar. Clarin*, p. 73)
          'In the end those who (lit.: who that) lose out will always be us.'

4.2.5 The chronological priority of interrogative chi che

Poletto and Vanelli (1995) note that the spread of *che* in interrogatives appears to start with *chi* 'who', but our textual analysis does not confirm such chronological

TABLE 7.3 Comparison of *chi* and *cosa*

Title of play + date	chi che	chi (chi sa)	*chi* cleft	*cosa* che	*cosa*	*cosa* cleft
La Cichin-a, c.1850	0	7 (2)	2	8	14	2
Guera o pas, 1859	5	4 (4)	1	8	25	4
Marioma Clarin, c. 1860	13	6 (5)	1	3	58	0

priority for Piedmontese. The number of tokens overall is admittedly not high. A bias in favor of using the complementizer with *chi*, however, does seem to emerge in the mid nineteenth century, as table 7.3 illustrates. Discounting the instances of *chi sa*, which represents a fossilized expression (figures in parentheses, also included in the totals for simple *chi*), one obtains an almost overwhelming use of *chi che* in two of the plays, compared to a far less frequent use of *cosa che*.

As to the reason for this preference, one might appeal to the animacy hierarchy and speculate that just as human beings (especially agents) tend to become the topics of discourse and therefore grammatical subjects as a result of the essential egocentricity of humans, so salience explains the greater prominence afforded to human rather than to other WH-proforms.[21] Also *chi?* may have been influenced by developments affecting headless relative *chi*, but *còsa* does not have this relative function in most Piedmontese varieties (instead, the determiner *lo(n)+che* is used; cf. Italian *ciò che, quello che*).

5. A syntactic note

The pragmatic analysis that has been presented above for the diachronic facts relating to the step-by-step emergence of *che*—which appeared first in exclamatives, then in interrogatives used as exclamatives, and finally in interrogatives presenting direct questions—finds a structural explanation in recent synchronic studies within the generative framework. As Benincà (1996) has demonstrated for Paduan (but her findings have more general relevance), WH-movement produces a particular ordering of the WH-elements within the CP. Tests show that the position occupied by the exclamative phrase is distinct from that occupied by the interrogative one and from left-dislocated elements, the exclamative position being further to the left (or higher in the structure) than the straightforward interrogative elements, so that we have the following sequence (Benincà 1996:41):

(68) /Hang. Topic/ /(Left Disloc.)/ /WH-exclam./ /Left Disloc./ /Wh-inter./[22]

In a detailed synchronic examination of northern Italian dialect data Poletto (2000) argues for a split CP analysis in which distinct functional projections are associated with different pragmatic interpretations of interrogative structures: to the left (or above) the CP associated with straightforward questions she postulates a CP associated with the expression of surprise, and above that a CP associated with modal questions.

Returning to the diachronic facts of Piedmontese, we see that in the traditional form of interrogation, the movement of a WH interrogative element to a focus position in CP was accompanied by raising of the verb to C (producing the familiar "inversion" of the subject clitic and verb). However, verb raising was not a feature of "true" exclamatives (see 4.2.1) or of WH movement in relative clauses (the position occupied by the relative operator is higher than left dislocation).[23] Instead, following the NP head of the relative clause, there was an overt complementizer *che*, which could be interpreted as a WH operator.[24] The early appearance of the complementizer in *che/quanto*+NP exclamatives may thus be attributable to the influence of relative clause structures, which shared with exclamatives the function of foregrounding one part of the sentence. The use of *che* in exclamatives as an explicit marker of foregrounding may have presented itself as a more economical strategy than inversion, thus encouraging its spread. In view of the ordering of WH-elements in CP seen above, it is to be expected that *che* first appeared in the higher position where most saving on movement was to be made—that is, in interrogatives used as exclamatives—and only later in the lowest CP, that associated with direct questions.

6. Conclusion

[WH+*che*] structures represent nowadays the unmarked option for formulating root WH questions in most Piedmontese varieties. It seems plausible, on the basis of Piedmontese data from dramatic texts of the late eighteenth and nineteenth centuries, to attribute their emergence to a process more complex than that of straightforward "copying" of subordinate structures. While the latter doubtless reinforced the use of *che* in main clauses, it is nonetheless more than likely that other factors both pragmatic[25] and syntactic served to initiate this change.

Notes

I am grateful to Kersti Börjars, Alda Rossebastiano, Cecilia Poletto, Rodney Sampson, and Nigel Vincent for valuable discussions and comments during the preparation of this chapter; all shortcomings are naturally mine. My debt to Paola Benincà far exceeds the knowledge gleaned from the works cited in the references—I warmly thank her for her generous encouragement and friendship since we first met at the First Diachronic Generative Syntax conference at York in 1990.

1. Monoclausal, typically modal, constructions involving *che* + subjunctive verb, such as polite imperatives and imprecations, are generally interpreted as being dependent on an elliptical main verb.

2. "An *x*-question is a many-valued function, which presupposes the disjunction of a set of propositions (positive or negative according to the form of the question), each

member of the set differing from the others in that it supplies a different value for the variable' (Lyons 1977:757–758).

3. So-called in situ interrogatives are found in echo questions but are not common in pragmatically unmarked interrogatives in Piedmontese, unlike in colloquial French. The term *in situ* relates to a movement analysis of interrogatives, as in current generative theory: according to this hypothesis, the interrogative element may remain in the position in which it originates in the underlying structure of the sentence (in situ) or, more usually, it moves to the focus, sentence-initial position (more precisely, to the specifier of the Complementizer (Radford 1988:504)). It may, however, be preceded by other topicalized constituents (hanging topics, left-dislocated items) which also move to CP (Benincà 1988:126).

4. Modern Piedmontese has obligatory subject clitics, at least in 2sg., 1pl., and 2pl., but phonetic change and processes of neutralization between the different persons have led to significant morphological differentiation between proclitic and enclitic forms (see Parry 1993).

5. Poletto (2000) accommodates such unusual structures as (10) and (11) by means of a split CP analysis. The fact, however, that these "inversion" structures have a proclitic subject in addition to the enclitic subject may induce a reinterpretation of the second as an affix.

6. In some northern dialects cleft structures are obligatory for interrogatives that relate to the subject (e.g., in central and southern Veneto; Poletto and Vanelli 1995:154–55). Ligurian has similar structures to Pied. *col che*, etc. meaning 'which?' (see Cuneo 1997:31–61).

7. Note that in this pragmatically marked context it is the *traditional* "inversion" structure that is maintained (verb-*scl*) in contrast to the modern type with proclitic and enclitic *scl* found in yes-no questions:

Et   fè-të   queicosa   staseira?
2sg.$_{scl}$ do-2sg.$_{scl}$ something   tonight?

8. This matches a parallel spread of [WH+verb] in the rest of northern Italy (Benincà and Poletto 1997:7).

9. The category [WH minus *che*] includes the two interrogative types, traditional [WH+inv.] and innovative [WH+verb]. It is not always easy, or necessary in our particular study, to distinguish between these two stages, since subject WH elements did not cause inversion originally and they persist in a number of common fossilized phrases such as *chi sa?* Only later when subject clitics occur obligatorily with quantifiers can this phrase be distinguished from *chi sa-lo?* with enclitic subject. Also, the fact that the enclitic 2pl. pronoun became incorporated into several originally monosyllabic verb forms can make it difficult to distinguish between these and "inversion" structures.

10. Except, as noted, in the case of some subject interrogatives, since prior to the generalization of the subject clitic to use with quantifier subjects, no inversion obtained when the subject was interrogated (as in English).

11. This construction recalls Italian exclamatives with *sì*, which are introduced by *che*:

Quello sì che è cretino!
'He's really stupid!'
Quelle sì che sono mamme!
'They are real mothers!'   (Baroni 1997:28)

Here the emphasized *sì* separates the demonstrative from the rest of the sentence introduced by the complementizer. This is rare in the texts analyzed, but in (32) a *sì* intervenes before the *che*; given the strong contrastive focus, this *si* corresponds probably to the equivalent of Italian *sì* 'yes' and is not the homophonous proximate locative adverb. In the Piedmontese plays *sì, nò, o* 'or', as well as focused adverbs, are regularly followed by *che* introducing sentential complements:

(i)　　　Martin, levte da sta ca, o ch' mi it levo la mia protession
　　　　'Martin, take yourself away from this house, or (that) I shall take away
　　　　　　(from you) my protection'　　　　　　(*Le ridicole illusioni*, p. 73)

(ii)　　　Già ch'l é vei
　　　　'Of course (that) it's true!'　　　　　　　　　　(*Ël nodar*, p. 56)

12. See Benincà (1995:134) and Portner and Zanuttini (1998:14) for this type.

13. Pied. *sòn* and *lòn* (with final epenthetic nasals) are, respectively, proximate and distal invariant demonstratives, the latter functioning also as a cataphoric pronoun.

14. In this text 16 of the 30 instances of causal *përché* are followed by the complementizer. The *ché* of *përché* functions here as a cataphoric pronoun, cf. Fr. *parce que*. It may thus seem strange that *përché* is singled out in some modern varieties spoken in Piedmont, Veneto, and Romagna for its lack of a following *che* (Poletto and Vanelli, 1995:149). This may be due to a dialect-specific constraint blocking the repetition of a phonetically identical form (cf. Fr. *j' ai besoin de (*du) fromage*).

15. "È plausibile ritenere che il fenomeno dei due introduttori nelle interrogative indipendenti sia del tutto analogo a quello riscontrato nelle subordinate perché la diffusione dei due introduttori nelle interrogative indipendenti è simile a quanto è stato descritto per le subordinate: se esiste almeno un caso di doppio introduttore, esso si manifesta con il sintagma interrogativo *chi*" (Poletto and Vanelli 1995:152).

16. English WH-exclamatives, unlike interrogatives, also lack inversion (*How nice she is! ~How nice is she?*), and it has been suggested that they represent cases of topicalization and adjunction rather than WH-movement (see Grimshaw 1997:380 for references).

17. See Benincà (1995:143) for a discussion of Italian verbless exclamatives.

18. See Givon (1995:217–218) regarding the rise of cleft and WH-Question constructions.

19. "While the basis for the foregrounding is quite different in the two cases, the foregrounding itself—the divisions of a sentence into a more prominent and a less prominent part—is essentially the same. And so the notion of foregrounding may well be the semantic correlate that we have been seeking for the syntactic property of promotion: the semantic property common to focus and relative constructions" (Schachter 1973:44). The complementizer that follows the subject in main clauses in Occitan (*U òmi qu'abè dus hilhs* 'A man (that) had two sons' (Ronjat 1937:536)) and Welsh "abnormal" sentences (*A Duw a ddywedodd...* 'And God (that) said...' (Gen.1:3, cited by Thorne 1993:347) may also have originated as a foregrounding device. I leave this topic for future research. For a recent foregrounding/promotion analysis of relative clauses, see Kayne (1994:chap. 8).

20. Portner and Zanuttini (1998:17) discuss the ambiguous categorial status (nominal or clausal) of exclamatives introduced by a complex WH-phrase which is an NP, followed

by *che,* such as Paduan:

> Che   libri   che   el leze!
> *what books that scl reads*
> 'The books he reads!'

21. "NPs higher on the inherent salience hierarchy tend to occupy more prominent syntactic positions than NPs lower on it" (Shopen, 1985:288). Munaro (1997:66) notes that in some Bellunese dialects subject interrogatives are always clefts, only the subjects of unaccusative verbs (whose subjects are considered to originate in the underlying object position) may occur in simple inversion structures.

22. See the following examples:

(i)   Che   bel libro, a to   sorela, che i   ghe   ga   regalà!
        what a fine book,to your sister, that they to her have given'
        (Exclam. – Left Disloc.)

(ii)   A to   sorela, che libro vorissi-   to   regalar- ghe?
        to your sister, what book would wish -you to give- to her?
        (Left Disloc. – Interrog.)

23. As can be seen in the following example (Rizzi 1997):

> Un   uomo a cui,   il   premio Nobel, lo   daranno   senz' altro
> *A   man to whom, the Nobel prize, it (they) will-give certainly.*

24. The merging of the relative pronoun *che* with the homophonous complementizer is a complex story; see Middleton (1999).

25. See Schwegler (1988) for the crucial role of pragmatic factors in the development of new strategies for negation.

Sources of diachronic data

Bottasso, Enzo (ed.) (1953) *Giovan Giorgio Alione: L'opera piacevole.* Bologna: Libreria Antiquaria Palmaverde.

Casalis, Carlo (1970) *La Festa dla Pignata ossia Amor e Conveniensse: Comedia 'n tre att e 'n vers piemontèis.* ed. R. Gandolfo. Turin: Centro Studi Piemontesi.

Faldella, Giovanni (1974) *Un bacan spiritual,* ed. Caterina Benazzo. Turin: Centro Studi Piemontesi.

Il Conte Pioletto, Commedia piemontese di Carlo Giambattista Tana. Turin: Briolo (1784); reprinted Turin: Viglongo (1965).

Le ridicole illusioni, un'ignota commedia piemontese dell'età giacobina, ed. Gianrenzo P. Clivio, Turin, Centro Studi Piemontesi, 1969.

Pegemade (1971) *Ël nodar onorà: Commedia piemontese-italiana del secondo Settecento,* ed. Gianrenzo P. Clivio. Turin: Centro Studi Piemontesi.

Teatro in piemontese: Antologia di testi con note storiche e di regia, ed. Massimo Scaglione. Turin: Daniele Piazza Editore, 1982: Federico Garelli, *Guera o pas?* (17–47); Vittorio Bersezio, *Le miserie 'd Monssù Travet* (53–130), Eraldo Baretti, *I fastidi d'un grand om* (133–88); Luigi Pietracqua, *'L Cotel* (193–212); Mario Leoni, *Ij mal nutrì* (250–297).

Toselli, Giovanni and Tommaso Villa (1979) *La Cichin-a 'd Moncalé*, ed. Albina Malerba. Turin: Centro Studi Piemontesi.

Zoppis, Giovanni (1986) *Marioma Clarin—La Neuja—La Vigna*, ed. Gualtiero Rizzi. Turin: Centro Studi Piemontesi.

References

ASIS   "Atlante Sintattico dell'Italia Settentrionale" (unpublished). Padua: Dipartimento di Linguistica dell'Università di Padova, Centro di Dialettologia del Consiglio Nazionale delle Ricerche.

Baroni, F. (1997) *Il sonno se n'è andato*. Padua: Unipress.

Battye, A. and M.-A. Hintze (1992) *The French Language Today*. London: Routledge.

Benincà, P. (1988) "L'ordine degli elementi della frase," in L. Renzi (ed.), *Grande grammatica italiana di consultazione*, vol. 1, pp. 115–225. Bologna: Il Mulino.

Benincà, P. (1995) "Il tipo esclamativo," in L. Renzi, G. Salvi, and A. Cardinaletti (eds.), *Grande grammatica italiana di consultazione*, vol. 3, pp. 127–52. Bologna: Il Mulino.

Benincà, P. (1996) "La struttura della frase esclamativa alla luce del dialetto padovano," in P. Benincà, G. Cinque, T. De Mauro, and N. Vincent (eds.), *Italiano e dialetti nel tempo. Saggi di grammatica per Giulio C. Lepschy*, pp. 23–43. Rome: Bulzoni.

Benincà, P. and C. Poletto (eds.) (1997) *Strutture interrogative dell'Italia settentrionale* (Quaderni di lavoro dell'ASIS 1). Dipartimento di Linguistica, Padua: Consiglio Nazionale delle Ricerche.

Benincà, P. and C. Poletto (eds.) (1998) *La negazione nelle lingue romanze: Atti della 3ª giornata italo-americana di dialettologia* (Quaderni di lavoro dell'ASIS 2). Dipartimento di Linguistica, Padua: Consiglio Nazionale delle Ricerche.

Brero, C. (1976) *Sintassi dla lenga piemontèisa*, suppl. of *Ij Brandé, Armanach ëd poesìa piemontèisa*. Turin: A l'ansëgna dij Brandé.

Brero, C. and R. Bertodatti (1988) *Grammatica della lingua piemontese*. Turin: Edizione Piemont/Europa.

Cinque, C. (1988) "La frase relativa," in L. Renzi (ed.), *Grande grammatica italiana di consultazione*, vol. 1, pp. 444–503. Bologna: Il Mulino.

Cuneo, M. (1997) "Il pronome interrogativo *'koelu (...ke)* nel dialetto di Cicagna," in P. Benincà and C. Poletto (eds.), *Strutture interrogative dell'Italia settentrionale* (Quaderni di lavoro dell'ASIS 1), pp. 31–61. Dipartimento di Linguistica, Padua: Consiglio Nazionale delle Ricerche.

Fox, B. and S. A. Thompson (1990) "A discourse explanation of the grammar of relative clauses in English conversation," *Language* 66:297–316.

Grimshaw, J. (1997) "Projection, heads, and optimality," *Linguistic Inquiry* 28:373–422.

Kayne, R. S. (1994) *The antisymmetry of syntax*. Cambridge, Mass.: MIT Press.

Lyons, J. (1977) *Semantics*, vol. 2. Cambridge: Cambridge University Press.

Middleton, R. (1999) "The last vestiges of *che* as a relative pronoun in Italo-Romance." Paper delivered to the *Society for Italian Studies Conference*, Bristol, April 9–11, 1999.

Munaro, N. (1997) "Proprietà distribuzionali dei sintagmi interrogativi in alcuni dialetti veneti settentrionali," in P. Benincà and C. Poletto (eds.), *Strutture interrogative dell'Italia settentrionale* (Quaderni di lavoro dell'ASIS 1), pp. 63–74. Dipartimento di Linguistica, Padua: Consiglio Nazionale delle Ricerche.

Parry, M. (1993) "Subject clitics in Piedmontese: A diachronic perspective," *Vox Romanica* 52:96–116.

Parry, M. (1997) "Variazione sintattica nelle strutture interrogative piemontesi," in P. Benincà and C. Poletto (eds.), *Strutture interrogative dell'Italia settentrionale* (Quaderni di lavoro dell'ASIS 1), pp. 91–103. Dipartimento di Linguistica, Padova: Centro Nazionale delle Ricerche.

Poletto, C. (1997) "I tipi di pronomi interrogativi in friulano occidentale," in P. Benincà and C. Poletto (eds.), *Strutture interrogative dell'Italia settentrionale* (Quaderni di lavoro dell'ASIS 1), pp. 75–88. Dipartimento di Linguistica, Padua: Consiglio Nazionale delle Ricerche.

Poletto, C. (2000) *The Higher Functional Field: Evidence from Northern Italian Dialects.* New York: Oxford University Press.

Poletto, C. and L. Vanelli (1995) "Gli introduttori delle frasi interrogative nei dialetti italiani settentrionali," in E. Banfi, G. Bonfadini, P. Cordin, and M. Iliescu (eds.), *Italia settentrionale: crocevia di idiomi romanzi. Atti del convegno internazionale di studi, Trento, 21–23 ottobre 1993*, pp. 145–158. Tübingen: Niemeyer.

Portner, P. and R. Zanuttini (1998) "The force of negation in wh-interrogatives and exclamatives," in P. Benincà and C. Poletto (eds.), *La negazione nelle lingue romanze—Atti della 3ª giornata italo-americana di dialettologia (Quaderni di lavoro dell'ASIS 2)*, pp. 1–37. Dipartimento di Linguistica, Padua: Consiglio Nazionale delle Ricerche.

Radford, A. (1988) *Transformational Grammar. A First Course.* Cambridge: Cambridge University Press.

Rizzi, L. (1997) "The fine structure of the Left Periphery," in L. Haegeman (ed.), *Elements of Grammar*, pp. 281–337. Dordrecht: Kluwer.

Roberts, I. (1997) *Comparative Syntax.* London: Arnold.

Ronjat, J. (1937) *Grammaire istorique des parlers provençaux modernes.* Montpellier: Société des Langues Romanes.

Schachter, P. (1973) "Focus and relativization," *Language* 49:19–46.

Schwegler, A. (1988) "Word-order changes in predicate negation strategies in Romance languages," *Diachronica* 5:21–58.

Shopen, T. (1985) *Language Typology and Syntactic Description,* Vol.1: *Clause Structure.* Cambridge: Cambridge University Press.

Thorne, D. (1993) *A Comprehensive Welsh Grammar.* Oxford: Blackwell.

8

Making Imperatives:
Evidence from Central Rhaetoromance

Cecilia Poletto and Raffaella Zanuttini

1. Imperative particles in Badiotto

In this chapter, we hope to contribute to a better understanding of the syntax of imperatives by analyzing the properties they exhibit in a Rhaetoromance variety spoken in northeastern Italy, in the Dolomites area, in a valley called Val Badia.[1] This language, which we call Badiotto, exhibits properties typical of verb second languages, as discussed in Benincà (1985/1986) and Poletto (2000).

For a positive imperative to be grammatical in this variety, one of the four particles *ma, mo, pa, pö* must be present, as exemplified in (1):[2]

(1) a.   Lî-l   *ma/ mo/ pö/ pa*! (Badiotto)
           read-it   prt
           'Read it!' (2nd sg)

     b.   Lié-l   *ma/ mo/ pö/ pa*!
           read-it   prt
           'Read it!' (2nd pl)

A positive imperative cannot consist of the verb alone (2), or of the verb and a pronominal clitic (3):[3]

(2) a.   * Ciara!
             look (2nd sg)

     b.   * Ciared!
             look (2nd pl)

(3) a.   * Lî-l!
            read-it (2nd sg)
            'Read it!'

    b.   * Lié-l!
            read-it (2nd pl)
            'Read it!'

This constraint does not stem from a phonological or prosodic restriction which
makes sequences such as the ones in (2) and (3) ungrammatical in this language.
Neither does it stem from a restriction against monosyllabic sequences, since
bisyllabic verbs are as ungrammatical as monosyllabic ones in positive imperatives
if they lack one of the particles. Moreover, it doesn't stem from a restriction which
rules out clauses consisting of a single word, since the same constraint holds even
in the presence of other lexical material, such as an adverb, as in (4), or an overt
object, as in (5). Finally, it doesn't stem from a restriction against sequences which
consist of only the verb and a pronominal clitic, since such sequences are
grammatical in nonimperative clauses, as shown in (6):[4]

(4) a.   Fà-l *(*ma*) atira!
            do-it   ma   right away (2nd sg)
            'Do it right away!'

    b.   Jit *(*ma*) zagn!
            go   ma   now (2nd pl)
            'Leave now!'

(5) a.   Lî   *(*ma*) l   liber!
            read   ma   the book (2nd sg)
            'Read the book!'

    b.   Liét *(*ma*) l   liber!
            read   ma   the book (2nd pl)
            'Read the book!'

(6) a.   Al vëgn.
            s.cl comes
            'He is coming.'

    b.   Al l' ó
            s.cl cl wants
            'He wants it.'

In light of the contrast between (1) on the one hand and (2) and (3) on the other, it
seems natural to think that the particles *ma, mo, pö,* and *pa* are required to mark
the clause as an imperative. There is, however, one syntactic environment in which
the particles can be missing. As shown in (7), in the presence of the sentential
negative marker *no,* the particles are not required (though they are possible):

(7) a.   No *(ma)* l lî!
           neg   *it read (2nd sg)*
           'Don't read it!'

     b.   No *(ma)* l liét
           neg   *it read (2nd pl)*
           'Don't read it!'

If the grammar of Badiotto requires the presence of one of those four particles to form an imperative, their absence in (7) should give rise to ungrammaticality, contrary to what is observed.[5]

To understand the syntax of imperatives in this language we will seek an answer for the following questions:

•   What is the semantic contribution of the particles which obligatorily occur in positive imperatives?

•   What is their syntactic characterization?

•   Why are they obligatory in positive but not in negative imperatives?

More broadly, in this work we will be asking the question of what makes a sentence imperative in Badiotto, with the hope of better understanding the properties of this clausal type in general. For example, it has been argued in the literature (see Rooryck 1992; Rivero 1994; Rivero and Terzi 1995; Graffi 1996; Han 1998, among others) that imperatives are characterized by verb movement to C. It remains to be established whether this is a necessary property or simply one of several ways of marking a clause as imperative. Because in Badiotto imperatives are characterized by the presence of certain particles, we should ask whether verb movement is nevertheless required or whether the presence of the particles makes it superfluous. The answer to this question is likely to help us better characterize the role of this syntactic property in marking a clause as imperative.

The chapter is organized as follows. In section 2, we provide an informal characterization of the contribution of the particles to the interpretation of the clause in which they occur. We suggest that the contribution of the two particles which are unique to imperatives is best expressed with the notion of point of view. We take point of view to be a modal notion and suggest that imperatives in Badiotto encode this notion in the syntax, via a functional projection with modal properties (ModP). In section 3, we turn to the analysis of the structural position of these particles, which sheds light on the structure of the clause in general and of imperatives in particular. We then discuss what our findings from Badiotto suggest about the syntax of imperatives. Finally, in section 4, we discuss negative imperatives, which contrast with positive imperatives in not requiring the presence of a particle and in the different extent to which the verb moves. We examine how these differences can be reconciled with the syntactic requirements on imperatives previously uncovered.

2. The contribution of the particles

In this section, we provide an informal characterization of the contribution of the four particles found in imperative clauses in Badiotto. We will discuss first the two particles which are unique to sentences with the illocutionary force of an imperative, then the two which are also found in other contexts.

One parameter which we will use in characterizing the contribution of the particles is that of "point of view." Informally, we can think of an order as being given either from the vantage point of the speaker or from that of the hearer. For example, "Bring me a cup of coffee!" can most readily be seen as a command given for the benefit of the speaker, whereas "Have a cup of coffee!" as one given for the benefit of the hearer. Imperatives expressing these two different points of view are often described as expressing an order or command, and giving advice or permission, respectively.[6] In what follows we will see how this simple distinction proves helpful in characterizing the intuitions of the informants concerning the contributions of the particles to the sentences in which they occur. We will then build on these intuitions to formulate our hypothesis on the properties of imperatives in Badiotto.

Let us start by examining the two particles unique to imperatives, *ma* and *mo*.

2.1 ma

Imperatives containing the particle *ma* are described by our informants as expressing advice or permission. This can be paraphrased in our terms by saying that *ma* signals a command given from the vantage point of the hearer. Both advice and permission can be seen as related to the notion of point of view, in particular as corresponding to an order given for the benefit of the hearer.[7] Some examples follow, illustrating the range of contexts in which imperatives with *ma* can occur:[8]

(8) a.   Màngel *ma* che   spo crësceste.
          eat-it   ma *that then grow (2nd sg)*
          'Eat it and you'll grow.'

    b.   Tèt   *ma* n dé   de   vacanza!
          take-yourself ma *a day of   vacation (2nd sg)*
          'Take a day off for vacation!'

    c.   Va *ma* tres   adërta   fora!
          go ma *always   straight ahead (2nd sg)*
          'Keep going straight ahead!'

In addition to co-occurring with imperative verbs, as in the examples just given, *ma* can also co-occur with subjunctives when the clause has the illocutionary force of an imperative, as in (9):

(9)   Ch'al   vëgnes   *ma* ince   osc   compagn.
         that s.cl come(subj.) ma *also   your   friend*
         'Your friend may come in as well.'

Characterizing *ma* as a particle which signals an order given from the point of
view of the hearer allows us to account for the ungrammaticality of imperatives
with *ma* in contexts where the order is given for the benefit of the speaker. The
judgements indicated here were given for a context where the employee clearly
wants to leave and the employer puts forward another request:

(10) a. * Puzenëime   *ma* ciamò i   ćialzà!
           clean-me   ma *yet   the shoes*
           'Polish my shoes!' or 'You still have to polish my shoes!

     b. * Arjigneme   *ma* cà   le   bagn!
           prepare-me ma *here   the bath*
           'Get my bath ready!'

Further support for the hypothesis that *ma* signals a command given from the
vantage point of the hearer comes from the fact that when the imperative with *ma*
is followed by the description of a negative consequence for the hearer, the sentence
is judged grammatical only if taken to be ironical. Some such examples are given
in (11):

(11) a. Fà-l   *ma* che spo   t'amareste.
         do-it ma *that then s.cl-get-sick*
         'Do it, and you'll get sick.'

     b. Dìjil   *ma* che spo s' ofëndel pa   bëgn.
         tell-him-it ma *that then s.cl offends quite well*
         'Tell him that, and he'll really get offended!'

2.2 mo

The particle *mo* is only found in co-occurrence with imperative verbs.[9] Imperative
clauses containing the particle *mo* are described by our informants as expressing
an order. This can be paraphrased in our terms by saying that *mo* signals a command
given from the vantage point of the speaker. This helps us account for the fact that
mo is possible in precisely those contexts where *ma* isn't possible, as shown in
(12):

(12) a. Puzenëieme *mo* ciamò i   ćialzà!
         clean-me   mo *yet   the shoes*
         'Polish my shoes!' or 'You still have to polish my shoes!'

     b. Arjigneme   *mo* cà   le   bagn!
         prepare-me mo *here   the bath*
         'Get my bath ready!'

Imperatives with *mo* are also possible when it is not clear from the context whether the order is given from the point of view of the speaker or the hearer; in such cases, they can only be interpreted as an order, and not as a piece of advice or as permission:

(13) a. Mànge-l *mo*
          eat-it   mo *(2nd sg)*
          'Eat it!'

     b.   Mangé-l *mo*!
          eat-it   mo *(2nd pl)*
          'Eat it!'

In such cases, *ma* would also be possible, but then the imperative would be interpreted as giving advice or permission.

There are two restrictions on the distribution of *mo* that deserve to be mentioned, although we do not know how to account for them at this point. First, imperatives with *mo* cannot be negated, thus differing from imperatives with the other particles. The second restriction concerns the type of clause which makes a grammatical continuation of an imperative with *mo*. As expected, it is impossible to follow up with a sentence which denotes something for the benefit of the hearer, as in (14), since it is incompatible with the point of view marked by *mo*. Moreover, a continuation expressing that the benefit is for the speaker, as in (15), must be introduced by the complementizer *che:* lack of the complementizer gives rise to ungrammaticality. This contrasts with imperatives with the other particles, which may have a continuation which is not introduced by the complementizer. Two examples of possible continuations are given in (15):

(14)   * Mànge-l *mo* ke   spo   crësceste.
           eat-it   mo *that then grow (2nd sg)*
           'Eat it and you'll grow.'

(15) a.   Fà-l   *mo*, *(che) i   l'adori!
          do-it mo,   *that* s.cl *it use*
          'Do it, I need it!'

     b. ? Fà-l   *mo*, *(che) i   l'ó   atira!
          do-it mo,   *that* s.cl *it want right now*
          'Do it, I want it right away!'

We speculate that these restrictions are syntactic in nature, though we will not provide an explanation for them at this point.

To summarize our discussion up to this point, we have suggested that the contribution of *ma* and *mo*, two particles unique to imperatives, consists in marking the point of view from which the command is expressed, as follows:

(16)

Point of view	Particle
+hearer	*ma*
+speaker	*mo*

We now turn to the other particles, *pa* and *pö*, which are found in positive imperatives though are not restricted to these contexts.

2.3 pö

Contrary to *ma* and *mo*, which are always found in clauses with the illocutionary force of an imperative, *pö* also occurs in other types of clauses (cf. the statements in (17)). It signals that the content of the proposition denoted by the sentence in which it occurs contradicts some proposition which is already in the discourse. We can thus call *pö* a presuppositional particle, in that it signals that the discourse contains a proposition which conflicts with the one denoted by the sentence in which it occurs.[10] For example, the sentence in (17a) asserts that something is good; because of the presence of *pö*, it is felicitous only if the discourse already contains the proposition that what is being discussed is not good. Similarly, the sentence in (17b) is felicitous if a proposition expressing that he's coming is already present in the discourse; (17b) asserts that he is not coming, and implicates that this is contrary to expectation:[11]

(17) a.   Al   é   *pö*   bun!
            s.cl   *is*   pö   *good*
            'Sure it's good!' (contrary to what was said)

    b.   Al   ne   vëgn   *pö*   nia.
            cl   *neg*   *comes*   pö   *neg*
            'He's not coming.' (contrary to expectation)

In imperatives *pö* has the same function, informally that of signaling that the denotation of the imperative sentence is in contradiction with some proposition already present in the discourse. In this case, if we view the contribution of the imperative to the discourse as that of adding an item to a list of things to do on the part of the hearer, we can view the role of *pö* as that of signaling that the discourse contains some proposition to the effect that the hearer was not planning or did not intend to do such a thing. This reflects the intuition of the native speakers, who describe an imperative with *pö* as indicating that the speaker is trying to convince the hearer to do something which wasn't part of his or her plans or desires.[12] The imperative in (18a), for example, is felicitous if, given the structure of the discourse up to this point, it is assumed that the hearer was not going to do what is being ordered. Similarly, the example in (18b) is felicitous if, given his/her knowledge of the road, the speaker has reasons to believe that the hearer might not go straight:

(18) a.   Fàl   *pö*   ch'al   é   na   buna   idea.
          do-it   pö   *that it   is   a   good   idea*
          'Do it, it's a good idea.'

   b.   Va   *pö*   tres   adërta   fora.
          go   pö   *always   straight   ahead*
          'Keep going straight ahead.'

We note that, though possible in general with positive and negative imperatives, the particle *pö* is not compatible with imperatives in the first person plural, as shown in (19c), for reasons which are not clear to us at this moment:[13]

(19) a.   Mànge-l   *pö*   che   sce   no   vëgnel   frëit.
          eat-it   pö   *that   if   not   gets-cl   cold (2nd sg)*
          'Eat it, or it'll get cold.'

   b.   Mangé-l   *pö*   che   sce   no   vëgnel   frëit.
          eat-it   pö   *that   if   not   gets-cl   cold (2nd pl)*
          'Eat it, or it'll get cold.'

   c.   * L mangiun   *pö*.
          it eat (1st pl)   pö

Finally, it is important to note that imperatives with *pö* are only possible in contexts where the order is given for the benefit of the hearer, while they are impossible when it is given for the benefit of the speaker. In this respect, then, they share the distribution of imperatives with *ma*. This is shown in the examples below, where the sentences in (20) are orders given for the benefit of the hearer, and those in (21) for that of the speaker:

(20) a.   Mànge-l   *pö*   che   spo   crësceste.
          eat-it   pö   *that   then   grow (2nd sg)*
          'Eat it and you'll grow.'

   b.   Tèt   *pö*   n dé   de   vacanza!
          take-yourself   pö   *a day   of   vacation (2nd sg)*
          'Take a day off for vacation!'

(21) a.   * Puzenëieme   *pö*   ciamb i   ćialzà!
          clean-me   pö   *yet   the   shoes*
          'Polish my shoes!' or 'You still have to polish my shoes!'

   b.   * Arjigneme   *pö*   cà   le   bagn!
          prepare-me   pö   *here the bath*
          'Get my bath ready!'

We will account for this aspect of the distribution of *pö* by assuming that, in addition to signaling a particular relation to the discourse, it also signals that the order is given from the point of view of the hearer, similarly to *ma*.

2.4 pa

The particle *pa* is the hardest one to characterize, since it occurs in a variety of contexts in Badiotto; hence, our description of its function is more tentative than the one given for the other three particles. When it occurs in statements, it is described by our informants as giving the sentence the character of an emphatic affirmation or of an emphatic negation, as exemplified in (22) and (23), respectively:[14]

(22)   Al é   *pa* bun!
            it is pa good
            'It IS good!'

(23)   Al n'é   *pa* bun.
            cl neg'is pa good
            'It ISN'T good.'

The sentences are perceived as asserting that the state of affairs they describe is the true one, in contrast with some other state of affairs. We take this as suggesting that *pa* signals that the entire sentence is focused.

Confirmation for this hypothesis comes from wh-questions. When *pa* is present, the sentence is interpreted as an unmarked wh-question; when it is absent, the wh-phrase gets contrastive focus, as if the rest of the sentence were known and the speaker only wanted the information corresponding to the wh-phrase. This is exemplified in (24); the sentence in (24b) is only grammatical with emphatic stress on the wh-phrase:

(24)a.   Can vaste *pa* a Venezia?
          when go-cl pa to Venice
          'When are you going to Venice?'

     b.   CAN vaste a Venezia?
          when go-cl to Venice
          'WHEN are you going to Venice?'

We view this as resulting from the fact that *pa* signals that the entire sentence is in focus; when *pa* is absent, then another constituent receives contrastive focus, as marked by intonational prominence.

Imperatives with *pa* can also be described as having the whole sentence in focus. The informants describe them as "stronger orders," in comparison with imperatives with the other particles:

(25)a.   Fà-l *pa* ch'al   é na buna idea!
          do-it pa that s.cl is a good idea (2nd sg)
          'Do it, it's a good idea.'

     b.   Fajé-l *pa* dessigÿ!
          do-it pa definitely (2nd pl)
          'Definitely do it!'

c.   Va *pa* tres   adërta   fora.
      go pa *always   straight ahead (2nd sg)*
      'Always go straight ahead!'

Moreover, they seem to be orders given from the vantage point of the speaker, as was the case with *mo*. This is suggested by their incompatibility with certain continuations which explicitly suggest that the order is for the benefit of the hearer, as in (26):

(26)   * Màngel *pa* che spo   crësceste.
          eat-it pa *that then grow*
          'Eat it and you'll grow.'

In sum, *pa* occurs in a variety of contexts, with the function of marking that the entire clause is focused. Moreover, in imperatives, it signals that the order is given from the point of view of the speaker.

The particles *pö* and *pa* thus maintain in imperatives the same discourse function they have in nonimperative contexts: *pö* signals that the sentence expresses a proposition which contradicts one already present in the discourse, while *pa* signals that the proposition expressed by the sentence is the true one out of a set of propositional alternatives. Moreover, in imperatives they take on the function of expressing the point of view from which the command is given, normally carried out by *ma* and *mo*: *pö* signals that the command is given from the point of view of the hearer, while *pa* from that of the speaker. This is summarized in the table in (27):

(27)

Particle	Relation to discourse	Point of view
pö	contradicts a presupposition	+hearer
pa	clause is in focus	+speaker

We can now go back to one of the questions raised at the beginning of the chapter—namely, why a particle is obligatory in positive imperatives in Badiotto. Given the data examined up to this point, we can formulate a preliminary hypothesis (to be revised in the course of the chapter): imperatives in Badiotto obligatorily express in the syntax the point of view from which a command is given. Because all of these particles can mark point of view, any one of them can satisfy this requirement and thus make imperatives grammatical.

Viewing point of view as a type of modality (cf. Kratzer 1981), we suggest that this requirement is syntactically encoded in the presence of a functional category of modal nature, which we label ModP for convenience. The projection ModP must be activated (in the terminology of Cinque 1999), or licensed. The reason one of these particles must be present in positive imperatives, then, is to activate, or license, this projection. In the next section, we will see more precisely how this is done.

3. The syntax of the particles

We begin this section by discussing the structural position of the imperative particles in Badiotto. We then put forward our proposal concerning the characteristic property of imperative clauses in this language. Throughout our discussion, we will assume that linear order reflects hierarchical relations (cf. Kayne 1994). Because the verb always occurs to the left of the particle in positive imperatives, we assume that the particles are not heads, which would interfere with head movement of the verb, but rather XPs in the specifier position of some functional projection.

3.1 The structural position of the modal particles

Let us start by analyzing the particle *ma*. The characterization of its meaning we have given in the previous section, in terms of the notion of point of view, leads us to propose that it occurs in a modal projection. Cinque (1999) discusses several kinds of modal notions argued to be encoded in the syntax. Though the one we used to characterize the imperative particles does not correspond exactly to any of the ones discussed in that work, if we are indeed dealing with a modal projection, following his proposals we expect it to be in the part of the structure where other modal projections are found, namely lower than CP and higher than TP.

Evidence that *ma* indeed occurs lower than CP is provided by sentences with the illocutionary force of an imperative and the verb in the subjunctive, which have an overt complementizer. Let us repeat here the example already given in (9):

(28)   Ch'al   vëgnes   *ma* ince osc   compagn.
        that s.cl come(subj.) ma *also your friend*
        'Your friend may come in as well.'

In this example, the particle *ma* follows the complementizer *che*, hence it is lower than *che* given our assumption concerning the relation between linear order and hierarchical structure.

Evidence that *ma is* located in the part of the structure argued by Cinque to be the one devoted to modal projections can be found by examining the relative order of this particle and certain adverb classes in the same part of the tree. The classes of adverbs that can be tested are limited in number, given that several never occur in imperatives (see Zanuttini 1997). One adverb that can be found is *doman* 'tomorrow'. Some examples are given in (29):

(29) a.   Fà-1   *ma doman!*
           do-it ma *tomorrow (2nd sg)*
           'Do it tomorrow!'

b.   Fajé-l *ma doman!*
         do-it ma *tomorrow (2nd pl)*
         'Do it tomorrow!'

We take the linear order exhibited in the sentences in (28) and in (29) as showing that the particle *ma* occurs in a position structurally lower than the one occupied by the finite complementizer *che* and higher than the one occupied by the adverb *doman* 'tomorrow'. Hence, we take these data to offer support for the hypothesis that the particle is in a functional projection lower than CP, within the part of the tree where the functional projections express modal notions. Following up on the suggestion we put forth on the basis of semantic considerations in the previous section, we hypothesize that *ma* is the specifier of a functional projection which expresses point of view and that it is found in the part of the tree which Cinque (1999) identifies as expressing modality. This can be summarized schematically as follows:

(30) $[_{CP} [_{C^\circ}$ Fa ... $[_{ModP}$ *ma* ... $[_{TP}$ doman $]]]]$

Turning now to *mo*, we find that its distribution is completely parallel to the distribution of *ma*: it occurs lower than the complementizer in imperative clauses with a subjunctive verb and it occurs higher than temporal adverbs like *doman:*

(31) a.   Ch'al   vëgnes   *mo*   ince osc   compagn.
           that s.cl come(subj.) mo *also your friend*
           'Your friend must come in as well.'

     b.   Fà-l   *mo doman.*
           do-it mo *tomorrow*
           'Do it tomorrow!'

As we have seen in section 2, *mo* shares with *ma* the property of expressing point of view: whereas *ma* signals that the order is given from the point of view of the hearer, *mo* signals that it is given from the point of view of the speaker. We take this similarity in function and the shared distributional properties mentioned here as evidence in favor of assuming that *ma* and *mo* occupy the same structural position—namely, the specifier of a modal projection lower than the complementizer but higher than TP.

The third particle we have examined in section 2—*pö*—displays the same distribution we have observed for *ma* and *mo*: it occurs higher than temporal adverbs but lower than the finite complementizer in imperative clauses with a subjunctive verb:

(32) a.   Ch'al   vëgnes   *pö*   ince osc   compagn.
           that s.cl come(subj.) pö *also your friend*
           'Your friend may come in as well.'

b.   Fà-l *pö doman.*
     do-it pö *tomorrow*
     'Do it tomorrow!'

Pö differs from *ma* and *mo* in function, however, since in addition to signaling the point of view from which the command is issued, it also signals that the proposition contradicts one already present in the discourse.[15] The question arises, then, of whether this difference in discourse function corresponds to a difference in structural position. After all, the two syntactic tests we used to determine the position of these particles (occurrence to the right of the complementizer but to the left of temporal adverbs located in Spec,TP) define a syntactic space which can be occupied by more than one projection. Cinque (1999) argues that at least four modal projections have to be postulated higher than TP but lower than CP, each of which encodes a distinct semantic feature. Therefore, *pö* could occupy a different position from *ma* and *mo* though one which cannot be precisely determined by our tests. For the time being, therefore, we should simply conclude from the examples in (32) that *pö* occurs in the same syntactic space where *ma* and *mo* occur while leaving open the possibility that they might not all occur in the same functional projection. We will see later that there is at least one reason to believe that *pö* is located higher than *ma* and *mo*, though still lower than CP (see the discussion concerning example (41)).

Let us now turn to examining the case of *pa*. If we apply the same two tests we used for the other three particles, we see that *pa* is located higher than temporal adverbs of the class of *doman*:

(33)   Fà-l *pa doman!*
       do-it pa *tomorrow*
       'Do it tomorrow!'

However, differing from the particles previously examined, *pa* is ungrammatical in an imperative with the verb in the subjunctive:

(34)   * Ch'al vëgnes *pa* ince os compagn.

Such ungrammaticality could be taken to stem from *pa* and the complementizer being in competition for the same structural position. If this is correct, then *pa* occurs in a position structurally higher than the one occupied by the other three particles. Independent evidence that *pa* is in C° can be found in data from another variety of central Rhaetoromance, spoken in an adjacent valley called Val di Fassa (hence the name Fassano for the language). This language differs from Badiotto in not being a verb second language. Hence, contrary to Badiotto, in wh-questions it can have a constituent other than the verb in second position. This is relevant for our purposes because, in these contexts, the language exhibits an alternation between the complementizer *che* and the particle *pa*, as shown in (35):[16]

(35) a.　　Olà　*pa* tu　vas?　(Fassano)
　　　　　　where pa *s.cl go*
　　　　　　'Where are you going?'

　　b.　　Olà　*che* tu　vas?
　　　　　　where that s.cl go
　　　　　　'Where are you going?'

　　c.　　* Olà *che pa* tu vas?
　　d.　　* Olà *pa che* tu vas?

If we assume that *pa* occupies the same position in interrogative and in imperative clauses, then these data suggest that *pa* occurs in the same functional projection as the complementizer *che* which introduces finite clauses.[17] Following Rizzi's (1997) proposal, this amounts to saying that *pa* occurs in one of the lower components of CP.[18]

If we are on the right track in assuming that *pa* occurs in one of the layers of CP and *ma* in the part of the structure devoted to modal projections, then the relevant part of the structural representation of a positive imperative in Badiotto is as follows:

(36)

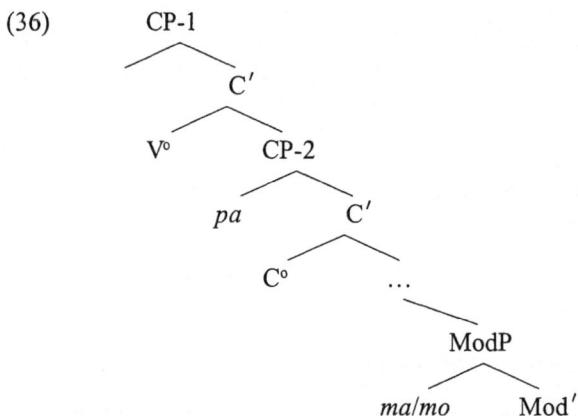

Given this structural representation, which involves two distinct structural positions for *pa* and *ma*, we would expect that the order in which they co-occur be fixed, with *pa* preceding *ma*. This is indeed what we find: *pa* obligatorily precedes *ma*, as illustrated in (37):

(37) a.　　Màngel *pa ma*!
　　　　　　eat-it pa ma
　　　　　　'Eat it!'

　　b.　　* Màngel *ma pa*.

The interpretation of the example in (37a) is the one we would expect given what we said in the previous section about the contribution of *ma* and *pa*: it is interpreted as a command given from the vantage point of the hearer (the contribution of *ma*) and the entire sentence has contrastive focus (the contribution of *pa*).[19]

We can now provide a partial answer to the question of whether the particles found in imperative clauses occur in the same or in different structural positions. Based on the examination of *ma*, *mo*, and *pa*, the answer is that they occur in at least two different structural positions: *ma* and *mo* occur in a modal projection lower than CP and higher than TP, while *pa* occurs in one of the CP layers.

Turning now to *pö*, we should come back to the problem of whether it occurs in the same position as either *pa* or *ma/mo*, or whether we need to invoke yet another position. If the latter, such a position will be lower than the position where *pa* occurs, namely C°, given that *pö* can co-occur with a complementizer, whereas *pa* cannot. Like *pa*, *pö* obligatorily precedes *ma* when they co-occur, as shown in (38):

(38) a.   Màngel *pö   ma*!
           eat-it   pö   ma
           'Eat it!'

    b.   * Màngel *ma pö*.

This sentence is interpreted as a piece of advice, hence a command given from the point of view of the hearer (the contribution of *ma*); moreover, it is felicitous if the discourse contains a proposition to the effect that the hearer did not intend to do what is being advised (the contribution of *pö*).

Pa and *pö* can themselves co-occur, as shown in (39):[20]

(39) a.   Màngel *pa   pö*!
           eat-it   pa   pö
           'Eat it'

    b.   * Màngel *pö pa*!

A precise characterization of the interpretation of (39a) proved to be a rather difficult task. What seems clear is that the two elements normally contributed by *pa* and *pö* are present: the sentence receives contrastive focus (contribution of *pa*) and is felicitous when it contradicts a proposition already present in the discourse (contribution of *pö*). Whether it takes the point of view of the speaker or of the hearer proved rather difficult to establish.

Given the co-occurrences just described, we can make three hypotheses on the structural position of *pö*:

1. *Pö* could be viewed as a modifier of the particle which it precedes: that is, $[_{XP} pö [_X ma]]$. This would straightforwardly account for the word order in (38a); however, it would do nothing to help us account for the co-occurrence of *pö* with *pa*, as in (39a).

2. *Pö* could be viewed as occurring at times in the position of *pa* (namely, one of the layers of CP) and at times in the position of *ma* (namely, in

ModP). It would be in CP when it co-occurs with *ma* (which is in ModP), as in (38a), and in ModP when it co-occurs with *pa* (which is in CP), as in (39a). This would seem to us to imply that *pö* can function exclusively as a marker of point of view when it is in ModP, and as a presuppositional marker when it is in CP. The interpretation of (39a) does not support this view, however: when *pö* co-occurs with *pa*, and hence should be in ModP it does not clearly contribute point of view. Rather, it maintains its usual function of signaling that the proposition being expressed contradicts one already present in the discourse.

3. Finally, *pö* could be viewed as occurring in a position structurally lower than the one occupied by *pa* and higher than the one occupied by *ma*, as indicated in the tree in (40):

(40)   CP-2

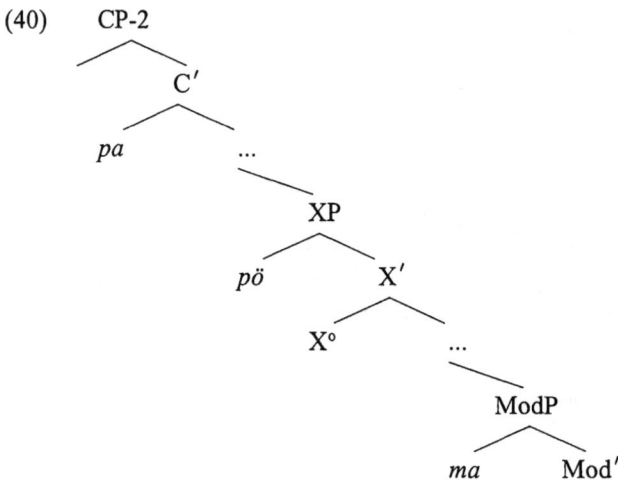

This view can account for the fact that these three particles can indeed co-occur, as in (41):[21]

(41)   Ah pu fà-l   pa pö ma!
       ah pu *do-it* pa pö ma *(2nd sg)*
       'Come on, do it!'

In the interpretation of this sentence, each particle seems to bring its usual contribution to the interpretation of the clause. The sentence is interpreted as receiving contrastive focus (*pa*), as requiring a context in which it was assumed that the hearer would not do it (*pö*), and as being a piece of advice, hence a command given from the vantage point of the hearer (*ma*).[22] If we take each contribution to correspond to a different projection, then this would support the hypothesis that three different functional projections are involved for the three particles.

At present, it seems to us that the third hypothesis is the best one and we thus suggest that the four particles which are found in imperatives in Badiotto occur in three distinct positions, as suggested in the diagram in (40).

3.2 Characterizing imperatives in Badiotto

The discussion concerning the structural position of the particles sheds some light on the structure of the clause in Badiotto, in particular insofar as the relative position of certain functional elements is concerned. This can help us better understand the position of elements which mark focus, presupposition, and point of view, as well as the clausal type under investigation. On the basis of the data and the analysis presented so far, we are now in a position to formulate a more precise hypothesis on the structure of imperatives.

Imperatives in Badiotto crucially involve two functional projections. One is CP, the site to which the verb moves in positive imperatives. Given that the verb occurs on the left of the particle *pa*, which we have seen to be in complementary distribution with the complementizer which introduces finite clauses, we conclude that it moves to a CP layer higher than the one where the finite complementizer occurs. Verb movement to C in imperatives has been invoked for several languages, so this property does not uniquely distinguish Badiotto from other languages examined in the literature.

The second functional projection involved in the syntactic makeup of imperatives, we hypothesize, is the one which expresses point of view; this proposal is based on the observation that, in positive imperatives, the point of view from which the command is given is always expressed. We identify such a projection with the one where *ma* and *mo* occur, which we have characterized as a modal projection expressing point of view.[23] Such a projection, ModP, can be licensed by one of the particles we have been discussing; if the hypothesis that these particles occur in three different structural positions is correct, then the licensing takes place in different ways:

1. ModP contains the particles expressing point of view, *ma* or *mo*.

2. ModP is licensed by *pö*, a presuppositional element which occurs in a structural position c-commanding it.

3. ModP is licensed by *pa*, a focus marker which occurs in a structural position c-commanding it.

One question which arises at this point concerns the exact mechanism which allows licensing, and also what enables these particles to license ModP.[24] Note that the fact that these particles are obligatory in positive imperatives suggests, under our hypothesis, that the verb cannot license the projection ModP: if it did, the particles would not be obligatory. As for the technical aspect of licensing, we can assume that it happens by virtue of these particles merging in ModP; while *ma* and *mo* stay in the specifier of ModP, *pa* and *pö* raise further, to check the features of higher projections $(pa/pö_i \, [_{ModP} \, t_i \,])$.[25] One way to think of this licensing is that it can happen because these particles are all endowed with features shared by ModP, in contrast with the verb which, crucially, must not be. We cannot provide a precise description of the features associated with each of these particles; they must either be a bundle of different kinds of features, or else rather abstract in nature, since they can check both a projection which is modal in nature and a higher projection related to presupposition (in the case of *pö*) and to focus (in the case of *pa*).[26]

Another question which arises is whether the need to license ModP reflects a purely syntactic constraint, or, rather, a constraint which is semantic or pragmatic in nature, to the effect that the point of view from which a command is given must always be expressed in this language (recall the preliminary hypothesis formulated at the end of section 2). A clearer answer to this question will come from the examination of negative imperatives, to which we now turn.

4. Negative imperatives

While examining negative imperatives, we will focus on two issues: the fact that the particles which are obligatory in positive imperatives are not obligatory in negative imperatives; and the relative position of the verb and the negative marker, which sheds light on the extent of verb movement (section 4.2).

4.1 Negative imperatives without a particle

Before we delve into the issue of negative imperatives, let us describe briefly how Badiotto negates a nonimperative clause.[27] The preverbal negative marker *ne* cannot by itself negate a clause (42a), but it can in co-occurrence with one of the three following elements: *nia, mine,* and *pa:*

(42) a.   * Maria   *ne*   vëgn   a   ćiasa.
            Maria   neg   comes   to   home

   b.   Maria   *ne*   vëgn   *nia*   a   ćiasa.
            Maria   neg   comes   neg   to   home
            'Maria isn't coming home.'

   c.   Maria   *ne*   vëgn   *mine*   a   ćiasa.
            Maria   neg   comes   neg   to   home
            'Maria isn't coming home.'

Let us examine first the difference between *nia* and *mine*. Whereas the co-occurrence of *ne* and *nia* yields a negative sentence with no particular discourse status, the presence of *mine* signals that the sentence contradicts a proposition already present in the discourse. In other words, *mine* behaves like one of the so-called presuppositional negative markers discussed in Cinque (1976, 1999) and

Zanuttini (1997). The sentence in (42c), for example, is uttered felicitously if the discourse already contains the proposition that Maria is coming home. Neither one of these postverbal negative markers can negate an imperative, as shown in the following examples:

(43) a.   * *Ne* le fà   *nia.*
          neg it do neg (2nd sg)
          'Don't do it!'

b.   * *Nia* le fà.

c.   * *Ne* le fà   *mine.*
        neg it do neg (2nd sg)

d.   * *Mine* le fà.

The preverbal element *ne* can also negate a clause in co-occurrence with postverbal *pa*. *Pa* differs from *nia* and *mine* in being able to occur with *ne* in imperatives (cf. (44b)):

(44) a.   Maria   *ne* vëgn   *pa*   a   ćiasa.
          Maria   neg   comes   neg   to   home
          'Maria isn't coming home.'

b.   *Ne* le fà   *pa*!
     neg it do pa
     'Don't do it!'

We might think that the *pa* which co-occurs with *ne* is a negative marker homophonous with the particle *pa* which occurs in positive imperatives. However, in both examples in (44) *pa* seems to make the same contribution to the interpretation of the clause we have attributed to this particle in nonnegative contexts, namely that of signaling that the entire clause receives contrastive focus. Thus, if we said that the *pa* found in negative contexts was a negative marker homophonous with the *pa* which marks contrastive focus, we would still have to attribute to it some of the same properties of the *pa* found in other contexts—a suspicious coincidence. Alternatively, given that the *pa* found in negative clauses differs from *nia* and *mine* precisely in being able to occur in imperative contexts, we might think that it is the same element that we find in positive imperatives. In that case, we would have to say that *ne* is the only negative marker in the clause, and that the reason it can negate the clause (contrary to what we saw in (42a)) is that it is licensed by *pa*. This solution (already mentioned in note 14) has the advantage of avoiding the postulation of an accidental homophony while having to attribute to the two elements certain shared properties. We will subscribe to this hypothesis.[28]

If we view *pa* in (44b) as the same as the *pa* found in positive imperatives, then we haven't yet encountered a case of a negative imperative which lacks a particle and is grammatical. Such a case is found when the imperative is negated by a negative marker unique to these contexts, namely *no*.[29] *No* can be either postverbal and co-occur with *ne,* or preverbal without *ne.*[30]

(45) a.   *Ne* le fà *no!*
           neg it do neg (2nd sg)
           'Don't do it!'

     b.   *No* le fà!
           neg it do (2nd sg)
           'Don't do it!'

Interestingly, these examples do not contain any of the particles we found in positive imperatives, and yet they are grammatical. Why are the particles required in positive but not in negative imperatives?[31] In the previous section we hypothesized that two functional projections are involved in the making of imperatives in Badiotto, CP and ModP. We further suggested that the particles are needed to license ModP. Maintaining that hypothesis, we now suggest that, in examples like those in (45), it is the negative marker which licenses ModP.[32] That is, in addition to the particles which mark point of view *(ma* and *mo),* presupposition *(pö)* and focus *(pa),* yet another functional element has the ability to license this functional projection—namely, the negative marker *no.* This amounts to saying that all these elements, including the negative marker, have features of the right kind to license ModP. The proposal that the negative marker *no* can license ModP is reminiscent of the proposal found in Kayne (1992) to the effect that, in Italian imperatives, the negative marker *non* can license an empty modal verb (which in turn takes an overt infinitive as its complement).

Viewing the negative marker as endowed with modal features is one way of expressing the fact that negative markers can be sensitive to the mood specifications of the clause in which they occur. It is well known that in Latin, for example, the negative marker *ne* was used in prohibitive sentences, a class which included imperatives and certain clauses in the subjunctive, whereas *non* was used in all other clausal types. In fact, Sadock and Zwicky (1985) point out that, cross-linguistically, when a language has two or more morphologically distinct negative markers, they are most often sensitive to mood distinctions and specialize accordingly. Badiotto *no,* in our view, is one instance of a negative marker which exhibits sensitivity to mood; such sensitivity is manifested in its ability to occur in sentences where the projection ModP is licensed (for example when *ma* is present), or to license it itself. This cannot be done by the other negative markers of Badiotto, *nia* or *mine,* which occur with other moods or, in our terms, do not have modal features which make them compatible with the ModP of imperatives.

How does *no* license the projection ModP? Because this negative marker only occurs in imperatives, it is difficult to establish where exactly in the structure it originates. We know that, when it is in postverbal position, it follows the modal particle *ma* and precedes adverbs corresponding to English 'anymore' and 'always':

(46) a.   *Ne* le fà ma *no* *plü*
           neg it do ma neg anymore
           'Don't do it anymore.'

b.   Ne le fà ma *no tres*!
        neg it do ma neg always
        'Don't always do that!'

Let us then assume that *no* merges in a position structurally lower than ModP and suggest that it licenses it either by overt raising, or by covert raising of the relevant features. When *no* occurs in preverbal position, as in (45b), such licensing can take place by the negative marker moving through the projection ModP on its way to a higher position (which we will discuss momentarily):

(47) $no_i\ [_{ModP}\ t_i\ [_{Mod^°}\ \cdots\ [_{NegP}\ t_i\ [_{Neg^°}\ \cdots\ ]]]]$

When *no* occurs in postverbal position and no modal particle is present, as in example (45a), it is difficult to know whether it is lower than ModP ($[_{ModP}\ \cdots\ [_{NegP}\ no\ [_{Neg^°}]]]$) or whether it has raised to ModP overtly ($[_{ModP}\ no_i\ [_{Mod^°}\ \cdots [_{NegP}\ t_i\ [_{Neg^°}]]]]$). If it is lower than ModP, then licensing must take place at LF via adjunction of the relevant features.

We can now go back to the question raised earlier of whether the requirement on the licensing of the projection ModP is syntactic or semantic in nature. That is, does it stem from a semantic/pragmatic constraint of Badiotto which requires that every command be specified as being either from the vantage point of the speaker or of the hearer, or does it stem from a purely syntactic requirement that the projection ModP be licensed? We think it is the latter, in view of the fact that negative imperatives which lack a particle are not clearly specified for point of view: they can be commands given from the vantage point of the speaker or of the hearer. If the negative marker can license this projection without specifying one of its values (point of view of the speaker versus point of view of the hearer), the requirement on licensing must be purely syntactic. That is, it cannot be the case that the language needs to specify, for every command, what point of view it takes; rather, it must be that the language needs to license, for every imperative clause, a certain number of functional projections, which include ModP.

4.2 Verb movement in negative imperatives

Besides not requiring a particle, negative imperatives in Badiotto are also worth examining because they appear not to be subject to the requirement that the verb move to C. When an imperative is negated by *no* in postverbal position, the verb appears to occupy the same position as in positive imperatives, immediately preceding the particles:

(48) a.   Ne le <u>fà</u> *ma no*!
        neg it do ma neg (2nd sg)
        'Don't do it!'

b.   Ne le <u>fà</u> *pa no*!
        neg it do pa neg (2nd sg)
        'Don't do it!'

This suggests that the verb is higher than ModP (recall that we are working with the assumption that *ma* is in the specifier of ModP). Moreover, if our hypothesis on the position of *pa* is correct, the verb is also higher than the CP layer which hosts either *pa* or the complementizer found in interrogative clauses.

The position of the verb is different when the negative marker *no* is in preverbal position; in this case, the verb follows the particles:

(49) a. *No   ma* le fà!
         neg ma *it* *do (2nd sg)*
         'Don't do it!'

    b.   *No   pa* le fà!
         neg pa *it* *do (2nd sg)*
         'Don't do it!'

That the verb is in different positions depending on whether the negative marker is pre- or postverbal is also shown by its distribution with respect to lower adverbs (see Cinque 1999). When the negative marker is postverbal, the verb precedes the adverb corresponding to 'anymore', as shown in (50). Assuming that adverbs of this class occur in the specifier of a functional projection higher than VP, this suggests that the verb has raised out of VP:

(50)   Ne le fà ma *no* plü!
         neg it do ma neg *anymore (2nd sg)*
         'Don't do it anymore.'

In contrast, when *no* is preverbal, the verb follows the adverb corresponding to 'anymore', as shown in (51). This suggests that the verb is in a lower position with respect to the adverb:

(51) a. *No* pa plü   le fà!
         neg pa *anymore* it do *(2nd sg)*
         'Don't do it anymore!'

    b.   *No* ma plü   le fà!
         neg ma *anymore* it do *(2nd sg)*
         'Don't do it anymore!'

    c.   No plü   le fà!
         neg *anymore* it do *(2nd sg)*
         'Don't do it anymore!'

The examples in (52) show that if the verb precedes the adverb, the result is ungrammatical:

(52) a. * *No* le fà plü!
         neg *it* do *anymore*
         'Don't do it anymore!'

b.   * *No*   pa   le   <u>fà</u>   <u>plü</u>!
           neg pa *it do anymore*

c.   * *No*   ma le   <u>fà</u>   <u>plü</u>!
           neg ma *it do anymore*

The same pattern holds when we observe the relative order of the verb and the lower adverb corresponding to English 'always':

(53) a.   Ne   le   <u>fà</u>   ma   *no*   <u>tres</u>!
           neg it do ma *neg always*
           'Don't always do that!'

b.   *No*   ma   <u>tres</u>   le   <u>fà</u>!
           neg ma *always it do*
           'Don't always do that!'

c.   * *No*   ma   le   <u>fà</u>   <u>tres</u>!
           neg ma *it do always*
           'Don't always do that!'

Here again, when the negative marker *no* is in preverbal position, the verb appears on the right of the lower adverb, thus suggesting that it is in a position lower than the adverb.

If the verb is required to move in positive imperatives, why does it fail to move in negative imperatives when *no* is in preverbal position, without giving rise to ungrammaticality? Along the lines of our proposal concerning the particles, here also we propose a solution to the puzzle that relies on the idea that the negative marker is able to carry out a function normally carried out by movement of the verb, thus rendering verb movement unnecessary. That is, we suggest that whatever triggers movement of the verb in positive imperatives, presumably certain strong features that need checking, can instead trigger movement of the negative marker *no* in negative imperatives.

We do not pretend to have a theory of what these features might be and of why *no* can check them. For the moment, we limit ourselves to pointing out that these data suggest an interaction between movement of the verb and movement of the negative marker to the effect that the latter can make the former unnecessary. Interactions of this sort have been invoked to account for the contrast between positive and negative questions as well. Independently, both Cheng et al. (1996) and Zanuttini (1997) have argued that the reason verb movement is obligatory in positive but not in negative yes/no questions in the languages they investigate is that the negative marker can move in the latter and satisfy the requirements otherwise met by movement of the verb. Similarly, here we are arguing that the negative marker makes verb movement unnecessary. This implies that the notion of what motivates movement in certain contexts must be construed broadly enough to include a range of values which can be satisfied by elements as different as the verb and (certain types of) negative markers.[33]

Before we conclude this section, we need to comment on the alternation exhibited in our data between movement of the verb and movement of the negative marker. The examples in (48) exhibit verb movement to C; those in (49), in contrast, exhibit movement of the negative marker to C, if our hypothesis is correct. If we think that the target in C attracts the closest element with the right kind of features, this alternation is puzzling: how can the closest element be sometimes the verb and sometimes the negative marker? In fact, this alternation is only apparent, as Badiotto speakers of different age groups tend to use only one of the two structures. That is, older speakers consistently use the structure exemplified in (48), which exhibits verb movement, whereas younger speakers can use, in addition to that structure, also the one exemplified in (49), which exhibits movement of the negative marker.[34] Hence we believe that the proper way of thinking of these data is not as a case in which the requirement of moving to C is optionally satisfied either by the verb or by the negative marker. Rather, this should be considered a situation in which the apparent optionality is, in fact, the result of the presence of two grammatical systems. In one grammar, that of the older speakers, the verb is the only element that can check the features in C, and thus it is the only element which moves to C in imperatives, positive and negative. In the other grammar, in addition to the verb, the negative marker is also endowed with the relevant features to satisfy the needs of the target C; because it is closer to the target than the verb (since the verb originates in VP), it is the element which moves to C. Whereas the older speakers consistently use one grammar, younger speakers can switch from one to the other, thus giving rise to apparent cases of optionality.

5. Conclusion

On the basis of data from a Rhaetoromance variety, Badiotto, in this chapter we have argued that the syntax of imperative clauses is characterized by the need to license two functional projections: CP and ModP.

Verb movement to C, motivated by the need to license (one layer of) CP, has been argued for in many languages to account for the fact that the relative order of the verb and the pronominal clitics is different in imperative and declarative clauses. We think of this property as some trigger for movement which is present in (one of the layers of) the CP projection. For the sake of concreteness, such a trigger can be thought of as some (strong) feature which needs checking. We leave aside the issue of whether this feature can be identified with the one expressing illocutionary force (as proposed in Rivero and Terzi 1995), and simply say that it distinguishes imperatives from declaratives. In Badiotto, the verb raises in positive imperatives and in negative imperatives in which *no* is postverbal. However, when *no* is preverbal, the negative marker raises instead of the verb. This leads us to conclude that the trigger which causes movement to (one of the layers of) CP can be satisfied by more than one element. In Badiotto, such an element can be either the verb (for all speakers, in positive imperatives) or the negative marker *no* (for younger speakers, in negative imperatives). The proper characterization of the trigger, and the issue of why it can be satisfied by both the verb and the negative marker, is left for further research.

The need to license a ModP projection in imperatives has not been widely discussed in the literature, to our knowledge. One such proposal is found in den Dikken (1992). On the basis of considerations having to do with right-peripheral NP-placement in Dutch, this chapter argues for the existence of a Mood and Modality Phrase (M&MP) whose head hosts imperative mood in imperatives (and can otherwise host focus, negation, and emphasis). We argue that a projection ModP must be licensed in imperatives in Badiotto based on the observation that a particle must be present in all contexts except the ones where the negative marker *no* is present. We interpret this as the manifestation of the requirement that a functional projection of modal nature is involved in making an imperative, one which we hypothesize to express the point of view from which the command is given. Such a modal projection can be licensed in Badiotto either by having lexical content or via raising of one of a fixed set of functional elements (the presuppositional particle *pö*, the focus marker *pa*, and the negative marker *no*). We further argue that the need to license this projection is purely syntactic, rather than semantic or pragmatic.[35]

This work also offers us the opportunity to make more precise the descriptive generalization concerning the incompatibility of preverbal negative markers and verbal forms unique to the imperative paradigm ("true imperatives"). The data from Badiotto show that such incompatibility does not extend to negative elements which are maximal projections that moved to preverbal position from a lower position in the structure. Therefore the generalization should be stated as follows: preverbal negative markers which are heads and which can by themselves negate a clause are incompatible with true imperatives.

Finally, we should note that we have not discussed the nature of the difference between a language like Badiotto, which needs to have the projection ModP licensed by a particle or by a particular type of negative marker, and the languages which do not show such a requirement, for example standard Italian or English. Nor have we addressed the question concerning why, assuming that our approach is on the right track, the imperative verb cannot license ModP in Badiotto, while certain particles and the negative marker *no* can. In a highly speculative vein, we would like to propose that, these two issues are connected as follows: in languages like standard Italian or English, ModP can be licensed by the imperative verb which adjoins to Mod° on its way to Comp. In contrast, in languages like Badiotto, movement of the imperative verb through the head of ModP is not sufficient to license this projection; a stronger requirement holds instead—namely, that the specifier be filled as well, by an element with appropriate features. Such an element can be one of the particles we have been discussing, the negative marker *no*, or their trace. This amounts to saying that the licensing of a projection can involve a different procedure in different languages, and even within the same language for different projections. In other words, the parameterization of the requirements on the licensing of a functional projection could be invoked to explain the different behavior of English and Italian on the one hand and Badiotto on the other.

Notes

It is our honor to dedicate this chapter to Paola Benincà, who is for us a teacher, a role model, and a source of inspiration. It is with great joy and enthusiasm that we write a chapter for her, grateful for the opportunity to show her our appreciation for being not only such a careful and sophisticated linguist but also a most gracious, patient, and generous mentor. This work was presented at the 24th *Incontro di Grammatica Generativa* (Verona, February 1998), LSRL 28 (Penn State, April 1998), and the *Quarta giornata italo-americana di dialettologia* (Padua, June 1998); we are grateful to those audiences for their comments. Moreover, we would like to thank Guglielmo Cinque, Robert Frank, Richard Kayne, Paul Portner, Yves Roberge, Vieri Samek and Laura Vanelli for more extensive discussions of this material. We also wish to thank Fabio Chiocchetti and Veronika Pedevilla for their help with the data from Pera di Fassa and from Corvara, respectively. Most of all, we are indebted to Daria Valentin, our main informant from San Leonardo: her sharpness and her natural gift for understanding the complexity of language, combined with her thoughtfulness and infinite patience, have enabled us to uncover the pattern we describe and understand it to the level to which we do. We could not have done this work without her. For the concerns of the Italian academy, Raffaella Zanuttini takes responsibility for sections 1 and 2, Cecilia Poletto for sections 3 and 4, and we jointly take responsibility for section 5.

1. Unless otherwise noted, all the data are from the town of San Leonardo in Badia. They were collected by Cecilia Poletto, with invaluable help from Daria Valentin.

2. Throughout this chapter, we write the examples following the orthographical conventions established by the *Istitut Cultural Ladin "Micurà de Rü" della Val Badia y Val Gardena* and the *Istitut Cultural Ladin "Majon di Fascegn" della Val di Fassa*. These organizations promote the preservation and the study of the varieties of Rhaetoromance spoken in the Dolomites. We will only use phonetic transcriptions when needed to mark a morphological distinction which is relevant for our discussion. We will, however, take the liberty to insert diacritics as needed; for example, in (1), we use a dash to separate the verb from the pronominal clitic.

3. The morphological form used for the second person imperative, both singular and plural, is usually distinct from that used for the corresponding form in the indicative and subjunctive, and from the infinitive. This is illustrated with the verb *arsi* 'to land':

(i)

	2nd singular	2nd plural
Imperative	arsësc	arside
Indicative	arsësces	arsîs
Subjunctive	arsësces	arsîs
Infinitive	arsí	

In contrast, the morphological form used for the first person plural imperative is for some speakers identical to the one used for the same person in the present indicative and subjunctive, while for others it is distinct (cf. Haiman and Benincà 1992:98). This split seems to be along generational lines, with the older speakers maintaining a distinct morphological form which the younger speakers have lost. In this chapter, we limit our discussion to the forms which are unique to the imperative for all speakers, namely second singular and second plural.

4. Regrettably, it is not possible to find nonimperative contexts in which the verb precedes the pronominal clitic, which would constitute a minimal pair with the examples in (3). This is because the verb follows the pronominal clitics with all finite verbs, as well as with infinitives and gerunds; moreover, Badiotto does not make use of clauses formed with gerunds (e.g., temporal adjuncts) or past participles (e.g., absolute constructions).

5. Another interesting property of the examples in (7) is that, even though the verbal form is morphologically unique to the imperative paradigm (hence they are "true imperatives"), they can be negated. At first sight, this seems to invalidate a robust generalization concerning true imperatives, namely that they cannot be negated by a preverbal negative marker (see Rivero 1994; Zanuttini 1997; Han 1998, among others). However, as will become clear in section 4, the negative marker *no* found in (7) is not a preverbal negative marker in the sense relevant for that generalization. Hence, these are not true counterexamples.

6. See Lewis (1979), and references therein, for a semantic characterization of imperatives that express orders in contrast with those that express permission.

7. In addition to Badiotto, our informants can speak Italian, which is, in fact, the language we use to interact. They would often translate Badiotto imperatives with *ma* into Italian imperatives with *pure*, a particle marking concessive or permissive imperatives, exemplified in (i) and (ii):

(i)   Siediti   pure!   (Italian)
        sit (2 sg) pure
        'Have a seat!'

(ii)   Che venga   pure anche il   vostro amico.
        that come(subj.) pure *also   the   your   friend*
        'Your friend may come in as well.'

8. For reasons of space, we give only examples with the second person singular; the same pattern holds with the second person plural.

9. The particle *mo* found in imperatives happens to be homophonous with the adversative element in Badiotto which corresponds to English *but* (cf. (i)), with which it can co-occur (cf. (ii)):

(i)   Al e bun   *mo* pesoch.
        it is good but heavy
        'It's good but heavy.'
(ii)   *Mo fàl   mo!*
        but do-it   mo
        'But do it!'

We take the homophony to be accidental and assume that, as a particle, it is unique to imperative clauses.

10. As was first pointed out to us by E. Herburger (p.c.), this is parallel to the function of German *doch*.

11. Badiotto has a special morphological form, *mine,* for a presuppositional negative marker, namely one which signals that the proposition expressed by the sentence contradicts a proposition present in the discourse. The negative marker *nia* in (17b) is not

presuppositional. Hence, in this example, the task of relating the proposition to the discourse in this particular way is carried out by *pö*.

12. The situation is slightly more complex, as it seems that imperatives with *pö* are compatible both with cases in which the hearer is neutral (for example, hadn't yet thought about it) and with those in which the speaker is unwilling to do what is being ordered. It is not clear to us what the contribution of *pö* is in the former case.

13. We note that, while *pö* alone gives ungrammaticality in co-occurrence with a verb in the first person plural, *pö* and *ma* together yield a grammatical sentence:

(i)   L mangiun *pö ma!*
        it eat   pö ma
        'Let's eat it!'

14. Though not directly relevant to the point under discussion, it is worth noting an interesting property of the sentence in (23). The only negative marker is the preverbal *n*. Like French preverbal *ne*, this element usually cannot by itself negate a clause; to do so, it requires the co-occurrence of another negative element. In this case, we speculate that the particle *pa* can license *n* and the negative features of the clause. See Ladusaw (1992) for a discussion of cases where the role of postverbal elements is that of licensing the negative features on IP.

15. In general, in translating examples with *pö*, we should indicate that some information already present in the discourse is being contradicted. We haven't always done so simply for reasons of space. In particular, example (32a) differs from example (28) in that it signals that the order conflicts with what was already in the discourse.

16. These data come from the village of Pera di Fassa and were collected by C. Poletto with help from Fabio Chiocchetti.

17. If *che* is an X° and *pa* an XP, as suggested at the beginning of this section, then the former will occur in the head and the latter in the specifier of this functional projection. Their lack of co-occurrence would then have to be related to incompatibility of some sort.

18. Note that if *pa* is in the same position in interrogatives and imperatives—namely, in the projection otherwise occupied by the finite complementizer—we are led to conclude that in imperative clauses the verb is in a head higher than the one of the complementizer, given that it always precedes *pa*.

19. This might seem problematic in light of what we said in the previous section and summarized in example (27)—namely, in imperatives, in addition to marking that the sentence is in focus, *pa* also signals that the command is given from the vantage point of the speaker. It seems that while this is true when *pa* is the only particle in a positive imperative, it is not true when it co-occurs with another particle, as in the example in (37a). We hypothesize that this stems from the fact that when *pa* is the only particle, it licenses the projection ModP, whereas in the presence of *ma*, a particle expressing point of view, the projection ModP is licensed by *ma*, which also determines its interpretation.

20. Like *pa*, the particle *pö* cannot co-occur with *mo*. For reasons that are not clear to us at present, *mo* does not co-occur with any other particle:

(i)   * Màngel *mo pa/pö/ma!*
           eat-it   mo pa/pö/ma
           'Eat it!'
(ii)   * Màngel *pa/pò/ma/mo!*

21. This example could be accounted for by the first hypothesis, i.e., by assuming that *pö* is a modifier of *ma*, but not by the second, which assumes that *pö* occupies the same position as either *pa* or *ma*.

22. Our informant found that the sentence was perfect if introduced by the exclamation particles *ah* and *pu*.

23. We have chosen this option, at least in part, for the sake of concreteness. Alternatively, we could hypothesize the need to license a functional projection which does not express point of view but rather some other (either interpretative or purely functional) property of imperatives, but which can be licensed by particles marking point of view.

24. In this discussion, we use the term "licensing" to refer to the ability of some element to activate a given functional head, following the terminology of Cinque (1999), or to license it by checking (some of) its features, following Chomsky (1995). In the literature, the term is also used to refer to the opposite situation, in which a head makes possible the occurrence of some lexical category, for instance a DP or its trace. Hoekstra's (1991) Uniquess of Licensing Principle, according to which a given head can license one and only one element, applies to the second type of licensing, and not to the one relevant here.

25. When *ma* is present in the specifier of ModP, *pa* and *pö* will presumably merge in a higher position.

26. We will see in the next section that another element has the relevant features which can license ModP—namely, the negative morpheme *no*, which is only found in co-occurrence with verbs in the imperative paradigm. This negative marker shares with the particles the property of being an XP in a specifier position, rather than a head. Based on this observation, one could speculate that the reason the particles and the negative morpheme *no* can license ModP, in contrast with the verb which cannot, is related to their X-bar status (rather than, or in addition to, their features). That is, the language could have a requirement to the effect that ModP can only be licensed if its specifier is not empty. We will leave this possibility for further investigation.

27. We will leave aside cases where the clause contains a negative indefinite.

28. If this proposal is on the right track, it has interesting consequences for the way we think about the restrictions on the possibility of negating imperatives. There is a body of literature which has focused on the fact that preverbal negative markers in Romance and in certain Slavic languages cannot negate a true imperative (see Rivero 1994; Rivero and Terzi 1995; Graffi 1996; Zanuttini 1991, 1997; Han 1998, among others). If *ne* is really the element which negates the imperative in example (44b), then the question arises of whether it constitutes a counterexample to that generalization. While it does at first sight, it is necessary to note that it is not a negative marker which can by itself negate a clause, like Italian *non* or Spanish *no*. Rather, it resembles French *ne* or Walloon *nu* (see Remacle 1952:11) in always needing to be licensed by some other element. Note that French *ne* can occur in true imperatives, in co-occurrence with *pas*:

(i)   *Ne* mange *pas!* (French)
        neg eat   *neg (2nd sg)*
        'Don't eat!'

Badiotto *ne* exhibits the same behavior as French *ne*. This suggests that the generalization still stands, though it strictly applies to those preverbal negative markers which can by themselves negate a clause, as already emphasized in Zanuttini (1997).

29. The only other context where *no* is found is when it occurs in isolation, for example as the negative answer to a question.

30. Going back to the discussion in note 28, one should ask whether the preverbal *no* of example (45b) constitutes a counterexample to the generalization that preverbal negative markers in Romance cannot negate a true imperative. We do not think it does, since the negative markers covered by that generalization are best analyzed as heads which originate in a structural position higher than the one occupied by the finite verb in a declarative clause, whereas *no* is a maximal projection originating in a lower structural position. The generalization concerning the incompatibility of preverbal negative markers and true imperatives should then be viewed as applying to preverbal negative heads, not to all negative markers which can occur in preverbal position.

31. The negative marker *no* may co-occur with three of the particles which mark an imperative, namely *ma*, *pa*, and *pö*:

(i)	Ne le fà *ma no*!
	neg it do ma *neg (2nd sg)*
	'Don't do it!'
(ii)	Ne le fà *pa no*!
(iii)	Ne le fà *pa mine no*!
(iv)	Ne le fà *pö no*!

The point is that it does not have to co-occur with one of these particles for the sentence to be grammatical.

32. In example (45b), *no* is the only negative marker, and thus it is straightforward to think that it is the one which licenses ModP. In the example in (45a), the issue is slightly more complex, as there are two negative markers, preverbal *ne* and postverbal *no*. In this case, it is difficult to ascertain which one licenses ModP: because pre-verbal *ne* is licensed by post-verbal *no*, it seems that the latter plays a role in the licensing, either by doing so itself or by doing so indirectly through the licensing of *ne*. In what follows, we will focus on licensing by *no*.

33. G. Giusti and R. Kayne (p.c.) pointed out to us an alternative way of viewing the data where *no* is in preverbal position, preceding the particle and the adverb (as in (51)). According to this view, the verb would raise and then the negative marker, the particle and the adverb, as a unit, would move to an even higher position. The main difficulty we see with this solution is in accounting for the fact that the negative marker *no* precedes the particle, given that, when it is in postverbal position, it always follows it (cf. (48)).

34. We note that in the variety of Rhaetoromance spoken in the nearby town of Corvara all speakers now use the counterpart of (49)—that is, a structure which exhibits movement of the negative marker.

35. Platzack and Rosengren (1994) propose the existence of a functional projection (labeled SP) which checks the feature related to sentence type: the imperative. Similarly to den Dikken's (1992) and to our proposal, this projection is said to be above VP and below CP. Further similarities with our proposal are difficult to see, however, given the difference in the focus of their work, which is mainly concerned with subjects in imperative clauses.

References

Benincà, P. (1985/1986) "L'interferenza sintattica: di un aspetto della sintassi ladina considerato di origine tedesca," *Quaderni Patavini di Linguistica* 5:3–15.

Cheng, L. L.-S., C.-T. J. Huang, and C.-C. J. Tang (1996) "Negative Particle Questions: A Dialectal Comparison," in J. R. Black and V. Motapanyane (eds.) *Microparametric Syntax and Dialectal Variation*, pp. 41–78. Philadelphia: John Benjamins.

Chomsky, N. (1995) *The Minimalist Program*. Cambridge, Mass: MIT Press.

Cinque, G. (1976) "Mica," *Annali della Facoltà di Lettere e Filosofia, Università di Padova* 1:101–112.

Cinque, G. (1999) *Adverbs and Functional Heads: A Cross-Linguistic Perspective*. New York: Oxford University Press.

den Dikken, M. (1992) "Empty Operator Movement in Dutch Imperatives," *Language and Cognition* 2:51–64.

Graffi, G. (1996) "Alcune riflessioni sugli imperativi italiani," in P. Benincà, G. Cinque, T. De Mauro, and N. Vincent (eds.) *Italiano e dialetti nel tempo: Studi di grammatica per Giulio Lepschy*, pp. 143–148. Rome: Bulzoni.

Haiman, J. and P. Benincà (1992) *The Rhaeto-Romance Languages*. London: Routledge.

Han, C.-H. (1998) "The Syntax and Semantics of Imperatives and Related Constructions." Ph.D. thesis, University of Pennsylvania.

Hoekstra, E. (1991) "Licensing Conditions on Phrase Structure." Ph.D. diss., University of Groningen.

Kayne, R. S. (1992) "Italian Negative Infinitival Imperatives and Clitic Climbing," in L. Tasmowsky and A. Zribi-Hertz (eds.) *Hommages à Nicolas Ruwet*, pp. 300–312. Ghent: Communication and Cognition.

Kayne, R. S. (1994) *The Antisymmetry of Syntax*. Cambridge, Mass.: MIT Press.

Kratzer, A. (1981) "The Notional Category of Modality," in H.-J. Etikmeyer and H. Rieser (eds.) *Words, Worlds, and Contexts*, pp. 38–74. Berlin: de Gruyter.

Ladusaw, W. A. (1992) "Expressing Negation," in C. Barker and D. Dowty (eds.) *Proceedings of the Conference on Semantics and Linguistic Theory 2*, pp. 237–259. Columbus: Ohio State University.

Lewis, D. K. (1979) "A Problem about Permission," in E. Saarinen, R. Hilpinen, I. Niiniluoto, and M. P. Hintikka (eds.) *Essays in Honour of Jaakko Hintikka*, pp. 163–175. Dordrecht: Reidel.

Platzack, C. and I. Rosengren (1994) "On the Subject of Imperatives. A Minimalist Account of the Imperative Pronoun and Negated Imperatives," *Sprache und Pragmatik* 34:26–67.

Poletto, C. (2000) *The Higher Functional Field: Evidence from Northern Italian Dialects*. New York: Oxford University Press.

Remacle, L. (1952) *Syntaxe du parler Wallon de La Gleize*. Paris: Société d'Edition les Belles Lettres.

Rivero, M. L. (1994) "Negation, Imperatives and Wackernagel Effects," *Rivista di Linguistica* 6(1):39–66.

Rivero, M. L. and Terzi, A. (1995) "Imperatives, V-movement and Logical Mood," *Journal of Linguistics* 31:301–332.

Rizzi, L. (1997) "The Fine Structure of the Left Periphery," in L. Haegeman (ed.) *Elements of Grammar: Handbook of Generative Syntax*. Dordrecht: Kluwer Academic.

Rooryck, J. (1992) Romance Enclitic Ordering and Universal Grammar," *The Linguistic Review* 9(3):219–250.

Sadock, J. M. and A. Zwicky (1985) "Speech Act Distinctions in Syntax," in T. Shopen (ed.) *Language Typology and Syntactic Description,* pp. 155–196. Cambridge: Cambridge University Press.

Zanuttini, R. (1991) "Syntactic Properties of Sentential Negation: A Comparative Study of Romance Languages. " Ph.D. diss., University of Pennsylvania.

Zanuttini, R. (1997) *Negation and Clausal Structure. A Comparative Study of Romance Languages.* New York: Oxford University Press.

9

Enclitic Subject Pronouns
in the Romance Languages

Giampaolo Salvi

1. Introduction

It is a well known fact that in many Northern Italian dialects the expression of a pronominal subject is obligatory even in the presence of a lexical subject:

(1) *Locarno (Canton Ticino)*
     a.   La me mam   la   riva   doman.
           the my mother   she arrives tomorrow

     b.   * La me mam riva doman.
     c.   La riva doman.

     d.   Nessün u vör   vegnii.
           nobody   he wants to-come

     e.   * Nessün vör vegnii.

Rizzi (1986) compares this fact with the French data in (2):

(2) *French*
     a.   Ma mère elle arrive demain.
     b.   Ma mère arrive demain.
     c.   Elle arrive demain.
     d.   * Personne il ne veut venir.
     e.   Personne ne veut venir.

On the basis of these and other syntactic facts, he claims that in French, subject pronouns are phonological clitics: in the syntax they occur in subject position and are therefore in complementary distribution with lexical subjects (cf. (2b,c)); when lexical and pronominal subjects apparently co-occur, as in (2a), the lexical subject is in reality left dislocated, and only the pronoun occupies the subject position. Thus, in the case of DPs that cannot be left dislocated (e.g., some negative quantifiers), the co-occurrence of lexical and pronominal subject is barred (cf. (2d,e)). Furthermore, Rizzi claims that in the Northern Italian dialects considered here, the subject pronouns are syntactic clitics: they are generated as part of Inflection and can freely co-occur with a lexical subject in subject position (cf. (1a,d)); as part of the verbal inflection, their expression is obligatory (1b,e), but they represent a strong agreement type, so the subject position may remain unfilled (1c).

Besides other inadequacies (see especially Benincà 1986 and the synthesis of Poletto 1993a), this account cannot straightforwardly explain the co-occurrence of lexical and pronominal subjects in the French Complex Inversion Construction:

(3) *French*

    a.   À   qui   Pierre a-t-il   parlé?
          to   whom P.   has he   spoken

    b.   À   qui   personne ne   veut -il   parler?
          to   whom nobody   neg. wants he   to-speak

In (3) the lexical subjects cannot be in a left dislocated position: they occur between the Wh-phrase and the inflected verb, and under current assumptions, left dislocated elements precede Wh-phrases in Comp. Furthermore, while Left Dislocation with *personne* is generally impossible, as (2d) shows, in Complex Inversion the co-occurrence of *personne* and a subject pronoun is perfectly grammatical.

One possible solution to this problem that could save the spirit of Rizzi's approach would be to conceive of enclitic subject pronouns as belonging to a syntactic category different from the one proclitic subject pronouns belong to. Notice that, while preverbal subject pronouns alternate with lexical subjects (2b,c), postverbal enclitic subjects do not:

(4) *French*

    a.   As -tu   vu   Marie?
          have you   seen M.

    b. * A   Pierre vu   Marie?
          has P.   seen M.

A possible explanation of this fact would run as follows: proclitic subject pronouns belong to the same category as lexical subjects and can occur in preverbal subject position (i.e. [Spec, IP], where they are assigned Case via agreement). A lexical subject in postverbal position is not permitted (because, say, it cannot be assigned Case by the verb in C via government), but a pronominal subject is permitted, so it is not of the same syntactic type as lexical subjects. The solution taken by Rizzi and Roberts (1989) is to assume that the pronominal subject is incorporated into the verb (it is thus analyzed as a sort of affix). In their solution this incorporation is performed in the syntax, so by D-structure preverbal and postverbal pronominal subjects belong to the same syntactic category (which explains why they are morphologically identical), while by S-structure they belong to two different categories: preverbal subject pronouns are D(P)s, and postverbal ones are affixes (which explains their different syntactic behavior).

This analysis nevertheless does not work in the case of Complex Inversion: to generate sentences like that in (3), it seems that the Numeration contains two elements with the same θ-role (i.e., the lexical subject and the pronominal one), in violation of the θ-criterion (cf. Kaiser 1996). The solution proposed by Kayne (1983) (namely, that *il* in these examples is an expletive pronoun), is not intuitively very appealing in light of facts such as that seen in (5) (*elle* is not otherwise an expletive):

(5) *French*
> Marie mange-t-elle?
> *M.   eats   she*

A more radical (and, by the way, traditional) approach would be to say that in French there exists an "interrogative" conjugation that we may use in questions. Under this analysis, the enclitic subject pronouns are not pronouns (nor subjects) at all, but rather verbal suffixes expressing an interrogative illocutionary force. This solution would be particularly suitable for popular French -*ti*, which functions as an interrogative suffix independently from the person of the subject:

(6) *Popular French*
> J' suis-ti   comme elle?   (Kayne 1972, n.35)
> *I am interr. as   she*

However, in Standard French this solution raises more problems than it can solve. We have first the problem of the relation between this putative "interrogative" conjugation and its "question" interpretation: in the spoken language the use of the interrogative conjugation is optional in main questions, but it is always impossible in embedded questions (the same holds for Popular French -*ti*):

(7) *French*
> a.   Je me demande quand il verra.
>   *I wonder   when he will-come*
>
> b. * ...quand   verra   -t-il.
>   *when   will-come he*

On the other hand, in Literary French the interrogative conjugation occurs in sentences that are not questions:

(8) *Literary French*
> Peut-être   viendra -t-il.
> *perhaps   will-come he*

Syntactically, this approach cannot explain why the interrogative conjugation may be used only when the subject is null (4a) or lexical (5), but not when it is a clitic pronoun:

(9) *French*

    * Tu   manges -tu?
      you eat   you

Furthermore, morphologically we find no explanation for the fact that in Standard French the interrogative conjugation suffixes have the same form as the subject pronouns.

We can see that this more radical approach is much worse than the generative one. Nonetheless, it has recently been revived by Fava (1993) in relation to the Northern Italian dialects, mainly on the basis of morphological arguments. Reviewing the facts presented in that paper and many other facts supplied by the Italian dialects (mainly from the unpublished materials of the *Atlante Sintattico dell'Italia Settentrionale* [*ASIS*], University of Padua), we will try to better assess (if not solve) the whole problem of enclitic subject pronouns in the Romance languages.

2. The two paradigms of subject pronouns

As noted already by Renzi and Vanelli (1983), the paradigm of proclitic and enclitic subject pronouns is often not the same (see also Fava 1993:2508–2509): one of the most typical configurations is the one exemplified in (10), where the proclitic series has only three members (II, III, and VI person), whereas the enclitic one is complete:

(10) *Padua* (Benincà and Vanelli 1982, sec. 2.5)

	I	II	III m/f	IV	V	VI m/f
procl.	-	te	el / la	-	-	i / le
encl.	i	to	lo / la	i	o	li / le

As can be seen, the very form of the pronoun may differ in the two positions (*te/to, el/lo, i/li*); this is general in the Northern Italian dialects that have enclitic forms; cf. (11), where the two series are complete, but only the II p. pronoun has the same form in proclitic and enclitic position:

(11) *Paluzza (Udine)* (ASIS)

	I	II	III m/f (/n)	IV	V	VI
procl.	a	tu	a - l / a / a	a	a	a
encl.	o	tu	al / e	o	o	o

This general non-correspondence between proclitic and enclitic forms (contrary to what happens in French) could be used as an argument against the hypothesis that proclitic and enclitic pronouns are the same elements at the moment of lexical insertion. In the dialects treated here, no independently motivated phonological rule can explain the variation in the form of the pronouns or their possible disappearance in preverbal position.

Other morphological arguments show that the relation between the enclitic pronoun and its host verb is stricter than the one between the proclitic forms and the verb (see also Fava 1993:2509–2513). As such, they may be taken not to be independent words but, rather, affixes that are an integral part of a morphological word. For example, enclitic subject pronouns can cause modifications in the phonological shape of their host. In some cases, this modification is regular from a phonological point of view. This can be seen in (12a), where the change in the final vowel of the verb is caused not only by enclitic subject but also by object clitic, as in (12b):

(12) *Venice*

    a.   i   magna / magne-i?
            they eat / eat   they

    b.   magna! / magne   -i!
            eat (imp.) / eat (imp.) them

In most cases, however, the modification is tied to the appearance of an enclitic subject pronoun. In this regard note the presence *vs.* absence of the *s* in (13):

(13) a. *Venice*   (Zamboni 1974:25)
        ti   magni / magnis-tu?
        you eat / eat   you

    b. *Cordenons (Pordenone)*   (ASIS)
        te   parlis / parli -tu?
        you speak / speak you

    c. *Paluzza (Udine)*   (ASIS)
        al e / es-al?
        he is / is he

In some cases the use of an enclitic pronoun may induce a reduced form of the host verb:

(14) *Valdagno (Vicenza)*   (Fava 1993:2512)
        te   voli / voli -to? ~ vu   -to?
        you want / want you ~ want you

Sometimes the subject pronoun is incorporated in the verb form:

(15) a. *Rocca Pietore (Belluno)*   (ASIS)
        i   magna / magnie?
        they eat   / eat-they

    b. *Sutsilvan*   (Linder 1987:88–93)
        i   savevan / savevin?
        they knew   / knew-they

The pronoun for one and the same person may have different forms, depending on the host verb. In general, the criteria are either lexical verb *vs.* auxiliary verb (cf. (15a,b)), or different auxiliary verbs (cf. (15c)):

(16) a. *Valdagno (Vicenza)*   (Fava 1993:2512)
           magne-li? / ga -i?
           eat   they / have they

    b. *Gherdëina*   (Anderlan-Obletter 1991:40)
           cherdov-i? / son-s?
           believed I / am I

    c. *Cordenons (Pordenone)*   (ASIS)
           e-lu? / as -i?
           is he / has he

In several cases enclitic forms exist only for the auxiliary verbs (17) or for certain tenses (18):

(17) a. *Venice*   (Zamboni 1974:25)
           magno? / so-gio?
           eat(-I) / am I

    b. *Laste (Belluno)*   (ASIS)
           magne? / e   -mi?
           eat(-I) / have I

(18) *Valdagno (Vicenza)*   (Fava 1993:2511)
           magnè-o? / magnavi?
           eat you.pl / ate(-you.pl)

All the facts reviewed in this section clearly show that the enclitic subject pronouns of the Northern Italian dialects may be morphological affixes: the degree to which they are identifiable (i.e., recognizable) with the proclitic forms may be very low (the corresponding proclitic form may be missing or very different), and the degree of morpho-phonological interaction (such as induced changes, morphological selection, and incorporation) with the host verb may be very high.

3. The affix status of enclitic forms

The morphological facts illustrated in the preceding section do not suffice to refute a syntactically based analysis of enclitic subject pronouns. Benincà and Cinque (1993) have convincingly demonstrated that proclisis and enclisis are two qualitatively different processes. In particular, proclitic elements act as independent words, and enclitic elements are more like affixes. Moreover, the differences in morphosyntactic behavior between proclitic and enclitic elements can be shown to exist even in cases in which no doubt has been cast on the identity of the proclitic elements and the enclitic ones. Here I remind the reader of Benincà and Cinque's (1993) arguments, which are exemplified with clitic object pronouns (to my knowledge, nobody has ever assumed that the use of enclisis with object pronouns is a type of "objective" conjugation!):

1. A proclitic object pronoun can be hosted by two coordinated verbs, an enclitic one cannot:

(19) *French*   (Benincà and Cinque 1993:2319, 2321)
    a.   Je le lis   et   relis.
          I it read and re-read

    b. * Lis   et   relis   -la!
        read (imp.) and re-read (imp.) it

Note that the same phenomenon exists with subject pronouns:

(20) *French*   (Benincà and Cinque 1993:2322)
    a.   Il chantera et   dansera   avec nous.
        he will-sing and will-dance with us

    b. * Chanteraet dansera -t-il avec nous?
        will-sing and will-dance he with us

In the Romance languages, an affix cannot be adjoined to two coordinated stems (cf. Italian*mangia- e bevo<u>no</u>*—for *mangia<u>no</u> e bevo<u>no</u>* 'they eat and drink').

2. Proclitic pronouns can be coordinated, enclitic ones cannot:

(21) *French*   (Benincà and Cinque 1993:2323–2324)
    a.   Je lui et vous   ferais   un plaisir.
        I him and you.pl would-do a favor

    b. * Écris   -nous et   lui!
        Write (imp.) us   and him

In the Romance languages, affixes cannot be coordinated (cf. Italian *mangiava<u>mo</u> e -<u>te</u>*—for *mangiava<u>mo</u> e mangiava<u>te</u>* 'we ate and you.pl. ate').

3. Proclitic pronouns can be separated from their host verb by a (light) word, enclitic ones cannot:

(22) *French*   (Benincà and Cinque 1993:2325)
    a.   Pour   le bien faire.
        in-order it well to-do

    b. * Fais   bien le!
        do (imp.) well it

Affixes cannot in general be separated from their stem by other words: cf. Italian *da-retta-vamo* (for *davamo retta* 'we followed (s.o.'s) advice').

4. Enclitic pronouns can attract stress, proclitic ones cannot:

(23) *Naples*   (Rohlfs 1966/1969, sec. 312))

        pìglia!   / piglia-tì-llo!
        take(imp.) / take(imp.)-yourself-it

In Romance, affixes can attract stress (cf. Italian *gàtto/gattìno* 'cat/little cat').

In light of these facts, we can conclude that showing that enclitic subject pronouns are affixes is not per se a sufficient argument to deny that they belong to the same category as proclitic subject pronouns: enclitic object pronouns are analyzable as affixes, too (but one would not deny their syntactic identity with the proclitic forms).

In spite of this, the differences that we have found in the two series of subject pronouns in the Northern Italian dialects (concerning both the inventory and the morphological shape of the single elements) are striking and have no parallel in the object pronouns' series. As such, it may be worth examining the problem a little more.

4. Inversion is syntactic

Before we introduce some new facts, it will be useful to show that the Northern Italian dialects, too, demand a syntactic analysis of the phenomena connected with enclitic subject pronouns.

The evidence is even more cogent than in French; inversion is obligatory in main questions, forbidden in embedded ones:

(24) *Padua*

    a.   Quando ze-lo vegnuo?
            when   is-he come(past part.)
            'When did he come?'

    b. * Quando el ze vegnuo?
            when   he is come(past part.)

    c. * Me domando quando (che) ze-lo vegnuo.
            I-wonder   when   that is-he come(past part.)

    d.   Me domando quando ch' el ze vegnuo.
            I-wonder   when   that he is come(past part.)

Here we find not only a beautiful example of complementary distribution (that we had not found in French), but also a clue to a nontrivial syntactic explanation: the inversion construction excludes the appearance of the complementizer *che* and vice versa. In the dialects in which *che* may appear in main questions, we find the same complementary distribution in this type of sentence:

(25) *Portogruaro (Venezia)*   (Poletto and Vanelli 1995)
    a.   Cossa che   te   fa?
            what   *that* *you* *do*

    b. * Cossa che fa-to?
            what   *that* *do you*

Following the standard analysis (see Poletto 1993b), in main questions the verb raises to the functional C position to the left of the subject. In embedded questions (and, in some dialects, in main questions; cf. (25)), this position is occupied by the complementizer, so no raising can take place, and we have no inversion. Note that an explanation of the complementary distribution of inversion constructions and complementizers is absolutely out of the range of a theory based exclusively on semantics: the link between the semantics of questions and its realization in the grammar passes through the syntax (Rizzi 1991).

Another argument for a syntactic analysis of inversion (and against a purely semantic analysis of the "interrogative" conjugation type) can be drawn from the structure of negative questions. In those dialects that have preverbal negation, inversion is impossible in normal negative questions (Benincà and Vanelli 1982, sec. 2.5; Poletto 1993b, sec. 3.4):

(26) *Padua*   (Benincà and Vanelli 1982, sec. 2.5)
    a. * No ve-to   via?
           not *go you* *away*

    b. No te   ve   via?
           not *you go* *away*

Here the negation could be a syntactic barrier to the raising of the verb past the subject pronoun.

5. Poletto's (1993b) hypothesis

In light of the evidence reviewed in sections 2 and 4, Poletto (1993b) proposes an analysis of the Paduan dialect that accounts for both the morphological facts and the syntactic ones. In particular, she adheres to the syntactic (verb movement) hypothesis, but she assumes that the two series of subject clitics belong to two different syntactic categories. The proclitic forms, following the hypothesis of Rizzi (1986), are agreement particles generated under Inflection, while the enclitic forms are genuine pronouns—that is, D(P)s generated in subject position. The proclitic forms contribute, together with the agreement suffixes, to the licensing and identification of the possibly null subject via agreement. When the verb raises to C, the enclitic forms can appear in subject position, but must be incorporated into the verb in order to receive Case (nominative Case cannot be assigned by the inflected verb in C via government, as we can see from the fact that lexical subjects cannot appear in inversion contexts; so incorporation is the sole way that subject clitics can comply with the Case Filter). The subject position cannot remain empty because, by hypothesis, the licensing and identification of a null subject, too, is only possible via agreement and not via government.

Poletto's analysis, which does not give up the advantages of a syntactic explanation, can account for the striking morphological differences between the two paradigms of subject clitics in an illuminating way: the enclitic forms are pronouns, so we have the complete paradigm, as is usual with pronouns. The proclitic series is part of the agreement system, so the paradigm does not have to be complete inasmuch as it forms a whole with the agreement suffixes: some persons may have only a suffix, others only a preverbal particle, others both or neither. In addition, the proclitic and enclitic forms do not have to be the same: they are different syntactical elements, but since they are both used to identify subjects, they may show formal similarities, of the type we observe between personal and possessive pronouns.

Nevertheless, Poletto's analysis leaves several questions unanswered and presents some inconsistencies. For example, she does not address the question of why the enclitic forms cannot occupy the subject position when the subject does not raise into C (perhaps because, being morphologically determined as enclitics [suffixes], they do not find to their left a possible host verb to cliticize to), nor why proclitic and enclitic forms cannot co-occur (as proclitic forms and lexical subjects co-occur; cf. (1a,d)). Concerning this latter problem, notice that, while Poletto (1993b) assumes Rizzi's (1986) theory of the proclitic forms in the Northern Italian dialects as agreement particles, in her book (1993a, sec. 2.3.1) she convincingly argues that in Paduan the proclitic forms are D(P)s generated in subject position and moved into Infl in the syntax (in Paduan, as in French, examples like (2d) are ungrammatical, which can be explained if the proclitic forms are generated in subject position by D-structure). This hypothesis would explain the complementary distribution of the two series of subject clitics (both are D(P)s generated in subject position); however, it voids the content of the previous analysis, which was based essentially on the observation that there is a diversity of subject clitics.

Even if we disregard these problems, the consideration of new evidence taken from the domain of Northern Italian dialects will show us that Poletto's (1993b) approach cannot be extended in a natural way to explain other types of enclitic subject pronouns.

6. New evidence: Gherdëina

I will now consider some facts relative to the use of subject clitics in Gherdëina, one of the varieties of Ladin spoken in the Dolomitic Alps (in the valley named Gherdëina/Gröden/Gardena [Bozen/Bolzano]). Gherdëina is a V2 language, as are other Romance varieties spoken in the Dolomites and in Graubünden. Gherdëina also has subject clitics, as do the majority of Northern Italian dialects (cf. Benincà 1985/1986; Haiman and Benincà 1992, secs. 4.1, 4.4; Salvi 1997:290, 293–294).

6.1 The forms

The paradigm of proclitic pronouns has the same structure as in Paduan, while the enclitic series is apparently quite different, having only four members:

(27) *Gherdëina*   (Anderlan-Obletter 1991:38)

	I	II	III m/f	IV	V	VI m/f
procl.	-	te	1 / la	-	-	i / les
encl.	i	-	(e)l / (e)la	s	-	i / (e)les

But comparing this paradigm with the parallel paradigms of the other Ladin dialects of the Dolomites (except Fashan; see table 9.1, based on Kramer 1976, sec. 4.5.1.1), we can see that the enclitic series is the result of a reduction of the complete paradigm as is present in Marèo, Fodóm, and, partially, Badiot/Ladin. Since IV person (with the enclitic pronoun) and V person both end in *-s*, we might suppose that these forms as the result of the dropping of a final *-e* preceded by an affixal *s* (we leave open here the question of the origin of the *-s* of IV person; the *-e* is historically attested for the XIX c. dialect of Gherdëina (Gartner 1879:76, 87):

(28) a.   cianton+se   →   cianton+s
     b.   ciantëis+e   →   ciantëis+Ø

The II person is more problematic (it was missing in XIX c. too—Gartner 1879:76), but the comparison with the other Ladin dialects, with the Romansh dialects of Graubünden (Linder 1987:53–62) and with many Southern German dialects clearly shows that in this geographic area there is a general tendency for the loss of II (and V) person enclitic pronouns (Haiman and Benincà 1992:202).

TABLE 9.1 Proclitic/enclitic subject pronouns in Dolomitic Ladin

	Marèo	Badiot/Ladin	Gherdëina	Fashan	Fodóm
I	i / i	i / i	- / i	- / -	- / jo
II	t(e) / te	t(e) / (te)	te / -	te / te	te / to
III m	1 / (e)l	1 / (e)l	1 / (e)l	el / (e)l	1 / lo
III f	la / (e)ra	la / (e)la	la / (e)la	la / la	la / la
IV	i / ze	(i) / ze	- / s	- / -	- / zo
V	i / e	(i) / e	- / -	- / -	- / o
VI m	aj / aj	aj / i	i / i	i / i	i / li
VI f	ales / (e)res	ales / (e)les	les / (e)les	les / les	le / le

If we accept that the loss of final -*e* is a rather superficial phenomenon (connected with the general tendency of Gherdëina to reduce unstressed *e*), we may reconstruct a paradigm for the enclitic subject pronouns which is very like the Paduan one—the sole exception is II person, whose absence seems to be an independent phenomenon:

(29) *Gherdëina*:

	I	II	III m/f	IV	V	VI m/f
encl.	i	-	l / la	s[e]	[e]	i / les

As for the proclitic series, we have no particular reason to think that a reduction of the forms has occurred. Table 9.1 shows that Gherdëina groups with Fashan and Fodóm in having a system with only three pronouns, like Paduan.

6.2 The use of subject pronouns

Although the systems of subject clitics in Gherdëina and Paduan are very similar, the use these dialects make of them is somewhat different.

6.2.1 Proclitic forms

Since Gherdëina is a strict V2 language, the proclitic forms are in complementary distribution with lexical subjects and tonic (free) subject pronouns:

(30) *Gherdëina*
    a.   L   / Ël   / L   dutor cianta.
           he (cl.) / *he (free)* / *the doctor sings*

    b.   * Ël l cianta. / *L dutor l cianta.

Sentences like (30b) are possible in Paduan as cases of Left Dislocation since clitic pronouns are in subject position by D-structure (see section 5). Note that with I, IV, and V person (for which there exists no proclitic form), tonic subject pronouns alternate with zero. In these cases the verb appears in first position in spite of the V2 constraint:

(31) *Gherdëina*
       Ie / Ø ciante.
       I / Δ sing

As in French, where subject clitics are phonological clitics (Rizzi 1986), but unlike Paduan, where subject clitics are syntactic clitics (Poletto 1993a, sec. 2.2.1), a subject clitic need not be used before a verb preceded by another verb with the same subject clitic (32a)–(33a) and the subject clitic precedes the negative particle (with some dialectal variation for II person; see (32b)–(33b)):

(32) *Padua*   (Benincà and Vanelli 1982, sec. 2.4)

    a.   El ze rivà   e   *(el) ga magnà.
            he is arrived and   he has eaten

    b.   No la   magna.
            not she eats

(33) *Gherdëina*

    a.   L ie jit   da n paur   i   l'   à   petlà.
            he is gone to a farmer and him has implored

    b.   Te ne foves nia ilò.
            you not were not there

Notice that in the coordinated structure it is indifferent whether the first subject pronoun is proclitic (33a) or enclitic (34):

(34) *Gherdëina*

        Finalmënter ie-l jit   da n paur   i   l'   à   petlà.
        in-the-end is he gone to a farmer and him has implored

6.2.2 Enclitic forms

Due to the V2 constraint, the enclitic forms are not used only in questions (35a), but also in those sentences in which the sentence's first position is occupied by a constituent different from the subject (35b,c). Notice that in questions an interrogative clitic particle *pa/'a* appears after the verb and the enclitic subject (cf. Siller-Runggaldier 1993):

(35) *Gherdëina*

    a.   Cómpr-el pa n liber?
            buys-he   pa a book

    b.   Sce l pluef, tol -i l' òmbrela.
            if it rains take I the umbrella

    c.   Ilò à -l scumencià a mené na stleta vita.
            there has he begun   to lead a bad live

But, surprisingly, enclitic forms are not in complementary distribution with free subject pronouns; actually a free subject pronoun in inversion constructions is always accompanied by the appropriate enclitic form (if there is one for the given person):

(36) *Gherdëina*

    a.   Cómpr-el   pa ël   n liber?
            buys he(cl.) pa he(free) a book

a'. * Compra pa ël n liber?

b.   Duman   va -1   ël   dal   dutor dai dënz.
      tomorrow goes he(cl.) he(free) to-the dentist

b'. * Duman va ël dal dutor dai dënz.

c.   Nsnuet jon-s   nëus   a maië na bona cëina.
      tonight go-we(cl.) we (free) to eat a good dinner

c'. * Nsnuet jon nëus a maië na bona cëina.

Co-occurrence of enclitic pronouns with lexical subjects is ungrammatical in Gherdëina:

(37) *Gherdëina*
    a. * Dlongia ruf   mët-eles la mutans doi banc.
        near   brook put-they the girls   two benches

    b.   Dlongia ruf mët la mutans doi banc.

Here we accept Siller-Runggaldier's analysis that in *Cueje-les 'a bele la bales?* ('are-cooking they *pa* already the *knödels*?'), the lexical subject is right dislocated.

Note, however, that in other V2 Ladin and Romansh dialects we find some evidence for this latter phenomenon (Haiman and Benincà 1992:191–192, 203–204; Linder 1987:146–162). For Dolomitic Ladin, see (38a); here the clitic may not be an expletive because the latter always has the unmarked III m. form (38b):

(38) *Ladin*
    a.   Canch'al ê   indô su,   l' damanâ-i   sü compagns
          when   he was again alone   him asked they his companions

          y   i   dódesc, ćaî   che chëstes paraboles orô dí
          and the twelve   what that these   parables   meant

    b.   Al ê   ailò inćo na ëra   che...
          it was there too a woman who

For Romansh see (39):

(39) *Sutsilvan*   (Linder 1987:86)
      Giou avànt la tgea   digl Bonati spitgeavan-i igls vituregns
      down before the house of-the B.   waited they   the coachmen

      cun tgar a   tgavagl.
      with coach and horse

Co-occurrence of enclitic subject and free subject pronoun is possible in Southern German dialects too (Renzi and Marx 1997); here the tonic form may appear in postverbal (40a) as well as in preverbal (40b) position:

(40) *Bavarian*   (Renzi and Marx 1997)
    a.   Do   geh-ma   mia   a hi.
        there   go we(cl.)   we(free)   too

    b.   Mia   mach-ma   des scho.
        we(free)   do we(cl.)   that already

Renzi and Marx assume that the enclitic forms of Southern German are not affixes, but merely reduced variants of the free forms, and that in examples such as (40) they are in subject position; but we have evidence that in Gherdëina the enclitic forms and the free forms occupy different positions. As (35a) shows, enclitic forms occur before the particle *pa*, while free forms occur after it (36a), as is the case for lexical subjects (41):

(41) *Gherdëina*
         Can   compra pa Piere n liber?
         when buys   pa   P.   a book

6.3 Poletto's (1993b) hypothesis applied to Gherdëina

At this point we can clearly see that Poletto's (1993b) approach cannot be transferred to the data of Gherdëina.

6.3.1 Proclitic forms

The proclitic forms are D(P)s at least by D-structure (i.e., they cannot co-occur with lexical subjects). They could be D(P)s by S-structure, too, since they count as the first constituent for the V2 constraint, but example (31) shows that a phonologically null element can also count as the first constituent, so by S-structure the proclitic forms could be heads (i.e., syntactic clitics), the sentence's first position being occupied by an empty category (cf. the analysis of Paduan proclitic subjects in Poletto 1993a). Note that in the varieties in which the II person pronoun follows the negation particle, only this latter solution is available.

6.3.2 Enclitic forms

The enclitic forms do not occupy subject position by S-structure, as can be seen by the contrast between (35a) and (36a)/(41). Whether they are in subject position by D-structure depends on the interpretation of the doubling facts reported in (36); if the free subject pronouns occupy subject position, clearly the enclitic forms cannot be D(P)s in subject position, by virtue of the Projection Principle. In this respect, the data from the other dialects seen in (38)–(39) are unambiguous: lexical subjects are to be generated in subject position, so the enclitic forms cannot be generated there. Subject pronouns, however, may apparently occupy other positions (Burzio 1986, sec. 2.3) and can co-occur with lexical subjects:

(42) *Italian*

Giovanni cucinerà lui la cena stasera.
G.   will-cook he the dinner tonight

In a framework where subjects are in [Spec,VP] by D-structure and in [Spec, IP] by S-structure, we could say that the lexical subject is generated in [Spec, VP] with a focus feature, and then moves to [Spec, IP], leaving the focus feature in situ, since the focus' unmarked position is postverbal in Italian; this feature is later realized as an emphatic subject pronoun. This approach accounts for the interpretation of the subject pronoun as focused, as well as for the fact that we always find the lexical subject in preverbal position and the free pronoun in postverbal position, and not the other way around.

In a similar way, in Paduan a free subject pronoun can co-occur with a subject clitic, be it proclitic or enclitic:

(43) *Paduan*   (Benincà and Vanelli 1982, secs. 2.4, 2.5)

a.   Te   rivi   tì.
      you(cl.) arrive you(free)

b.   Parcossano ve-to   anca tì?
      why   not go you(cl.) also you(free)

In fact, here too the evidence is more complicated: in the case of a postverbal focalized lexical subject, the expression of an enclitic subject pronoun is always possible (but in general optional): *Vien(-li) anca i tosi?* 'come(-they) also the boys?'; *Te scrive(-li) anca i tosi?* 'to-you write(-they) also the boys?'; *Te lo ga-li scrito anca i tosi?* 'to-you it have-they written also the boys?', while the expression of a proclitic subject pronoun is possible only in some cases: *(La) me lo ga dito to sorèa* '(she) to-me it has told your sister' vs. **La ga telefonà to sorèa* 'she has phoned your sister'; **I ze saltà fora do gati* 'they are jumped out two cats'—cf. Benincà and Vanelli 1982, sec. 2.4, especially n. 5.

In any case, there seems to be an essential difference between the data from Italian and Paduan, on the one hand, and those from Gherdëina and the other Ladin and Romansh dialects, on the other: while in the former doubling is always tied to focalization (cf. (42)–(43)), in the latter this is not the case (cf. (36), (38), and (39)). In these examples, at least for some speakers, the postverbal subject is not necessarily interpreted as focused, such that (36b), for example, may be continued as follows: ... *ajache l à scialdi mel* 'since he has much ache', which makes clear that the focus is on going to the dentist, and not on who goes.

The comparative evidence shows that the cases of focalization require a different analysis, one that permits doubling without violating the Projection Principle (in the case of pronouns, this might perhaps follow the lines traced in the text following (42); for the case of lexical subjects referred to in the text following (43), I have no suggestion). On the other hand, the facts from Dolomitic Ladin and Romansh do not need this special treatment, and we may assume as the null hypothesis that they fall within the scope of the Projection Principle.

On the basis of this evidence, we can tentatively conclude that the enclitic forms of Gherdëina cannot be generated in subject position since they can co-occur with the free subject pronouns generated in subject position. This conclusion is even more solid for the other Ladin and Romansh varieties, in which the enclitic forms cooccur with lexical subjects.

6.3.3 Conclusion

We have thus reached the conclusion that the proclitic forms of Gherdëina are D(P)s in subject position by D-structure (and perhaps by S-structure, too), while the enclitic ones may not be in subject position, neither by S-structure nor by D-structure: this is exactly the contrary of the analysis Poletto (1993b) proposes for Paduan.

7. More comparative evidence

At this point, in lieu of an alternative analysis (I do not offer one which could do better work than the reviewed one), I will propose some general considerations that can possibly help future research on this topic.

7.1 Celtic synthetic verb forms

The behavior of enclitic subject pronouns in Gherdëina resembles the alternation of synthetic and analytic verb forms in Welsh as described by Rouveret (1992). Synthetic verb forms in Welsh are inflected for mood, tense, and person and are used when the subject is null or pronominal (44a,b). Analytic forms are inflected only for mood and tense (the person is the unmarked III), and are used when the subject is lexical (44c):

(44) *Welsh*   (Rouveret 1992:539, 542)

    a.   Darllenasant   y   llyfr.
             read-past-VI   the book
             'They read the book.'

    b.   Darllenais i   y   llyfr.
             read-past-I I   the book
             'I read the book.'

    c.   Darllenodd   y   plant y   llyfr.
             read-past-III the boys   the book
             'The boys read the book.'

In the verbal morphology of Gherdëina, III and VI person are never distinct and have no personal endings, so the verbal forms that lexical subjects occur with are always unmarked for person: *l mut cianta / i mutons cianta* 'the boy sings / the boys sing.' If we now consider only the cases in which the subjects are postverbal (which is the normal subject position in Celtic), we may see that, in Gherdëina, too, verb forms with personal endings and/or incorporated pronouns are used when the subject is null or pronominal; verb forms without personal endings are used when the subject is lexical:

(45) a.   Ilò   à   -l   scumencià a mené na stleta vita.   (= (35c))
        there has he begun   to lead a   bad   life

     b.   Duman   va -l   ël   dal   dutor dai dënz.   (= (36b))
         tomorrow goes he(cl.) he(free) to-the dentist

     c.   Dlongia ruf   mët la mutans doi banc.   (= (37b))
        near   brook put the girls   two benches

It is interesting to note that Hale (1990) derives the synthetic forms of Irish by a process of incorporation into the verb of the pronominal features of the (subject) argument position. Rouveret (1992) does not accept this approach because in Welsh the synthetic forms can co-occur with pronouns in subject position (which is not the case in Irish), and he proposes a more complex analysis in which he assigns lexical subjects and pronominal subjects to two different categories (DPs and NumPs, respectively), and then derives their different properties from the different relations they have to inflection.

The case of Gherdëina is more complicated in this respect since subjects may be preverbal, too; in this case, the verbs never incorporate a clitic pronoun, and the verb form is not a function of the subject type (null, pronominal, or lexical), as is the case with postverbal subjects (in addition, subjects may be null only at I, IV, and V person). The comparison is interesting, however, in the parallelism we observe when the verb governs the subject position and, in a diachronic perspective, for the cues it may give us in the explanation of the origin of inflected forms.

7.2 Doubling constructions: two typological implications

Doubling constructions with subjects show some parallelism with doubling constructions with non-subjects, a parallelism which in general is not paid attention to in the analyses of the phenomena individually, mainly because the case of subject clitics is often discussed in relation with agreement phenomena, while in the case of object clitics, agreement is not taken into account, at least in Romance.

If we examine the possibilities of co-occurrence of a clitic and the related DP, we may distinguish different cases:

  1. If there is a clitic, the full DP may occur only in a left or a right dislocated
     position (indicated here with a comma), but not in an argumental position:

(46) *Italian*

    a.   Il   pane, l' ho   comprato. / L'ho   comprato, il pane.
        the bread it I-have bought / it I-have bought   the bread

    b. * L'ho   comprato anche il   pane.
        it I-have bought   also the bread

(47) *French*

    a.   Pierre, il verra   demain   / Il verra   demain,   Pierre.
        P.,   he will-come tomorrow / he will-come tomorrow P.

    b. * Personne il ne   verra.
        nobody   he not will come

  2. Free pronouns in argument position must cooccur with a clitic, lexical DPs may not:

(48) *Portuguese*

    a.   Vi   -te   a ti.   / *Vi   ti.
        I-saw you(cl.) a you(free) / I-saw you(free)

    b.   Vi   o   João. / *Vi   -o (a)o   João.
        I-saw the J.   / I-saw him (a) the J.

(49) *Gherdëina*

    a.   Cómpr-el pa ël   n liber? /
        buys he(cl.) pa he(free) a book /

      * Compra pa ël n liber?   (= (36a,a'))
        buys   pa he a book

    b.   Dlongia ruf mët la mutans doi banc. /
        near   brook put the girls   two benches /

      * Dlongia ruf mët-eles la mutans doi banc.   (= (37))
        near   brook put they the girls   two benches

  3. All DPs in argument position must co-occur with a clitic:

(50) *Locarno (Canton Ticino)*

           A g   dò i   danee al   me fradel. /
           I to-him give the money to-the my brother/

        * A dò i   danee al   me fradel.
         I give the money to-the my brother

(51) *Locarno (Canton Ticino)*

           La me mam la riva   doman. /
           the my mother she arrives tomorrow /

* La me mam   riva   doman.   (= (1a,b))
the my mother arrives tomorrow

There may be an asymmetry between preverbal and postverbal position in the case of subjects which is not found in the case of objects, but this can be due to the fact that the argument position of objects (direct and indirect) is only postverbal in Romance. There is normally an asymmetry between proclitic and enclitic subject pronouns which is not found in the case of object pronouns, but this may be due to the fact that proclitic subject pronouns are normally tied to a preverbal subject position and an enclitic pronoun is normally tied to a postverbal subject position, while an object pronoun (proclitic or enclitic) is always tied to a postverbal argument position. Some examples for these asymmetries:

- Gherdëina doubling of the postverbal pronominal subject by an enclitic pronoun (36) vs. the absence of doubling with preverbal subjects and proclitic pronouns (30b);

- Paduan (optional) doubling of a postverbal focalized subject with an enclitic pronoun: *Vien(-li) anca i tosi?* 'come(-they) also the boys' vs. the absence of doubling with proclitic pronouns and preverbal subjects: *I tosi i vien* 'the boys they come' (only analysable as a case of Left Dislocation; doubling of a postverbal focalized subject by a preverbal clitic is in some cases optionally possible—see the examples above in the text following (43));

- French doubling of a preverbal subject (only III and VI person) by an enclitic pronoun (3), (5) vs. the absence of doubling with a proclitic pronoun (2d).

All these facts permit two tentative generalizations that we may express in the form of implications:

1. If a language allows doubling of lexical DPs in argument position by a clitic pronoun, it allows doubling of pronominal DPs, too;

2. For a language X which has proclitic and enclitic pronouns: if X allows doubling of DPs in argument position by proclitic pronouns, it allows their doubling by enclitic pronouns, too.

Note

The bulk of these rather inconclusive notes was born on the occasion of a course on Ladin Philology I held at the University of Trento in 1994; they were later presented at the *XXV Romanistentag* (Münster, 1995) and at the University of Amsterdam (1996). They are largely inspired by the work of Paola Benincà, Lorenzo Renzi, and Laura Vanelli on Northern Italian dialects (much more than the cited references can show). I decided to publish them in spite of their scarce originality because it was Paola who gave me the opportunity to work on these topics, and these notes may perhaps show that her confidence was not completely misplaced.

Data on Gherdëina stem from Anderlan-Obletter (1991) and from the kind communication of Heidi Siller-Runggaldier. Data on the dialect of Locarno are my own. If the source is not indicated, data from Paduan were fraudulently elicited from Paola Beninca.

References

Anderlan-Obletter, A. (1991) *La rujeneda dla oma: Gramatica dl ladin de Gherdëina.* Urtijëi: Istitut Pedagogich Ladin—Lia Maestri de Gherdëina.

Beninca, P. (1985/1986) "L'interferenza sintattica: di un aspetto della sintassi ladina considerato di origine tedesca," *Quaderni Patavini di Linguistica* 5:3–15.

Beninca, P. (1986) "Punti di sintassi comparata dei dialetti italiani settentrionali," in G. Holtus and K. Ringger (eds.), *Raetia Antiqua et Moderna: W.Th. Elwert zum 80. Geburtstag,* pp. 457–479. Tübingen: Niemeyer.

Beninca, P. and G. Cinque (1993) "Su alcune differenze fra enclisi e proclisi," *Omaggio a Gianfranco Folena,* pp. 2313–2326. Padua: Editoriale Programma.

Beninca, P. and L. Vanelli (1982) "Appunti di sintassi veneta," in M. Cortelazzo (ed.), *Guida ai dialetti veneti,* IV: 7–38. Padua: CLEUP.

Fava, E. (1993) "Sulla pertinenza della pragmatica nell'analisi grammaticale: un esempio dalla cosiddetta coniugazione interrogativa nel dialetto alto-vicentino," *Omaggio a Gianfranco Folena,* pp. 2495–2520. Padua: Editoriale Programma.

Gartner, T. (1879) *Die Gredner Mundart.* Linz.

Haiman, J. and P. Beninca (1992) *The Rhaeto-Romance Languages.* London: Routledge.

Hale, K. (1990) "Some Remarks on Agreement and Incorporation," *Studies in Generative Grammar* 1:117–144.

Kaiser, G.A. (1996) "V2 or not V2? Subject-Verb Inversion in Old and Modern French Inerrogatives," in E. Brandner and G. Ferraresi (eds.) *Language Change and Generative Grammar,* pp. 168–190. Opladen: Westdeutscher Verlag.

Kayne, R. S. (1972) "Subject Inversion in French Interrogatives," in J. Casagrande and B. Saciuk (eds.) *Generative Studies in Romance Languages,* pp. 70–126. Rowley, Mass.: Newbury House.

Kayne, R. S. (1983) "Chains, Categories External to S, and French Complex Inversion," *Natural Language and Linguistic Theory,* 1:107–139.

Kramer, J. (1976) *Historische Grammatik des Dolomitenladinischen. Formenlehre.* Gerbrunn bei Würzburg: Lehmann.

Linder, K. P. (1987) *Grammatische Untersuchungen zur Charakteristik des Rätoromanischen in Graubünden.* Tübingen: Narr.

Poletto, C. (1993a) *La sintassi del soggetto nei dialetti italiani settentrionali.* Padua: Unipress.

Poletto, C. (1993b) "Subject Clitic/Verb Inversion in North-Eastern Italian Dialects," in A. Belletti (ed.), *Syntactic Theory and the Dialects of Italy,* pp. 204–251. Turin: Rosenberg and Sellier.

Poletto, C. and L. Vanelli (1995) "Gli introduttori delle frasi interrogative nei dialetti italiani settentrionali," in E. Banfi, G. Bonfadini, P. Cordin, and Maria Iliescu (eds.), *Italia settentrionale: crocevia di idiomi romanzi,* pp. 145–158. Tübingen: Niemeyer.

Renzi, L. and S. Marx (1997) "Pronomi personali congiunti in varietà dialettali tedesche e italiane." Ms., University of Padua.

Renzi, L. and L. Vanelli (1983) "I pronomi soggetto in alcune varietà romanze," *Scritti linguistici in onore di Giovan Battista Pellegrini*, pp. 121–145. Pisa: Pacini.

Rizzi, L. (1986) "On the Status of Subject Clitics in Romance," in O. Jaeggli and C. Silva Corvalan (eds.) *Studies in Romance Linguistics*, pp. 391–419. Dordrecht: Foris.

Rizzi, L. (1991) "Residual Verb Second and the Wh Criterion," *Technical Reports in Formal and Computational Linguistics*, no. 2. University of Geneva.

Rizzi, L. and I. Roberts (1989) Complex Inversion in French. *Probus* 1:1–30.

Rohlfs, G. (1966/1969) *Grammatica storica della lingua italiana e dei suoi dialetti*. 3 vols. Turin: Einaudi.

Rouveret, A. (1992) "La nature des prépositions conjuguées," in L. Tasmowski and A. Zribi-Hertz (eds.) *Hommages à Nicolas Ruwet*, pp. 529–555. Ghent: Communication and Cognition.

Salvi, G. (1997) "Ladin," in M. Maiden and M. Parry (eds.), *The Dialects of Italy*, pp. 286–294. London: Routledge.

Siller-Runggaldier, H. (1993) "Caratteristiche della frase interrogativa a soggetto inverso nel Ladino Centrale," in R. Lorenzo (ed.), *Actas do XIX Congreso Internacional de Lingüística e Filoloxía Románicas* IV, pp. 289–295. A Coruña: Fundación Pedro Barrié de la Maza.

Zamboni, A. (1974) *Veneto*. Pisa: Pacini.

10

The Misunderstood Double Marking of Indirect Objects and New Infinitive Strategies in Unexpected Places: A Brief Study of Romance Variation

John B. Trumper

1. Differential Marking of Indirect Objects

Rohlfs (1968, 3 §632) discusses the normal marking of DOs that are [+human] with prepositions, usually *a*, in Southern Italian dialects, including the Calabrian varieties. I have already addressed a few brief comments to this topic in Trumper 1996.[1] The phenomenon, which syntactically binds Southern and some Central dialects to Sardinian, to Corsican, to Ibero-Romance, and to Romanian, is also present, albeit with more restrictions, in Northern Italian dialects.[2] Rohlfs is essentially correct when he states that the preposition used is not always *a* but sometimes *da* ("Gallo-Sicilian"), sometimes *per*, not only in Romanian (*am văzut pe tine*) but even in the Mediterranean "lingua franca" or sabir described in detail in Cifoletti (1989) with examples such as *genti mirado per mi andar con ti* = "mi s'è visto andar via con te": the example *mi ablar per ti* adduced by Rohlfs doesn't exhibit this particular construction but only the generalized use of the preposition *per* to mark both IO's ("io *ti* dico": *mi ablar per ti*) and DOs ("io *ti* vedo": *mi mirar per ti*), provided they be [+human]. The particular preposition used seems to be irrelevant; more important is the fact of marking a distinction between types of DO/ IO [+human] vs. [-human], not always with the restriction [+human] to the names of persons or the Pro-forms that substitute them, but often with an extension to kinship terms, occasionally to place names (personification?) and, usually to professions or roles. That it is a question of differentiating [+human] from [-human] complements is also brought out in Sornicola (1997:335–336). The Neapolitan dialect, probably all Campanian, does not distinguish the clitic pronoun in *(N)cə tələfunájə a Ggiuánnə* from that in *(N)cə tələfunájə allə Cummúnə* ('I phoned up John', 'I phoned up the Town Hall'), whereas in the absence of the head NP referencing the proclitic pronoun a structure such as *O tələfunájə* can only refer to the former, with a human IO ('I phoned him up'), and *(N)cǝ talǝfunájǝ* can only reference the latter case, with a nonhuman IO ('I phoned up', e.g., the Town Hall). A. N. Ledgeway reminds me that the differential marking of human complements leads in some dialects to ambiguous situations, where one doesn't know whether regional Italian *Ho detto a te* means, in an Italian sense, "Ho detto té <non lui>" ('I said you <not him>'], with *a te* DO, or "Ho detto a té" ('I said to you'), with *a te* IO. In fact, as he points out, Neapolitan can disambiguate by re-marking the IO with a different choice of preposition, whether it be *vǝcínǝ, 'mpìettǝ* or *'nfaccǝ*, as in *L'aggǝ rittǝ vǝcin'a mmuglièrǝmmǝ* ('I told my wife')—cf. the use of *incóntro* in rural Veneto dialect, as in note 2. Both northern Calabrian with *T'aju dittu'nt' a facce* and southern Calabrian with *T'u dissi 'nt' a fácci* can occasionally distinguish the dative/beneficiary function (IO) from others by using, exceptionally, *'nt' a facce [-i]* (= to you; lit.: in your face]. This seems to be the only prepositional phrase allowed. Usually, however, in Calabrian dialects potential ambiguity remains. Further complication may be caused by the existence of two distinct types of dative, one inherently dative (to say *to* someone, to speak/talk *to* someone, to give *to* someone, etc.), the other not inherently a dative, however one may wish to label them. The situation is often more complex than supposed and should be analyzed in more detail.

Two further cases might be added. The first is that being able to reference [+human] IO's with either an object or dative form of the proclitic pronoun leads to a new pragmo-semantic distinction in the majority of Calabrian varieties and may be illustrated as follows:

(1) Transitional dialects between the Lausberg Area and North Calabria (e.g., Castrovillari, CS)[3]

    a.   'On **ci** pparlu, tantu 'on zènti/

           'On **ci** parlu, picchí 'ollu stavu vidènnu pròpiu

    vs.

    b.   'Oll**u** parlu, picchí è cciu:tu/

           E' nna vita c' oll**u** parlu, picchí mi fa 'ncazzá

(2) North Calabria

    a.   'Un **ci** parru, tantu 'u' ssènta[di],

           'Un **ci** parru, tantu 'unn' asulíja[di]/

           'Un **ci** parru, picchí 'unn'u staju vidíennu pròpiu

    vs.

    b.   'Unn'**u** parru, picchí è cciúotu/

           'Unn'**u** parru picchí mi fa 'ncazzá[re]

(3) Mid Calabria

    a.   'On **ci** parru, tantu 'on zènta/
         'On **ci** parru picchí 'onn'u staju vidèndu pròpiu

vs.

    b.   Esta na vita ca 'onn'**u** parru/
         'Onn'**u** parru, picchí hácia ma mi 'ncazzu[4]

The opposition seems to be between (a) the physical possibility of talking to someone, which is marked by a dative proclitic form, and (b) the desire to talk or not to talk to someone, marked by an object proclitic form, with the possible distinction between a physical and a psychological act being syntactically and morphologically marked. Once again, the whole question has to be gone into in a more in-depth manner. However, it might also be noted that this possible distinction does not seem to be implemented in southern Calabrian varieties, at least at the current stage of our research. The dialects of the Locride (RC), for example, only have *Non ci parru*, never **No' llu parru*, in all such instances, even where the non-desire to talk is underlined by the fact of negative relations—for example, in *Non ndi parramu picchí ndi liticammi* ('We aren't talking because we've argued')—this is not particularly obvious, as it is in *Non ci parru picchí ndi liticammi* ('I'm not on talking terms with him because we've argued') and would be equivalent to *'Ollu parlu picchí nn'amu liticatu / 'Unn'u parru picchí nn'amu liticatu / 'Onn'u parru picchí ndi liticamma* in the other varieties described above,[5] these last all with object and not dative pronouns.

    A second case of such marking human IOs but with different prepositions is noted and labeled by Rohlfs (1968, §639) as a "dativo greco" and is dealt with by him as a case of supposed substratum in the following terms: "Nei paesi che sono stati romanizzati nel corso degli ultimi due secoli, l'uso in parola venne trasferito, durante il periodo di bilinguismo, alla parlata italiana, e vi rimase, anche dopo che il greco fu del tutto spento." At §639 note 1 Rohlfs notes a parallel use between Calabrian dialects like those of Bagaladi, S. Lorenzo, Brancaleone, Palizzi and Bovalino (RC) and the morphological merger in Albanian and Romanian between "dative" and "genitive," a merger apparently caused, according to him, by Greek influence. He might, therefore, at this point have introduced the same "substratum" factor as being concausal of a similar merger between dative and genitive in late Latin, but here he wisely limits his comments to a discussion of the already operative merger of the two cases involved in the first declination as the possible cause of a chain merger (1968, §631): "Nel latino tardo la coincidenza formale tra genitivo e dativo nella declinazione in -*a* (*puellæ* 'della fanciulla' e 'alla fanciulla') condusse, nelle altre declinazioni, a confusioni nell'uso dei due casi."

    There is, however, a slight flaw in Rohlfs' argument. The [+human] IO is marked with the same preposition as the [+human] DO in the Tyrrhenian dialects of the province of Reggio Calabria (e.g., Melicucco/Polistena (RC)):

(4)   Nci rissi ô figghjòlu 'u si ndi vaci/
          Nci rissi ô figghjòlu 'u mi faci ssu favuri

Here ô represents the monophthongization of all unstressed occurrences of *a* (prep.) + *u* (def. art.), as in the marking of DOs in cases such as

(5)   U vitti ô figghjòlu/
         [U] vitti a Ggiuánni/
         Ggiuánni viri a mmía

This example (5) has an exact correspondence in the city dialect of Reggio Calabria:

(6)   Nci rissi ô figghjòlu mi si ndi vài/
         Nci rissi ô figghjòlu mi mi fài ssu faúri

Plus, both have the same marking by the same preposition in

(7)   Vitti a Ggiuánni/
         Ggiuánni viri a mmía

This situation holds as far as Melito Porto Salvo, at the toe of Italy, but it is not the case in dialects north of Melito and of Ionian dialects in general, at least as far as Siderno. In the Ionian dialects of S. Ilario, Locri e Siderno, for example, while there is a unique marking of [+human] DOs with the preposition *a*, a double contrastive [+human] IO marking is exploited; in other words, we have cases such as the following:

(8)   Si dissi <u>ô</u> figghjòlu 'u si ndi vaci/
         Si dissi <u>ô</u> figghjòlu 'u mi faci ssu favuri

This is the UNMARKED INSTANCE, without any pragmatic or information presuppositions. This prepositional use contrasts with the structures

(9)   Si dissi <u>d'u</u> figghjòlu 'u si ndi vaci/
         Si dissi <u>d'u</u> figghjòlu 'u mi faci ssu favuri[6]

In these latter structures there are clear implications that we are dealing with a case of anaphora, with information about the "lad" already contained in previous text and therefore known or contextually "given," or the "lad" is so well known to the interlocutors that his very existence is given as known or old information from the general context of village life or even of relatively close kinship relations. That this is not necessarily a calk on any Balkan language merger is demonstrated by the fact that the preverb pronominal clitic is always the "dative" (*si* in these dialects = *nci/cci* in other Calabrian dialects); it cannot be a "genitive" pronoun. If we were to substitute a "genitive" form of the pronoun, then we would have an ungrammatical utterance (*<u>Ndi</u> dissi <u>d'u</u> figghjòlu 'u si ndi vaci* with *ndi* the partitive/genitive form). This sufficiently differentiates the Romance strategy from the modern Greek one: for example, Εἶπα τοῦ παιδιοῦ νά πάε 'I told the lad to go', with pronominal prefix Τοῦ 'πα νά πάε 'I told him to go', where formally and historically we have genitive forms both in the noun and pronoun. The Calabrian dialect situation is nearer that of Romanian where the noun is ambiguously genitive/dative and the pronoun unambiguously dative (*Zisei copilui să meargă/ <u>Îi</u> zisei copilui să meargă*), with the sole pronoun <u>Îi</u> *zisei să meargă*, as is the case in

Albanian *U i thash djalit t'iki,* with pronoun substitution and not as an echo form *I thash t'iki.* In both cases the pronoun is decidedly an indirect form (dative). Rather than with Greek, parallels can be drawn, then, with Romanian and Albanian. In these last cases, however, there is no contrastive prepositional or case use. We are dealing, in other words, with a differential marking of IOs as a strategy operated by the Ionian Romance dialects of the province of Reggio Calabria that deserves detailed study and not hasty labeling as a case of "substratum" influence, as handbooks have so far done, and that without any in-depth pragmo-syntactic analysis. My proposals tentatively open a series of questions which must be discussed in greater detail.

2. Phonological and syntactic variability: Reggio Calabria, a case of dialect reaffiliation

In Trumper (1997) and in greater detail in Trumper and Chiodo (1997) it was argued that the dialect of Reggio Calabria is structurally and phylogenetically different from other Calabrian dialect groupings on the basis of a certain number of dialect phenomena discussed in greater detail in these papers. Some of the phonetic and phonological phenomena are echoed in the regional Italian of Reggio Calabria and differentiate it from the regional Italian of other Calabrians. In a first pilot study we tested a number of variables using small regional population samples—that is, 12 males from Reggio Calabria, 18 males from Catanzaro, 18 males from Cosenza, 16 males from three Pre-Silan villages near Cosenza (Pietrafitta, Aprigliano, Pedace), 6 males from the Mittelzone of the Lausberg Area (Rotonda, Rotondella), 10 Sicilian males from Messina (born and brought up there), and 10 males from Naples (born of Neapolitan parents and brought up there). Speakers' variability was estimated in recorded spontaneous conversations of about 30–35 minutes. The following variables were tested:

Var. 1–3: the lenition (voicing) of the single (short) voiceless stops /p, t, k/
Var. 4: fricativization of the single (short) voiceless alveopalatal affricate /tʃ/
Var. 5–6: voicing of short voiceless continuants /f, s/
Var. 7–9: variable lenition of the single voiced stops /b, d, g/ realized as continuants [υ/β, ð/ð, ɣ/ɰ], in which the second option is an approximant realization, the first presenting slight friction
Var. 10: variable gemination (lengthening) of the single voiced stop /b/
Var. 11: variable voicing of postnasal voiceless stops
Var. 12: variable aspiration of postnasal voiceless stops as a reaction to variable 11.

In the history of some Romance dialects there has evidently taken place a wholesale lenition process that involves voiceless stops and continuants, so that intervocalically

(10)   a.   /p, t, k/   →   [b, d, g]

b.   /b, d, g/   →   [β, δ, ɰ]
c.   /f, s, ʃ, ç/ →   [v, z, ʒ, j]

both word-internally and word-initially within the utterance. It seems to characterize not only Sardinian, Corsican, and dialects of Central-South Italy from Umbria as far down as Naples, but it also seems to have characterized dialects of the Lausberg Area as well: evidence is given in the Trumper and Chiodo (1997) paper discussed at a European Science Foundation Symposium. The process may, however, be interpreted as two ordered subprocesses of the type:

R1:   /b, d, g/ →   [β, δ, ɰ]   →   ([v, r, j] with variable
                 rephonematization → /v, r, ɟ/)

R2 (variable): /P, T, K/ → [b̥/b, d̥/d, g̥/g] > where /P, T, K/ are "lax"
                 segments no longer marked for the "voice" feature. Hence
                 "voice" is the variable feature and not "tension."

This is the situation that appears to occur in East Sicilian dialects (Messina) and hence in the Calabrian dialect of the city of Reggio Calabria. For the situation at Reggio Calabria see as a first study Maddalon and Marafioti (1991), and for Sicily D'Agostino (1997), with geolinguistic distribution in her map 3 (p. 111). As D'Agostino points out, the intervocalic "laxing" observed in East and West Sicilian is not a recent phenomenon, but has gone relatively unnoticed because of "normative" dialect transcriptions, largely the responsibility of G. Rohlfs et al. (the *Italo-Swiss Atlas*, Rohlfs' *Grammatica Storica*, etc.). It needs to be noted that such processes have intervened after the Romance merger between b-/-b- and v-/-v- in Latin. Examples from the Reggio dialect are "b," "v" (Latin) → /b/ (Romance) → /v/ in *virdi* 'green', *virdísca* the shark *Prionace glauca* (L.); /bb/ in *bbèrtula* 'sack', *bbaciàri* 'kiss'; /Nb/ in *mbivìri* 'to drink', *mbistìnu* 'shark' (generic); but /P/ in /Puttˢu/ 'dingy' (< *buzzu, guzzu* in other Calabrian dialects; *buzzettu* is given in Mandalari (1881) as the Reggio form) = ['b̥ut:ˢʊ], "d" (Latin) → /d/ (Romance) → /r/ *renti* 'tooth', *runari* 'give'; /dd/ in *ddisertari* 'abort'; /nd/ in *nduccu* 'marsh owl' (*dduccu/duccu* in other Southern Calabrian dialects), but / T/ in ceramita /tˢera'miTa/ 'tile' (< *ceramida, ceramila* in other Calabrian dialects) = [dʒera'mI:d̥a], *na ceramita* 'a tile' [naʒera'mI:d̥a]; "g" (Latin) → /g/ (Romance) → /ɟ/ *in jatta* 'cat', jattupárdu *Scyliorhinus* sp., *jad̥d̥u* 'cockerel', *jad̥d̥ína* 'hen'; but Ø in *aúgghja* (1) 'needle', (2) *Belone belone* (L.), *úrdu* 'voracious', 'hungry', *ámburu/ámbaru* 'shrimp'. Other Southern Calabrian dialects have, respectively, *agúgghja, gúrdu, gámbaru/gámburu*, Ø → /v/ between two identical vowels, e.g., *fravágghja* 'fry' (other dialects *fragáglia, fragágghja*), *pavári* 'to pay' (other dialects *pagári*), but /K/ in, say, *cájula* = ['g̥ajʊla] *Lithognatus mormyrus* (L.) (other dialects *gájula*). These dialect phenomena have created a series of variable processes in such speakers' regional Italian, which I have studied: the above processes are labeled 1–3, 5–6, and 7–9 in this study. I have added the fricativization of the single voiceless affricate /tˢ/ that urban Sicilian and more recently Reggio Calabria have in common with Neapolitan and Central Italian dialects, as well as the variable voicing of postnasal voiceless stops that characterizes both the dialect and regional Italian of many South Italian speakers, together with its converse— that is, the variable aspiration of voiceless stops in the same context.

In a previous study (Trumper and Chiodo 1997, still unpublished) we also included three other variables: the gemination or phonemic lengthening of the alveopalatal voiced affricate /dʒ/, the unvoicing of postnasal voiced stops as a reaction to variable 11, and the retroflex realization of the clusters /str, tr, dr/, which were analyzed together with the other 12. Results were less homogeneous inasmuch as they did not indicate an easily interpretable affiliation of the Catanzaro subgroup or of its variability. Intra- and interregional results were given in table 5 of Trumper and Chiodo (1997). The results for linear r-coefficients are given here in table 10.1. Results for r significant at the 1% level ($F_{1\,10}$ = 10.0) are marked with a double asterisk, those significant at the 5% level ($F_{1\,10}$ = 4.96) with a single one. Though values of r that range from .58 to .7 are significant at the 5% level, I have decided to treat .7 as a pertinent divide between linear correlation coefficients, given that for significance at the 1% level one needs an r-value of .71. To construct our relation diagram I postulate a significant but weak correlation between groups for values $.6 > r > .57$ (a single line), a significant and medium strength correlation for values $.7 > r \geq .6$ (a double line), a significant and extremely strong linear correlation for values $.85 > r > .7$ (a triple line). The relations between three natural groupings, from the point of view of their variability in regional Italian (not in dialect), would thus be as in figure 10.1.

In figure 10.1, Catanzaro is now well linked up with the rest of the region, from the point of view of variability in regional Italian, while Reggio Calabria has been strongly captured by a southern urban group (Naples and densely populated Sicilian urban agglomerations), though it still keeps a significant even if tenuous correlation with the Italian spoken by co-regionals in the Sila Range and at Catanzaro.

TABLE 10.1 Results for linear r-coefficients

	Pre-Sila	Lausberg Area	Cosenza	Catanzaro	Reggio Calabria	Naples
Lausberg Area	.6*					
Cosenza	.84**	.82**				
Catanzaro	.74**	.27	.6*			
Reggio Calabria	.59*	.54	.29	.58*		
Naples	.44	.78**	.4	.19	.7*	
Messina	.3	.48	.04	-.03	.7*	.62*

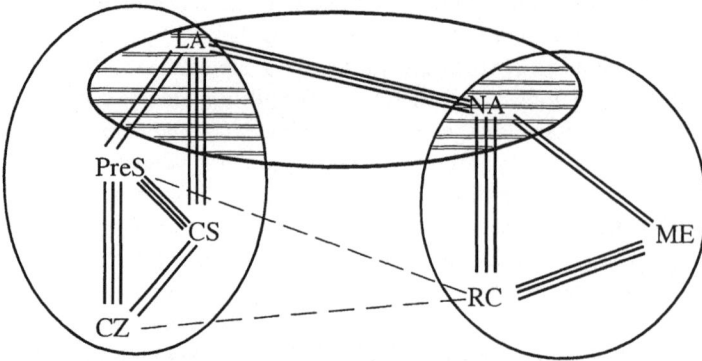

Fig. 10.1 Relations between three natural groupings (LA, Lausberg Area; PreS, Pre-Sila; CS, Cosenza; CZ, Catanzaro; NA, Naples; ME, Messina; RC, Reggio Calabria)

An elaboration of the sample population scores has been further developed by applying well-known cluster analysis methodology. On the basis of the scores for 11 variables (var. 1–6, 8–10, 12–13), over seven communities (Cosenza, Pre-Sila villages, Catanzaro, Reggio Calabria, Messina, Naples, and the Lausberg Area), adding to the data scores for the northeastern population (27 males) as a control group, a squared Euclidean dissimilarity coefficient matrix was obtained, as in table 10.2. Averages scores were not weighted except in terms of the dispersion of variability within each subsample (s values) and calulations and elaboration carried out with usual cluster analysis software.[7]

Using the centroid method applied to such a matrix we obtain the following dendrogram of clusters as in figure 10.2. It is very much evident from the dendrogram in figure 10.2 that Reggio Calabria forms a unique cluster with Messina and Naples rather than with the other Calabrian dialects. The Catanzaro sample is now marginally connected with the Calabrian cluster at whose center we have Cosenza and the Pre-Sila villages, with which the Lausberg Area is associated, thus expliciting what was expressed in a more vague fashion in figure 10.1.

TABLE 10.2 Squared Euclidean dissimilarity coefficient matrix

Variable	LA	CS	CZ	ME	NA	PA	RC
Cosenza	5924.27						
Catanzaro	8767.8398	8998.5303					
Messina	10859.3398	17512.5293	18383.5				
Naples	7828.1899	11331.3799	14852.3496	5947.1499			
Padua	14335.3604	19485.0508	18999.2207	17082.2207	25906.6699		
Reggio Calabria	7098.5898	11557.4805	7044.25	5536.25	3575.3	22408.7695	
Pre-Sila	6345.3398	3739.53	4474.5	13289.0	10678.3496	14757.8203	6963.25

Rescaled Distance Cluster Combine

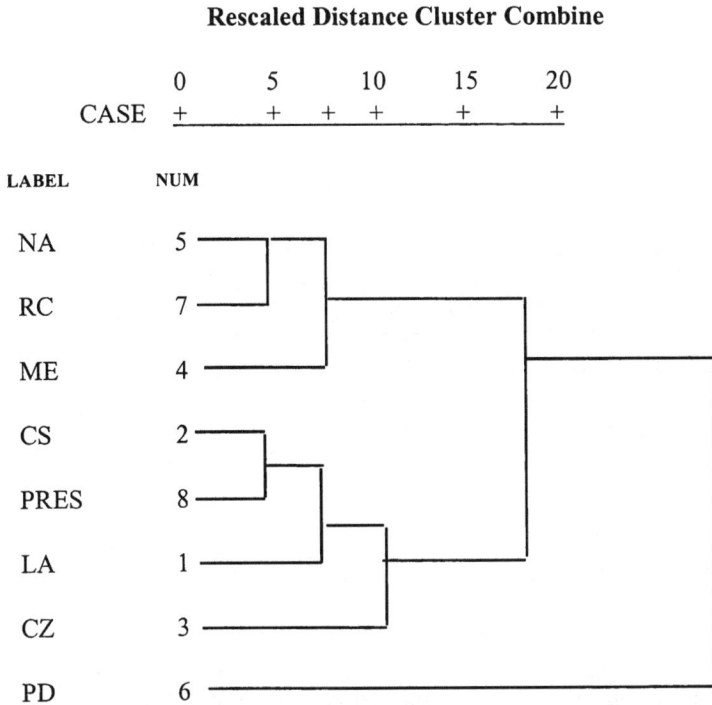

Fig 10.2 Dendrogram of clusters

These clusters can now be projected and plotted in a two-dimensional variability space where the relevant positioning of the members of each cluster within each separate cluster and across clusters is made even more evident, as in figure 10.3. It is even more obvious in this case that the maverick groups with respect to the two Southern Italian geolinguistic clusters are, on the one hand, speakers from the Pollino Lausberg Area and, on the other, the population sample from Reggio Calabria. In the first case, positioning can be calculated in a more decisive fashion by increasing the population sample, which is being done in ongoing research. An in-depth analysis may also help group the Reggio speakers in a clearer fashion. However, it can already be stated that there is a Calabrian regional Italian cluster to which Reggio Calabria does not belong and an urban Sicilian-Neapolitan cluster to which Reggio does belong, though at the present state of research in a more peripheral manner. Further investigation, as we have suggested, is needed, though our main point on dialect and regional Italian affiliation seems to need no further proof. The neo-Venetian group (Padua sample) is something quite separate, from the point of view of variability in regional Italian, and serves merely as a control group with respect to clustering patterns established by the Southern varieties and by their Italian variability under investigation. For more precise judgements on Veneto phonological-phonetic variation, see Trumper and Maddalon (1991).

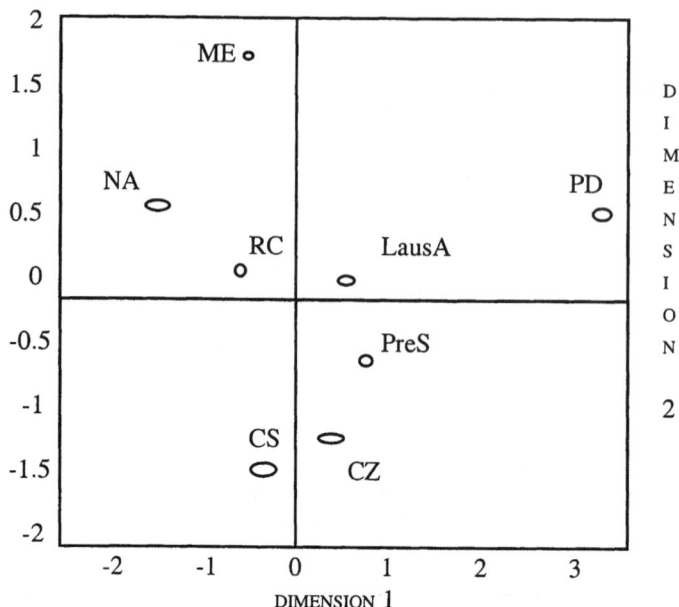

Fig 10.3 Clusters plotted in a two-dimensional variability space

The major factor in separating Reggio Calabria from the rest of Calabria, both from the dialectal point of view and from that of variability in regional Italian which directly reflects dialect processes and associating it with a linguistic model typical of urban eastern Sicily in particular and with that of the large urban agglomerations of the erstwhile Kingdom of the Two Sicilies, with Naples and Palermo as "parlers guide," was considered in Trumper and Chiodo (1997) to be the spate of earthquakes in the period 1905–1908.[8] Details are in Boschi et al. (1995).[9]

In Trumper and Rizzi (1985) the question of the non-use of infinitival strategies in mid and southern Calabrian was tackled at some length and taken up from the point of view of Salento (South Apulian) dialect varieties in Calabrese (1993). Infinitive strategies seem to be impossible in such dialects except after their equivalents of *potere* 'can/may', in some cases after *dovere* 'have to/must/ought to' and marginally in constructions that depend on "perception" verbs ('hear', 'feel', 'perceive'). It was pointed out that in the first case the relevant distinction was not between "physical possibility" and "permission" as respective components of 'can' and 'may' but between optative and non-optative aspects of both verbs (Trumper and Rizzi 1985:68–70 §3), in the last that infinite strategies were allowed in cases where the perception verb was directly subcategorized to take an infinitive verb phrase which represented a sort of unspecified "hanging" phrasal complement (Trumper and Rizzi 1985:70–73 §4). When the complement phrase has a subject and an object NP beyond the straightforward verbal action, relativization or some other alternative strategy immediately substitutes this "hanging" infinitive. Alternatively, in the vast majority of cases where a finite verb strategy is required, there seems to be no clear-cut semantic criteria to distinguish verb complements with *ca* + finite phrase from those with *'u/mu* + finite phrase. There may well be an underlying opposition between future-oriented, or perhaps modally oriented, predicates, that require a *mu/ma/mi* complementizer, and predicates that cannot be so labeled, requiring *ca/chi* complements, as others suggest, but I would prefer to leave the details of such a distinction open at the present.

From the point of view of the refusal to use infinitive strategies and the particular distinction between *ca*-complements and *mu*-complements, the Reggio Calabria dialect described in Mandalari (1881) seems to be no different from the present-day dialects of the lower Tyrrhenian coast, say those of Melicucco and Polistena, or those of the lower Ionian coast, for example, those of S. Ilario and Locri. We can compare strategies within these three groups with Italian and similar strategies in the dialects of Vibo Valentia (mid Calabrian, Tyrrhenian coast) and Catanzaro (mid Calabrian, Ionian coast) as in table 10.3. Examples from the Vibo Valentia and Catanzaro dialects will not be given here since they can easily be checked in Trumper and Rizzi (1985). Obviously, more cases could be tested and control checks can easily be extended with native speakers. In cases where one or two dialects differ in strategy from at least three others, the divergent strategy has been scored in cursive script in the table.

There is, of course, a current discussion on whether the construction *(m)u* + finite phrase really involves a finite verb or represents, in some way, an inflected infinitive: arguments are given in Ledgeway (forthcoming). At present, we may acknowledge three points in favor of this argument:

1. This type of strategy does not permit temporal oppositions within the verb; that is, we have

> Ti dicu ma/ (m)u/ mi ti ndi vai/
> Ti dicía [Ti diciva] ma/ (m)u/ mi ti ndi vai/
> Ti dissi ma/ (m)u/ mi ti ndi vai/
> T'avia dittu ma/ (m)u/ mi ti ndi vai

In other words, the second (dependent) verb is not inflected for a TIME component, but only for PERSON.

2. Both *ca* and *ma/mu* may co-occur in constructions such as

> 'O ffai atru *ca ma* ciangi (mid Calabria)/
> No' ffai attu *c'o* chjangi   (south Calabria, e.g. the Locride,
>   where *c'o* < *ca* + *'u*) = "Non fai altro che piangere"
>   ('You do nothing but cry')[10]

3. Negation precedes *mu/ma/mi*: for example, we have *nommu/nomma/nommi*, which, as Ledgeway emphasizes, would be "strange" if *mu/ma/mi* were straighforward complementizers: *ca/chi*, usual finite

complementizers, precede the negative. However, even where temporal inflection is missing, there is still a significant morphological distinction between infinitives inflected for person, as in Portuguese or Old Neapolitan, and inflected verbs, inflected at least for person, such as *parru/parri/parra/parramu/parrati/párranu [párrunu]*, so the question of whether *mu/ma*-clauses are in fact inflected infinitival clauses or not will be waived at the present, and I will continue to list such clause structures as finite clauses until the whole matter has been hammered out.

TABLE 10.3 Infinitive and non-infinitive strategies[11]

Governing verb	Italian	Vibo Valentia	Catanzaro	Melicucco/ Polistena	S. Ilario/ Locri	RC1880
DIRE1 (non-jussive)	*che*+F	*ca*+F	*ca*+F	*ca*+F	*ca*+F	*chi*+F
DIRE2 (jussive)	*di*+I	*[m]u*+F	*ma*+F	*'u*+F	*'u*+F	*mi*+F
ACCORGERSI	*di*+I (E) / *che*+F (O)	*ca*+F	*ca*+F	*ca*+F	*ca*+F	*chi*+F
CREDERE	*di*+I (E) / *che*+F (O)	*ca*+F	*ca*+F	*ca*+F	*ca*+F	*chi*+F
PENSARE	*di*+I (E) / *che*+F (O)	*ca*+F	*ca*+F	*ca*+F / *'u*+F	*ca*+F	*chi*+F / *mi*+F
TEMERE / AVERE PAURA	*di*+I (E) / *che*+F (O)	*ca*+F	*ca*+F	*ca*+F	*ca*+F	*chi*+F
SPERARE (=CREDERE) (=AUGURARSI)	*di*+I (E) / *che*+F (O)	*ca*+F / *'u*+F	*ca*+F	*ca*+F	*ca*+F	*chi*+F
DECIDERE1 (for s.o. else)	*che*+F	*ca*+F	*ca*+F	*ca*+F	*'u*+F	*chi*+F
DECIDERE2 (for oneself)	*di*+I	*'u*+F	*ma*+F	*'u*+F	*'u*+F	*mi*+F
ESSER SICURI/ ESSER CONTENTI	*di*+I (E) / *che*+F (O)	*ca*+F	*ca*+F	*ca*+F	*ca*+F	*chi*+F
DOPO	+I (E) / *che*+F (O)	*ca*+F	*ca*+F	*ca*+F	*ca*+F	*chi*+F

TABLE 10.3 (continued)

Governing verb	Italian	Vibo Valentia	Catanzaro	Melicucco/ Polistena	S. Ilario/ Locri	RC1880
APPENA	+F	*ca*+F	*ca*+F	*ca*+F	*ca*+F	*chi*+F
CONVINCERE/ PERSUADERE	*di*+I	*'u*+F	*ma*+F	*'u*+F	*'u*+F	*mi*+F
DOVERE	I	*'u*+F	*'e*+I	*a*+I	*'u*+F	*a*+I / *mi*+F
POTERE1	I	I	I	I	I	I
POTERE2	I	I	I	I	I	I
POTERE3	I	*'u*+F	*ma*+F	*'u*+I	*'u*+I	??
LASCIARE	I	*'u*+F	*ma*+F	*'u*+F	*'u*+F	*mi*+F / I
FARE	I / *che*+F (subj)	*'u*+F	*ma*+F	*'u*+F	*'u* = *pemmu*+F	*mi*+F
VOLERE	I / *che*+F (subj)	*'u*+F	*ma*+F	*'u*+F	*'u*+F	I / *mi*+F
jussive/ imperative subjunctive	*che*/imp. (subj)	*'u*+F	*ma*+F	*'u*+F	*'u*+F	*mi*+F
VENIRE	*a*+I	*pemmu*/ *'u*+F	*pimma*/ *ma*+F	*pemmu*/ *'u*+F	*'u*+F	*mi*+F
ANDARE	*a*+I	*'u*+F	*ma*+F	*'u*+F	*'u*+F	*mi*+F
IN MODO DA	*da*+I	*pemmu*+F	*pimma*+F	*pemmu*+F	*pemmu*+F	(*pirchi*) +*mi*+F
COMINCIARE	*a*+I	*'u*+F	*ma*+F	*'u*+F	*'u*+F	*mi*+F
CONTINUARE	*a*+I	*'u*+F	*ma*+F	*'u*+F	*'u*+F	*mi*+F
FINIRE1	*di*+I	*'u*+F	*ma*+F	*'u*+F	*'u*+F	??
FINIRE2	*con*+art +I	*'u*+F	*ma*+F	*'u*+F	*'u*+F	??
AIUTARE	*a*+I	*'u*+F	*ma*+F	*'u*+F	*'u*+F	*mi*+F
PERMETTERE	*di*+I	*'u*+F	*ma*+F	*'u*+F	*'u*+F	*mi*+F

— Continued

TABLE 10.3 (continued)

Governing verb	Italian	Vibo Valentia	Catanzaro	Melicucco/ Polistena	S. Ilario/ Locri	RC18-80
PROVARE/ CERCARE	a / di+I	'u+F	ma+F	'u+F	'u+F	mi+F
RIUSCIRE	a+I	'u+F	ma+F	'u+F	'u+F	??
final/causal	per+I	pemmu-+F	pimma+F	'u+F pemmu+F	'u+F pemmu+F	mi+F
passive	da+I	'u+F	ma+F	'u+F	'u+F	mi+F
before + gerund/temporal clause	prima di+I(E) prima che+F	prima mu+F	prima ma+F	prima +'u+F	prima +'u+F	prima +mi+F
SENTIRE+ single complement	+I	I	I	I	I	I
SENTIRE+ XP compl. 2 elements	+I +NP	ROC	ROC	ROC	ROC	I
SENTIRE+ XP compl. 2+elements	+I +NP + (PREP) NP	ROC	ROC	ROC	ROC	ROC
SENZA	I(E)/ che+F subj (o)	senza+ (m)u+F	senza+ ma+F	senza+ (m)u+F	senza+ 'u+F	senza+ + mi+F

Examples from the Melicucco/Polistena modern dialects are respectively: Ti ricu ca staju jendu / Ti rissi 'u vai rá / M'addunái ca nd'avía raggiúni / Criju [Nun criju] ca nd'avía raggiúni / Penzu ca 'nci vaju = Penzu 'u 'nci vaju / Speramu ca chjòvi / Reciría ca tu 'nci vái / Reciría mu 'nci vaju, Recíriti 'u vái / Sugnu cuntentu ca vinni; Statti attentu ca mi struppíji / Roppu ca mi vitti, si 'ndi jíu / Appena ca mi vitti ... / Mi cunvincíu (m)u vaju / Mi fici nu piaciri e mmò m'aju a ddisubbrigari / U figghjòlu potarría pisari cinquanta chili / Ti pòi levari 'i rocu, si bbòi / Potarría 'u chjòvi ≠ Potarría chjuvíri / Mi rassáu 'u vaju / Fici 'u mi 'ndi vaju / Vogghju 'u mi ricògghju / M'a pòi fari ssa cosa [= M(u) + a...] / Vinni pemmu ti mbitu = Vinni 'u ti mbitu / Jíu m'u pigghju / U fici 'u m'ajuta / Ncignáu 'u chjòvi / Cuntínua 'u chjòvi / Finíu ca lijíu a líttara (Finì col leggere la lettera) / Finíu mu lèji a líttara (Ha finito di leggere la lettera) / M'ajutáu mu nchjanu / Mi permittíu (m)u mi ndi vaju / Circáu 'u ndi sparti; Cerca 'u 'nci 'u rici / Riuscíu 'u si ndi vá / M'u fà 'u 'nci fazzu nu favúri / E' ffácili 'u si lèji / 'Nci 'u rissi prima 'u mi ndi vaju / Sentu cantári (= sentu ca cántanu); No' ssentu cantári / Sentu accèri chi ccántanu; Sentu a Mmaría chi ccanta; No' ssentu a nnuru chi ccanta/ Sentu a Mmaría chi ccanta na canzuni / 'U fici senza 'u mi viri; 'U fici senza 'û viju.

Their equivalents in the present day Locri/S. Ilario dialects are: Ti dicu ca jía / Ti dissi 'u vái / M'addunái [= M'accorgía] ca i[]u vinni / Criju [Non criju] ch'è 'a veru / Penzu ca 'ndaju 'u vaju / Sperámu ca chjòvi = Cridímu ca chjòvi / Decidía ca 'ndái 'u vái / Decidía 'u vaju; Mòviti 'u vái / Signu cuntentu ca vinni / Doppu ca mi vvitti, si 'ndi jíu / Appena ca mi vitti... / Mi cunvincíu 'u vaju / 'Ndaju 'u mi 'ndi vaju / Gianni potarría nd'avíri vint'anni / Tu ti poi jurgíri, si bbòi ≠ Tu pòi 'u ti jurgi, si bbòi / Potarría 'u chjòvi ≠ Potarría chjuvíri / Mi dassáu 'u vaju / Mi fici 'u mi 'ndi vaju / Vogghju 'u ricògghju / M'a fái ssa cosa [= M(u) + a]/ Vinni 'u ti 'mbitu ô matrimmòniu / Jía m'u pígghju / S'u fici pemmu mi fái nu favúri / 'Ncignáu 'u chjòvi / Cuntínua 'u chjòvi / Finía ca lijía a líttara / Finía 'u lèju a líttara; Sta 'ttentu ca vái 'u finísci ca mi ciúnchi / M'ajutáu 'u 'nchjanu / Mi permittíu 'u vaju / Cerca 'u si 'u dici / Rinuscíu 'u si 'ndi vái / M'u fici pemmu si fazzu èu nu favúri / E' ffácili 'u si lèji / S'u dissi prima 'u mi 'ndi vaju / Sentu cantári / Sentu cantári arcè[]i; Sentu cantári na canzuni but Sentu a Mmaría chi ccanta; Sentu ca María canta / Sentu ca María canta na canzuni; Sentu a Mmaría chi ccanta na canzuni / U fici senza 'u mi vidi; U fici senza m'u viju.[12]

In the case of the 1880 Reggio Calabria dialect described in detail in Mandalari (1881) a certain number of cases can be found. The general picture that emerges is that of a dialect not essentially different from the others in table 10.3, with variation in the case of strategies with *pensare* like Melicucco/Polistena and with *dovere* as in the dialects of Catanzaro and Melicucco/Polistena. However, three differences are already recorded: double (variable) strategies, admitted with *lasciare* and *volere*, while the infinitive strategy is seemingly normal in the case of *sentire* when two following complements are involved. Straightforward examples with *chi* + finite clause will not be given here, only some involving *mi* or alternative strategies, as given in the source of this 1880 dialect, i.e.: **dire 1** (narrative) with *chi* (*dissi chi era tempu pirdutu... / dissi chi ê tempi... succidìu...* in Novella IX) vs. **dire 2** (jussive with *mi*:: *Dinci mi nesci fora...* Raccolta di XXXI); **pensare** with *chi* (*Pensu chi ndi vardàvamu...*, Raccolta di Canale XLII), as well as with *mi* (*pinsau mi vai...* Novella IX); **dovere** with both infinitive (*andaju a diri*), as well as with a finite complement, with *potere* only examples with infinitives are to be found. With **lasciare** we have a double strategy (finite clause in *dassati [mi] nci curpati vui*, Raccolta di Canale VIII, in other cases *si dassa guardari, mi mi dassa jri* etc.), as with **fare** (finite clause in *Fai, co li toi modi, mi ammarruna*, Canti Calabresi, Mandalari 1881:384 elsewhere with the infinitive) and with **volere** (*t'u vurria cumprimentari*, Novella IX, but *mi* + finite clause in *vurria mi sacciu*, Raccolta di Canale XXXIII etc.). Other such cases are: jussive uses as in *A ferma fidi mi mi teni a mmia* Raccolta di Canale XVII, *Mi mi dassa jri* id. XVIII, *Ddiu mi mi scanza* id. XLVIII etc., with **venire** (*vegnu cca nda tia mi ottegnu vinditta*,

Novella IX, *Vinisti mi mi vidi*, Raccolta di Canale VII); **andare** (*Vai mi ricurri ô Re*, Novella IX etc.), with final clauses (*...mi partia pirchì cantandu / Mi ti lu dicu cu la bbucca mia..., pi 'na mia sodisfazioni mi m'ansigni*, Novella IX); **provare** (*nc'è cu cerca mi ndi sparti*, Raccolta di Canale XXXV = 'There is someone who's trying to split us up'), even with passive constructions as in *Non eppi mbasciaturi mi ti mandu* 'Non ebbi ambasciatori da mandarti' = 'I had no ambassadors to send you'). In the case of the verba sentiendi class, there seems to be no block to the infinitive strategy if the infinitive represents a "hanging" sentence or even if there are two complements—for example, *si vvo' sentiri cantari* (Raccolta di Canale XXXVIII), *si sintìu pirdiri 'u cori* (Novella IX)—while in the case of more complements, relativization strategies intervene, as in *ddi 'mproperii chi sentu diri chi ti càntinu 'i genti* (Novella IX) 'quelli improperi che ti sento dire cantare dalla gente'. Obviously, the dialect equivalent of an Italian infinitival subject or object (*Mangiare mi piace*, etc.) is a finite clause preceded by *mi*, as in Mandalari (1881), Raccolta di Canale XXXV / *Mi ndi spàrtinu a nnui non nci sunn'arti /* "Separarci non ci sono arti," as in the modern dialects of table 3.1, for example, *Ma ndi spártanu non è pussíbbila* (CZ), *'U ndi spártinu non è pussíbbili* (Vibo/Polistena/Melicucco/Locri/S. Ilario) = "Separarci non è possibile." Rural East Sicily presents a similar picture of dialect syntactic strategies; see Varvaro (1988 §10.3.9) ("Il triangolo nord-or. usa la fora del cong. ottativo, che qui, per un tipico fenomeno di sostrato greco, è **mi trasi.** . . . **mi si setta** 'si segga'." etc.). As in Trumper and Rizzi (1985), and later in Calabrese (1993), it is argued that this is not so much a question of substratum as of Sprachbund phenomenology and syntactic strategies over the last millennium, and formally, in a morphological sense, dialects differ on whether the finite verb is subjunctive or not. It may be so in the Apulian case, not in the Calabrian and E. Sicilian one, for instance, though this could be argued as being true diachronically. Varvaro's criticisms of earlier attempts at description of these dialects might be leveled at his own efforts. However, it may well be the case that urban Eastern Sicily has undergone a historical conflict between rural strategies without infinitives and urban Sicilian koiné where such strategies are extremely common. Unfortunately, no in-depth studies are available to date on this topic, though the present situation seems to show a Messina dialect which has long ago left behind its rural dialects and their specific syntactic strategies to follow an urban originally upper- and middle-class norm with a basically different syntax.

The modern situation at Reggio Calabria has gone further in the direction of Sicilian urban dialect syntax. In fact, though a large number of cases with *mi* + finite clause are kept, there is much more flexibility in the modern dialect with regard to infinitive strategies and in some cases they have now become the norm. Examples of identical *mi* strategy to that observed in the 1880 dialect are cases such as the following:

- **dire 2**   (jussive: *Ti ricu mi ti ndi vái* "Ti dico di andartene")

- **pensare** with variable strategies (*Penzu chi vaju rumani = Penzu mi vaju rumani* "Penso di andare domani")

- **decidere 2** (*Riciría mi mi ndi vaju* "Ho deciso di andarmene")

- **persuadere** (*Mi cunvinciu mi mi ndi vaju â casa* "Mi ha persuaso di andarmene accasa"), jussive uses

- **venire** + infinitive (*Vinni ccá mi travagghju* "Sono venuto qui a lavorare")

- **andare** + infinitive (*Jiu mi trova a sso zziu* "E' andato a trovare suo zio"), modal uses (= in modo che/ da..., cf. *Ffácciti â finestra mi ti vardu* "Affácciati alla finestra in modo che io ti veda")

- **cominciare** + a + infinitive (*Ncignáu mi chjòvi* "Cominciò a piovere")

- **continuare** + a + infinitive (*Cuntinuváu mi chjòvi* "Continuò a piovere")

- **aiutare** + a + infinitive (*Mi jutáu m'u fazzu* "Mi ha aiutato a farlo")

- **permettere** + di + infinitive (*Permentíu mi mi ndi vaju â casa* "Mi ha permesso di andare accasa")

- **provare/ cercare** + a + infinitive (*Circáu mi vái, ma non 'nci riniscíu* "Ha provato ad andare, ma non c'è riuscito"; *Nd'eppi cu circáu mi ndi sparti* "C'è stato chi ha provato a separarci"; *Staju circandu mi t'u trarúciu* "Sto cercando di tradurtelo"), final clauses, passive constructions (*Esti bbonu mi si mangia* "E' buono da mangiare")
- **prima** + di + infinitive (*Prima mi ti ndi vái, dinci tuttu* "Prima di andartene, digli tutto!")

Some identical uses of the infinitive are kept, as in the 1880 model—'must/ have to' (*Ndaju a ffari ḍḍa cosa* "Devo far quella cosa"), with **potere** 'may/can', without distinction between optative and non-optative uses. Innovations consist in a new obligatory use of the infinitive strategy with verbs such as **lasciare** 'allow/ let' (*Mi rassáu fari chiḍḍu chi vvuliva* "Mi ha lasciato fare ciò che volevo"), **fare** 'make' (*Ti fici fari tuttu chiḍḍu chi vvulivi* "Ti ho fatto fare tutto ciò che volevi"), and **volere** (*Mi vò ccuntintari* "Mi vuole accontentare"), as well as with verbs such as **finire** and **riuscire** (*riniscíri*). There now seem also to be no bounds on the use of the infinitive after the *verba sentiendi*, even when there are two or more complements, without recourse to alternative syntactic strategies. In addition, one might add that modern Reggio speakers are much more "possibilistic" on extending the infinitive strategy to new cases not formerly contemplated by dialect syntax, a completely different attitude to speakers from the rest of the southern part of Calabria. All in all, one might conclude that Reggio Calabria has been groping for new syntactic strategies that are in line with urban Sicilian models, as well as with the supravernacular "siciliano aulico" of historical fame, a tendency that is now reinforced by its being in line with syntactic strategies in the national language. I would, however, suggest that this gradual change in syntactic patterns, associated with a change of dialect affiliation, is due less to postwar Italianization, with obvious reference to the Second World War, than to the demographic upheaval that was consequent on the earthquakes and tsunami of the 1905–1908 period. One feels that this situation should be looked at in greater detail and not "overlooked" as it has been in Italian dialectology.

Notes

Anrheg addas i ti, i'th ddoniau tawel teyrnged. Per Paola, affettuosamente.

1. DO = direct object, IO = indirect object. Phonetic conventions used in the transcriptions of Calabrian dialects follow those of usual Italian orthography except that 'chj' and 'ghj' represent palatal stops (respectively, /c/ and /ɟ/), ô, â, and ê represent monophthongizations usual in such dialects in contractions of the preposition 'a' with the definite article (from, respectively, a + u, a + a, a + i), otherwise IPA conventions are followed, as in the case of retroflex /ɖɖ/, /ʎʎ/. In the dialect of Reggio Calabria -ci- does not represent an affricate, as usually, but its allophonic intervocalic variant, a lax alveopalatal fricative. I am indebted to Adam Ledgeway for comments on a first draft of this chapter: obviously he is not responsible for any interpretative errors on my part.

2. Rohlfs 1968 vol. 3 §632 errs in limiting the phenomenon to the dialect of Triest: he also furnishes examples in the Genoan dialect, in Ligurian and the so-called "Gallo-Sicilian" of Nicosia, which should ideally have prompted an in-depth analysis of this particular grammatical strategy, both in Southern and Northern Italian Romance varieties. Unfortunately, the details of this strategy are discussed in a completely inadequate way. It is interesting to note that the two instances in Triest dialect quoted by Rohlfs in the above paragraph (i.e., *no stéme lassar fora a mi* and *mi te go pregà a ti de farme sto piassèr*) correspond perfectly to constructions in all neo-Venetian dialects and some Friulian ones (the Isonzo transitional dialects quoted in Trumper 1996:354). These constructs are almost exactly identical to those of other dialects of the Veneto region (cf. PD/VI *no stè-me lassar fóra a mi/ mi te go pregà a ti de farme sto piassère*, etc.). To distinguish between a real "dative" *a* marking an IO in *Te go dito a ti* 'It's you I told' and the marking of an anticipated DO in *Te go visto a ti* 'It's you I saw', the rural varieties of older PD/VI informants use *incóntro* to mark IO's: for example, *Te go dito incóntro a ti / Te go dito incóntrote, Ghe go dito incóntro a me mojére, Ghe go dito incóntro a uno, Ghe go dito incóntro a élo / Ghe go dito incóntroghe*. The preposition *incóntro* cannot so mark a DO. In other words **Te go visto incóntro a ti* is ungrammatical in anyone's Veneto dialect, and *Te go dito incóntro a ti* is perfectly grammatical in the markedly rural dialect of older country folk.

3. Pertinent geolinguistic divisions are explicated in Trumper (1997).

4. Lit.: 'I don't talk to him because he doesn't listen'; 'I haven't been talking to him because I haven't been seeing him lately'; 'I'm not talking to him because he's stupid'; 'I'm not talking to him because he makes me livid'.

5. "To argue" is a reflexive verb in Calabrian but not in Italian (*litigare*).

6. Examples come from fieldwork carried out in the last fifteen years in which I have lived regularly in Calabria: translations 'I told the lad to go' and 'I told the lad to do me a (= this) favor', respectively.

7. I wish to thank G. A. Mian and S. Cannazza of Padua University's Engineering Faculty for a discussion of the multidimensional and cluster analysis most suitable for processing this type of linguistic data and for its elaboration.

8. The last on 28 December 1908 was an earthquake of intensity XI MCS,

magnitude 7, one of the strongest earthquakes recorded at worldwide level, its shockwave being measured in 103 stations around the globe; it caused a catastrophe in the Strait of Messina in which 42% of the population of the city of Messina died, ca. 25% of the population of Reggio Calabria.

9. More damage and deaths were caused by the later 10–15 m high tsunami or shock tidal wave that occurred in the contiguous strip of sea in the strait extremely early on the following morning, completing the destruction in its wake. For precise measurements see Platania (1908, 1909, 1914): at Pellaro and Gallico, slightly south of Reggio, the wave was registered as 10 m high 1/4 km inland, so out at sea at that point it must have been considerably higher, which is why we have suggested a minimum of 10m (inland), a maximum of 15 m (at sea-level) as the height of the shock wave. A brief example: at Lazzaro, slightly further south, the picture is exactly the same as at Pellaro, if not worse; see Baratta (1910:367): "LAZZARO.—Il maremoto si presentò come una colossale ondata, che molti rassomigliarono ad una cupa muraglia con varie lingue, la quale in alcuni punti si inoltrò per 250 m. circa. Altezza dell'acqua m. 10 circa. Tutto il paese inferiore, che si distendeva lungo la Provinciale, più che dal terremoto è stato raso al suolo dalla violenza del maremoto, che quivi ha prodotto quasi gli stessi effetti osservati in Pèllaro." The tsunami caused approximately 2,000 deaths, though this is probably an underestimate. What is more important, from the demographic point of view, is that although only one working-class "rione" of Messina was destroyed (the "rione Paradiso"), all the working-class "rioni" of Reggio were destroyed and had to be rebuilt, causing an enormous influx of outside population employed in the reconstruction. Although part of this incoming population was from the surrounding Calabrian countryside, it must be remembered that 40,000 people escaped from Messina in this period, 10,000 going to Palermo, the rest toward other Sicilian cities and to the Calabrian mainland where they were used as part of the workforce employed in the post-earthquake rebuilding project. Some details are in Restifo (1995).

10. I am not at all sure that *ca* in such cases is the normal finite complementizer *ca/ chi*, so that an argument based on such a co-occurrence with *ma/mu/mi* does not seem to me to be convincing: I await further proof on this score.

11. Abbreviations in table 10.3 (pp. 240–242) are as follows: F = finite, I = infinitive, E = equideletion, O = otherwise, and ROC = relativisation of complement.

12. Rough translations are, in order: I tell you that I'm going (that I went) / I told you to go / I realised he was right (that he'd come) / I think he's right (it's true) / I think I'll go; I think I must go / We hope it'll rain / I decided you go (you must go) / I decided to go; Make up your mind to go! / I'm glad you came (Careful you don't lame me) / After he saw me, he left / As soon as he saw me... / He persuaded me to go / He did me a favour and I have to reciprocate (I must leave) / The lad could just weigh 50 kg. (John could be 20 years old) / You can leave, if you like (≠ I wish you'd leave!) / It might just rain (≠ I wish it would rain!) / He let me go / He made me leave / I want to go home / Would you do me this! / I have come to invite you (to the wedding) / He went to get it / He did it in order to help me (to do me a favour) / It began to rain / It continues raining / He ended up reading the letter / He finished reading the letter (Take care: you'll end up laming me) / He helped me to get down / He allowed me to leave / He tried to split us (Try to tell it him) / He succeeded in leaving / He did it so that I'd do him a favour / It's easy to read / I told him before I left / I hear singing / I hear birds singing; I hear Mary singing (I hear noone singing) / I hear Mary singing a song / He did it without seeing me; I did it without seeing him.

References

Baratta, M. (1910) *La Catastrofe Sismica Calabro-Messinese (28 dicembre 1908)*. Rome: Società Geografica Italiana.

Boschi, E., G. Ferrari, P. Gasperini, E. Guidoboni, G. Smeriglio, and G. Valensise (eds.) (1995) *Catalogo dei forti terremoti in Italia dal 461 a.C. al 1980*. Rome: SGA Editore. Also on CD ROM, available from the Istituto Nazionale di Geofisica, Rome.

Calabrese, A. (1993) "The Sentential Complementation of Salentino: A Study of a Language without Infinitival Clauses," in A. Belletti (ed.), *Syntactic Theory and the Dialects of Italy*, pp. 28–98. Turin: Rosenberg and Sellier.

Cifoletti, G. (1989) *La lingua franca mediterranea*. Padua: Unipress.

D'Agostino, M. (1997) *Aspetti della variabilità: Ricerche linguistiche siciliane*. Palermo: Centro di Studi Filologici e Linguistici Siciliani.

Ledgeway, A. N. (forthcoming) "Variation in the Romance Infinitive: The Case of the Southern Calabrian Inflected Infinitive," in *Transactions of the Philological Society*.

Maddalon, M. and C. Marafioti (1991) "Proposte preliminari per una ridefinizione dei confini meridionali di alcuni fenomeni di lenizione," *Quaderni del Dipartimento di Linguistica, Serie Linguistica* 3:27–48.

Mandalari, M. (1881) *Canti del popolo reggino*. Naples.

Platania, G. (1908) "Il maremoto dello stretto di Messina del 28.12.1908," *Bollettino della Società Sismologica Italiana* 13:369–458.

Platania, G. (1909)"I fenomeni marittimi che accompagnarono il terremoto di Messina del 28.12.1908," *Rivista Geografica Italiana* 16 fasc. 3:3–8.

Platania, G. (1914) "Le recenti variazioni del livello del mare in Italia e la causa del terremoto di Messina e Reggio," *Rivista Geografica Italiana* 20:561–566.

Restifo, G. (1995) "Local Administrative Sources on Population Movements after the Messina Earthquake of 1908," *Annali di Geofisica* 38(5–6):559–566.

Rohlfs, G. (1966, 1968, 1969) *Grammatica storica della lingua italiana e dei suoi dialetti*, 3 vols. Turin: Einaudi.

Sornicola, R. (1997)"Campania," in M. Maiden and M. Parry (eds.), *The Dialects of Italy*, pp. 330–337. New York: Routledge.

Trumper, J. (1996) "Riflessioni pragmo-sintattiche su alcuni gruppi meridionali: italiano 'popolare'," in P. Benincà, G. Cinque, T. DeMauro, and N. Vincent (eds.), *Italiano e dialetti nel tempo: Saggi di grammatica per Giulio Lepschy*, pp. 351–367. Rome: Bulzoni.

Trumper, J. (1997) "Calabria and Southern Basilicata," in M. Maiden and M. Parry (eds.), *The Dialects of Italy*, pp. 355–364. New York: Routledge.

Trumper, J. and G. Chiodo (1997) "A Changing Europe: The Presence vs. Absence of Drastic Events Provoking or Blocking Internal Migration and Their Possible Contribution to Linguistic Change or Conservation." Paper given at the *Divergence/Convergence ESF Symposium*, University of Heidelberg.

Trumper, J. and M. Maddalon (1991) "Il problema delle varietà: l'italiano parlato nel Veneto," *Società Linguistica Italiana* 25:159–191.

Trumper, J. and L. Rizzi (1985) "Il problema sintattico di *calmu* nei dialetti calabresi mediani," *Quaderni del Dipartimento di Linguistica (Università della Calabria), Serie Linguistica* 1:63–76.

Varvaro, A. (1988) "Sizilien," in G. Holtus, M. Metzeltin, and C. Schmitt (eds.), *Lexicon der romanistischen Linguistik*, vol. 4, pp. 716–731. Tübingen: Niemayer.

Appendix: Publications by Paola Benincà

1969 "Commenti all'ASLEF: Sezione Entomologica," *Studi Linguistici Friulani* 1:67–98.

1970 "Note in margine alle 'Etimologie venete' di Angelico Prati," *Atti dell'Istituto Veneto di Scienze, Lettere e Arti* 128:673–704.

1972, 1974 (in collaboration with others) *Redazione dell'Atlante Storico Linguistico Etnografico Friulano (ASLEF)*, directed by G.B. Pellegrini, vol. I, Padova-Udine 1972; vol. 2, Padua-Udine 1974.

1973a "Osservazioni sull' 'Unità Lessicale Ladina,'" *Studi Linguistici Friulani* 3:121–132.

1973b "Ascoli e Manzoni: Due Terapie per l'Integrazione Linguistica," in *Graziadio Isaia Ascoli e l'"Archivio Glottologico Italiano"* M. Cortelazzo (ed.), pp. 139–150. Udine: Società Filologica Friulana.

1974 (in collaboration with others) "Italiano standard o italiano scolastico?" in *Dal dialetto alla lingua* (Proceedings of the *IX Convegno di Studi Dialettali Italiani*). Pisa: Pacini. Reprinted in *Guida all'Educazione Linguistica*, A. Colombo (ed.), pp.162–178. Bologna: Zanichelli, 1979.

1975a (in collaboration with L. Vanelli) "Elementi per un Dibattito sull'Educazione Linguistica," *La Ricerca Dialettale* 1:303–345.

1975b Review of G. B. Pellegrini, *Saggi sul Ladino Dolomitico e sul Friulano* [Bari 1972], in *La Ricerca Dialettale* 1:567–575.

1975c "Dialetto e Scuola: Un Rapporto Difficile," in *L'Educazione Linguistica* (Proceedings of the *Giornata di Studio Giscel*), pp. 35–41. Padua: CLEUP. Reprinted in *Guida all'educazione linguistica*, A. Colombo (ed.), Bologna: Zanichelli, 1979.

1976a (in collaboration with L. Vanelli) "Un'Innovazione nel Dominio Romanzo: la 1. Persona del Presente Indicativo di I Coniugazione," in *Problemi di Morfosintassi Dialettale* (Proceedings of the *XI Convegno per gli Studi Dialettali Italiani*), pp. 213–226. Pisa: Pacini.

1976b (in collaboration with L. Vanelli) "Morfologia del verbo friulano: Il presente indicativo," *Lingua e Contesto* 1:1–62.

1976c Review of M. Iliescu, *Le Frioulan à Partir des Dialectes Parlés en Roumanie* [The Hague 1972], *Bollettino dell'Atlante Linguistico Italiano* 3,1:52–55.

1977 (in collaboration with others) "101 Modi per Richiedere," in *Aspetti Sociolinguistici dell'Italia Contemporanea* (Proceedings of the *VIII Congresso Internazionale della Società Linguistica Italiana*), pp. 501–533. Rome: Bulzoni.

1978a (in collaboration with L. Vanelli) "Il Plurale Friulano: Contributo allo Studio del Plurale Romanzo," *Revue de Linguistique Romane* 167–168:241–292.

1978b "Sono tre ore che ti aspetto," *Rivista di Grammatica Generativa* 3(2):231–245.

1978c Review of U. Weinreich, *Lingue in Contatto* [Turin 1974], *La Ricerca Dialettale* 2:448–455.

1979 (in collaboration with *il Gruppo di Padova*), "Aspetti dell'Espressione della Causalità in Italiano," in *La Grammatica. Aspetti Teorici e Didattici* (Proceedings of the *IX Congresso Internazionale di Studi della Società Linguistica Italiana*), pp. 325–375. Rome: Bulzoni.

1980 "Nomi senza articolo," *Rivista di Grammatica Generativa* 5:51–62.

1981a Review of J. P. Rona and W. Wölck (eds.) *The Social Dimension of Dialectology* [in *International Journal of the Sociology of Language* 9, 1976], *La Ricerca Dialettale* 3:593–608.

1981b (in collaboration with R. Peca Conti) Review of T. Bynon, *Historical Linguistics* [Cambridge 1977, Italian translation: Bologna 1980], *Studi Italiani di Linguistica Teorica e Applicata* 10:482–486.

1982a (in collaboration with L. Vanelli) "Appunti di Sintassi Veneta," in M. Cortelazzo (ed.), *Guida ai Dialetti Veneti IV*, pp. 7–38. Padua: CLEUP.

1982b (in collaboration with Rita Peca Conti) "Teorie linguistiche e cambio linguistico," *Linguistica e Letteratura* 7(1–2):261–278.

1983a "Il Clitico *a* nel Dialetto Padovano," in *Scritti Linguistici in Onore di G. B.Pellegrini*, pp. 25–35. Pisa: Pacini.

1983b "Osservazioni sulla Sintassi dei Testi di Lio Mazor," in C. Angelet, L. Melis, F. Mertens, and F. Musarra (eds.), *Langue, Dialecte, Littérature: Etudes Romanes à la Mémoire de Hugo Plomteux*, pp. 187–197. Leuven: Leuven University Press.

1984a (in collaboration with L. Vanelli) "Aspetti Sintattici del Portogruarese tra Veneto e Friulano," in R. Sandron (ed.), *Atti del Convegno "L'Area Portogruarese tra Veneto e Friulano."* Portogruaro: Comune di Portogruaro.

1984b *Dizionario Etimologico Storico Friulano* vol. 1 (ed. entries from *bifòlc* to *breùte*), pp. 216–266. Udine: Casamassima.

1984c "Un'Ipotesi sulla Sintassi delle Lingue Romanze Medievali," *Quaderni Patavini di Linguistica* 4:3–19.

1984d Review of B. Terracini, *Linguistica al bivio* [in G. L. Beccaria and M. L. Porzio Gernia (Naples 1981); and F. D'Ovidio, *Scritti Linguistici* in P. Bianchi (ed.), Introduction by F. Bruni (Naples 1982)], *Romance Philology* 37(3):336–341.

1984e "Uso dell'Ausiliare e Accordo Verbale nei Dialetti Veneti e Friulani," *Rivista Italiana di Dialettologia* 8:178–194.

1985a "L'Interferenza Sintattica: di un Aspetto della Sintassi Ladina Considerato di Origine Tedesca," in *Quaderni Patavini di Linguistica* 5:3–15. Also in Proceedings of the 14th *Convegno di Studi Dialettali Italiani*, vol. 2, pp. 229–239. Pisa: Pacini, 1988.

1985b (in collaboration with L. Vanelli and L. Renzi) "Typologie des Pronoms Sujets dans les Langues Romanes," in *Actes du 17ème Congrès International de Linguistique et Philologie Romanes*, vol. 3., pp. 164–176. Italian translation in *Quaderni Patavini di Linguistica* 5:49–66.

1986a "Il Lato Sinistro della Frase Italiana," *ATI Journal* 47:57–85. Also in *Balkan Archiv* 11:213–243.

1986b "Punti di Sintassi Comparata dei Dialetti Italiani Settentrionali," in G. Holtus and K. Ringger (eds.), *Raetia Antiqua et Moderna: W. T. Elwert zum 80 Geburtstag*, pp. 457–479. Tübingen.

1987 "Due Nomi Friulani per *ape*: Etimologie Morfologiche," *Ce Fastu?* 63:59–61.

1988a Review of D. Santamaria, *Bernardino Biondelli e la Linguistica Preascoliana* [Rome, Cadmo, 1981], *Romance Philology* 41(3):337–340.

1988b "L'Ordine degli Elementi della Frase e le Costruzioni Marcate," in L. Renzi (ed.), *Grande Grammatica Italiana di Consultazione*, vol. 1, Bologna: Il Mulino, pp. 115–195 (pages 119–129 in collaboration with G. Salvi).

1988c *Piccola Storia Ragionata della Dialettologia Italiana*. Padua: Unipress.

1988d "Friulanisch," in *Lexikon des Mittelalters*. Munich: Artemis.

1989a "Friaulisch: Interne Sprachgeschichte I: Grammatik," in G. Holtus, M. Metzeltin, and C. Schmidt (eds.), *Lexikon der Romanistischen Linguistik*, vol. 3. Tübingen: Niemeyer.

1989b (ed.), *Dialect Variation and the Theory of Grammar*, Proceedings of the *Glow Workshop* in Venice. Dordrecht: Foris.

1989c "Note introduttive a un atlante dialettale sintattico," in G. Borgato and A. Zamboni (eds.), *Dialettologia e Varia Linguistica per Manlio Cortelazzo*. Padua: Unipress.

1989d "Qual è l'Invidia che Può Dire il Nome," in V. D'Urso (ed.), *Imbarazzo, Vergogna ed Altri Affanni*. Milan: R. Cortina.

1990a "Alcune Precisazioni su Due Articoli di Paolo Di Giovine e Giovanni Petrolini" [in *Italia Dialettale*, 1988], *L'Italia Dialettale*:269–271.

1990b Review of L. Burzio, *Italian Syntax: A Government Binding Approach* [Dordrecht: Reidel, 1986], *Lingua Nostra* 2–3:82–85.

1990c Review of G. Lepschy, *Nuovi Saggi di Linguistica Italiana* and *Sulla Linguistica Moderna* [Bologna: Il Mulino, 1989], *L'Indice*: May.

1990d "La Variazione Linguistica del Friuli e la Linguistica Romanza: La Posizione del Friulano Occidentale," *Ce Fastu* 66:219–232.

1991a (in collaboration with E. Magno Caldognetto, eds.) *Atti del Convegno "L'Interfaccia tra Fonologia e Fonetica."* Padua: Unipress.

1991b "L'Interfaccia tra Fonologia e Fonetica. Dal Lato della Fonologia," in E. Magno Caldognetto and P. Benincà (eds.), *Atti del Convegno "L'Interfaccia tra Fonologia e Fonetica,"* pp. xiv–xxiii. Padua: Unipress.

1991c (in collaboration with L. Vanelli) "La Fonologia Autosegmentale Come Interfaccia tra Morfologia e Fonetica: Saggio di Analisi del Friulano," in E. Magno Caldognetto & P. Benincà (eds.), *Atti del Convegno "L'Interfaccia tra Fonologia e Fonetica,"* pp. 3–18. Padua: Unipress.

1991d "Qualcosa Ancora sulla Koiné Medievale Alto-Italiana," in G. Sanga (ed.), *Koiné in Italia dalle Origini al Cinquecento* (Proceedings of the *Convegno di Milano e Pavia*). Bergamo: Lubrina.

1991e (in collaboration with G. Cinque) "Il Participio Presente," in L. Renzi and G. Salvi (eds.), *Grande Grammatica Italiana di Consultazione*, vol. 2, pp. 604–609. Bologna: Il Mulino.

1991f "Su una Nota Sintattica di Carlo Salvioni," in *Saggi di Linguistica e Letteratura in Memoria di Paolo Zolli*, pp. 43–52. Padua: Antenore.

1991g (in collaboration with L. Vanelli) "Il Friulano del Trecento Attraverso il Commento agli 'Esercizi di Versione'," in *Per Giovan Battista Pellegrini. Scritti degli Allievi Padovani*, pp. 3–74. Padua: Unipress.

1992a "Geolinguistica e Sintassi," in G. Ruffino (ed.) *Atlanti Linguistici Italiani e Romanzi*, pp. 29–41. Palermo: Centro Studi Filologici e Linguistici Siciliani (CSFLS).

1992b "Whither Dialectology?" Round Table of *Quaderni di Semantica* 12 (1991):215–218; 13:102–105.

1992c (in collaboration with J. Haiman) *The Rhaeto-Romance Languages*. London: Routledge.

1992d (in collaboration with G. Cinque) "Sur l'Ambiguité Structurale des Verbes Météorologiques en Italien," in L. Tasmoswsky-De Ryck and A. Zribi-Hertz (eds.), *De la Musique à la Linguistique*, pp. 154–162. Ghent: Communication and Cognition.

1992e (in collaboration with C. Poletto), "La Dialettologia e il Modello Generativo," *Rivista Italiana di Dialettologia* 15:77–97.

1993a (in collaboration with G. Longobardi, eds.) *Paradigmi Glottologici: Documenti di Storia del Pensiero Linguistico*. Milan: Led.

1993b (in collaboration with G. Cinque) "Su Alcune Differenze fra Enclisi e Proclisi," in *Omaggio a Gianfranco Folena*, pp. 2313–2326. Padua: Programma.

1993c "Sintassi," in A.Sobrero (ed.), *L'Italiano: le Strutture, la Variazione*, pp. 247–290. Bari: Laterza.

1993d Review of T. De Mauro, F. Mancini, M. Vedovelli, and M. Voghera, *Lessico di Frequenza dell'Italiano Parlato* [Milan: Etas libri, 1993], *Lingua e Stile* 4:590–593.

1994a "Che Cosa Ci Può Dire l'Italiano Regionale," in T. De Mauro (ed.), *Come Parlano gli Italiani*, pp. 157–165. Florence: La Nuova Italia.

1994b "Le *Postille Etimologiche* di Giovanni Flechia: Riflessioni sul Metodo," in U. Cardinale and M.L. Porzio Gernia (eds.), *Per Giovanni Flechia nel Centenario della Morte* (Proceedings from the *Convegno a Ivrea e Torino*, December 5–7, 1992), pp. 217–225. Turin: Edizioni dell'Orso.

1994c (in collaboration with C. Poletto) "*Bisogna* and Its Companions: The Verbs of Necessity," in G. Cinque, J. Koster, J.-Y. Pollock, L. Rizzi, and R. Zanuttini (eds.), *Paths towards Universal Grammar: Studies in Honor of Richard S. Kayne*, pp. 35–58. Washington, D.C.: Georgetown University Press.

1994d *La Variazione Sintattica: Studi di Dialettologia Romanza*. Bologna: Il Mulino.

1994e "Linguistica e Dialettologia Italiana," in G. C. Lepschy (ed.), *Storia della Linguistica*, vol. 3, pp. 525–644. Bologna: Il Mulino.

1995a "Il Friulano dalle Origini al Rinascimento," in G. Holtus, M. Metzeltin, and C. Schmidt (eds.), *Lexikon der Romanistischen Linguistik* 2, pp. 42–61. Tübingen: Niemeyer.

1995b "I Dati dell'ASIS e la Sintassi Diacronica," in Proceedings of the *Convegno Internazionale su L'Italia Settentrionale: Crocevia di Lingue e Culture*, pp. 131–141. Tübingen: Niemeyer.

1995c (in collaboration with L. Vanelli) "Saggio di Analisi Autosegmentale di Morfologia Friulana," in *Scritti di Linguistica e Dialettologia in Onore di Giuseppe Francescato*, pp. 25–46. Trieste: Edizioni Ricerche.

1995d "Indeur. *dw-* > Armeno *erk-*: Un Mutamento Naturale," *Quaderni del Dipartimento di Linguistica* 11 (Serie Linguistica 5, Università della Calabria), *Festschrift in Onore di J.Trumper*. Rome: Herder.

1995e "Complement Clitics in Medieval Romance: The Tobler-Mussafia Law," in A. Battye and I. Roberts (eds.), *Clause Structure and Language Change*, pp. 325–344. New York: Oxford University Press.

1995f "Il Tipo Esclamativo," in L. Renzi, G. Salvi, and A. Cardinaletti (eds.), *Grande Grammatica Italiana di Consultazione*, vol. 3, pp.127–152. Bologna: Il Mulino.

1996a "La Frase Esclamativa alla Luce del Dialetto Padovano," in P. Benincà, G. Cinque, T. De Mauro, and N. Vincent (eds.), *Italiano e Dialetti nel Tempo: Saggi di Grammatica per Giulio Lepschy*. Rome: Bulzoni.

1996b "Agglutination and Inflection in Northern Italian Dialects," in C. Parodi, C. Quicoli, M. Saltarelli, and M.L. Zubizzareta (eds.), *Aspects of Romance Linguistics* (Selected Papers from the *Linguistic Symposium on Romance Languages XXIV*), pp. 59–72. Washington, D.C.: Georgetown University Press.

1996c *Piccola Storia Ragionata della Dialettologia Italiana*. 2nd ed. Padua: Unipress.

1996d (in collaboration with Piera Rizzolatti) "Note Quattrocentesche Inedite in un Laudario dei Battuti di Pordenone: Annotazioni Linguistiche," in *Il Quattrocento nel Friuli Occidentale*, vol. 1 (Proceedings of the *Convegno a Pordenone*, December 3–4, 1993), pp. 237–252. Pordenone: Biblioteca dell'Immagine.

1997a "Sentence Word Order," in M. Maiden and M. Parry (eds.), *The Dialects of Italy*, pp. 123–130. London: Routledge.

1997b "Conjunctions," in M. Maiden and M. Parry (eds.), *The Dialects of Italy*, pp. 131–136. London: Routledge.

1997c (in collaboration with C. Poletto) "The Diachronic Development of the Italian Verb *bisogna*," in A. van Kemenade and N.Vincent (eds.), *Parameters and Morphosyntactic Change*. Cambridge: Cambridge University Press.

1997d "Note di Dialettologia Lombarda," in R. Arena, P. Bologna, M. L. Meyer Modena, and A. Passi (eds.), *Bandhu: Studi in Onore di Carlo Della Casa*. Alessandria: Edizioni dell'Orso.

1997e (in collaboration with C. Poletto, eds.) *Strutture Interrogative dell'Italia Settentrionale (Quaderni di Lavoro dell'ASIS* 1), Publication of the *Centro di Studio per la Dialettologia Italiana*. Dipartimento di Linguistica, Padua: Centro Nazionale delle Ricerche.

1997f "La Frase Interrogativa nel Dialetto di Monno," in P. Benincà and C. Poletto (eds.), *Strutture Interrogative dell'Italia Settentrionale (Quaderni di lavoro dell'ASIS* 1), Publication of the *Centro di Studio per la Dialettologia Italiana*. Dipartimento di Linguistica, Padua: Centro Nazionale delle Ricerche.

1998a Review of Gian Luigi Beccaria, *I Nomi del Mondo: Santi Demoni, Folletti e le Parole Perdute* [Turin: Einaudi, 1995], *Romance Philology* 51:484–490.

1998b (in collaboration with G. Salvi, eds.) *Romance Syntax: A Reader*. Doctoral Programme in Romance Philology. Budapest: L. Eötvös University.

1998c "Lombard, Dolomitic Ladin, Venetan," in G. Price (ed.), *Encyclopedia of the Languages of Europe*, pp. 261–265. Oxford: Blackwell.

1998d (in collaboration with C. Poletto) "A Case of *do*-support in Romance," The University of Venice Working Papers in Linguistics.

1998e "Le Lingue Romanze Medievali," in R. Lorenzo (ed.), *Atti del XIX Congresso Internazionale di Linguistica e Filologia Romanza*. University of Santiago de Compostela.

1999a (in collaboration with C. Poletto, eds.) *La Negazione nelle Lingue Romanze: Atti della 3ª Giornata Italo-Americana di Dialettologia (Quaderni di Lavoro dell'ASIS 2)*, Publication of the *Centro di Studio per la Dialettologia Italiana*. Dipartimento di Linguistica, Padua: Centro Nazionale delle Ricerche.

1999b (in collaboration with L. Vanelli) *Esercizi di Versione dal Friulano in Latino in una Scuola Notarile Cividalese (sec. XIV)*. Udine: Forum.

1999c "Between Morpholohy and Syntax: On the Verbal Morphology of Some Alpine Dialects," in L. Mereu (ed.), *Boundaries of Morphology and Syntax*, pp. 11–30. Amsterdam: John Benjamins.

2000 (in collaboration with L. Renzi) "La Venetizzazione della Sintassi nel Dialetto Cimbro," in G. Marcato (ed.), *Isole Linguistiche? Per un'Analisi dei Sistemi in Contatto* (Proceedings of the *Convegno di Sappada/Plodn*, July 1–4, 1999), pp. 137–162. Padua: Unipress.

2001a "The Position of Topic and Focus in the Left Periphery," in G. Cinque and G. Salvi (eds.), *Current Studies in Italian Syntax: Essays Offered to Lorenzo Renzi*, pp. 39–64. Elsevier North Holland: Amsterdam.

2001b " 'Lingua' e 'Dialetto' alla Luce della Teoria Linguistica," in G. Marcato (ed.), *I Confini del Dialetto* (Atti del Convegno di Sappada 2000), pp. 13–24. Padua: Unipress.

2001c (in collaboration with L. Renzi) "Sintassi Romanza e Germanica nelle Interrogative del Cimbro," *Romanistik in Geschichte und Gegenwart* 6(1):146–165

2002a (in collaboration with G. Borgato) "Sintassi," in C. Lavinio (ed.), *La Linguistica Italiana alle Soglie del 2000*, pp. 353–372. Rome: Bulzoni.

2002b "Antiche e Nuove Linee di Ricerca della 'Nostra' Dialettologia: Le Radici Storiche della Sintassi Dialettale a Padova," in G. Marcato (ed.), *Dialetti e Dialettologia: Oltre il 2001* (Atti del convegno di Sappada 2001), pp. 15–23. Padua: Unipress.

2002c (in collaboration with M. Vai) "Sintassi e Lessico delle Esclamative: Caratteristiche Romanze ed Indeuropee," in G. Marcato (ed.), *Dialetti e Dialettologia: Oltre il 2001* (Atti del convegno di Sappada 2001), pp. 199–208. Padua: Unipress.